T0320346

THE ORGANIZATION OF THINGS

This is a book about knowledge and how it is organized.

The business school has captured ideas about organization, and reduced them to questions of formal structures, documented processes, logistics, and operations. This book shows how the concept can be understood more generously by illuminating the fundamental importance of culture to our understanding of organization. Using the idea of a cabinet of curiosities, the author shows how we can learn a lot about authority from choirs of angels, about secrecy from shipping containers, or work from art galleries. In disorganizing categories, forcing unusual conjunctions, the work opens itself to organization studies and studies of organizing, as well as cultural sociology, human geography, and social theory.

Bringing together arguments developed over the last two decades, this book brings together and updates work that will provide a unique and valuable reference for students and scholars of management and organization around the world.

Martin Parker is Professor in the Business School at the University of Bristol, UK.

THE ORGANIZATION OF THINGS

A Cabinet of Curiosities

Martin Parker

Routledge
Taylor & Francis Group

LONDON AND NEW YORK

Designed cover image: cyano66 / iStock / Getty Images

First published 2025
by Routledge
4 Park Square, Milton Park, Abingdon, Oxon OX14 4RN

and by Routledge
605 Third Avenue, New York, NY 10158

Routledge is an imprint of the Taylor & Francis Group, an informa business

British Library Cataloguing-in-Publication Data
A catalogue record for this book is available from the British Library

ISBN: 9781032714271 (hbk)
ISBN: 9781032714240 (pbk)
ISBN: 9781032714288 (ebk)

DOI: 10.4324/9781032714288

Typeset in Sabon
by Newgen Publishing UK

CONTENTS

PREFACE

For quite a few years now I have been indulging certain obsessions. Alongside my day job writing worthy things about business ethics, the politics of the business school and how we might build a low-carbon, high-inclusion, high-democracy economy, I have been burrowing away at some peculiar fascinations. This book is a catalogue of some of them, a cabinet of the curiosities which have interested me, and that I hope will interest you.

I never quite know what I am going to get absorbed by, and it feels to me that there is nothing that predictable in the way that the fascination chooses me. That is to say, I'm not conscious of it. It's not intentional. Rather, it fastens itself to me, perhaps because it's something that smells of my childhood, results from a particularly interesting conversation or art work, or I am captured by an image that won't let me go. The fastening begins like a tick buried in the skin, but it then fattens as I gradually collect a swaying pile of academic books, novels, DVDs, magazines, printouts of quotes and articles, comics, poems, and so on. After a few years, because it does take a while, the tick has become a growth, an excrescence that must burst, and so eventually I begin burrowing through the pile, making notes, turning over the corners of pages, writing marginalia and hopefully beginning to work out what it is about this thing that has captured me.

To be clear, I don't know before I begin. I can't explain 'the argument'. (In academic terms, that's the expected throat clearing that might be written in an abstract, or grant application.) Indeed, I don't want to know what the end looks like because that would be dull. For much of my day job, I do know what I am going to write before I start. This is because I want to persuade people of a particular point of view. I might want to explain to them that the business school is an institution that needs radical change, or that cooperative forms of business are likely to be kinder to human and non-human entities, or that all this talk of (business) ethics needs to become talk about (business) politics. I'm not unhappy that I write these other things, because I would like to believe that they matter, but they are different from the curiosities you will encounter here. When I am being an angry business school professor, I am unrolling an argument towards a destination that I have already determined, writing in a straight line. I'm happy if I do that well, but often slightly bored because I know where I am going. Here, in these less directional pieces, the joy is in beginning to think and write about my beloved object, if by love I mean an inability to let something go, a kind of pinioning which continually draws me back, and refuses escape.

It means that the blank screen, the blinking cursor beckoning my attention, which is a source of terror for some, is an invitation for fun because I can then begin to arrange my thoughts about my obsession. It means I can play, put ideas in play, moving glinting fragments, arcana, quotes and vague images until they assume a kind of order, a sequence which allows me to travel from origins in mystery to a kind of stabilization, however fragile. I'm turning the object over, and around, looking at it through my loupe and my telescope, smelling and rubbing myself against it. It's an intimate process because I write for me, to explain to myself why I care about whatever it is. There's a shamelessness in saying that, as if writing for yourself was the rather sinful, intellectual masturbation that it is. Writing for joy, for its own sake, just as one might go for a walk because you wanted to go for a walk. It's a process, a practice, a habit – an itch that is lovely to scratch. Once I have done that, and once the writing can stand up on its own, boredom begins to lurk again. At that point, the reader must be admitted, and for the purposes of these essays the reader was very often the rock tumbler of editors and reviewers in academic journals who often end up grinding down the rough surfaces into 'an argument', or connecting it to 'organization theory', or the 'readers of this journal' or somesuch. (And this sometimes meant that ideas that began with a faraway look in the eye ended up being rather professional, wandering words ordered into regiments, full of references and explanations.)

Then the thing is finished, written, accepted in some academic journal or edited collection where it can sit behind a screen (probably behind a paywall too) and occasionally be visited by an academic or someone who wants to be one, browsing casually or intentionally in the gigantic virtual stacks of knowledge that are produced as a by-product of rankings in the global university system. My fascination now lies there smugly and silently under its vitrine, complete, not to be touched or changed, and my interest in it dramatically wanes. It can't speak to me anymore from behind its glass. It is as if publication were a kind of inoculation, or an exorcism which places a stake through the heart of whatever it was, reducing it from greedy technicolour life to black-and-white still.

Indeed, when kindly people then keep sending me images of tower cranes, or a book on the circus, or recommend a film about Billy the Kid, I almost feel nauseous. (After I had finished writing about James Bond, I was simply disgusted with him, and with myself for being interested in that sort of stuff.) But even if I'm not repulsed by my immersion, I don't want any more now, because it's over and done. Why are you trying to drag me back there? Or are you suggesting that there is something that I have missed, showing me something that might help make my grasp of the phenomenon more complete? I don't want to know about things that I have missed. I feel exhausted being dragged back to that stuff again. I resent it, so I smile nicely, tell them that sounds fascinating, and then ignore them. It's done. OK? Leave me alone.

The exciting thing is the next project, not the last one, and at the present moment I have piles in various states of maturity. Zombies, Andy Warhol and Concorde are for the future, but I am currently working my way through comic book villains. I think the thing will be about villains and dis/ organization, because some of them just want to snarl and smash things up, whilst others want to glue all the Lego bricks together so that no one can rearrange them. At least I think that's what it will be about, but I don't know yet. That's what makes me want to do it. Because the cursor is blinking, beckoning me to build sandcastles, stir the soup, splash the paint.

This book is something different though, because it feels like a way of stitching together these individual granny squares to make something bigger. I could have left them alone of course, rather than narcissistically building this little edifice, a temple to me. I suppose some justification is required, some sort of 'argument'. Well, I think this was worth doing because when I look back at my writing over the last few decades, I realize that it's not just a pile of random fascinations. It just feels that way at the time, in the middle of each one, when I can't pull my head out and notice that I have been here before. It's more like a series of walks that intersect in places that I am particularly drawn to, a ramble away and back, through some clearing or viewpoint where I always pause, point, and mumble something *faux* profound.

If I had to hazard a guess, and I'm hesitant at doing this, I think I am generally fascinated by how the sublime is produced, with the machineries, lies and money that end up producing something beautiful or strange. So the Apollo space programme, the skyscraper, the circus, the zoo and so on are all incredible parlour tricks that make me feel strange inside. It always begins with this sense of the extraordinary – in the art gallery, the angels on the front of a Gothic church, the inaccessibility of a shipping container. I'm a sucker for the impression of disorganization, of something excessive and mysterious that seems to escape order and organization. Pulling the curtain aside is both a way of getting closer, being more intimate, but also has the consequence of demystifying whatever goes on backstage. That might explain my feeling of boredom, even revulsion, once I have 'worked out' whatever it is. I end up being indifferent to what I once loved, pulling the wings off the beautiful butterfly to understand how it flies.

The other justification for this book does connect to my more directional work on alternative organizations, economies and education. It has long seemed to me that one of the extraordinary limitations of conventional business school thought on such matters was that it tends to assume so much – only investigating certain sorts of organizations in certain sorts of ways. Assuming that 'management' and 'leadership' were the propellers that make the world move, that corporations are the most important forms of organization, and that the logic of 'the market' should be the logic of the world. I have written lots on this elsewhere, but I think that these chapters are a sort of demonstration that organizing happens all over the place, and that it is baroque and multiple and strange. I find this inspirational because it helps me push back against the high-carbon, high-exclusion and low-democracy travesty of work and economy that masquerades as natural law, as if there were no alternatives. Learning from secret societies, the Gothic and weeds might sound unlikely, but the cabinet of curiosities teaches curiosity and variety, that there are many things under the sun, and under the moon. Organizing is never merely an efficient response to a particular problem, a straight path between a and b, but is politics made durable.

Enough of the throatclearing then. Versions of these chapters, these fragments of butterfly wing under glass, have been published elsewhere with appropriate reference given in an endnote at the start of the chapter.[1] Exuberant thanks to everyone who commented on written or spoken versions at the time. We might sometimes write alone, but we are all always doing this together. All these chapters have been revised quite a bit for this volume, with lots of excess being trimmed so that the reader just gets the good stuff. Now it's up to you to decide whether it's a masterpiece or a piece of shit with no value or meaning whatsoever. Or, I suppose, somewhere in between, because I'm only the author and I don't get to decide.

Note

1   The chapters, apart from 1 and 15, were originally published between 2005 and 2022, and have been edited from the pre-publication versions. I have tried to get rid of repetition, maximize the connections between them and stop them feeling quite so academic. In terms of the latter, this has involved taking out quite a lot of 'signposting' and words like 'hence' which appears to be the scaffolding that allows me to tell reviewers in journals what I am doing. Oddly, given that it's a mark of scholarly writing, it seems to involve treating readers like idiots.

PART I
Fascinations

1

CONCEPTS AND METHODS

After the rather too intimate throat-clearing of the Preface, here's the beginning of the real content. Never mind all that *faux* writerly stuff, I expect you want to know what this book is actually about, what holds this gallimaufry of nonsense together and gives it the weight to be published by a publisher as august as Routledge. Many of my readers (though I very much hope not all) will be busy business-school people after all, and they don't have time to waste.

Concepts

This is a book about knowledge and how it is organized. It seems to me that people often need to be reminded that the world does not appear to us in the same shapes and consistencies as academic disciplines, with 'tear here' dotted lines between biology and chemistry, politics and economy, psychology and sociology. After all, inter-, multi- and trans-disciplinarity have been spoken about for many years, largely because most of the interesting problems, as well as the urgent ones, don't fit into the boxes we construct for them. This book is an extended demonstration of this fact, often using knowledge produced within the business school as an illustration of how ideas can tangle and catch, growing tendrils that do not respect disciplinary boundaries. Connection seems to be the dominant practice here, as opposed to disciplinary discipline, the sort of thought that makes sure that people stay within their fields, and don't push down the barbed wire and start grazing elsewhere.

I think this sort of work could be done with many different concepts, ideas that are generous enough to hold multitudes, but the one that has fascinated me for many years is 'organization'. It is probably fair to say that it has

DOI: 10.4324/9781032714288-2

possessed me. It is a word that, over the past few decades, has come to belong to the business school, and has tended to be attached to 'organizations', entities which are seen as containers for particular kinds of work-related activity. This is not incorrect of course, because language is what language does, but it is limiting, because 'organization' is also used as a verb, as in 'organizing', and this verb can be applied to many contexts which are not remotely recognizable as formal organizations. The rules for an English bus queue or a Swedish Hells Angels gang, the segmentary lineage systems of the Pashtun peoples of Afghanistan and Pakistan, the social arrangements of chimpanzees, or the repeated patterns of flowers and waggle dances of bees. All can be understood as organization, as pattern repeated in time and space, as difference and repetition recognized as difference and repetition.

So, given the capaciousness of the concept, why might we assume that ideas about organizing would and should only refer to formal organizations? The social and natural world is 'organized' in so many different ways, yet the word 'organization' is usually imagined to be something that applies to certain formal organizations – corporations, companies, businesses and so on. This has always struck me as a very limited empirical and theoretical focus, because so many of the words that we use to think about the human and more-than-human world refer to patterns, relationships and forms. Ordering and classification are methods to organize human understandings of the world and all that is in it, whether manifest in a museum or a strategy document, a map or a census, a taxonomy of supply chains or of polyploidal grasses. And ordering and organization are close synonyms, particularly in their verb forms. As a concept, 'organization' is such an useful term, one that is both noun and verb, object and action. It offers a generous terrain to think about the structuring of relationships between people and things, both empirically and theoretically, in the past, present and (perhaps most importantly) the future.

'Organization theory' is now usually understood to be a theory of work organizations, or of forms of organizing that take place in, between and around work organizations, and it is a form of knowledge production that is imagined to belong in the business school. Related terms do similar work – organizational behaviour, organization studies, organizational analysis – all tending to focus on how human beings think and act within organizations and institutions. Of course they exclude far more than they include, but that is the nature of academic disciplines, being pizza cutters for slicing knowledge into digestible chunks. Think, for example, about the divide between 'culture' and 'organization'. The former is a term which is sometimes attached to practices which are symbolic, artistic, aesthetic and so on. Its distinctiveness is often enough marked by its difference from the vulgar world of business, money and organizing, as if each marked the boundaries of the other. Yet (as Andy Warhol demonstrated and asserted) it is obvious that art and money are absolutely entangled, and it is clear enough that culture does not end at the door to the factory or the office (Parker 2000). Indeed, we could treat this distinction as itself an example of how different practices are categorized in human societies by making some things similar and other things different. If we want to understand the rules for the Brazilian dance fight *capoeira*, how meals are arranged in different human societies, or the carvings on the front of a medieval cathedral, then we will be trying to understand a structure of similarities and differences. We might call this order, classification, pattern – but in this book I will explore what it means to think of these relationships as forms of organization.

Of course I'm not the first person to try and connect 'culture' and 'organization'. This is a book which is quite deliberately attempting to connect and sit between things, but other people have done that too. The longest-standing academic example of this is the Standing Conference on Organizational Symbolism (SCOS) which has been holding events across Europe since 1981 and spawned the academic journal *Culture and Organization* (first published in 1995). SCOS grew out of early work in 'organizational symbolism' and then 'organizational culture', with much of the work paying attention to the culture, ritual, ceremony, and symbolism of organizations in an anthropological sense. A very substantial literature on organizational culture followed, both popular managerialist and critical, but much of the consultancy-focused work pursued the idea of organizations as 'containers' for culture, and moreover that culture in that sense was something that managers could change. 'We want a new organizational culture' is best translated as 'get rid of behaviours that management don't like.'

In this book I start with the opposite assumption: trying to think of culture as the container for organizing. That is to say, to understand organizing and organizations as manifestations of cultural practices, so that the pernicious distinction between culture and economy is exorcised. As you will see in the next chapter, this means that I do have something of a debt to ideas from cultural studies which, from the 1970s onwards, was using a combination of sociology, history and literary theory to think hard about the everyday. As with many other intellectual currents, this work appears in business schools a few decades later, as people like me get jobs teaching the 'people and organizations' courses in a part of the Northern European university system which was expanding very quickly indeed. This means that there is work which is similar to this book, driven by an attempt to achieve the same sort of interdisciplinarity and to take an anthropological sense of culture seriously.

For example, Emma Bell (2008) has written about films which show representations of management and organization, Smith and colleagues (2001) edited a book on science fiction, Marek Korczynski (2014) has done the same with pop music in and about work, and a few books have been written on humour at and about work (Westwood and Rhodes 2007, Plester

2016). To this we could add a few books on organizations and popular culture (Hassard and Holliday 1998, Rhodes and Lilley 2012, Rhodes and Westwood 2008). These are all great books, though they largely focus on cultural forms which comment on work and organization, rather than trying to think about how the concept 'organization' (and also 'disorganization') might help us think about culture itself. I think the closest to what I am trying to do here is probably Gibson Burrell's experimental book *Pandemonium* (1997), Philip Hancock's book on the organization of Christmas (2023) in which he focuses on the labour and economics that produces the modern global Christmas and Timon Beyes' lovely book on colour and organization (2024). In the journal *Organization Studies*, there have also been some strange and beautiful writings on airports (Knox et al. 2015), ruins (De Cock and O'Doherty 2017) and atmospheres (Steyaert and Michels 2018), as well as attempts to reach towards the arts and humanities in the theory and practice of thinking about organizing (Steyaert et al. 2016).

Like some of this work, I want to push against any sense of there being a boundary (however porous) between 'inside' and 'outside' organization. I want to try and treat organizing as necessarily cultural, and to demonstrate this by bringing together topics like angels, astronauts and secret societies as examples of making sense with (in those three cases) spirit beings, NASA and invisible institutions. If, as the anthropologist Claude Levi-Strauss suggested, culture is that which is 'good to think with' (1966), then almost anything can find a place in the ordering and classifying systems of culture. This tells us nothing other than that ideas, materials, people, animals, plants, tower cranes and shipping containers are elements in culture, and can be understood as contained within it, and being made comprehensible through it. I want to explore what is kept apart and what is brought together, made visible or invisible to who, and where and when this happens. I want to put the concept of organization to work in these inquiries, and help to rescue it from what I see as its present limiting tendencies.

It seems to me that, in the present context, the business school has captured ideas about organization, and reduced them to questions of formal structures, documented processes, logistics and operations. This book is an attempt to show that organizing can be understood far more generously, and that doing so allows us to 'see' things that we might not otherwise notice, as well as relations between those things. All of the chapters that follow treat various elements of culture as 'organized', in the sense that I use them to think about various principles – mobility, hierarchy, separation, visibility and so on. It has long seemed to me that we can learn a lot about authority from choirs of angels, about secrecy from shipping containers, or work from art galleries. Indeed, there is a certain perversity in this project, trying as it does to conjoin matters that usually seem to exist in different parts of the culture that I inhabit, and consequently of different parts of the university too. In disorganizing these categories, forcing unusual conjunctions, I pull things into proximity and see what effect it produces. These chapters are a bit like a series of experiments in which I have brought together something that I find odd and fascinating, and then tried to understand its principles of organization. Does it stay still or move? Does it advertise its existence or hide? What happens backstage in order to produce the effects and affects it generates for its audiences?

I also think that there is a common method in these chapters and bringing them closer together might allow that to be seen more clearly. Which, of course, is a way of describing a principal of organization itself, a collection of something that was previously more dispersed, such as happens in archives, zoos, galleries, museums, and cabinets of curiosity. Each of the six parts that follows is intended to draw attention to a particular theme or movement and they are arranged deliberately in a kind of sequence. I have also emphasized the connections between parts and chapters, as these pieces cross and re-cross common themes, and use similar approaches in order to understand the particular object of my temporary and mobile fascinations.

Method

A few notes on method seem appropriate, but these are not really the sort of 'research methods' that are employed to adjudicate the merits of 'findings' within the social sciences more widely. I do believe that understanding and practicing more conventional methods is important to establish a warrant for the claims that people make, and that can potentially distinguish the sort of things that social scientists claim from the sort of conversations that we might have on a bus or in the pub. But that wasn't what I did, which was often methodical, but in a rather different way. When I was writing about the 1969 moon landings, I made a plastic model of an Apollo-Saturn launch vehicle. When I was trying to understand the image of a person alone at the top of a tower crane or a piece of performance art, I did some interviews with crane drivers and museum information assistants. If I wanted to inhabit conspiracy theories, I needed to read magazines about UFOs. When I got obsessed with outlaws, I obsessively watched films and TV shows about the mafia, cowboys, pirates and assorted robbers. To understand the circus, or zoo, you need to spend time in circuses and zoos.

My 'method' was more like a kind of immersion, one stimulated by no more than the idea that I wanted to write something about a particular object or phenomenon. It began with the object, not a 'research question' that required me to surface some epistemological assumptions, which in turn implied a 'research design' and the selection of appropriate 'research methods'. So when, for example, I was writing about tower cranes, I began with an image from a beautiful film I had seen which documented 24 hours in crane cabs over London – floating above the bustle, watching the sun rise and the sun set, the imperceptible twitch of a hand resulting in the motion of massive girders from the street, and the coded radiostatic instructions from voices hundreds of metres down on the ground, like mission control a quarter of a million miles away. That was all that captured me at that point, wanting to understand this strange isolation in the heart of the city – like a guardian angel, or superhero, looking down at us from a ledge far above.

It is common enough for academics, particularly those who work in business schools, to moan about the restrictions in topic and style that follow from the expectations of disciplines and journals and publishers and the research excellence framework and journal rankings list and promotion and citation and, and, and. I should know, I've done enough of that moaning myself, but these chapters were relatively unconstrained by such considerations. I'm well aware that asking what topics, materials, concepts commonly get addressed can result in a charge sheet of constraint, as the controversial, difficult, or arcane gets ignored in favour of moulding some words that fit into place like a jigsaw piece. 'Finding gaps in the literature', 'joining the conversation', 'making a contribution', 'adding to the literature', 'continuing the debate': these are all fine metaphors which share a sense of needing to fit in, finding a small crevice in the book stacks and citation webs that thought can wriggle into. Elbowing your way into the middle of the crowd, like a penguin huddling in from the storm. This is often what research questions do because they are different from ordinary questions. They are more specific, more bracketed. 'How is the experience of the crane driver similar or different from that of other isolated occupations?' 'Does the national and global movement of cranes reflect flows of global capital?' 'What architectural forms became possible as a result of the invention of the self-jacking crane?' 'How do birds and bats respond to cranes as potential nesting sites?'

I like all of those questions, but each of them also feels a little small, a bit too restricted. They focus my attention in ways that mean I might be missing things, blinkered by my particular question and consequently not capable of seeing all the other questions out of the corner of my eye, or in the vibrations of my body. My question was just 'cranes?' Or perhaps 'why am I fascinated by cranes?'. In other words, I wanted to read about and think about cranes for a bit. That was all. And I wasn't quite sure why.

As you can see in the chapter on tower cranes in this book (Chapter 5), I always liked seeing them on the horizon. They spoke of a certain strangeness and possibility, jutting from the ground like giant trees, promising to grow something new next to them. They seemed temporary and permanent at the same time, massive and fragile, offering a sublime viewpoint for dull machine-minding labour. Often, the crane seemed to me much more exciting than what it was building which, when complete, sat there with a dull smugness, finished and complete and radiating whatever cliché its compromise between money and architecture could achieve. So perhaps my question, my question to shape a 'research strategy', was 'What are the ways of seeing cranes?' What sorts of research, practice, writing, thinking allow me to write about cranes in a way that I think would be interesting to me and illuminate its object in some way? To catch the cranes in a spotlight, to see them as culture, to exorcise my fascination, and (later on) to encourage readers to see cranes again, to see them in a new light.

So what did I do? Well, over a period of about four years or so, I collected things. An amazing bumper-sized book on the history of cranes that I saw in the window of a closed second-hand bookshop in Lancaster. (Who writes a book on the history of cranes? Is this a joke?) I walked away, telling myself that it would be another pointless book that I would never actually read. Then, being unable to shake the need to open that magic box, I asked my friend who we had been visiting to buy me the book. (He was a professor of English literature, and continues to smile tolerantly when I describe the latest farrago of nonsense I intend to write about.) I emailed Eva Weber to get a copy of her wonderful haunting documentary 'The Secret Life of Cranes' and she kindly sent me a CD copy in return for some money and a promise not to screen it for public viewing. In another second-hand bookshop, I came across a small blue 1849 book by Joseph Glynn titled *A Rudimentary Treatise on the Construction of Cranes and Machinery*. It was quite expensive, but the owner was prepared to haggle, so I spent more than I intended and added it to the pile.

What method is this? What procedure I am describing? If by method we mean something planned from the start, written down in an ethics application or methodology chapter of a PhD, then I suppose this is no method at all. More like waiting for cultural detritus to drift past me in the current, and then pulling it in and hoarding until I was ready to start chewing on it. It has always been really important to me to preserve the strangeness of the topic, so I rarely do anything like a systematic literature review. I don't want my thinking and writing to be too disciplined, to operate from a visibility which has been predictably produced and that gives me a lot of work to do. I don't want to be bored before I begin, but remain enchanted for as long as possible.

I emailed my son's school asking them about whether they used toy cranes in the classroom. In return I got a picture of Cranky from Thomas the Tank Engine and was told that the first episode of the cartoon series 'Mary, Mungo and Midge' was about cranes. I endlessly talked to people about cranes and tried to remember what they said, sometimes writing cryptic notes about our conversations on my phone at the time, or on scraps of paper for the pile afterwards. I joined a crane driver Facebook site and contacted the trade union UCATT. That led to phone and skype interviews with five crane drivers. I interviewed another son, who was a high rope access worker on tall buildings in Vancouver, British Columbia at the time. I read a piece of journalism that one of his friends wrote about him, because she was studying for a qualification in creative writing at the time.

Despite the fact that I was the Director of Research when I was doing this, I didn't fill in an ethics form for any of my interviews or online lurking. I remember wondering what would happen if it was revealed, particularly since (at the time) I was having to endlessly nag people to make sure that all student and staff research went through our ethics audit.[1] It's almost as if I didn't regard this as 'real' research, the sort of work that needed to go through the anxious and paranoid machineries of the university, but instead was some sort of hobby, an activity done for pleasure. More like creative writing than academic writing (a distinction that is itself rather instructive).

I subscribed to a crane magazine – *International Cranes and Specialised Transport* – and various crane-marketing mailing lists and social media feeds. I read things about urban explorers who love to climb cranes, crane accident statistics, crane worker health and safety manuals and crane training programmes. This led me to a trail of images and writings about cranes, construction, radio towers, electricity pylons and girders in art, sculpture, poetry, novels. It seemed that other people had been interested in these icons of twentieth-century modernity too, and they formed a catalogue of artistic clans with shouty manifestos – constructivists, rayonnists, vorticists, orphists, suprematists, futurists. I interviewed a composer who had done a piece of music about cranes. I thought about assemblage theory, and networks of actants, and what it must be like to want a piss when you are a hundred metres in the air.

And finally, when the pile was big enough, I started taking it apart again, turning down the corners of pages, underlining things and inserting yellow sticky notes, beginning a document of thoughts, which gradually grew subheadings. I suppose we might understand this as different ways of seeing the same materials, a sort of perspectival view, but I was just as excited by the idea of making the materials into different sorts of exhibits in different worlds. What resulted, after the pile had been reduced to rubble and then built into a different shape, was itself an assemblage of bits and pieces, making connections both fleeting and durable, combing words into straight lines. I was organizing my materials into themes in a fairly typical 'data analysis' way I suppose, but always wanted the themes to contain mysteries and contradictions themselves. The point was not to tidy up the crane, to box it, but to ensure that its mystery did not collapse beneath the weight of analysis.

I wanted to be able to see the crane, for my writing to not get in the way too much. Or rather, for my writing to provide a series of ways of seeing, like rays which illuminated something that could never be understood as a totality, never finally caught and explained away. I constructed the tower crane as something produced by mathematical calculations for stress and pullies, knowledge about the ways to connect metal, flows of capital and people, city boosterism in the downtown core, the labour process of a fat bloke in a cab, aesthetic responses to modernity and the temporality of something so huge arriving and disappearing in a day.

And all the way through, appearing and reappearing like a structure swaying in the wind, these metaphors of construction, as both noun and verb. The structure that makes a structure, something temporary that produces a pool of order, a stabilization of things. Rusting metal vibrating, creaking, moaning as flakes of paint flutter to the ground. The straight lines that frame dizzy triangles of air and provide a perch for birds and someone with their lunch in a plastic box. An assemblage that is self-jacking, autopoetic, and that makes it possible for a something that looks like a permanent assemblage to be built. (Even though that will, because of land values going up, and decay pulling down, probably be demolished by a wrecking crane one day too.) And so eventually back then to organization, as process and structure. And to organization studies, and a journal article. Coming back down to ground, with both relief and sadness as the crane lets me go.

Now this is all rather vague, open, undefined. My account above doesn't really encourage the sort of methodical repetition that is usually described as method. It seems undisciplined, an insistence on responding to the object, or rather to the different ways in which the object might be caught. It also rests on writing as a practice of producing a temporary stabilization of ideas, a scaffold for thought as a technique for producing combinations of concepts and images, and soliciting some response from writer, and reader. In that sense, writing is also a form of exploration, a method of inquiry, a mode of research itself, and not something that happens *after* the real work has taken place (Richardson and St Pierre 2005, Parker 2014). It is itself productive, not merely 'writing up' (or 'writing down').

All of the pieces in this collection, I hope, have a different style, a different taste to them. Nonetheless, there are certainly recurring themes – organization/ disorganization, the engineered and the sublime, mystery and secrecy – and a fascination with objects and practices that attract me emotionally but repel me intellectually. But this circling around certain concerns doesn't mean that each return feels the same. It's important to me that the outcome of writing as a method of inquiry should be that the text somehow echoes its object, that it produces a surface which allows the object to emerge in its distinctiveness and not to smooth off the writing so that the crane, choir of angels, or Apollo Saturn Launch Vehicle simply take their places in a catalogue which insists on taxonomy, on measuring differences and similarities. Or a museum in which all the pieces are dusted and positioned in symmetrical vitrines, together with labels that explain them.

I was aware that I wanted a piece about the Gothic to be dark, whilst writing about angels should evoke the mysteries of the air and whispers of half-understood messages. Or that trying to understand James Bond would lead to a series of presentations of office life interiors and a stilted formality, whilst shipping containers demanded a series of images of global flows of treasure and danger. I don't know whether I was successful in doing this but would be disappointed if all these pieces felt the same, as if I only responded to all these different practices, phenomena, images, concepts in the same way. (Which seems to me like it would be a way of saying that I didn't respond to them at all, merely captured and exhibited them.)

Which is to return to academic capitalism, the production of journal articles for research assessment, careers, salaries, and university rankings. It might be thought difficult to do such vague and floaty work as I have described here in such a defined context. A context in which thinking and writing is already prefigured in terms of the recognizable research questions associated with particular disciplines and outputs. A context in which the focus on the production of 'outputs'[2] often means that what is written, and how it is written, are much less important than the mere fact that it is published, and counted, and fed into various algorithms to produce scores which in turn feed into tables of rankings that themselves drive movements of students, and staff, and money. This is all true, and it is depressing when I think about it. But, as this book documents, every form of organization brings with it its own disorganization, the ghost that haunts the corridors of the bureaucracy, the migrants in the shipping container, the wildness in the zoo, the uncanny goal of the moon race. 'When you invent the ship, you also invent the shipwreck; when you invent the plane you also invent the plane crash; and when you invent electricity, you invent electrocution' (Virilio 1999, 89). That which underpins order also undermines it.

In focusing on the many ways that the organization (in this case, 'the university') controls and domesticates, we might not be able to see the space for thinking otherwise. In imagining organization as something complete and totalizing, we fail to realize that even such a thought – the very possibility of such a thought – demonstrates the limits of control. As Gibson-Graham and Dombroski (2020), the originary theorists of postcapitalism and diverse economies, have argued, if we only look for capitalist economic and cultural practices then that is all we will see. Their invitation to displace 'capitalocentricism' (in order to be able to see non-capitalist economic practices such as barter, volunteering, self-provisioning and so on) is not that dissimilar to my suggestion that we might displace 'the work organization', with 'organizing', dissolving it into a flow of cultural practices, a temporary assemblage of people and things. And, of course, to dissolve the 'common sense' of the business school, refuse the insistence that organization is limited to studying human beings collected together in containers for work, and open the door to a much more mysterious wilderness of stories. Such a shift encourages us to be attentive to the ways that organizing is never complete, always haunted by its other, by escape and decay and the cracks that let some strange light in. I think that it is only by recognizing this incompleteness that we can see things that are difficult to see, even something as a big as a crane.

Notes

1 I assume some sort of statute of limitations means that I will not face disciplinary action for this breach of academic procedure.
2 A word that always makes me think of shit, and why we might measure how much a person was producing.

2

THE CULTURE OF ORGANIZING

If you walk down the small high street of one of the districts of the city of Stoke-on-Trent where I used to live, you see promises of escape in shop windows and on billboards. Stoke is a poor city which used to be the heart of the UK ceramics industry and has not recovered from the industrial collapse of the 1970s.[1] There are no tower cranes in Stoke. About half the shops are boarded up or empty. Even the Subway sandwich shop has closed,[2] but there are drinkers in some of the pubs from mid-morning onwards. It is shit. A city which has been let down and left behind, and in which the factories have no roofs, the pits are closed and in the steelworks grow grass and brambles. The text on a mug made here says 'If you work and do your best, You'll get the sack like all the rest, But if you laze and bugger about, You'll live to see the job right out. The work is hard, pay is small, So take your time and sod 'em all. Cause when your dead you'll be forgot.'

But imagine yourself here, and you will be surrounded by promises. The betting shops have displays which hint at the mountains of cash on offer to someone who picks the right odds, and show pictures of steel-thighed footballers slamming the ball into the back of the net. The travel agent has pictures of a golden beach and a blue sky, a huge cruise liner in an exotic port, the skyline of New York, glittering like a Christmas tree. A newsagent's window tells you that *you* could be a millionaire next week if you scratch the right card or tick the right box, and inside sells a lot of cigarettes and porn. Several massage parlours offer a simulation of the real thing, under signboards saying 'Executive', 'Little Tingles' and 'Head Office'. A billboard invites you to share the glory of the local football team, another invites you to a blockbusting film in which determined-looking men escape from somewhere or somebody, and an off-licence

DOI: 10.4324/9781032714288-3

shows fun and laughing friends with white teeth and boasts of knockdown bargain prices. On the bus stop, an advert for an employment agency with a smiling white man looking at the camera, inviting you to work. Someone has added teeth and glasses, an ejaculating cock and balls, and written 'WANKER' underneath. People in this city seem to exist on promises nowadays, on the idea that there could be an alternative to being here, now, on a pavement dotted with chewing gum and sparkling splinters of last night's glass bottles.

For those who don't have the time, resources, or power to debate, argue and dialogue, there seem to be at least two ways in which social arrangements can be contested. One is a strategy of graffiti, laughter, ridicule in which the figures of power appear with horns or big noses and the bus stop becomes obscene. This is criticism through representation, a form of thumbing your nose at those people and things which make everyday life difficult or objectionable. The other is escape, an attempt to take yourself away from the grating sounds and fatty smells of the present in order to be somewhere else, doing something else. Exit and absence don't have to be physical, but can also take the form of dreams, fantasies and promises. In this chapter, I want to explore both of these strategies as elements in what I will call the 'counter-culture' of organizing. There has been a fair amount of work done on the ways in which films, songs, comic books and so on very often contain negative representations of management and organization, and I will lean on some of this work in this chapter. What I want to add here is some sense of escape as being understandable in these terms too. I want to understand the graffiti and the betting shop as different solutions to the same problem.

I begin by quickly outlining some of the historical moves which have allowed the innocuous word 'culture' to carry such political weight. This means thinking about the word as a term which produces 'us' and 'them', either in spatial and institutional terms (the culture of Stoke, the culture of an organization), or in moral terms (they are like that, we are like this). I then move on to discuss how the idea of a counter-culture of organization reproduces this 'us' and 'them' in representational terms, and show how I think this counter-culture works. But I don't believe this exhausts the ways in we can think about a culture which opposes the present, but not directly, in the terms of a resistance which pushes back against power. The following section begins to explore escape as a form of politics too, what the anthropologist James Scott (1990) calls an 'infrapolitics', an exodus from the spaces and terms which define what it means to be a subject in a managed society. Of course the conditions for these escapes are often managed too, which is a potentially tragic end to this chapter, but one that I try to avoid by insisting that we can never know (for once and for all) what is political and what is not.

Culture and Politics

Culture, like many words, can mean many things (Williams 1976, 87). In its most general sense, it refers to an anthropological understanding of the way of life of a people and also suggests some sort of distinctiveness between what different peoples do in different places and times. It includes forms of song, dance, myth and so on, but also topics which observers might put in other boxes – technology, economy, organization and so on. In principal, the anthropological sense of culture would leave nothing out. It attempts to capture a whole way of life without making any particular distinctions between different parts of that life. This is because the different forms of anthropological culture intermingle. A marriage ceremony might embed assumptions about power and inheritance, and a story about the gods tells us why we are at war with the people over the river. Wherever we begin, every other aspect of that life is implicated, because the social world does not come with lines that allow us to separate economics, from politics, from culture and so on.

However, it seems to have been easier to maintain this holistic sense of culture when the object of enquiry was 'others'. Anthropology grew out of the colonial encounter which identified 'them' as different from 'us', and perhaps *their* lives looked undivided when 'we' viewed them from a distance. Once the social sciences began to emerge in the imperial nations in the second half of the nineteenth century, forms of specialization began to produce diverse fields of enquiry which made a series of increasingly definitive claims about the separation of different elements of human life. The disciplines of economics, psychology, politics, sociology and so on were each predicated on the idea that they were investigating different sites or institutions, or were doing so in a distinctive way. At the same time, the humanities were increasingly demarcating those aspects of cultural life with which they are concerned – history, literature, music, visual art and so on. Whilst such distinctions were certainly helpful for claims to expertise, they also segmented knowledge in ways that made certain matters evident and obvious, and other ideas difficult to think at all.

In the case of the humanities, they also sedimented the idea of an implicit class distinction which became a way of understanding who has culture and who does not. We can see this in the second common meaning of culture as a label for *particular* and *preferred* cultural forms and practices – opera and not popular song, literature and not detective novels or penny-dreadfuls. In general terms, this implies an epistemological distinction between 'culture' and the everyday, and a distinctive set of research sites where such work could be done – museums, galleries, certain theatres and universities themselves. To speak of someone as 'cultured' means that they are knowledgeable about what Matthew Arnold called 'the best that has been thought and said'.

More generally, it also becomes a way of gesturing towards the manners of the upper and middle classes,[3] referring to particular forms of supposedly timeless comportment and attitude. The raucous and ephemeral vulgarities of the people were not culture at all in this second sense, and certainly not worthy of serious study. Since trivia had nothing timeless to say about the human condition, it could easily be dismissed as crude 'mass' culture.

Combining disciplinary division with a cultural politics based on exclusion meant that academic ideas about culture have tended to bear all sorts of half-hidden assumptions. Within studies of organizations within the business schools of the Global North, for example, the use of the term 'culture' begins to be applied in quite specific ways from the 1980s onwards. Though earlier writers from organizational sociology, occupational psychology and industrial anthropology had already referred to organizational 'climate', 'atmosphere' and 'personality', the growth of the idea of 'organizational' culture within the growing business school was driven by the claim that culture could be a source of value (Parker 2000). In practice, what was being studied were usually the accounts of management and professionals. Older traditions of occupational community studies and shop-floor ethnographies (Brown 1992) began to be eclipsed and the organization tended to be imagined as a container, a time and place where a particular sort of culture happened. Despite Linda Smircich's (1983) often repeated insistence that organizations don't *have* cultures, they *are* cultures, the tendency was to assume that culture began at 9 and ended at 5, and could be found within the boundaries of the workplace. The multiple intersections between a particular organization and that of a wider culture were rarely explored, perhaps because they were assumed not to be relevant for a business-school audience. If it was work and organizations that was being studied, then the research needed to take place *in* work organizations and not between or outside them.

The politics of (management) knowledge framing the word 'culture' was both elitist and partial, but the 1970s had already seen a series of movements in sociology, history and literature which were beginning to undo both the epistemological and institutional divisions which had produced such a complex terrain for a reasonably simple concept.[4] The result was what is now usually called cultural studies, and (to simplify considerably) this was a new interdisciplinary space where an anthropological definition of culture was being applied to the way of life of the people of modern societies. Social historians began to investigate the common people, rather than kings and generals, sociologists began to relax the distinction between culture and structure which had produced their discipline, and literary critics began to pay attention to chapbooks, popular ballads and comics (Storey 1993, Lewis 2008). The result was an opening for a different understanding of culture, one which refused epistemological and disciplinary difference in favour of an engagement with everyday materials, with the celebration of the popular rather than the denigration of the mass (Rhodes and Parker 2008). This was work that came with a leftist political stance, in which popularity was not seen to be a problem, and populism was not an insult. One might have imagined that this would include work on work, but in practice, organizations were rarely considered to be of interest in themselves in early cultural studies, more the backdrop to research on youth culture or education, or the unexamined places which produced the clothes, TV programmes and pop music which were the object of analysis (Hall and Jefferson 1976, Willis 1977). In a sense, the focus was on what happened *outside* work, in the 'leisure' time of the weekend and the spaces of the shopping mall, in the places of consumption rather than the places of production.

And so now we can return to where we began, with the question of how to deal with what I saw all around me in Stoke when I lived there, both the promises and the graffiti. It seems that this place and these phenomena don't fit well into the sorts of boxes that the university provides, which makes it interesting in all sorts of ways. This is a place in which was made by industrial labour, and in which 'high' culture is mostly absent. Instead we have examples of a variety of popular cultural practices and representations most of which aren't even clearly 'about' work and organizations. The promises don't seem to be related to the claims made by the proponents of free markets, a knowledge economy, self-management and so on. These are utopias of work (Grey and Garsten 2002), but the billboards sell us Cockayne and Arcadia, the lands of plenty, and the graffiti, the cock and balls on a suit, rejects the idea that the world of work can provide you with money and smiles. Both, it seems to me, are examples of the counter-culture of organizing, but they are not the same. If the spray-paint is an example of opposition, then the betting shop and travel agent are not explicitly 'against' something. If the former is an example of resistance, then the latter is an example of escape, not so much pushing against but rather an exodus into the arms of something different. Yet I think that they can both be understood as attempts to resolve some of the undesirable aspects of working life, and are 'political' in different ways. Phil Cohen, in an early paper that prefigured some key ideas from the Birmingham Centre for Contemporary Cultural Studies, suggested that youth subcultures offered magical resolutions to the contradictions of the everyday: 'It seems to me that the latent function of subculture is this: to express and resolve, albeit "magically", the contradictions that remain hidden in the parent culture' (1972/1997, 94).

Cohen suggests that the procession of subcultures represented structural transformations of 'the basic problematic or contradiction which is inserted in the subculture by the parent culture' (ibid.). Rather than seeing subcultures as pathological, he tries to understand them as imaginative responses to structural tensions and contradictions in the social. I want to adapt Cohen's argument here and apply it to the promises of Cockayne and Arcadia being sold in the shop windows in Stoke. To do this I will use another rather classic paper from cultural studies, Richard Dyer's 'Entertainment and Utopia', originally from 1977/1993). Dyer argues, using various media theorists, that there is a promise of something different, something better, in much that is dismissed as mere entertainment: 'Alternatives, hopes, wishes – these are the stuff of utopia, the sense that things could be better, that something other than what is can be imagined and maybe realised' (Dyer 1977/1993, 273). His example is the musical, but it seems to me that this sort of argument can also be used in the context of betting shops, travel agents and pubs – any cultural formation which promises escape and articulates 'now' as a problem.

For those without the resources to engage in debates with the powerful, resistance can be understood through these ideas from early cultural studies. Both graffiti and the betting shop can be imagined as ways to magically resolve the present, whether through opposition or exit to a place for us, a new way of living. I will say some more about these ideas as we go along, but want to first outline the sort of objects which I think are important when we consider these questions. I'll start with a genre of oppositional cultural representation which comments on work, management and business, but in ways that are often satirical and extraordinarily hostile to authority.

Resistance

It seems to me that the counter-culture can be set against a 'culture *for* organizing', which contains many images of work and management which are broadly positive. Think of the sorts of ideas you find in orthodox textbooks, in the marketing claims made by business schools, business magazines and newspapers, and the shelves full of strident 'one-minute manager' books. Rather like the utopian dreams of escape offered by musicals, fashion, holidays, or betting shops, this is mirrored by a set of representations which combine first-class lounges, expensive watches and exclusive credit cards with the idea of being a special person. Certain people are part of the star system within this arena – management consultants with international tours delivered to packed conference rooms in expensive hotels, 'outlaw' entrepreneurs who can afford private jets, business-school professors who can charge extraordinary fees for their creamy wisdom. Embedded among these images are other more mundane ones – well-dressed people looking at laptops, workplaces with water coolers and pizza Fridays, and apartments offering lifestyle living in the heart of the city. This is all part of a cultural genre in which organizations, management and work are regarded as central to the reproduction of what is good, and the faraway look of a (male) executive gazing out of an aeroplane window as a (female) member of the aircrew passes by smiling tells us what our dreams should be.

However, as is obvious, this culture for organizing is hugely contested. Take a delightful comic called *The Adventures of Unemployed Man* (Origen and Golan 2010). It tells the story of a smug middle-aged white superhero – 'Ultimatum' – who passes through the city at night with messages of self-help for the poor and deviant. However, after being fired from a company he thought he owned and as it dawns on him that that he can't get another job, he gradually comes to realize that the problem is the inequalities of capitalism, and not the indolence of the poor. Fighting the forces of the 'Invisible Hand' and the 'Free Marketeers', he becomes 'Unemployed Man' and defeats evil through collective organization. Just about everything in this comic contests ideas about work which underpin pro-managerialism utopianism. I do not believe that this is an unusual or anomalous example. Indeed, the counter-culture of organizing is actually just as important and widespread as that which it opposes, and perhaps even more so. It is as if ideas about organization produce their own resistance.

Just to take some examples – in films as diverse as *Brazil* (1985), *What Women Want* (2000), *Monsters, Inc.* (2001) and *Fun with Dick and Jane* (2005) – we have plots that are developed around the idea that the work organization is the problem. In popular film, most organizations are managed by bureaucrats, careerists, or criminals, and freedom can only be found by telling the boss what you really think and then walking out, or pushing him out of the skyscraper window. In much storytelling, this is now no more than the deployment of a very common stereotype. If you want a bad guy, then make him a company executive (Bell 2008, 65 *passim*). So, when *The Muppets* film was being made in 2012 , the plot revolves around an evil oil baron called Tex Richman, and the 2014 *Lego Movie* has Lord Business as the baddie. In science fiction movies, many now-classic films have shadowy evil corporations as the ultimate source of the problem that needs to be overcome – The Tyrell Corporation in the *Bladerunner* films, Omnicorp in *Robocop*, Skynet in *Terminator* and The Weyland-Yutani Corporation in *Alien*. Our heroes are pirates and outlaws who fight against the corrupt state and greedy corporations (Parker 2012), and films about work are explorations of the meaninglessness of routine, boredom and humiliation – *Clerks* (1994), *Office Space* (1999), *Waydowntown* (2000), *I Really Hate My Job* (2007), *Horrible Bosses* (2011) and many others.

I think we can add to this list a whole series of ways in which the same generalized scepticism is routinely deployed in endless acts of production and consumption – for example, a badge that simply says 'Fuck Work'. I have one, and think of it as an impossible object (or at least, a hypocritical one), since it in some sense attempts to deny the very labour that went into its production. Like the mug from Stoke, someone designed it and chose a colour and typeface that someone else had designed, marketed it, optimized the production schedule, pressed the button that made the machines run, packed it, designed a website, distributed it, sold it and collected the profit, or even the interest from their investment. Whilst the 'Fuck Work' example is rather extreme, a lot of money is clearly made through selling other examples of the counter-culture of organization. C. Northcote Parkinson's *Parkinson's Law* (1958) was an early example of a book-length view of organizations as inane bureaucracies populated by pompous and stupid men in suits. More recent examples are books with titles like *Bureaucrats: How to Annoy Them*; the *Bluffer's Guide to Management*; *The Little Book of Management Bollocks*; *The Little Book of Office Bollocks* and *Bullshit Bingo*. Found in a similar place in the book or gift shop might be *Mr Mean's Guide to Management*, *The Tiny Book of Boss Jokes*, or *250 Dumb Dares for the Workplace*, which is 'guaranteed to keep the office entertained'. *The Office Kama Sutra* contains instructions for the 'dance of a thousand sticky notes' and suggests many ways in which offices can become sites of libidinous excess. It also has a reversible book jacket which will allow you to pretend that you are actually reading a book called *Getting What You Want at Work: Ten Steps from Fantasy to Reality*. Or you might choose 'Voodoo Lou's Office Voodoo Kit' containing a corporate doll (with male and female sides), pins and 'Executive Spellbook'. The book explains what is wrong with bosses (playing golf, eating big lunches, driving a Lexus), their assistants, the computer nerd and so on. It then proposes various voodoo remedies that will deal with them, and provide the owner with 'your ticket to the corporate high life'. The same is probably not true of the 'Office Profanity Kit', containing a mini-talking punchbag which swears at you when you hit it, and three stamps with the mottos – 'This is F**CKING URGENT'; 'Complete and Utter BULLSHIT'; and 'I haven't got time to read this CRAP'.

Television is another place to find examples of similar sentiments, such as the 2004–05 US reality TV show *I Hate My Job*. A similar show was aired the year before in the UK – *Office Monkey*. Each episode was a TV version of giving the boss the finger: 'Offices are dull dreary places where nothing ever happens. That's why we bribed two members of offices around the country to disrupt their work places in the funniest ways possible. The winner gets a holiday, and the right to call themselves: Office Monkey.'[5]

The squirming embarrassment that accompanied victory was painful to watch, but tapped into some deeply rooted assumptions about what work is, and what work does to people. Office humour is generally spiteful, a form of vengeance that punishes hypocrisy and pomposity. This has been exploited by many British situation comedies in their portrayal of figures of authority.[6] *On The Buses* (1969–73), *Are You Being Served* (1972–83), and the Reginald Perrin shows (1976–79) all contained various supervisory or management characters whose vacuous vanity is regularly exposed (Hancock 2008). Often, these dramas were also post-war satires of social class in an era of accelerated social mobility, particularly of the 'jobsworth' who is acting up in terms of status and authority. So, Captain Mainwaring, the bank manager in *Dad's Army* (1968–77), or the leisure centre manager Gordon Brittas in *The Brittas Empire* (1991–97) are both claiming airs and graces which they clearly do not possess. Nowhere was this better satirized recently than in the mock reality TV show *The Office* which ran for two series on the BBC between 2001 and 2003, and then was remade for US TV, running for nine seasons between 2005–13. The US show, featuring the Dunder Mifflin company, has led to a video game, board game, nodding models of the characters, T-shirts, fake Dunder Mufflin websites and parodies of motivational posters.

Another iconic anti-work satire of the last few decades has been the Dilbert cartoons by Scott Adams. Co-opted by an entire generation of management academics and trainers, Adams' syndicated strip explores the stupidities of office life through the eyes of a naïve junior (Ackroyd and Thompson 1999, 116–118). Many episodes of *The Simpsons* picked up on similar themes concerning Homer's work at Mr Burns' power plant and the characteristics of the various professionals who work in Springfield (Rhodes 2001, Ellis 2008). These ideas were prefigured in Matt Groening's 1980s cartoons such as the *Work is Hell* collection (1986). Senior managers read articles titled 'How to Make the Veins in Your Forehead Throb Alarmingly' in a magazine called *Lonely Tyrant*. An even more surreal portrayal of work is David Rees *my new filing technique is unstoppable* (2004) which contains assorted employees abusing each other about their filing systems, computers that insult you profanely, and a character called Dr Niles Fanderbiles from the Quality Perfection Department who delivers self-righteous homilies in a Chinese accent. These satirical portrayals of work can also be found in plenty of underground comics and zines, such as the sad quietness of Stephen Knowles *five days out of seven* (2004). Celebrations of sabotage and slacking, and descriptions of alienation and boss hatred are a powerful theme, as Stephen Duncombe catalogues (1997, 79 *passim*). Less ribald, but just as powerfully, Matanle and colleagues have also shown how Japanese salaryman manga comics are plotted around our hero getting the better of corrupt or lazy bosses (2008).

Given its easy access at most workplaces and relative anonymity, it is hardly surprising that the internet has become a site for the counter-culture of organizing, as well as many ways to practically avoid working. The circulation of various anti-management spam mails is now a routine part of office life. Surfing during work time is a problem for organizations in itself, and various snooping technologies have been developed to prevent it, just as other counter-technologies have been developed to allow rapid movement between illicit web trivia and 'real' work on the computer. After all, if you were playing 'Whack Your Boss', you would almost certainly not want your superiors to know. This is a downloadable, and very disturbing, game that lets you kill your boss by using ordinary office equipment: 'So one can enjoy the numerous ways of whacking your boss. You can smash his head to the wall repeatedly, you can squish his egg head in the drawers of your office table. There are actually twenty different types of whacking your boss.'[7]

Bored with watching the blood splatter, you might go and have a look at websites and blogs like i-resign.com, worktotallysucks.com, and mybossisanidiot.com. The last allows you to send a letter from the site to your boss, anonymously of course, and helpfully provides templates and examples of other people's letters. There are some particularly nice examples on the site worksucks.com, which encourages obscene venting of various kinds:

> Every single thing we do here is scrutinized, analyzed, and just not allowed to proceed until the boss gets his fucking hands and opinion on it. He is a terrible business person and he fucks up so much here.
>
> It was his Daddy's business, a successful business, and this control freak, asshole, narcissistic abusive dickhead is just running it into the ground. And bringing us down with it. Every single day. And torturing us in the process.[8]

All these examples work so well precisely because the counter-culture of organization is embedded into so many assumptions about what work is and what it is not. We don't need to employ a huge amount of interpretive labour to make sense with them, or to explore their assumptions. They are the equivalent of the bus-shelter graffiti, a representational politics which gives power to the finger. So how does this sort of politics connect with the promises made by the betting-shop window?

Escape

In the mid-1970s, as cultural studies was in its infancy, the criminologists Stanley Cohen and Laurie Taylor wrote a book called *Escape Attempts*, subtitled 'The theory and practice of resistance to everyday life' (1976/1992). In characterizing everyday life as an 'open prison', Cohen and Taylor then go on to explore the various ways in which people cope by escaping into theatres of the imagination – through routines, distancing, fantasy, satire, inner identities – as well as caravans and hobbies (' … yoga, martial arts, dancing, occult, drugs, sexual workshops, discovering wild flowers, eating, boating, fishing … ' (ibid., 155). Cohen and Taylor present an account of escape in which resistance may well not be visible at all, being perhaps a question of distancing oneself from a work role which is played 'with detachment, with irony, even cynicism' (ibid., 54), or a form of fantasy or identification (with a football team or film star perhaps), which begins to insulate someone from a 'paramount reality' which is degrading and damaging. If paramount reality tells us that we are no more than puppets being moved around by others, then no wonder we want to becomes heroes in another drama. The most important point here is that the escape might be invisible, it might manifest as no more than going to see a film in which some good people beat some bad people, or a musical in which there is dancing and beauty, or the promise of a golden beach.

Nearly 30 years after *Escape Attempts*, Papadopoulos, Stephenson and Tsianos published their *Escape Routes*, a book which reframed 'paramount reality' in terms of Foucault's formulation of the move from sovereign to versions of capillary power structured as what they call 'postliberal aggregates' (Papadopoulos et al. 2008, 25). If Cohen and Taylor's book was predicated on a social phenomenology which insisted that social construction wasn't the same as determination, then this one is predicated on a poststructuralism which assumes that structures are always leaky, incomplete and can be escaped from. Post-Marxists or autonomists like Papadopoulos and colleagues talk more about the state than Cohen and Taylor, but the message is not so different. They suggest that we can classify itineraries of escapes as being concerned with new forms of life, migration and mobility, and a precarious relation to labour which produces new forms of sociality. Their routes are often (but not always) escapes in space, prefigured by vagabonds and nomads, because 'Escape is about energy, whilst discipline is about rule and labour is about static abilities' (Papadopoulos et al. 2008, 52):

> Our interest in escape is not that it culminates in a *better* configuration of life. Rather, the concept enables us to examine the often neglected engine of transformation which occurs without a master plan and without guarantees. Escape is a means, not an end ... '
>
> *(Papadopoulos et al. 2008, 61)*

Escape, in other words, is not the absence of politics, but an example of politics.

Cohen and Taylor are more pessimistic than Papadopoulos and colleagues' – compare their 'attempts' to the latter's 'routes' – but in both cases, escape is a form of resistance, though often an invisible one which does not involve the activism of graffiti-ing a bus shelter. The etymology of resistance is a sense of standing against something. It is a stance, a positioning which makes a standpoint clear, and implies some sort of force against force, a resistance. But the etymology of escape suggests leaving your pursuer clutching at your empty cloak whilst you vanish elsewhere. This is flight, a form of mobile politics that takes us elsewhere, and could easily not even be understood to be political at all, in the sense of a politics of manifestos and demands. Yet as James Scott suggests, there is much resistance which is documented in what he calls the 'hidden transcript' – 'the often fugitive political conduct of subordinate groups' (Scott 1990, xii). For Scott, these 'weapons of the weak' include folk tales, disguises, sarcasm, the occupation of different spaces and so on (1985). Scott's is a politics of the trickster, both in terms of what the trickster can do but also a sense in which it is often a politics that doesn't (at first glance) seem to be political at all. Another version of this is Judith Halberstam's queer version which explores illegibility and failure as statements of refusal and escape too. Judged by a culture which defines success in terms of production and reproduction, a refusal to play the game looks like an 'art of failure' (2011).

This sort of work, describing a politics that appears to be concerned to vacate The Political, helps me understand what I saw in Stoke, and what I think is a strong impulse towards escape in much of the counter-culture of organization. Unlike the explicit resistance we can see in many of the oppositional examples above which stand against work, the boss, the organization and so on, this seems to me to be a form of politics which shows itself as refusal through departure. In that sense, the promise of something else is predicated on an acknowledgement that the present doesn't work, and going absent is a reasonable response.

Consider this example. In May 2004, the English theme park Alton Towers, based near Stoke, put up a website titled ihatework.co.uk, which encouraged employees of other organizations to 'escape the workplace rat-race' by printing off a coupon for a cheap day out. The clear implication of the site was that you might pretend to be ill that day, and this provoked a small media storm with the Confederation of British Industries claiming that Alton Towers was acting irresponsibly in encouraging unauthorized absences. The PR people from the theme park of course denied this was the case, but one might wonder how tolerant the park management would have been if other organizations had encouraged Alton Towers' own employees to take time off work and go and have some fun.

Indeed, much popular culture that addresses work does trade on precisely these senses of escape from the 'open prison' as the hook for selling whatever is being sold. For example, an advert for a discount airline suggested that you could 'Tell the boss to stick it ... where the sun don't shine' because the holiday is largely made meaningful as a way of escaping from the times and places of work. Or a promotion for Christmas parties is called 'P45' (the UK tax form you get when leaving, or being sacked from, work), 'because you never liked your boss anyway'. Even the advertising for a chocolate bar can be articulated in terms of what it promises – 'Have a break. Have a Kit Kat' – because having a break from work is part of the routine of work itself. Almost any leisure-related product can make an useful reference to the repressive structure of the working week, such as the restaurant chain 'TGI Fridays' (Thank God It's ...), the TV show 'TFI Friday', or the hundred-and-one pop songs that have Friday on their mind, and are waiting for the weekend when we can dance, party, escape, or be together with the one we love (Rhodes 2007). In The Animals' 1965 song 'We Gotta Get Out of This Place', the singer begins by watching his father in bed, tired and hair greying, because he's been working and slaving his life away. Getting out is the best thing you can ever do.

Turning back to Stoke, that route to escape is written on the shop windows, on the billboards, and in the discarded lottery scratchcard on the pavement. It is precisely this impulse which so much of popular culture employs to 'magically resolve' the problems of the present (Cohen 1972). I assume that Cohen uses the word 'magically' here because there is no obvious mechanism which might allow such a resolution to take place. Instead, there is a desire for exodus, to be somewhere else, doing something else. So the promises in the betting-shop window, massage parlour, travel agent and off-licence are of escape from now through the mechanisms of luck, sex, aeroplanes and alcohol. It might not only be the work organization that needs to be escaped from, because there are possibilities for misery in unemployment and human relationships too, but there are enough references to relaxing, treating yourself, deserving a break, Friday night and the weekend to understand that the articulation of this escape is at least partly against work, against being in the organization.

There are other escapes here too, those of popular entertainment, as suggested in Richard Dyer's essay on musicals. He uses a series of structural oppositions in order to illustrate the sort of politics he sees in 'entertainment', a category almost intrinsically defined as trivial. If the social tension is defined by inadequacy and absence, then the solution proposes its opposite. Scarcity is remedied by abundance, exhaustion by energy, dreariness by intensity, manipulation by honesty, and fragmentation by community (Dyer 1993, 278–279).

In his examples, Dyer very often mentions work or the implications of work – 'unequal distribution of wealth … work as a grind, alienated labour … monotony, predictability, instrumentality of the daily round … advertising … job mobility … '. So, he argues, what entertainment does is to 'solve' issues:

> To be effective, the utopian sensibility has to take off from the real experiences of the audience. Yet to do this, to draw attention to the gap between what is and what could be, is, ideologically speaking, playing with fire. What musicals have to do, then (not through any conspiratorial intent, but because it is always easier to take the line of least resistance, i.e., to fit with prevailing norms), is to work through these contradictions at all levels in such a way as to 'manage' them, to make them seem to disappear.
>
> *(Dyer 1993, 279)*

So much of what we find on the billboards in Stoke dramatizes just this sort of gap, between the dull or oppressive present, and the drama of an alluring woman in a red dress with perfect makeup, or the cool gaze of a spy, superhero, or pirate. Even the posters advertising the local football team seem airbrushed, with bronzed demi-gods in taut poses, and wearing brightly coloured shirts sponsored by an online betting company. As they gaze at us, we might dream of such lives, of a kind of social and spatial mobility that would take us from here to there, to a life of energy and intensity, to become someone who was respected and popular, and could afford a big house and a shiny car.

Whether oppositional or utopian, it seems to me that the politics of popular culture is to question work, organization and management. It can do this through explicit satire, the wit of the trickster, or through a form of imagination which takes us elsewhere. This elsewhere, which Dyer sees as utopian, is a criticism of the present through its very existence, almost as if the more that the everyday world becomes a place of promises, the more obvious it is that those promises will never be fulfilled. As the National Lottery hailed its subjects – 'It Could Be You!!' – it could, but it probably won't.

Somewhere Else

Stephen Sondheim's lyrics to the 1957 musical *West Side Story* play with a particular notion of escape, a spatial one which is outside the experience of the poor who lived in the Upper West Side of New York City in the 1940s. In the song 'Somewhere', with soaring strings behind, his characters sings of having time together, time to look and time to care, of a new way of living. It is a powerful and beautiful cry for a sort of utopia from mean streets in which violence seems to prevent the endurance of love. In this chapter, I am trading on the idea that this is a form of culture which has historically been ignored by the university, and is still largely ignored by the business school. This aspect of popular culture has a politics which is in general opposition to a 'culture of organizing' which celebrates management and the market and can be found in the business school and other sites where the ideologies of capitalism are reproduced. Sometimes its complaints are voiced loudly, in graffiti on a bus stop, caricatures of evil bosses, or a mug that tells you that hard work is pointless. At other times, and perhaps more often, the strategy is to withdraw, to imagine, to hope that promises can come true because the present is too grey and heavy to bear. So when Cohen and Taylor, criminologists remember, describe their escape attempts as attempts to go 'over the wall' (1976/1992, 187), we get a nice sense of what the possibilities for escape might be, and an echo of other outsiders, vagabonds and outlaws (Becker 1963/1982, Parker 2012).

So far so good, but let's reflect on what this sort of argument does to ideas about a cultural politics of organization. For a start, most of my reference points have been unapologetically nostalgic – three works from the high point of leftist optimism in British social science from 1972, 1976 and 1977. In each of these works, there is a sense that the struggle for hegemony could be aided by taking 'culture' seriously. They assume that it is possible to understand a popular consciousness which is otherwise dismissed as mere entertainment, the product of culture industries which stupefy with bread and circuses (Horkheimer and Adorno 1944/2002). Though it is easy enough to sniffily dismiss all this as a romanticism of trash, I value this 1970s sense in which a politics can then be found in the trivial, in comic books and graffiti, as well as in musicals and betting shops. It echoes Halberstam's fascination for the 'silly' archives – animated film in her case – as being examples of 'low theory' (2011, 15). However, one of the problems is that such a 'culturalist' politics (hers included) runs the risk of ignoring the ways that the market itself produces and exploits desires for rebellion and escape, and then sells them back to us. Stories of surveillance and co-optation are common nowadays (Heath and Potter 2004, Boltanski and Chiapello 2005) and cultural politics more timid as a result. People pay money to place a bet or buy a lottery ticket, and their escape attempts seem to merely result in a move from one courtyard of the open prison to another. Cohen and Taylor are well aware of this problem: ' ... to say that everything can be an escape is as unhelpful as it is to assert that there is no need to look for escapes, that life offers everything' (1976/1992, 155). Or, to use the same equation, if we call everything politics, then perhaps it becomes harder to identify a politics that makes a difference, a politics that changes things, rather than merely leaves its graffiti on the skyscrapers of the powerful, or distracts us from the iron cage.

Perhaps, but this is to assume that we already know what 'politics' looks like, which is a general problem for this book. I have a simple suggestion for such difficulties of definition which end as counsels of despair. We could add some of the contingency of poststructuralism to these 1970s cultural studies arguments, and simply assert that to decide what counts as political in advance is already to narrow the possibilities of action. We cannot know, here and now, what graffiti might do, or what effects withdrawal might have. We cannot know what forms of organizing, or disorganizing, might help us build liveable worlds: 'The art of escape is the art of constructing an indeterminate form of energy from the encounter and interference with a regime of control.' (Papadopoulos et al. 2008, 52). This, I think, is similar to what Scott calls 'infrapolitics ... a wide variety of low-profile forms of resistance that dare not speak in their own name' (Scott 1990, 19). To decide what is 'political' is itself a political moment, and the sorts of decisions we make will show us the possibilities of the world in different ways. If we are to understand Scott's 'weapons of the weak' we cannot use the criteria established by the state, the town hall, the university, or the political party (Scott 1985, 1998). Then, instead of seeing Stoke as a place of despair and defeat, a place of empty promises and futile gestures, we might see it as a site in which cultural political struggle against hegemonic ideas about work and organization are written on bus stops and shop windows, as well as glittering on the early morning pavement.

Notes

1 This chapter is based on (2015) 'A Cultural Politics of Work: Resistance and Escape in the Counter Culture of Organizing', in A. Pullen and C. Rhodes (eds), *Companion to Ethics, Politics and Organization* (pp. 399–412). London: Routledge.
2 And, since Subways are normally more resilient than rats after a nuclear apocalypse, this tells you something about Stoke's economy.
3 Not just class, though this does seem to have been the most important organizing concept, but also gender, race and ethnicity too.
4 I'm not sure that culture is a particularly complex concept. Rather, its wide application results in it being a word with many different antonyms, prefixes and suffixes which result in it being a family of inflected terms rather than a single word.
5 https://en.wikipedia.org/wiki/Office_Monkey.
6 Apologies for the ethnocentricity of the following examples. Popular culture of the TV variety is rarely genuinely global.
7 Available on various websites at the time of writing, such as www.crazygames.com/game/whack-your-boss.
8 https://worksucks.com/work-rants/the-worst-person-i-have-ever-met/, accessed April 2024.

PART II

Assembly

3
ART

In a room, someone is sitting on a chair.[1] They are dressed in unremarkable clothes. Every 15 minutes or so, the person moves the chair, then moves again, and then again. After the third move, they sit for another 15 minutes. On the floor of the room are 400 dots, each in four-dot squares of the same colour. The legs of the chair have to rest on one of these squares, and the colour determines which direction the chair faces – red for south, blue for north, yellow for west and green for east. The room is in the Tate Gallery in the port of Liverpool in the post-industrial north west of England, 50 miles from the city of Stoke that we met in the previous chapter, and the people who sit on the chair are the Information Assistants (IAs) who work at the gallery. The IAs are almost all artists too – filmmakers, painters, writers, musicians and so on. Some are full time, but most work part time at the Tate in order to subsidize their own art work. The chair piece is one of the elements in a room curated by the English performance artist Tim Etchells. The chair positions are odd. People visiting the gallery often think that the person on the chair is performing some sort of security function. If they notice the strange movements and placements at all then they tend to observe from a distance. Only a few ask the person on the chair what they are doing.

Institutions like the Tate Gallery are, by definition, organized in some way. This doesn't mean that everything is organized, but it does mean that there must be some rules that can be explicated in a more or less coherent fashion. The rules might be written down as 'rules', perhaps numbered, or they might be visualized as organograms, flow diagrams, embedded in materials, in the design of buildings, or might be implicit in informal ways, in who wears what, and who says what to who. The general point is that it is impossible to imagine a formal organization with no rules, with no guides

DOI: 10.4324/9781032714288-5

to behaviour, no system which moves people around doing reasonably predictable things in time and space. However, this does not mean that there are any organizations that are entirely determined by formal rules. There are both practical and theoretical reasons for this. Practically, it is impossible to make sure that people follow every rule all of the time. In all but total institutions, the costs of surveillance would usually exceed the benefits of better rule following. In any case, it is theoretically impossible to write a set of rules to deal with every possible occurrence, such as the escape of a tiger in an art gallery, or the sudden appearance of His Majesty the King. This is simply because we cannot predict or describe every occurrence. Rather like Gödel's theorem, which proposes that no mathematical system can prove every statement within that system, no organizational system can propose rules for everything. For both these reasons, organizational rules are normally rather generalized, often containing broad guides to the aims of behaviour rather than details.

Tim Etchells' moving chair piece 'In Many Ways' is a simple set of instructions which can be performed in many ways. I found it very moving, hence this chapter, but I also focus on it to provoke questions about rules, questions which might be asked of organizations where the rules are more complicated, and there are no coloured dots on the floor telling us where to go next. Organizations like Henry Tate and Sons, sugar importers and refiners; the Tate Gallery Liverpool and DLA Piper, the sponsors of the 'DLA Piper This is Sculpture' series, of which Tim Etchells' piece was a part, and one of the largest legal services providers in the world. When I saw the piece, in June 2009, I watched the person moving around in the gallery, and was transfixed. Who was sitting in the chair, and were they getting paid? What were the rules for the movement, and for the pay? Most importantly, what did this piece suggest about the rules which produce something as 'work', or something as 'art'? Those were the questions that I asked in interviews with seven of the people who sat in the chair, as well as their supervisor, the artist, and the Head of Exhibitions and Displays.[2]

This chapter places the chair piece in the context of the other forms of organizing which were necessary in order that this 'work' could be done, in the space of art, of 'high' culture. It seems clear that both work and art are predicated on rules. Rules allow sameness and difference to be clearly identified, and production to become possible by repeating the same, or making something differently. In structural terms, it's pretty clear that we can only know that something is 'new' if we already know what the 'old' looks like. We need to know the rule before we know whether it has been broken, just as we can only classify something as organized in contrast to some notion of disorganization.

Nowadays, it might be argued that a common distinction between the cultural domain called 'work' and that called 'art' rests on assumptions about sticking to the rules. Being an artist is supposed to involve exposing the constraints of rules by breaking conventions and this usually happens outside organizations. Since the Industrial Revolution, work has conventionally been articulated as an organized place where repetition is encouraged, and rule breaking discouraged or punished. The space of the creative arts is supposed to be different, a space of freedom and play. No wonder that more recently there has been a sustained attempt to rebrand much middle-class labour as creative, as a site for self-expression and the engagement of passion (Hesmondhalgh 2018, Kane 2004, Bain 2005). What seems to be happening here, I think, is that ideas about the idealized freedoms and passions of 'art' are being used to symbolically ameliorate the pains of 'work', most particularly in the figure of the creative worker, the cultural quarter, the creative city and so on. Creative labour then sits between the autonomy of the artist and the slavery of the worker, a category which magically resolves some of the contradictions of capital by presenting much contemporary work as better than that which preceded it (Boltanski and Chiapello 2005).

'In Many Ways', as an example of 'art', is a phenomenon that necessarily echoes the work organization that allows it to be possible but cannot entirely explain it, any more than the organization can entirely determine the work of the receptionist or the security guard. As the institutional theory of art suggests (Danto 1964, Becker 1982, Dickie 1997), art is made in and by organized contexts – 'artworlds'. I want to add to this a more fine-grained and empirically detailed assertion – that art is work and involves rules, and work is creative and produces difference. This is an argument that also resonates with the suggestion that the economy is cultural, and culture is economic (du Gay and Pryke 2002, Amin and Thrift 2004), but with the important difference that I want the art itself to be part of the evidence here. Much of the cultural economy literature has been concerned with an anthropological sense of culture, but this has sometimes come at the cost of ignoring the texts of culture. Here, I want to think about both at the same time.

Work

The Tate Gallery Liverpool is based in the Albert Dock complex, on the north bank of the River Mersey. In order for the dock to be opened in 1846, a public house, several houses and a previous dock had to be demolished. One of its major commodities was sugar, and Henry Tate was one of those who used the docks to import the sugar needed for his business. The sugar initially came from cane cut by slaves on the plantations of the Caribbean. In 1889, Tate donated a collection of 65 contemporary paintings to the nation, together with a substantial bequest for a gallery to show them, and in 1897, the National Gallery of British Art opened in Millbank, London, on the north bank of the River Thames. Fifty years after its opening, Albert Dock could no longer be used by the new larger steamships since the gates were too small and the basin too shallow. By the 1920s, there was no shipping using the dock anymore and it was only being used for storage. After many years of decay, in 1988, the Tate Liverpool opened, receiving annual funding from the Department of Culture, Media and Sport. The Albert Dock is now the centre of a series of developments that include bars and restaurants, two hotels and various shops, and is surrounded by new offices, apartments, an events arena and a new shopping centre.

For two centuries, this has been a place of work, and its past is a tangle of institutions. Companies, firms, trusts and non-departmental public bodies have moved iron, stone and steel, ships, sugar, silk, paintings and people. The silt of the Mersey was dug, stone was lifted and placed, canvas was stitched, bails and boxes carried. Rhythms of labour, tonnes loaded and rates of pay. And this work was connected to other work by the labour of the vessels that tied the north bank of the Mersey to other organizations, in other places, where slaves were taught how to cut cane, and daily targets were set, and plantation rules were posted.[3] All work organizations are about rules, whether they have employees as property or employees as formally free. Rules for where to dig, the best way to drive a pallet truck, the expected amount of material to be moved in a day. Times of opening, and closing, of bells, horns, lock gates and doors, and harbour masters' offices. Places to walk, and not to walk – all involve the deployment of rules, of decisions about what and who moves where, and when.

Art

Tehching (sometimes Sam) Hseih is a Taiwanese American artist:[4]

> Between September 1978 and July 1986, Hsieh realized five separate yearlong performance pieces, in which he conformed to simple but highly restrictive rules throughout each entire year. In the unfolding series of these projects, punctuated by smaller intervals of unmarked life, Hsieh moved from a year of solitary confinement in a sealed cell without any communication with anyone, to a year in which he punched a worker's time clock in his studio on the hour every hour, to a year of itinerancy spent living without shelter on the streets, to another year in which he was tied closely with a rope to the artist Linda Montano, whom he was not allowed to touch, and lastly, to a year of total abstention from art activities and influences.
>
> *(Heathfield and Hsieh 2009, 11)*

On each occasion, Hsieh began by signing a piece of paper in which he outlined the rules for the performance:

'September 30th 1978

STATEMENT

I, Sam Hsieh, plan to do a one year performance piece, to begin on September 30, 1978.

I shall seal myself in my studio, in solitary confinement inside a cell-room measuring 11'6" X 9'X 8'.

I shall NOT converse, read, write, listen to the radio or watch television, until I unseal myself on September 29, 1979.

I shall have food every day.

My friend, Cheng Wei Kuong, will facilitate this piece by taking charge of my food, clothing and refuse.

Sam Hsieh

111 Hudson Street, 2nd/Fl. New York 10013'

(Heathfield and Hsieh 2009, 66)

Each of the performances involved some process of witnessing, getting an attorney to sign pieces of paper attesting to the truth of something, producing maps showing where he has been, stamped timecards or photographs, and asking an audience to be present in particular times and places.

Hsieh's 'work' is extreme performance art – life lived according to a minimal set of rules. At the time he performed these pieces, he was an illegal migrant in the United States, so it would be possible to see his art as political – as concerned with questions of shelter, incarceration, precarious labour – but Hsieh denies this:

You could see my work in some part as being about or representing the illegal immigrant, the refugee or the homeless person. But I don't think of art from this view, I think of it being about the struggle in life, and I'm inside it. You could say a work is about this or about that. It is not about something only. It continues to be open. It is possible for you to see it in many ways.

(Hsieh 2009, 326)

Hsieh appears to be more interested in the work as a demonstration of a certain sort of interiority, a truthfulness that simply is what it is, but at the same time shows the impossibility of knowing what it is. It doesn't need an audience, because it will carry on without them, but is nothing without an audience, though he is not interested in telling them to think in a particular way about what has happened. Its documents, such as the book produced over thirty years after the performances began (Heathfield and Hseih 2009), are 'proof' that the life was lived in the way promised, and nothing else. There is no other institutional product that might allow us to identify this as 'art', apart from our own speculations on what it would be like to do this ourselves, and how we would cope. Our thinking is perhaps the product, as 'the artist's thinking process becomes a work of art' (Hsieh 2009, 327).

Oddly, it is in the final piece that the rules become vague and in a sense unenforceable. On 1 July 1985, he signed a statement which said that he would not 'do ART, not talk ART, not see ART, not read ART, not go to ART gallery and ART museum for one year' (Heathfield and Hsieh 2009, 296). The other constraints were testable because they involved a certain fidelity to materials – a cage, a time clock, buildings and a rope. But art, and not-art? It is often enough assumed that there is a difference between life, work and art, but the previous four pieces of rule following have made such common sense unstable. So if art is life, and art is work, then how can there be a time when there is no art? How would we decide if Tehching was doing art? 'There is no accurate rule formulated in this piece; the rule cannot give this piece powerful support, it is just used for distinguishing life and art' (Hseih 2009, 336). Rules make distinctions between this and that, but even Tehching cannot construct this sort of rule with any accuracy.

Work

In 1959, the US sociologist Donald Roy wrote about how workers made repetitive jobs bearable. His answer was that they played games. His job involved working on a machine that punched out pieces of leather and plastic and meant performing the same task, all day, every day – 'click, ... move die, ... click, ... move die' (1959, 160). To ameliorate the boredom and exhaustion, he would give himself targets in response to the shape and colour of the materials he was working with. These might be expressed as 'as soon as I do so many of these, I'll get to do those' (ibid., 161). So, after doing a thousand brown rectangles, he would have the pleasure of some white circles. Another strategy involved the patterns he could create by using and filing the wooden cutting block in different ways – concentrating on putting as much wear and tear into the upper left-hand corner as he could and then sanding it down, for example. The patterns created by the different textures on the block, combined with the variations of leather or plastic, and trapezoid or square helped Roy play with the minimal intellectual demands of the job. It helped him stick it out, and quietened his thoughts about quitting.

Most of Roy's article is really about the social side of work and involves stories about the three other people who worked in his room of the factory. The patterns of time – peach time, banana time, window time, lunch time, coke time – and the structures of jokes and story telling, conversational themes and nonsense sounds, were what really quietened the 'beast of boredom' (1959, 164). Roy concludes, rather managerially, that these games prevented higher rates of labour turnover, and that any workgroup has a social equilibrium which is maintained through making a game of work. Work out when you are halfway through the pile, a quarter of the way, an eighth. Do all the red ones first. See how many plates you can balance on the rack before drying any. Race to see who can finish clearing the tables first. Leave the blue ones until last. How many chapters have I edited and how many do I have left? How many chapters have I read and how many do I have left?

The standard story about modern management is that it was not until the early twentieth century that a systemic approach to work organization was introduced. The work of people like Taylor, Gantt, Bedeaux, Ford, Urwick and others starts to introduce terms like 'scientific management' and 'time and motion' as descriptions of techniques for maximizing worker efficiency. Whether the origin story is true or not, it is clear enough that there was a lot of interest in how the spacing and timing of work could be engineered to minimize unproductive space and time. This might involve determining the pattern of breaks an employee was permitted, or re-designing their chair, or thinking about the movements of paper within an office. Tables of timings, photographs, films and floor plans of offices and factories would allow for work to be designed in every detail. Guidelines, instructions and rules are formulated which determine how movement through space happens, whether of people or things, machines or products, and a new class of expert is produced. At the same time, various authors were beginning to apply these techniques to the domestic sphere too, suggesting the most efficient way to organize a kitchen, a household, or the routines of a child (Dale 2009). The contemporary elaboration of these timing and spacing techniques in the workplace is often visual, with 'Just-in-Time' forms of production control involving painting coloured lines on a factory floor in order to show where and how many parts should be placed, and how stock should move around. The workplace becomes a diagram showing how work should be performed.[5]

Theatres, museums, zoos and art galleries are workplaces too. At the time of my research, there were about 40 IAs working in the Tate Liverpool, with about a quarter of them being full time. Part-time workers were given contracts for a certain number of hours which then allowed the construction of a rota for gallery and foyer duties which determined when and where people will be. Most of the time IAs spend time pacing the galleries telling people not to touch, not to bring food or drink into the galleries, not to run, not to take photographs. All these instructions for being a visitor could be found in the 'Tate Liverpool Visitor Regulations',[6] and they are one way of tracing the rules for the work of IAs.

Oddly, a document called the 'Information Assistant Job Description' is rather vague as to what IAs actually do, so the 'Gallery Procedure' effectively contains the rules for IAs, though it makes reference to other documents as well. It begins by noting that visitors will probably not be aware of the 'Visitor Regulations':

> Staff should always assume that the visitor is unaware of any Gallery rules and regulations. Every opportunity should be taken to impart suitable information to the visitor about the works on displays in a positive and informed way. When appropriate our aim should be to stop a visitor doing something that may be in breach of the Gallery's rules and regulations, but in such a way that does not embarrass them or make them feel uncomfortable but still leaves them feeling positive about the Tate.

The short document then covers, in 19 numbered points, the opening and closing of a Gallery, including equipment, appearance, patrolling, signing the check books, and so on. It also includes the checking of the 'Gallery rules and regulations' and ensuring that the Information Assistant is aware of these rules, particularly the visitor regulations. The document makes reference to other documents as well – an 'uniform instruction note', a 'fire evacuation procedure', and a 'bomb procedure'. Other implicit rules are referred to, such as 'crowd control' and the 'closing procedure', but no documents are mentioned for these.

Art

In 2008, the new Head of Exhibitions and Displays began to think about what to put in the gallery displays when they were re-installed in mid-2009. She had decided to focus on sculpture, and tried to think of as many ways of looking at this term as possible. This developed into the idea of having co-curators from other cultural areas – a filmmaker, a designer, a cook and so on – in order to move away from the traditionally chronological structure of these sorts of displays. Tim Etchells was asked to work to the title 'Performing Sculpture', for a small fee, some expenses, and a production budget for an original work of art. The Head was very pleased with the result, which she understood to be a way of challenging the conventional rules of gallery movement. Rather than the sideways shuffle along the walls, Tim's piece showed all sorts of spatial relations and trajectories. It challenged the visitor to think about what it means to look at art works in a gallery.

The set-up costs for 'In Many Ways' were not high – 400 coloured dots and a simple wooden chair – but the running costs were substantial. There were discussions about using students or volunteers to staff the chair, but it was unclear how a reliable rota could be developed which would ensure that there were trained people there every day for the next twelve months. Tim did not want people 'performing', so rejected the idea of using volunteers in favour of paying the IAs as part of their normal work. 'There's already an employer-employee relationship and all the responsibilities that go with that', he said. The Head of Exhibitions was aware, from a previous work, that it was difficult to sustain both budget and enthusiasm over a long performance. She also encouraged Tim to use people who were already on the payroll system and known to be reliable, who were (as Tim said) 'part of the machinery at Tate Liverpool'. This left her with the budgeting problem. How many hours of pay were required, for how many months, and at what cost? Her subsequent decision that the work should run from 11–3 every day then became a scheduling problem for the Information Assistant's Supervisor, Oren.[7]

Tim had only ever done the performance as a test when there was no one in the gallery. Once he had decided what to do, he outlined the idea in a meeting with the IAs who volunteered. Tim used the meeting to refine the instructions for the performance and the IAs who attended asked various questions which allowed Tim to specify both the rules and the freedoms more precisely. He was aware that he was 'paying performers to do this job' and wanted to provide them with 'a set of constraints within which you are free to operate, and to play'. After the meeting, he produced a written sheet titled 'Instructions for the performance'. It begins:

In this work a single performer moves a chair around 100 different positions marked on the floor of a gallery space, sitting in different positions and then, after a time, moving again. It's a simple task, the rules of which open many possibilities. The idea in a sense is to create a kind of ripple in the room – something just slightly out of the ordinary – an only-just-visible game that makes visitors to the gallery think about the space, and how they themselves are occupying it.

The sheet of instructions for this simple task take three-and-a-half pages, with an additional diagram and a page of sample answers to questions that the performer might be asked by gallery visitors. Clothing is specified as black trousers and an 'ordinary' top; knitting, reading, texting and so on are prohibited; visitors are not allowed to sit in the chair, and too much talking with visitors is discouraged, though simple questions can be answered. Much of the instruction sheet actually points out the choices and variations that the performers have. The rules are designed to be noticed by visitors, hence the three-hop movement, but the timing of the hops of the chair is not meant to be precise. Fifteen minutes is the maximum, but less is fine, and performers can sit in any way that they want, have their eyes closed or open, cross their legs or not, and so on. They also have complete freedom to move in whatever way they want within the 100 positions. Tim told me that he is interested in how different people will play with long hops, or short hops, staying on yellow, or moving from yellow to red to blue to green, moving away from visitors, or towards them, or refusing any discernible pattern apart from staying within the rules. As he said, 'according to different people's characters they would gravitate to certain ways of playing.' The same people might even be different on different days and might 'bring a different energy to it'. Tim wants them to have 'fun with the structure'.

There are certainly rules being followed here. Rules concerning paid employment, and time and space, all nested inside other rules, and others. But there are also endless holes in the rules, spaces where difference can be recognized. Tim's rules don't mention what happens if a fire alarm goes off, or if the King arrives, or if an academic wants to interview you about what it is like to sit in the chair. Perhaps we can never explain all the rules that matter within one system, and need to have recourse to other systems in order to find rules to apply. And once the economy of rules has been summoned, other paradoxes surface. Within Tim's elegant system, he needs to tell performers when they are free, and where they are constrained, as if freedom required a rule too, as if freedom had to be organized. As if we could only recognize freedom when it is pointed out to us, and play when it is different from work. And art when it is in a gallery, different from work.

Work

After his meeting with the IAs, Tim was not involved in the detailed planning concerning the rota for the performances and so on. He has watched them do it, and when they see him watching they nod and carry on. He is uncertain of people's motives for volunteering but doesn't mind if people only think – 'It's an extra shift. It'll be boring, but what the hell.' They don't need to feel like they are being 'art' in order to do it, and he also knows that people do things in different ways and that they might not stick to the rules. Oren, the supervisor, often walks through the gallery and occasionally has had to 'remind' people that this is a performance, and sometimes to stop them from chatting. Sometimes they are sitting rather too casually, with their 'arm over the back of the chair', so she tells them to sit up a bit in a stage whisper as she goes past. She isn't surprised that 'bad habits' come in when the performance lasts for a year, though she has told people that she doesn't really mind what they do if there is no one in the gallery. The Head has tried to watch too, but she thinks that they perform differently when she enters the room . If there were no visitors in the room, and the person in the chair has been chatting with one of the other IAs, they break off awkwardly and begin to perform. She doesn't like watching because it feels like a kind of control. But she knows that people do it differently anyway. Some are timid, and don't make eye contact with visitors, others like to communicate.

For example, Spike, one of the seven IAs I interviewed and who volunteered to perform 'In Many Ways', spent most of his time at work 'guarding the art', but really enjoyed doing talks and 'interpretation' when visitors asked him questions. He felt that most of his job was governed by written procedures, apart from these aspects which couldn't be the subject of a script and relied on his artistic knowledge. Both Spike and Jude, another Assistant, had been at the Tate for a long time. Jude felt that the job had become more deskilled as the Tate had become more like a business. All the Assistants looked forward to days when they were performing, rather than pacing the galleries. Spike enjoyed doing the piece because it got him away from the routine and doing something different. Max also said that he liked it because 'you get time to think', and Zoe that it's a 'nice little change of pace to look forward to', even though you don't get paid extra to be a performer. Assistants also liked the artist when he presented his ideas. Spike said, 'it felt as if [Tim] was asking us to do him a favour.'

Each of the Assistants followed the rules for 'In Many Ways' differently. Spike follows what he calls the 'guidelines' 'out of respect'. He sits relaxed, and interacts with people, seeking eye contact. He deliberately invades visitor's space, often making his moves more rapidly than the maximum 15 minutes in order to draw attention to himself. He talks to people when they talk to him and finds it hard not to be an IA when he sees people trying to take photos and so on. It's almost as if the rules for being an Assistant and the rules for performing interfere with each other. Jude thinks about what to wear, because 'it's a draughty gallery.' She also disrupts people's progress but doesn't follow the rules. She can't remember which way which the colours are supposed to face, so decides for that day, and ignores the timings in favour of getting in people's way, and sometimes echoing the shapes and attitudes of some of the artworks around her. But she thinks she performs the piece in a 'rigorous' way. When there are no visitors in the gallery, other IAs come over for a chat, and this annoys her a little because she is 'in the zone'.

Ben doesn't follow the rules either, and doesn't think most people do. He just follows people around, and delighted in telling me how he chased two French girls around the gallery one day. He 'abandoned the rules straight away' because it would be dull to stick to them. Martin saw the rules as a 'loose set of guidelines'. He will sometimes pick a colour to stay on or sometimes be deliberately obstructive, and see whether people will block his view of an artwork. Or he might look intently at a blank wall and try and encourage visitors to do the same. He doesn't try to look different and tries to be 'an unremarkable body'. Changing from his Tate uniform into the everyday clothes he wears for the performance makes him think of the 'separate sort of uniform that I have to wear for Etchells'. He is restless when sitting on the chair and often wants to stretch, 'break free', and walk around.

Abby thinks that 'every person makes their own rules'. She does 5–10 minutes between moves, avoids subsequent identical colours, and likes the odder placements of the chair. Once, she went and sat right next to a 'snogging couple' to see what would happen. The rules are leaking back into her job. She is now much more aware of her movements as she paces the gallery, and whether she is facing the blue way, or the red way, and so on. Zoe follows the rules, even if there is no one else in the gallery, but then gave an example of breaking the rules for a school talk, and not being able to time the moves very well. She tries to project a bland but not threatening persona – 'meditative', 'like solitaire' – but does sometimes do an 'outward performance' if there are people watching. She enjoys the 'absolute freedom to move wherever you want, how often you want', and this makes her feel as if she is in control of the space. This seems to have resulted in some odd responses from the public. Once, a woman came so close to her sitting on the chair in order to look at a Cindy Sherman photo behind her that she put her breasts in Zoe's face as if she wasn't there. Another man went 'mental' because she had claimed in response to a question that the movements were random, and he loudly insisted that they weren't, and that she shouldn't be doing the performance because she didn't understand it.

Despite these encounters, most members of the public didn't engage with the performance directly. Oren said that it was mostly young people, as well as some visiting staff from the Tate Modern in London, who questioned the employees sitting on the chair. Kids would ask Ben, 'are you Art?' One asked Jude, 'what *are* you?' Or perhaps they would question the experience, asking 'don't you get bored sitting there all day?' There were also questions about the performance as if it were a job – 'do you get paid extra for this?' Max told me about an incident with a casually employed Assistant called Fizz. One day in the summer, he was sitting in the chair and was surrounded by a group of rather sarcastic teenagers. They asked him 'why are you doing that?' And then, 'how much do you get paid?', and 'haven't you got anything better to do?' He had to be rescued by the IA on duty at the time.

Most of the IAs did understand the chair piece as a sort of art which was aimed at altering space. Spike, for example, said that he followed the rules out of respect for the art, not because it was work. This was something that he had volunteered for, and that allowed for freedom in choosing where to go. Zoe thinks about the piece as a 'subtle ripple in the normal social fabric', and Jude thinks about the way it changes space too. Doing it makes her feel powerful, but she doesn't feel it is work. The piece also did make many of the IAs think about rules, and about the routines that shape our use of space. Martin, for example, said that 'we don't realize how much we are manipulated by other people.' He seemed to mean that he could move people around through his own movements on the chair, but also widened the idea to refer to the physical characteristics of the space too. As he said, 'you are being determined by the wall.' Zoe said something similar: 'Most people, most of the time, follow most of the rules. And for sure, within work, because if you don't, you don't have the job.' But, she said, for 'In Many Ways' the rules are only a skeleton, and it's different every time you do it.

When I asked them whether 'In Many Ways' was 'work', or 'art', quite a few simply denied the separation. Spike, for example, pointed out that it might be conceptual art, not art that required craft, but that there are rules that govern the use of paint and surfaces too. He knew this because he was a painter himself. It wasn't a question of being constrained at work, and free in art, because there is a 'compliance needed for a piece of art'. Max noted that just because rules become so instilled in you that you don't think about them anymore doesn't mean that you aren't following them: 'It's all work isn't it? It's just that some work is more enjoyable than others.' Max was a painter too and said that 'painting can sometimes feel like it's a job. You've got to get up in the morning', and that 'you're producing a product at the end of the day that you hope will sell.' Most of the IAs didn't see any particular difference between following Tim's rules, and the work they did as artists. As Abby said, there are plenty of examples of art practice where someone follows someone else's rules, such as Sol LeWitt's instructions for his wall paintings, one of which had been exhibited at the Tate earlier in 2009. In that sense, following these rules was no different. Ben said that he was 'just a cog in the machine that [Tim] has set up' but wasn't resentful about this because he enjoyed it most of the time: 'Its not very hard work but it is work', and 'nice work if you can get it'. It was art, and work. The same as his own artwork, apart from the fact that he never gets paid in the middle of the night in his studio.

Artwork

Tim Etchells likes watching people work, and he told me a story about visiting a theatre in Vienna in between performances and sitting in the stalls watching thirty or forty people putting up the set, the lights, the props and so on. Unlike theatre, which has a 'declared energy', watching people who aren't very bothered about you has a very enigmatic character. There is a choreography to following rules, a drama unfolding, but you need to work out what is going on. Something is happening, but what? Tim characterized this as a 'blankness'. When I asked Ben what he thought about when he was hopping around the gallery on his chair, he seemed to find the question puzzling: 'What do I think about? [...] I need to go over there because I haven't been over there [...] I'm certainly not sat there thinking "I am art and I am important. Look at me". It's somewhere in between "what's for tea" and "I am art".'

Perhaps the gap between 'what's for tea?' and 'I am art' isn't a very wide one. Tehching Hseih was no doubt thinking about his tea often enough, locked in his cell, stamping the time clock, sleeping on a bench. His performance pieces might often remind us of 'monastery, religious order, messed-up cult, labour camp and terrible prison' (Etchells 2009, 357), but they can be understood in many ways. They were 'done quietly, with love and for art', but seem to call up conceptions of machinery, system, and 'conditions of physical and mental duress, isolation or hardship' (ibid., 357–358). Tehching made the rules, and then lived within them, and then stopped. But the sheer horror of those rules, of doing that to yourself, of alienating yourself in that way, somehow makes his performance even more frightening. There was no institution to enforce the rules, no social sanctions, no commission from an art gallery, no fifty lashes or docking pay. The 'artworld' that made this art was very minimal indeed (Becker 1982). 'It is just what it is', as Tim put it. Though we might speculate on Tehching's motives, his cultural influences, the political points he was making, he actually tells us nothing of that:

> There is only the submission or control of body, time and space, the endless regulation of and tracking of (human) resources. The work is time served. A perfect model of late capitalism perhaps in its product-less purity. All the discipline without the pay-off of an object. Prison labour organized by Samuel Beckett. Pointless non-manufacture. Absurd.
>
> *(Etchells 2009, 357)*

'In Many Ways' is an echo of Tehching's 'work', but it works because it is already embedded in a network of institutions, in an artworld. The Tate is less frightening than Hsieh's cage because there is already so much in place which organizes the work. Ben told me that 'it's art because Tim Etchells says it's art', but that was really only the beginning of the story. In order for Etchell's system to become art, the Head of Exhibitions, the Tate Liverpool and DLA Piper had to agree that it was too, and then space, money and other rules had to be organized in order that it might be hard to mistake it for work (Danto 1964, Becker 1982, Dickie 1997). Yet the Etchell's piece intrigues me precisely because it then leaks back into the matrix of rules and institutions, and it seemed to trouble the myth of artistic identity for those sitting in the chair too. Visitors would often mistake the person for someone guarding art, rather than art itself. There is a central position in the opening between the two sections of the gallery where the chair can be placed and looks like an obstruction. When sitting there, Spike is often asked, 'can we go in?', so used are the visitors to obeying rules that they have never seen. And when naïve children and rude teenagers demand to know what is going on, how much someone is getting paid, and why they can't get a better job than this, the boundary between art and work once again begins to look rather fragile, as if the careful construction of an artworld could suddenly collapse back into the world of work because of some minor disruption experiment. So we can watch someone work, as art, but it helps if they are on a stage, or in a studio or gallery. This is probably why we find it hard to imagine watching someone cutting sugar cane in a plantation, or even making cups of tea in the Tate café, as art. Unless we imagine that they are travelling along lines of coloured dots?

In part, this is because the idea of art usually comes into being through a certain sort of distinction from work. This is in part an economic difference. If art were the same as work, it would no longer have any distinction, and any market value beyond that given to other products or services of that sort:

> While art serves private functions of decoration, entertainment and investment, its difference from 'ordinary things' is signalled by providing special places for its display, where it sits simply to be studied and admired, not bought or consumed in any obvious way.
>
> *(Siegal and Mattick 2004, 17)*

The effacement of economic relations is part of the trick that produces economic distinctiveness, but so too is a certain sort of myth about the craft of the artist: 'It is more like the work done in a workshop in pre-modern times: volume is small, and each object has a unique status as the product of an individual, the artist' (Siegal and Mattick 2004, 17).

Older meanings of the word 'art' tend to associate it with work-based skill, as in the word 'artisan', but by the late seventeenth century, the word was increasingly being applied to some skills rather than others (Williams 1976, 41; Bain 2005, 27 *passim*). As industrialization progresses, 'art' and 'work' become differentiated, perhaps because the sort of autopoetic self-expression of the artist appeared to contrast so starkly with the repetitive and allopoetic rule following of everyone else:

> Art came to appear as the highest form of human productive activity, the model against which other forms of work could be measured, in particular the routinized, divided, manager-directed labour that came to dominate the factories and offices of developing capitalism.
>
> *(Siegal and Mattick 2004, 20)*

As Siegal and Mattick's book goes on to show, much of the history of the past century of conceptual art has been concerned to question these distinctions. They focus on the ways in which questions of production, circulation and business have been the focus of a variety of artists. As well as 'performance art', Marcel Duchamp used manufactured products, Piero Manzoni sold his own shit in identical tins, Mierle Laderman Ukeles cleaned a gallery as 'maintenance art', and Roxy Paine made a 'Painting Manufacture Unit' machine. Not only are these artists often worrying away at what counts as art, but often also something about the nature of the artist. Takashi Murakami sells figures, key rings and mousepads made in his own factory, Santiago Sierra hires prostitutes and illegal migrants to do things for money, and numerous artists become project managers working with specialist art fabrication companies (Molesworth 2003, Artforum 2007). If the gallery was once somewhere that concealed its own relations to work, now, it seems that the exposure of these relations in specific contexts is often the conjuring trick that produces art. Andy Warhol was ahead of the game here, with his insistence on wanting to be a machine, and desire for boredom and repetition as values in themselves (Bergin 1967). As he famously put it,

> Business art is the step that comes after Art [...] During the hippie era people put down the idea of business – they'd say, "Money is bad", and "Working is bad", but making money is art and working is art and good business is the best art.
>
> *(Warhol 2007/1975, 92)*

Both the institutional theory of art and elements of cultural economy are now playing catch up with conceptual artists in attempting to unmake these distinctions. But, even if we dissolve these divisions, in the name of creativity, critique, or social-scientific understanding, we are always left with rules. It is the exposure of the rule, through its stressing, that makes shit in tins interesting. At one level, we could say that these are rules for determining what work is and what art is. Lurking behind this distinction is the idea that art somehow bends and breaks rules, or lives between rules, or makes spaces that are not governed by the old rules. The myth of art and creativity then makes rules and freedoms, organization and disorganization, into oppositions, rather than showing how they make each other. Though art might sometimes look as if it is pushing itself away from conservative constraint, and towards the realm of pure freedom, it can do only so precisely because of the prior existence of something to kick against. In other words, we can only understand a rule if we can imagine breaking it, and only understand freedom in the context of its denial. If Tehching speaks, interacts, or leaves his 'cell-room', he will have broken his rules, but beyond that he is free to do and think what he wants within the cage. The very sharpness of that freedom is accentuated by the bars of the iron cage.

Tim Etchells captures this rather well when he talks about the way in which being trapped, compelled, and constrained itself opens possibilities, permissions, re-inventions: 'Without constraint there is no such thing as meaning, and I don't think there is any such thing as freedom, really.' Despite the detail of the rules of 'In Many Ways', all the IAs I talked to performed it differently. Between the dots, and the timings, there were styles, motivations, stories, and finally the obsessive-compulsive image of one of the assistants moving a chair in an empty and echoing gallery, as if in a dream, while outside the rain stippled the river. In working to rule, she broke the rules.

Organized Labour

In empirical terms, in work, and in art, there is no pure freedom, and no pure constraint. As Tehching put it – 'I am as free in the cage as outside' (Hsieh 2009, 328). We are always, as Tim put it, 'working inside rules, performing inside rules, behaving inside rules'. The rules tell us where here is, and where there is, and allow us to move faster, or slower, and to decide which colour to aim at today. But because there can never be enough rules, and because people forget and break the rules, or kick against the rules, the systems and structures are always decaying into something different. Just as organization is parasitic on disorganization (Cooper 1986), so is the decay, stress and failure of rules productive of events and artefacts that we can recognize as new, as well as forms of routine that then in turn become new rules. Oren the supervisor told me that IAs gradually developed ideas about how they might pace a newly installed gallery, in order to find ways of making friendly contact with visitors but not to break their sight lines. Tips are passed on to other IAs, and they become routines which might eventually be sedimented as informal rules, and perhaps even written ones too. Many of the IAs also told me how they gradually found the Etchells performance more routine, and less embarrassing. If embarrassment is a sense of having broken some rules, then routine is already halfway to boredom. To avoid the boredom of repetition, of 'click, … move die, … click, … move die', all the Assistants, and Donald Roy, made freedom by playing games.

This is just someone sitting on a chair. That's all. Just as I was when I was interviewing people and writing this book. But the very fact that they were doing it in an art gallery made it interesting, both in the sense that it broke the rules for an art gallery, and also that I know that if I come across work in an art gallery, it will very often be breaking some rules. That is often the rule, for art galleries nowadays, and it lies at the heart of other institutions too, like the circus and the zoo. In order to make the rule of rule breaking happen, Oren needed to put together a rota, and attend to all the relevant rules of employment and inevitable financial constraints. As 'In Many Ways' shows, the relation between work and art, economy and culture, is very unstable. Both involve the construction of a system, often stabilized and ramified into being an organization for a while. We cannot say that one involves repetition and the other makes difference, or that one is constrained whilst the other is free. What counts as work or art depends on institutional context, which is another way of saying that it depends on the rules that suspend all our performances in grids of intelligibility. Tehching Hseih 'chose' the year-long cage and the time clock, just as the IAs chose to subject themselves to Tim Etchells' rules because it was a change from their ordinary jobs.

The distinction between slavery and twenty-first-century work is that we are formally free. These formal freedoms are often mistaken for a lack of constraint, with the work of the artist often being held up as the model for a creative post-industrial workplace or creative city (Bain 2005, Boltanski and Chiapello 2005), just as it emerged from an idealization of the pre-industrial craft worker. But the 'wage slave' and the artist are both following and making rules, both being worked on and working. The distinction between the plantation slave who was freed to become a wage slave, the IA, the performance artist and the writer of this book can never really be about the substance of what their work involves, whatever they might claim, because there is no intrinsic difference to be found in what is actually done.[8] Donald Roy's work was as creative as Tehching Hseih's, and just as rule-bound too. If the institutional theory of art shows us that what counts as 'art' is made by social contexts, then symmetrically, it shows us that 'work' is made by that context too.

At night, after the visitors have gone home, and the IAs have left the building, I was told that someone takes the chair from the gallery to a disabled toilet where it stays overnight, for health and safety reasons. The Tate Gallery, built on industrial labour and now a creative hub for a creative city, runs on rules like this one, even though no one could tell me why a chair sitting in an empty gallery would be a heath and safety risk. Someone moving the chair to the art gallery's toilet every night, though there were no coloured dots to guide its passage and no audience to see it happen, is art itself.

Notes

1 This chapter is based on (2013) 'Art as Work: Rules and Creative Labour', *Journal of Cultural Economy* 6/2: 120–136.
2 All the interviews were taped and lasted between 20 minutes and an hour. I interviewed the artist in Sheffield in July 2009 and again briefly by telephone in December 2009. Everyone else I interviewed at Tate Liverpool in October and November 2009.
3 There are many examples of such plantation rules. See Bennet H Barrow's 'Rules of Highland Plantation' at www.sjsu.edu/faculty/watkins/barrowrules.htm; Mr St George Cocke's 'Plantation Management' at http://invention.smithsonian.org/centerpieces/whole_cloth/u2ei/u2materials/deBow.html; or Alexander Telfair's 'Plantation Rules' at http://invention.smithsonian.org/centerpieces/whole_cloth/u2ei/u2materials/prules.html (all accessed 9 December 2009). Rule 2 in the latter is 'No Negro to have more than Fifty lashes inflicted for any offence, no matter

how great the crime.' For more on the relations between management and slavery, see Cooke (2003).

4 Thanks to Tim Etchells for drawing my attention to this work. If you are interested, you might also have a look at artists like Marina Abramović, Benjamin Bennett and Alastair MacLennan.

5 The materialization, on a smaller scale, of the 'time geography' developed by Torsten Hägerstrand. See Pred (1981).

6 These are no longer available but are probably similar to the 'Tate Visitor Regulations', which can currently be found at www.tate.org.uk/visit/tate-gall ery-rules, accessed 19 July 2024. The previous versions which I allude to in this chapter are no longer available online.

7 I have given all my interviewees pseudonyms.

8 The key question is whether they can stop doing work or art if they get bored. Clearly, most people cannot easily stop working because they can't afford to.

4
THE ZOO

Classification and organization are co-produced.[1] The beginnings of classification are the beginnings of organization, and when we attend to organization, whether in a mug factory in Stoke or an art gallery in Liverpool, we are in the presence of systems of classification. That is to say, organizing is a process that can be recognized by its attention to collection and distribution; to claims about similarities and differences; to the boundaries that keep some elements together and other elements apart. The map of a zoo that you are given on entering is a representation of this sort of classification, one in which the separations between (mostly) humans and (mostly) non-humans are constitutive of the organization. The bars, palisades, glass and moats which separate the paths and cafes for the visitors from the cages of the visited define the zoo, because the zoo is brought into being by bringing things together and then keeping them just slightly apart.

Such matters might seem too obvious to remark upon, but for those interested in organizing, it is worth considering how an institution such as a zoo emerges from a series of antecedent institutions with slightly different forms of classification, both for people and animals (Ritvo 1997). The zoo did not spring into being as it is, fully formed, but is the result of a series of mutations which result in its current manifestation. My approach in this chapter is historical and requires that I explore how the zoo came to be possible, placing it within the genealogical context of other forms of collecting and ordering, particularly with reference to non-human animals, but also other non-human materials (Foucault 1989b, 1991). By genealogy, Foucault intends us to investigate the 'the history of the present', that is to say, to provide an account of how we have come to be what we are.

DOI: 10.4324/9781032714288-6

I want to understand how a particular form of organizing has emerged and congealed, using the zoo to help me think about the relation between organization and disorganization (Cooper 1986), rule and rule breaking, order and disorder (Foucault 1989a), the production of ideas about civilization and wilderness.

In what follows I will offer a chronological account of what seem to me to be the conditions of possibility of the modern zoo, beginning with the collection, then discussing the landscape park and the menagerie, and finally the carnival and fair. This leads to a discussion of its foundation in the nineteenth century, its engagements with capitalism and spectacle, and a few comments about the problems it faces in the twenty-first. Throughout, I consider how this organization grows from prior understandings of the classification of people and other things. I end with some reflections on the strange dialectic between order and disorder that the zoo exemplifies, an organization which is constructed to civilize and contain, but which is always haunted by the financial need for spectacle and the production of the idea of the absolute other of the wild non-human.

The Cabinet of Curiosities

Keeping animals in predictable places is common to all pastoral societies, but the keeping of non-native or spectacular animals for pleasure is something that, until the nineteenth century, was only practiced by the wealthy, and usually in private parks or palaces (Foucault 1986, 25; Baratay and Hardouin-Fugier 2004, 17). Persian *paradeisos* were wooded gardens populated with animals. Sometimes, the animals would be made to fight each other, or with humans. Ancient Romans would often parade wild beasts along with conquered people, and then use both in entertainments. This celebration of excess continues into the early modern period. In Italian, from the fourteenth century, a *seragli* was a place for the exhibition of animals. In French, and then English, the word commonly used was *menagerie*. These were spectacular displays of wealth and power, showing off the conquests of the hunt, gifts from supplicants, or the loot from places that had been plundered. By the sixteenth and seventeenth century in North Western Europe, such collections were quite common amongst popes, monarchs, and members of the landed gentry. Often these animals were assembled for staged fights, in which the generosity of the host would be measured by the amount of blood that was spilt. However, despite similarities, I don't think that this is the best place to look for a genealogy of the zoological garden. The seraglio of kings is a form of display designed to symbolize power and excess, not a systematic collection which is open to some kind of public.

A common reference point to begin to understand the idea of the collection in the early modern period is what is commonly called the 'Cabinet of

Curiosities' or *Wunderkammer* (Shelton 1994, Mauriès 2002, Bowry 2014). This assemblage brought together selected objects in a particular space, both natural wonders and curios made by people. By the sixteenth century, it appears that the very idea of curiosity is becoming possible for the emergent bourgeoisie in a way that it was not in medieval times. Clerics such as St Augustine, St Bernard, Pope Innocent III and many others had been keen to stress that idle questioning was a distraction from God's law and it was the Devil who incited prying (Blom 2004, 19; Dillon 2013, 214). The only collections that had been common were conspicuous displays of wealth, or religious reliquaries and representations of sacred and instructive scenes. The Renaissance inaugurates a context in which explorers' tales, new plants and animals and even different kinds of people were becoming permissible objects of interest. The accumulation of things without clear utility from other places can perhaps be understood as a way of claiming a particular kind of identity, a way for men (usually) to discuss and demonstrate taste and knowledge, to compare and contrast.

Unlike collections of art which required a large house and a great deal of money, the cabinet was something that could be assembled by someone with more modest means. Sometimes they were housed in pieces of furniture, sometimes rooms (as in the Italian *studiolo*), but always an arrangement of that which was defined as unusual and rare. If the cabinet was in a room, then images of them suggest that every surface – even the ceiling – was filled and covered with objects. There are differences between the cabinets found in different parts of Europe, particularly in terms of whether they contained *artificialia* (man-made objects) or *naturalia*, or some combination of those two categories. Typically, *naturalia* might include interesting rocks or stones, stuffed birds or pickled embryos, shells, skeletons, unusual plants and so on, whilst *artificialia* might be medals, exotic objects from other places, medicines, paintings and whatever. There were helpful texts that assisted with classification, suggesting certain orders of objects, and the taste of a gentleman was displayed in his cabinet, made material in assumptions about what was interesting and what was common, about what should be adjacent to what (Shelton 1994, Blom 2004, 239; Zytaruk 2011, Bowry 2014).

Mauriès describes the cabinet of curiosities as a 'carefully arranged profusion' (2002, 10), an artful chaos of things which employs the room, niche, frame, box and drawer to separate and conjoin. It is an assemblage which requires something be seen as 'other' in order that it can then be captured within the confines of a collection. It is parasitic on travel, trade and all the unknowns and unfamiliarities which that brings. The idea of the cabinet of curiosities is a helpful place to begin thinking about the emergence of many different institutions, such as the art gallery and museum, but is particularly relevant to the zoo because of the way it establishes the possibility of collecting being a bourgeois practice, undertaken for its instructive and social functions:

> A display of fearsome Turkish weapons; certain monsters or sports of nature, both human and animal, as, for instance, a doe with antlers or a dessicated Cyclops; a stuffed armadillo from Brazil; a stone carved with a hundred facets; an Italian spinet that played three tunes of its own accord by a secret automatic mechanism; divers automata; a collection of polyhedral crystals; Roman medals lately dug out of the earth; a small picture made of the root of an olive tree upon which nature had wrought a human figure; a mummified monkey's claw ...
>
> *(Dillon 2013, 18)*

As Dillon suggests, the collection is an invitation to a list, an inventory which is both its means and end. If it is to be understood a more than just a pile of matter out of place, a hoard of random junk, then its logic must be explicated in some sort of taxonomy.

Jorge Luis Borges, in his 1942 essay 'The Analytical Language of John Wilkins', nicely illustrates the arbitrariness and cultural specificity of any attempt to categorize the world. Borges writes of a classification supposedly taken from an ancient Chinese encyclopedia – the 'Celestial Emporium of Benevolent Knowledge'. It divides all animals into 14 categories:

> Those that belong to the emperor; Embalmed ones; Those that are trained; Suckling pigs; Mermaids (or Sirens); Fabulous ones; Stray dogs; Those that are included in this classification; Those that tremble as if they were mad; Innumerable ones; Those drawn with a very fine camel hair brush; *Et cetera*; Those that have just broken the flower vase; Those that, at a distance, resemble flies.
>
> *(Borges 1942/1964, 103)*

It's a marvellous list, and one that Foucault uses to begin his classification of classifications in *The Order of Things*:

> This book first arose out of a passage in Borges, out of the laughter that shattered, as I read the passage, all the familiar landmarks of thought— our thought, the thought that bears the stamp of our age and our geography—breaking up all the ordered surfaces and all the planes with which we are accustomed to tame the wild profusion of existing things and continuing long afterwards to disturb and threaten with collapse our age-old definitions between the Same and the Other.
>
> *(Foucault 1989a, xvi)*

The process of organizing makes things the same and different. As Robert Cooper explored in a series of essays (Burrell and Parker 2016), this means paying particular attention to the 'labour of division', to the boundaries and bars that produce difference by constituting insides and outsides, us and them, organization and disorganization. Such organizing demands the classification of people, methods and objects of enquiry, and (when successful) produces systematic distinctions and unities, theories about why particular boundaries and genealogies matter, and the keeping of records which assist the reproduction of the practice through time. There are two important changes here. One is the legitimacy of the very idea of collecting for reasons of curiosity, and the second is systematic reflection on the system which organizes the collection.

Within this period, there does appear to be a move from the idea of collecting many particular and wonderful items, to the collection of a series of items which could be compared for their forms and functions. Kaulingfreks and colleagues suggest that this is an example of the decline of wonder, and the move towards the production of institutions that address 'a hidden correspondence, an underlying classification, a secret relationship.' (Kaulingfreks et al. 2011, 322). For them, the *Wunderkammer* is the origin of a process which disenchants the world, and which results in the museum and gallery, both primarily based on the dull principal of compare and contrast. For example, the foundation of botanical gardens or herbariums began from the late 1500s onwards, laid out with care to ensure the separation between different forms and functions and often being established within universities. As the legitimacy of academic enquiry becomes more established, so does the idea that scholars should have access to, or even management of, menageries and botanical gardens. In his utopia *New Atlantis* of 1627, Francis Bacon describes Saloman's House – a massive scientific institution – with 'parks and enclosures of all sorts of beasts and birds which we use not only for view or rareness, but likewise for dissections and trials' (in Blom 2004, 183). This was collection for empirical purposes, and an implicit critique of past ignorance. A few years later, Chapter 3 of Thomas Brown's *Pseudodoxia Epidemica* of 1646 bemoans the vulgar errors which have allowed people to believe in griffins, unicorns, the phoenix and so on, as well as correcting fallacies, such that elephants have no joints, or that salamanders can live in fire. If nature is to be properly understood, it must be subject to the tests of experience, and that means collecting things in order to understand them, to place them in a series, in a classification (Ritvo 1997).

The London doctor Hans Sloane (1660–1753) collected over 70,000 objects which eventually became the foundation bequest of the British Museum, opened in 1759. He was a collector of other people's collections, and also kept a menagerie and herbarium next to his house in Chelsea (Blom 2004, 77 *passim*; Grigson 2016, 60). As Walter Benjamin suggested in his essay on libraries, a collector 'is engaged in a dialectical tension between the poles of disorder and order' (1999, 62). 'The collector, like the reader, seeks to convince himself that there is structure, that things can be ordered and understood, even if they seem to obey alien rules, or no rules at all' (Blom 2004, 206) So, what are the principles that organized the collection of living *animals* for reasons of curiosity, and what system could hold confusion at bay?

Management and the Menagerie

While Western European menageries had existed for some time, such as the collection in the Tower of London established in 1204, the creation of the landscaped park in the seventeenth century announces a different way of thinking about space and the control of animals. The idea of a view, a perspective, as well as attempts to prevent the escape of livestock or poaching, means that the involuted woodland of the hunting forest becomes increasingly bisected by avenues, observed by towers and enclosed by walls and ditches. A garden was a contrived work which combined paths, views, sculptures, grottos and water features – organizing space according to a plan and demonstrating wealth and taste. Foucault suggests that it was heterotopic in its ambition, an attempt to make many places occupy one space (1986, 25). A common feature was a square (*parquet*) often with criss-cross paths making stars or an octagon and centred on some sort of pavilion or tower which would allow the owner and his friends to observe the land around, including the animals, whether grazing or intended as objects for hunting.

Jeremy Bentham, in the late eighteenth century, proposed a design for a building – the Panopticon – which most historians have accepted as radical, though acknowledging the influence of his brother Samuel, an engineer who had previously suggested a circular building in the middle of a compound to observe the workforce. The Bentham brothers' radial plan, with a central tower for observation and walls to detain animals, had actually been common in the design of parks for well over a century (Baratay and Hardouin-Fugier 2004, 27). It was also given architectural form in the most common structure for a menagerie. Louis XIV had one built at Vincennes around 1661 which had a two-storey rectangular building in the centre of a courtyard with cells for the animals which radiated outwards from the middle. A few years later, with the development of Versailles, the architect Louis le Vau refines this structure even more clearly (see the plan in Robbins 2002, 42):

> An interior staircase led to the first floor [...] Seven of the eight sides of its sole room, called the '*salon de la ménagerie*', had windows that that opened onto a balcony that looked out onto an octagonal courtyard surrounding the pavilion on seven sides, around which, in turn, seven

animal enclosures were arranged [...] The animal yards – equipped with huts, ponds and fountains, and planted with turf – were separated from each other by walls and enclosed by iron railings to allow visitors to see into them ... .

(Baratay and Hardouin-Fugier 2004, 48)

The animals, previously distributed around the park, are now collected together to maximize visibility but species are (mostly) separated from each other. We can see the same sort of design in the eighteenth-century menageries of London's Kew Gardens, the Tower of London, Coombe Abbey in Warwickshire, Schönnbrunn near Vienna, Buen Retiro near Madrid, Holland's Het Loo and many others (Grigson 2016, 169).[2] Prince Eugene of Savoy's Schloss Belvedere menagerie, for example, was built in the 1720s, and was arranged as a series of views into animal pens from a first-floor balcony in the palace (Rothfels 2002, 29). It can also be seen in the architect Charles Percier's drawing 'Plan for a Menagerie', probably published in 1783.[3]

Foucault, in *Discipline and Punish*, does briefly note that Bentham could have been influenced by Le Vau's work at Versailles, suggesting that:

By Bentham's time, this menagerie had disappeared. But one finds in the programme of the Panopticon a similar concern with individualizing observation, with characterization and classification, with the analytical arrangement of space. The Panopticon is a royal menagerie; the animal is replaced by man, individual distribution by specific grouping and the king by the machinery of a furtive power.

(Foucault 1991, 203)

More likely, Bentham was influenced by other English menageries, particularly Lord and Lady Shelburne's menagerie in Bowood, Wiltshire which he visited very regularly (Bowring 1843). He is recorded as donating a white fox to the menagerie and stroking a 'tiger' (probably a leopard) on a visit there in 1781 (Grigson 2016, 134). In a 1790 letter to one of the ladies of Bowood – Caroline Fox – he playfully suggests that she find a spare 'den' in a menagerie for him 'because he is growing more and more savage every day' (Milne 2017, 120).[4]

The word 'management' comes from the same etymology as menagerie. The common Latin root for hand (*mano*) leads to the French *manier* (to handle), *mener* (to lead) and *ménager* (to economize). The fourteenth-century French *ménages*, or housekeeping, transitions from the verb to the noun, and by the seventeenth century it meant a site near a country house for the feeding of cattle and poultry. The word does some different work in other places. In Italy it is *maneggiarre*, the activity of handling and training a horse carried out in a *maneggio* – a riding school. In English, it becomes a skill – management or managery[5] – and then (in the same movement to the noun) a class of people who organize matters, initially in a theatre. From this sense of manual control, the word has expanded into a general activity of training and handling people. It is a word that originates with ideas about a docile or wilful creature that must be subordinated to the instructions of the master (Parker 2018, 99 *passim*). The panoptic structure of the seventeenth century menagerie makes this clear – a material technology for the observation and management of wild beasts that could then be applied with little alteration to prisons, factories, schools and hospitals.

This is a structuralist account of power, of the ways in which space and epistemology, Foucault's power/knowledge, produce forms of domination, but in the next section I will let the wildness back in to disturb this rather neat account.

The Fair

It seems to me that the zoological garden was the product of the idea of the collection combined with the panoptic park, but both of these were emplaced cultural forms which were only available to the elites and the emerging bourgeois. They were fenced off from the casual gaze. There is a much earlier institution which also shaped the early zoo. For most ordinary people, their only contact with extraordinary creatures would take place through the showman's animals that travelled around Europe, as well as exhibits in the fairs that took place regularly in every town. The fair or carnival was an important site for all sorts of novelties, entertainments and displays of human and animal freaks and curiosities. As Stallybrass and White characterise it:

> Carnival in its widest, most general sense embraced ritual spectacles such as fairs, popular feasts and wakes, processions and competitions [...], comic shows, mummery and dancing, open-air amusement with costumes and masks, giants, dwarfs, monsters, trained animals and so forth [...] in fact all the 'low' and 'dirty' sorts of folk humour. Carnival is presented by Bakhtin as a world of topsy-turvy, of heteroglot exuberance, of ceaseless overrunning and excess where all is mixed, hybrid, ritually degraded and defiled.
>
> *(Stallybrass and White 1986, 8)*

From the early modern period onward, there is much evidence of people travelling with animals to fairs and charging for them to be seen, touched, or ridden on. For centuries, elephants, lions and tigers, and monkeys were paraded for the financial benefit of their owners. Hyperbolic claims were made about these animals, and they were expected to do extraordinary things. It was common for monkeys to dress up and do tricks, for bears to fight or dance, hares to play drums and birds demonstrate their skills in counting (Baratay and Hardouin-Fugier 2004, 60). This would be alongside strongmen, acrobats, conjurers, fire eaters, freaks and monsters (Ritvo 1997, 134). A good show would involve an animal demonstrating the characteristics of a human being or mythological creature, or a human being demonstrating inhuman qualities: the world turned upside-down.

Importantly, these were mobile forms of organization. The journeys of a rhinoceros called Clara are a remarkable example. Between 1741 and 1758, she was shown across Europe, moved in a specially built wagon pulled by eight horses. Her owner, a Dutch sea captain called Douwemout Van der Meer, distributed handbills and posters to advertise her visits to various fairs in Vienna, London, Naples and many other places. In France, she was popular enough to cause 'rhinomania'. Souvenir medals, prints, plates and clocks were commissioned, and fashionable women adopted a style of hair and clothing *à la rhinocéros* (Robbins 2002, 94–5; Ridley 2004).[6] In England, travelling menageries, such as Wombwell's Royal, had three shows permanently on the road, and would travel from fair to carnival to festival (Cowie 2014, 61 *passim*). In 1858, the one that visited Windsor had 15 vans pulled by 45 horses and up to 40 keepers. The elephants did not travel in the vans but walked inside a structure which concealed them from public view so that only their feet were visible. As in the fair, the animals were presented in the context of a spectacular display, with extraordinary claims being made about their mythical origins, their capacities and propensities (Ito 2014, 61).

Though the fairs continued, as did their travelling menageries, urban animal collections began to take root in the eighteenth century. In Amsterdam – an important port for the animal trade – 'Blauuw Jan' was an inn which served drinks and displayed animals. An admission fee was paid, and the drinkers could then see the animals, many of them waiting to be sold to the seraglio of the wealthy. In London, above the shops on The Strand, the 'Exeter Change' established in 1765 displayed animals in small cages for the price of admission. In 1778, it was advertised as:

A Grand Collection of living Beasts and Birds, selected from Asia, Africa, and America, and is allowed to be the finest assemblage offered to the inspection of the curious this twenty years [...] the creatures are well secured in iron dens – Ladies and children may see them with the greatest safety.

(Grigson 2016, 98)

The proprietors of the Change were also buying and selling animals. The length of an animal's stay depended on whether it died (and then its body would quite likely be sold on for taxidermy or dissection), or whether someone offered a good price for it, and finally whether the paying public wanted to see it. Visitors needed to be got through the doors by whatever means necessary, and if animals weren't enough, then other displays would be employed. In 1793, the Change was also showing a model of 'the French beheading machine from Paris', organ performances and an optical machine with 'moving animations' (Grigson 2016, 106–107).

At the same time, other settled entertainments which used animals were being established too. Philip Astley's Amphitheatre opened in London in 1773, and he developed 18 other permanent hippodromes in other European cities. These were largely displays of horse-riding skills, of *maneggiarre*. So when the idea of the public urban zoological garden emerges in the late eighteenth century, it was into an institutional environment which non-native animals were already routinely understood to be objects of entertainment and spectacle.

The 'Zoological' 'Gardens'

It was founded in 1752, but from 1779, the menagerie at Schönnbrun Palace in Vienna had been sporadically open on certain days to members of the public, if they were dressed appropriately. However, the first institution that looks like a modern public zoo is the result of revolution. In 1793, the French Committee of Public Safety passed a decree which prevented any wild animals from being exhibited on public roads and mandated their transportation to the *Jardin des Plantes* in Paris. Under its previous name, the *Jardin de Roi*, this had been the King's Botanical Gardens since the seventeenth century. The remaining animals from the Versailles menagerie were transported there, as well as some from clearances of aristocratic seraglio and foreign conquests. It was described as a new democratic institution for research, science for the people not spectacle for royalty (Robbins 2002, 213 *passim*). Importantly, the evolving design of the *Jardin* over the following decades was picturesque and romantic, not regal. The grand perspectives and radial geometry of the neo-classical were replaced with a geography that was irregular and winding, not subduing nature into straight lines but enhancing its asymmetry and variety. This 'English style' had a further important consequence, which was the distribution of animals across the landscape, often with stylized pavilions which stressed the distinctiveness of each enclosure, with lakes, waterfalls and irregular planting of trees. Panoptic principles of collection and display no longer functioned, since vision was not concentrated in one central point but instead was as multiple as the curving paths. The architecture of the menagerie was reversed, with the animal at the centre and the humans looking in from outside.

The London Zoological Society opened its doors in Regent's Park in 1828, directly influenced by a visit that its founder, Sir Stamford Raffles, made to the *Jardin des Plantes*. The spatial layout was also that of a picturesque garden with architecturally distinctive animal houses spread across the landscape. From its conception in 1825, it was initially called 'the Gardens', 'Gardens and Menagerie', or 'the Vivarium', and it wasn't until 1829 that the condensation 'Zoological Gardens' was used (Ito 2014). The rapid diffusion of this institution – initially in port cities (Dublin 1831, Liverpool 1833, Bristol 1835, Amsterdam 1838, Antwerp 1843) – effectively meant that the modern zoo had now congealed in terms of its spatial form.[7] It was an institution which was firmly attached to the urban bourgeoisie, which included professional and business classes, with capital coming from donations or subscriptions. Bristol's zoo, for example, was founded and managed by a joint stock company, a vehicle which allowed for the pooling of capital and the minimizing of risk (Flack 2018). The development of a zoological park on the edge of a city was also a powerful incentive for nearby development, particularly housing aimed at the same social class that financed and used the park (Baratay and Hardouin-Fugier 2004, 83, 101). Most of these early parks were only open to subscribers, though the lower classes were allowed in on specific days on payment of a charge.

The explicit rationale was a claim about education and science, not wonder or freakery, and hence they often claimed attachment to learned societies, museums and universities. As Sir Stamford Raffles put it in a letter of 1825:

> I am much interested at present in establishing a Grand Zoological collection in the Metropolis, with a Society for the introduction of living animals, bearing the same relations to Zoology as a science that the Horticultural Society does to Botany. [...] Sir Humphrey Davy and myself are the projectors, and while he looks more to the practical and immediate utility to the country gentlemen, my attention is more directed to the scientific department.
>
> *(in Vevers 1976, 14)*

The observation and detailed pictorial representation of animals and the dissection of their corpses, or the establishment of a library, laboratory, or museum was a way of sustaining such a claim to scientific or educational aims. It was also a claim that this institution was not a fair or menagerie, and that its audience was not intended to come from amongst the sort of people that attended those other places. However, the evidence that early zoos were actually of any use for zoological research is limited. Attempts to deal with startlingly high mortality rates certainly led to developments in veterinary science, and their failure provided many specimens for dissection and taxidermy which allowed for developments in comparative anatomy (Woods 2018). The common factor here is death, because the observation of animal behaviour in the field, or of interactions with their native environments could not be performed on captive animals. The claim to be engaged in research seems to have been mostly about legitimation for the bourgeoisie.

Despite attempting to maintain a degree of exclusivity with regard to their visitors, zoos were (and have always been) primarily reliant on gate receipts. Given the running expenses, many were financially very fragile, some only lasting for a few years, and Brighton Zoo for only six months (Cowie 2014, 48). London was an institution that initially only allowed entrance to visitors who had been signed in by a member. It was aimed at polite society, a fashionable place to promenade (Ito 2014, 81). There was also a policy of not selling food and drink within the grounds, which meant that various vendors set up on the pavements outside the main gates. However, by 1847, its finances were so poor that it had to open to the general public and start making money by selling refreshments. This reliance on visitors also meant that decisions about how to display 'the attractions', were increasingly made with spectacle in mind. Cages were designed with thin bars and wire to maximize visibility and were often small and open on all sides. There was an emphasis on ensuring that the animals were entertaining, so bears were fed buns, elephants gave rides and chimpanzees dressed in clothing and had tea parties:

On a single day in Brussels in 1855, a bear was given five hundred bread rolls, and on 19 June 1959 in Antwerp, an elephant wolfed down 1,704 peanuts, 1,089 pieces of bread, 1,330 sweets, 811 biscuits, 198 orange segments, seventeen apples, seven ice creams and one hamburger!
(Baratay and Hardouin-Fugier 2004, 183)

Most zoos couldn't afford to only be a zoo, so it was common to diversify into other leisure activities and services – concerts, meetings, restaurants, exhibitions and so on. Competition with other urban entertainments – winter gardens, pleasure parks, fairs, sporting events – meant that the public continually needed fresh reasons to visit. Two early English zoos, Liverpool and Belle Vue in Manchester, both had primitive roller coasters built by the late 1840s.

Baratay and Hardouin-Fugier call this opening up a 'forced democratization' (2004, 104), and the case of the Surrey Zoological Gardens is an useful example. In 1831, the owner of the Exeter Change – Edward Cross – opened a new garden in south London, intending to compete directly with London Zoo. The Change was being demolished and Cross saw a market for a new attraction. At his new gardens, a domed glass conservatory was built to contain separate cages for the animals, as well as protecting them against the Northern European weather. The grounds were planted with native and exotic trees and plants, and dotted with pavilions in the picturesque style. Though the Surrey Gardens began by providing entrance to visitors only if they were signed in by a subscriber, the revenues were insufficient to cover costs, and it rapidly became a pleasure garden providing spectacle for half the price of a visit to its competitor. In 1835, Jacopo the monkey was advertised as ascending in Mr Charles Green's balloon and then descending to earth on a parachute. By 1837, the gardens were being used for large public entertainments – dioramas simulating the eruption of Mount Vesuvius and the Great Fire of London, as well as firework displays and promenade concerts (Cowie 2014, 28; Ito 2014, 41). Following a particularly bad year in 1851, when the Great Exhibition at the Crystal Palace took all the visitors, the zoo closed in 1855 and the animals were sold. Without gate revenue, they could not be fed. The neatness of a genealogy of the zoo as an amalgam of collection and park aimed at the bourgeoisie, as a scientific institution with living exhibits, was continually disturbed by the commercial realities of the carnival and fair, places that demanded wonder and were aimed at the common people, the masses who demanded popular entertainment as escape. These tensions were to continue through the following century, an era in which the zoo becomes more directly shaped by capitalism.

Animal Capitalism and the Spectacle

The importation of animals was a corollary of the globalization of international trade. Though it wasn't until the nineteenth century that specialist animal merchants developed their trade, the transportation of animals was common in early commerce. In medieval times, Asian animals were probably brought along spice routes, and conveyed into Europe by Venetian or Genoese merchants. African animals would have moved through North African ports, along with slaves, ivory and gold. From the Americas, the trade was controlled by the Spanish and the Portuguese, with Lisbon having several menageries in the royal parks (Grigson 2016, 3, 5). The first main suppliers for North Western Europe was probably the Dutch East India Company, which by the sixteenth century had built animal pens alongside its quays in Amsterdam (Baratay and Hardouin-Fugier 2004, 22), as well as the Antwerp branch of the Fugger Bank, which also kept cages next to their offices. The trade in animals appears to have been one element in colonial commercial relationships, initially organized as part of a barter system with local elites, or later a tax system for extracting wealth from the colonized, and then gradually becoming arranged and financed on an industrial scale by merchants specializing in animals or animal products (particularly ivory and skins).

The Hagenbeck family of Hamburg was the most influential of all, displaying seals (described as mermaids) on the quayside in Hamburg from 1848, and then becoming specialists in supplying zoos and circuses as they became the dominant customers for wild animals (Reichenbach 1996;

Rothfels 2002, 44 *passim*). The trade was huge. Between 1866 and 1886, Carl Hagenbeck's firm sold around 700 leopards, 1,000 lions and 400 tigers, 1,000 bears, 800 hyenas, 300 elephants, 80 rhinos, 300 camels, 150 giraffes, 600 antelopes, tens of thousands of monkeys, thousands of crocodiles and large snakes and over 100,000 birds. But these are only the ones who survived to be sold, because the slaughter of animals to stock zoos was extraordinary. An entire family might be killed in order that a baby could be caught, and then at least half of the animals died whilst in transit. It has been estimated that this meant than an average of ten creatures would have perished in order that one could be displayed (Baratay and Hardouin-Fugier 2004, 118). If we add to that the mortality rate of about one in three animals per year for early zoos (Woods 2018), then the zoo must be seen as a major cause of animal deaths, with the violence of the capture celebrated in popular culture. The great white hunter, with his big guns and stories of cowardly natives and charging animals, would often be working to contract for a particular company. Their published accounts are extraordinary assertions of imperial power and righteousness, of the violent subjugation of both wildlife and of inferior humans (Rothfels 2002, 59 *passim*).

It was a complex business model, but the profits were substantial. In 1876, an elephant could be purchased in Kassala in the Sudan for between 80–400 German marks and then sold in Europe for between 3000–6000 marks (Rothfels 2002, 57). There were two key problems: the logistics of long-distance travel and coordination; and attrition of the products due to disease or difficulties in transportation. A few specialist firms dominated the market, such as the Hagenbecks, the Jamrach family in London and Liverpool, and the 'Zoological Institute' and later the 'Flatfoots' in New York City in the 1830s–1870s. The latter were effectively a cartel who were not above using violence to ensure that they continued to control the importation of animals into the growing zoos of the US. Gradually, the increasing number of railway lines and more rapid sea transport produced lower attrition rates, and zoos got better at not killing their charges. There were now too many animals, and this resulted in a price deflation by the late 1870s. For Hagenbeck, the answer was a return to the travelling fair, showing extraordinary people and animals.

The first of these were a group of Sami with reindeer who he exhibited in Hamburg and then toured around Europe. The idea was financially successful and it grew. Hagenbeck's 'Ceylon Caravans' of the 1880s had up to 200 people on show, including snake charmers, acrobats, dancers and acrobats, as well as decorated elephants and a native camp. The presentation of these 'people shows' was of simple exotics from the dawn of time, underdeveloped children who were grateful to travel. There was a great deal of interest from university anthropologists, who took photographs and studied language, artefacts and behaviour, and at the end of the show, the travellers' artefacts often became part of ethnographic museum collections (Ritvo 1997, 125 *passim*; Rothfels 2002, 91 *passim*). Hagenbeck also invested in an ill-fated circus, various touring panoramas and a highly profitable touring lion exhibit which led into a Roman-themed performing animal show at the 1893 Chicago Columbian Exposition. A contemporary visitor recounts bears walking the tightrope, camels on roller skates and tigers pulling crowned lions in chariots (Rothfels 2002, 151).

So when Hagenbeck opened the Stellingen Zoo outside Hamburg in 1907, it should be understood as a development which incorporated the spatiality of the zoological garden with the spectacle of the travelling show and the panorama (Rothfels 2002, 42). The *Tierpark* used a fake mountain made from concrete, as well as an arrangement of lakes and trenches disguised with artificial rocks, to present a view of animals apparently living together in harmony in naturalistic settings. The site was designed so that the visitors would see the various displays from vantage points. Rather than bars, the animals and people were provided with simulations of nature, a display of free enclosures, *Freianlage* (Reichenbach 1996; Baratay and Hardouin-Fugier 2004, 244). Hagenbeck cultivated the idea that his zoos were an ark, and zookeepers were Noah-like friends of animals. Indeed, it was often claimed that the animals were happier and healthier in captivity than they would be in the wild.

Hagenbeck's trained animal shows were supposedly achieved with kinder methods of management (*zahme Dressur*) than the violence of the club, and the moats at the Tierpark were designed using observational data about the jumping abilities of different species (Rothfels 2002, 163). Of course the changes that produced this new zoo were not simply driven by altruism because the park was also a showroom in which all the livestock was for sale. Indeed, by this point Hagenbeck was marketing the sale of groups of animals, together with the cages and wagons needed to make them into components of a travelling menagerie, circus, or show. The design of the displays at the new park was also meant to acclimatize the animals to Northern European weather, making them more saleable, as well as being cheaper on heating. There were sound business reasons for the new model zoo, as well as for the repeated attempt to sell an account of happy animals living in *semi-liberté* (Rothfels 2002).

Yet, in order for this account of the zoo as an asylum for animals to become credible, it was necessary to conceal the trade that made it possible. A 1902 letter from the Director of the Bronx Zoo, William Hornaday, to Hagenbeck, asks him to be quiet about the fact that forty Indian rhinos had to be killed in order to get three infants, one of which was to be brought by the Bronx Zoo:

> There are now a good many cranks who are so terribly sentimental that they affect to believe that it is wrong to capture wild creatures and exhibit

them, – even for the benefit of millions of people. For my part, I think that while the loss of the large Indian rhinoceroses is greatly to be deplored, yet, in my opinion, the three young ones that survive will be of more benefit to the world at large than would the forty rhinoceroses [...] seen only at rare intervals by a few ignorant natives.

(Rothfels 2002, 67)

The History of the Present

It is hard to imagine such colonial violence being expressed by anyone in a contemporary zoo, yet Hagenbeck's naturalistic display of animals, together with the idea of the immobile ark, was hugely influential in shaping the contemporary zoo. It underpins a progressive narrative in which the cruel travelling menagerie is replaced by the civilized zoological gardens, which is in turn replaced by the sensitive biopark or conservation centre (Hosey et al. 2013, 14; E. Garrett 2014, 214 *passim*). Zoos have always been described by their supporters as places to cultivate a sensitivity to nature, and since the 1970s, this romantic sensibility has been augmented by an emphasis on sustainability and the environment, with displays aimed at demonstrating human entanglement in the web of life and performing the functions of an ark for endangered animals. The zoo continues to articulate itself as a site for civilizing human beings, using animals in order to do so, and stressing that 'science' is the justification (Braverman 2012).

The problem for zoos is that there isn't a great deal of evidence that they are very good for animals. The complaints go back a long way. For Victorian critics, the death rates in zoos showed a clear parallel with the people who lived in overcrowded dwellings, workhouses, barracks and asylums (Ito 2014). The zoo was compared to a factory where the lack of light and air caused the concentration of miasmas. When a British Royal Commission sat in 1875 to consider the regulation of animal experiments, its members suggested that the zoo was a gigantic pathological experiment, of which death by tuberculosis was the result. Their incarceration in the zoo had transformed wild, foreign creatures into sickly slum dwellers (Uddin 2015, 34; Woods 2018, 54). While zoos are evidently different now, their critics continue to accuse them of being primarily attractions not arks. The animals that live in zoos often undergo physiological changes due to lack of exercise or the impossibility of flight, and there are commonly changes in breeding patterns as well as well-documented psychological problems. To make matters worse, the evidence for the success of reintroduction of endangered species into the wild is patchy, and there are continuing concerns concerning the sourcing and display of animals – particularly what are usually referred to as 'charismatic megafauna' – for captivity (Braverman 2012). Yet without the 'biocapital' of the big animals (Flack 2018, 44), most zoos would be bankrupt. For critics of zoos, their exhibits are cruel simulations of something that has never existed, 'like dysfunctional theater productions in which the actors neither stir nor speak but pose mutely among inedible props' (Spotte 2006, 100). Zoos do not present or protect the wild because they are not the wild, and never can be: 'A captive Alpine ibex *by itself* tells us as little about goats as the *Mona Lisa* reveals about women' (ibid., 45).

The contemporary response to these accusations is always to further enrich the cages with foliage and landscaping, and build more naturalistic enclosures, hiding the bars in order to produce 'island sanctuaries in a burgeoning sea of anthropogenic desolation' (Flack 2018, 14). The explicit justification is to continue to move away from being merely an 'attraction' and towards becoming a conservation park (Beardsworth and Bryman 2001, 43; E. Garrett 2014, 114 *passim*), but spectres of other institutions continue to shape this development. The zoo has never really differentiated itself from the fair, the circus and the pleasure gardens, and contemporary zoos often have sea lion shows and fairground rides, cross-marketing or sponsorship with brands, as well as a great deal of emphasis on eating and shopping. In his earliest writing on 'Disneyization', Alan Bryman (1999) suggested that this sort of commercialization was an example of the 'dedifferentiation' of cultural forms. Dedifferentiation is an interesting concept because it contests the idea that modernization is always about the differentiation of social systems, producing an ever more elaborated division of labour within multiplying types of institution. The sociologist Edward Tiryakian proposed that this was an empirical question, since there was no necessary reason to assume that differentiation was always a one-way process (1992). What Bryman saw as the contemporary merging of theme park, mall, zoo, circus and so on suggests exactly this sort of reunification of what had, for a while, been distinct social forms.

However, I think the question is really whether the zoo has ever really escaped from the influence of the fair, and consequently from all the popular social forms that owe more to carnival than museum. Could the zoo ever escape its genealogy? Was it ever differentiated? In 1870, the US showman Phineas T. Barnum advertised his 'Grand Travelling Museum, Menagerie, Caravan and Circus'. The following year he expanded this to 'Museum, Menagerie and Circus, International Zoological Garden, Polytechnic Institute and Hippodrome'. Barnum was actively engaged in the marketing of dedifferentiation because he knew that the only thing that really mattered was getting the punters in and paying the bills. The more you offered, the more likely they were to come. The original 1825 prospectus for London Zoo claimed that the animals will be 'brought from every part of the world to be applied either to some useful purpose, or as objects of scientific research, not of vulgar admiration' (in Vevers 1976, 15). At the present time, despite continued and insistent claims to the contrary, critics of zoos still suggest that they are merely places of public entertainment, theme parks by another name. The spectre of the carnival still haunts the cages, because the contemporary zoo cannot escape its history. The zoo, as Elizabeth Hanson puts it, is a ' "hybrid" institution' somewhere between 'science and showmanship, high culture and low, remote forests and the cement cityscape, and wild animals and urban people' (2004, 7).

The Great Institutionalization

In *Madness and Civilization*, Foucault writes of a 'great confinement' taking place from the seventeenth century onwards (1989b). Those who offended bourgeois reason and morality had special buildings constructed for them – prisons, hospitals, schools and so on. This has been an influential idea, but it seems to me that it was not only deficient humans who were collected during this period, but that it is a time of a wider 'great institutionalization' for collections of all kinds, in which various activities, people, animals and materials had special structures constructed for them – whether parks with pavilions, rusticated neo-classical buildings, or a grand marquee. The architect of the menagerie at Versailles, Louis Le Vau, was also responsible for the design of the gigantic *Hôpital de la Salpêtrière*[8] twenty years previously. In the decades around the founding of the London Zoo, the National Gallery, British Museum, Natural History Museum, Victoria and Albert Museum and many other institutions were founded or moved to new grand buildings (Ito 2014, 7). The centralization of the state, donations from wealthy industrialists such as Henry Tate, and the urbanization of the population appears to have provided the finance and justification for collecting things together in grand places – whether they be animals, paintings, or traders. This is what Tony Bennett (1995), extending Foucault's argument, calls the 'exhibitionary complex', a display of power/knowledge which is public, spectacular and emplaced. The zoo shares much with these other institutions – the archive, theatre, museum, gallery, opera, covered market, amusement park, stock exchange, public park, library, even the university.

This genealogy of the zoo is partly an account of the way that a particular modern institution emerges from earlier cultural forms – the collection and parkland. But the neatness of this story is also disrupted by its debt to the travelling fair – episodic, nomadic and open to the common people. In *Rabelais and his World*, first published in English in 1968, Mihail Bakhtin appeared to be suggesting[9] that the laughter and disruption of the carnival had disappeared with industrialism as a result of the strengthening of the power of the state (1984). Stallybrass and White (1986) disagree, suggesting that the carnival is better thought of as a principle which continues to disrupt and upset established social relations. It is not in the past, but forms part of every present, disorganizing organization. To adapt their terms to the case at hand,

the civilizing process of the zoo, its moral architecture, is continually troubled
by the exotic beasts that it requires in order to get the punters through the
gates. It seems that spectacle is required to pay the bills and that the zoo can
never really exorcise the ghost of the menagerie (Cowie 2014, 205).

As I suggested at the beginning of this chapter, zoos are exercises in
classification. Like the cabinet of curiosity (Zytaruk 2011), the zoo brings
things together in a particular place and then keeps them slightly apart. The
internal boundaries are supposed to ensure that animals do not fight or eat
each other; zoo staff and visitors are clearly distinguished; backstage and
frontstage paths, moats and fences ensure the orderly movement of creatures
and materials. Just as the menagerie appears to have been part of the genealogy
of the Panopticon, so does the architecture of collection and observation
produce the similarities and differences, movements and impasses, which are
constitutive of formal organization. As Foucault suggests 'the Panopticon
also does the work of a naturalist' (1991, 203), inspecting the creatures in the
cells, observing behaviour and judging symptoms. For its exhibits, the zoo
seeks to be a total institution (Beardsworth and Bryman 2001, 88; Woods
2018, 31), but perhaps it can be better understood as an assemblage which
co-produces both non-human and human. As Irus Braverman expresses
it, relying again on Foucault, 'the naturalization, classification, naming,
identification, recording, registration, legalization, and reproduction of zoo
animals are also various technologies for disciplining *humans* into proper
human-nature relations' (Braverman 2012, 20)

But this structuralist account of the zoo as a form of thought made durable
tends to overstate the stability of this – of perhaps any – institution. The
mystery at the heart of the zoo is why we look at animals at all, and this is
a question that connects to the wonders of the carnival. It is often suggested
nowadays that the reason that we visit is because it connects us to nature,
perhaps by cultivating an imaginative identification (McKenna et al. 1987).
This is a nicely domesticated account of something much stranger, of the
presentation of something alien, even to the extent of their being a threat
to our lives. Because identification must fail. As Peter Berger suggested in
his essay 'Why Look at Animals?' (2009), the reality of the zoo is that the
animals don't see us because we do not share the same life world. That's why
they look through us, or eat us.

The ordered imaginary of the zoo requires the existence of this alien, the
other of order and organization. The zoo, to balance the costs of animals and
keepers against ticket prices and the sale of Hippoburgers with a plastic toy,
must produce and contain the idea of the exotic, of beauties and monsters,
of a spectacle that is frightening and wonderful, and of a strangeness
that allows spectators 'to travel by means of thought alone' (Baratay and
Hardouin-Fugier 2004, 151). This is why the zoo can never become fully

insulated from carnival, why it has never achieved the sort of differentiation achieved by similar institutions such as the museum or art gallery, because it requires the creation of this otherness at its very heart. So when Beardsworth and Bryman, in their analysis of the Disneyization of the zoo, point to the 'wild' as something which is now themed, they neglect the extent to which a fundamental strangeness underpins and undermines the institution (Beardsworth and Bryman 2001, 98). The history of the zoo is a history of attempts to tame the wild but it must always fail, otherwise there would be nothing to see. The tiger needs to stay dangerous, and the intelligence of dolphins must remain a mystery. Wonder, in the sense used by Kaulingfreks et al. (2011) must not be expunged or suppressed, but is actually required if the zoo is to provide a spectacle to justify the entrance price. This is not some metaphysical wildness, something pre-social, but something that must be conjured, produced by the institution in order that it can be recognized as distinctive, a structured encounter between humans and their others. Another way of putting this is to say that 'human exceptionalism' (Flack 2018, 28) is required in order that the zoo has a reason to exist. If 'they' are too much like 'us', then why are we there at all?

The visitors to zoos are part of this dialectic of organization and disorganization too. Since the foundation of London Zoo, it has been part of a civilizing mission, though one which had a complex relationship to the rowdy white working class and displayed some predictable racial prejudices towards non-white citizens (Uddin 2015). Just as zoo managers try to contain, observe and diagnose those in their custody, so do they endlessly complain about visitors who feed or throw stones at animals, drop litter, drink alcohol or eat food they haven't purchased, and climb across barriers. But when a human gets killed by an animal, the danger involved in bringing things together and keeping them slightly apart is displayed, and the imaginary of the zoo is reaffirmed.

The words 'menagerie' and 'circus' contain traces of alternate meanings, of chaos and disorganization, as does 'zoo' in certain sentences. When Dr Roderick McDonald, a former Harvard professor of zoology, resigned as Director of the Philadelphia Zoo in 1935, he said 'I didn't come here to run a menagerie or a circus' (Baratay and Hardouin-Fugier 2004, 215). The paradox is that the zoo needs the spectacle of the menagerie, not only to pay the bills, but to be the disorder that makes the order possible. The history of the present of the zoo shows that it is a form of organization that explicitly seeks to tame, but also requires the manufacture of the wild, the sniff of the sublime, the unpredictable other. It teaches us that the present is a particular arrangement of materials and assumptions that reassembles past arrangements in new ways. And it teaches us that organization and disorganization require each other, and can be made with bars, moats and glass.

Notes

1 This chapter is based on (2021) 'The Genealogy of the Zoo: Collection, Park and Carnival', *Organization* 28/4: 604–620.
2 We can also see the influences of this design in later zoos too, such as the 1875 plan for Melbourne (Gillbank 1996, 84).
3 See http://c7.alamy.com/comp/KNP86G/plan-for-a-menagerie-artist-charles-perc ier-french-paris-1764-1838-KNP86G.jpg, accessed March 2018.
4 Though there are no records as to the design of the three different versions of the Bowood menagerie in existence. I am grateful to Cathryn Spence, Bowood's archivist, for clarification of this point.
5 Menagerie was sometimes spelled managery or menagery. See Grigson 2016, 77, 87.
6 In 1827, a giraffe called Zarafa did a similar tour of France, causing the production of giraffe songs jewellery, textiles and hair styled *á la giraffe* (Ito 2014, 53; Grigson 2016, 235).
7 For an account of the later development of the North American zoo, and its connection to travelling circus and menageries, see Hanson 2004.
8 Also the hospital where Foucault died in 1984.
9 Though it has often been suggested that he may have been doing this to prevent his work being seen as critical of the Soviet Union.

5

TOWER CRANES

Consider the strange double life of the tower crane.[1] In any large city, they are ubiquitous. Solid and gigantic structures of steel, bristling on a bustling skyline, swinging over the streets. Even children know about cranes, and many may well possess one. A toy in yellow plastic, or one with a face on, like Cranky the Crane from Thomas the Tank Engine. Cranes are just too big to miss.

The word comes from the Old High German *krano* or *kran* for a large wading bird, perhaps an echo of its cry across the flat wet marshes. The usage, to mean a 'machine with a long arm', is first seen in the late thirteenth century, and followed by the extension to the human body ('craning your neck') as a verb at the beginning of the nineteenth century. Like many words and their associated concepts, the etymology documents mutability – from sound to animal to machine to the human body. This is suggestive, because despite the solid clarity of their existence, cranes are curiously ephemeral objects, lacy sketches of lines which can disappear overnight, unnoticed, and materialize somewhere else a few days later. You can see the sky through them, or the structures that they grow next to them, before they vanish like embarrassed parents or guilty lovers. And, unlike the buildings themselves, the pride and joy of city boosters and the object of glossy skyscraper porn – the light bouncing off their self-important glass and stone surfaces – the cranes have been folded away from history. Almost no one writes about cranes, apart from instruction manuals or professional magazines. Almost no one makes art with them,[2] or music about them, or dances for them. They are modest giants, hiding in the light.

Almost no one. In Eva Weber's beautiful documentaries 'City of Cranes' (2007) and 'The Solitary Life of Cranes' (2008), tower crane drivers sit in their cabs impassively observing the city below.[3] As the sun chases the shadows of the buildings, the crane makes its episodic moves, a chess player strategizing

DOI: 10.4324/9781032714288-7

with steel. Like the watchful angels in Wim Wender's haunting film *Wings of Desire* (1987), or a superhero standing on the ledge of a skyscraper with their cape fluttering in the wind, the operators look down on the bustle. Their hands twitch on the two tiny joysticks and far away and below, motors purr and cables whine whilst the wind makes the crane twitch and buck. What can they see from up there? What perspective does such elevation provide? Do they imagine themselves to be gods, or are they stuck up there, wishing to be down here, with us?

The crane is part of the sociotechnical assemblages of the modern world. As we will see, its manufacture, mobility, economics and operation are all staggeringly complex and necessarily global. It is one element in the entangled processes that make the modern city, as well as the power plants, bridges, container ports and electricity pylons that allow the city to live. The crane stands at the heart of these systems, and I employ it here as an object which allows me to unfold the movements of the world. I want to show that the crane makes, and is made. One of Bradley Garrett's 'place-hackers', or 'urban explorers', looks down from a crane across London at night at and comments that, like the river, 'it's all flow' (2014, 84). A century before, Umberto Boccioni, an Italian Futurist, suggested that any entity can be treated like this, as a temporary stabilization of that which surrounds it. He goes on:

> No one still believes that one object finishes off where another begins or that there is anything that surrounds us—a bottle, a car, a house, a hotel, a street—which doesn't cut into and sectionalize us with its arabesque of curves and straight lines.
>
> *(Boccioni 1912, 115)*

This is a relational ontology, one in which the object is always and necessarily part of that which surrounds it. It is also an organized world, but not simply in the sense of being a world of organizations (though it is). I think we can reveal the processes of organizing in this more general sense by trying to understand the various ways in which the crane can be seen (despite its persistent tendency to disappear) through different lines of sight as a topic of engineering, economics, labour, and aesthetics. As Boccioni suggests, I want to 'open up the figure like a window and enclose within it the environment in which it lives' (1912, 115). These are different ways of making something visible, or making different visibilities possible from the same materials. The philosopher Henri Bergson, who had some influence on the Italian Futurists, as well as contemporary theories of organization (Hernes et al. 2014) was keen on this sort of relational understanding:

> Does not the fiction of an isolated object imply an absurdity, since this object borrows its physical properties from the relations which it maintains

with all the others, and owes each of its determinations, and consequently its very existence, to the place which it occupies in the universe as a whole?
(Bergson 1911, 11–12)

I will return to what this suggests about the ontology of cranes later, but first I want to move through a series of perspectives which spotlight the crane as borrowing properties from its relations with a series of different ways of seeing – engineering and mathematics, capitalist economics, and a workplace labour process. Along the way, I will be using a variety of sources, including some interviews that I have done with crane drivers. To synthesize these different accounts, I then move to aesthetic perspectives, particularly Italian Futurism and Soviet Constructivism. The latter provide the hints which allow me to see the crane as a temporary stabilization of structure, and structure as an arrangement of planes and lines of force which allows certain moves, just as it prevents others. This aesthetics allows me to present a relational ontology which encourages us to think that different ways of seeing produce different objects (Mol 2003, Barad 2007). Concluding by borrowing some ideas from Deleuze and Guattari, I suggest that cranes are good to think with, but that any assemblage would do the job. Now, we must slew back to the beginning, to a someone eating a sandwich in a tiny cab, while below him the networks of the city gradually illuminate in the gathering gloom.

Engineering

It's all very well being romantic about this *man*, alone with his intensity, his perspective, his power, while the wind circles his lonely dwelling.[4] It feels like one of those Caspar David Friedrich paintings on the front cover of a paperback by Nietzsche, in which the hero reflects on mountain tops and fears nothing, apart from mundanity. Meanwhile, the masses chatter around in the streets like ceaseless insects, never looking up. But you wouldn't hear an engineer talking like that, any more than Neil Armstrong could write poetry about landing on the moon (Mailer 1971).

A tower crane is an engine on stilts. To make one, you need a lot of steel, as well as bolts, washers, gaskets, welding gear, presses, wiring, bearings, anti-corrosion paint, hydraulic rams, tubing, steel cables, glass, printed circuit boards, concrete counter-weights and so on. Imagine placing your hand on the base of a crane and feel the cold materiality of metal and the vibration of motors making the structure shiver slightly, and creak as it responds to wind and stress. The contemporary language of cranes is not the language of the romantic sublime, but of the technologies of the material. The operator hoist, pipe grabs, manriding cage, automatic hook, Ultraview cab, Manitowoc Crane Control System. They are made by companies with names that might be familiar from illuminated signs hanging over cities – Potain,

Linden Comansa, Wolffkran, Liebherr, Terex, XCMG – but could be global corporations that do pretty much anything. There is an older language buried there too, one that echoes its nautical origins (Glynn 1849, 9; Bachman 1997, 65). Cranes have spreader beams, spars, jibs, slings, shackles, booms and rigging. They slew and luff, and their ropes reeve, they have outriggers and ballast, and they sometimes oversail properties.

The first structures that look anything like modern cranes were permanent hammerhead port cranes at the beginning of the twentieth century. Gigantic constructions of steel with names like 'Titan', 'Ajax' and 'Hercules': these were built to last and stay in one place. When the tower crane moved inland to construction sites a decade or so later, it was in a much more slender form which allowed it to be moved from site to site. Even so, the problem of assembly and disassembly wasn't really solved effectively until the 1950s, with German manufacturers working on post-war reconstruction. Oddly perhaps, despite the building of skyscrapers in North America from the early twentieth century onwards, tower cranes were first used on European building sites. The Empire State and the rest had been built with derrick cranes and hoists attached to the structure, combined with a great deal of cheap labour. Thirty years later, in Europe, the rise of modernist tower blocks that soon surrounded war-damaged cities meant that the market for the manufacture and hire of tower cranes boomed. The invention of the self-jacking crane, which could insert sections into its tower, or the crane which could move up inside a lift shaft, meant that construction could be fast and require less labour. Effectively, the tower crane becomes mobile, a temporary structure which could move between sites. By the 1980s, this was becoming true on a global scale, as tower cranes were engineered to fit into shipping containers in order to follow the tides of the construction industry to Sydney, Shanghai and Dubai.

It's not enough to imagine that this engineered metal is the bottom line of the crane though, because underpinning it is the mathematics of weight, mass, stress and angle. In a book on cranes from the middle of the nineteenth century, Joseph Glynn is at pains to note that the angles of materials and distribution of stress should not be understood through mere experience (though he recounts a fair amount of that) but through tables and calculations. To begin, to understand how a crane works at all, we need to understand what a pulley does, and what combinations of pulleys do. Second, we need to know that lifting a weight causes stresses in materials, and the nature of these stresses depends on the material, and on its angles and bracing:

> If man were furnished with no other means of defence, or of assistance to his physical strength, than those which his own organization supply, he would be one of the most helpless creatures existing [...] The pole in his hands becomes a lever to remove the trunk of the fallen tree, and the rope

of twisted thongs or fibres of bark, thrown over the fork of an extended branch, probably formed the first crane.

(Glynn 1849, 1)

In his *Rudimentary Treatise on the Construction of Cranes and Machinery*, Glynn provides us with a table which shows weights raised, time taken, the resistance of the handle and different sorts of men, in order to come up with an assessment of the power of different men:

> The subject of this Treatise is the construction and use of machines which diminish toil, and facilitate and lessen labour without superseding it; enabling men to perform what they could not accomplish without such aid.
>
> *(Glynn 1849, v)*

According to Glynn, 11,550 lbs was raised by one foot in one minute 'easily by a stout Englishman', whilst 15,134 lbs was achieved 'with the utmost exertion by a Welshman' (Glynn 1849, 27). His book proceeds from such simple experiments with 'man-machines' to more complex calculations of the strength of wood and metal in different configurations, the difference between compression and transverse stresses, the power and problems of hydraulics. This leads us into a different language, that of mathematics, and the sort of alchemy which compares the strengths of cast iron, wrought iron, cast steel, Dantzic oak and red deal in order to understand the relative breaking weight of solid columns and hollow columns:

> From what has already been stated, it is evident that all crane jibs, acting on the thrust, should have their diameter largest on the middle and tapering in a curved form, approximating to the parabolic, towards the ends, which should be about 2/3 the diameter of the middle, and also in order to obtain the greatest strength with the least material, in a cast iron crane job, acting on the thrust, it should be made hollow, and the ends should be fixed, so that the stress shall be taken directly through the axis of the pillar, or that the ends of the pillar shall be flat, and their planes at right angles with its axis.
>
> *(Glynn 1849, 69)*

Glynn also reports the experiments of others, such as the late Mr. John Kingston in the dockyard at Woolwich and reported in the *Transactions of the Society of Arts*, Volume 51, 1837 (Glynn 1849, 71) Founded in 1754 as the 'Society for the Encouragement of Arts, Manufacture and Commerce', the *Transactions* began to be published annually from 1783 and contained articles usually classified under the headings 'Agriculture: Including

Planting, Gardening and every Branch of Rural Economy', 'Manufactures', 'Chemistry and Minerology', 'Mechanics: Including Hydraulic, Pneumatic, Optical, Mathematical, Astronomical, and Surgical Apparatus', 'Fine Arts', 'Colonies and Trade'. Volume 51 appears to be missing, but volume 52 (part one) contains articles such as 'Instrument For Ascertaining The Stability Of A Ship', 'A Resonant Spring For Table-Clocks', as well as 'Marble Tablets For Miniature Painters', 'Making Casts from Soft Anatomical Specimens' and a paper on 'Hoeing Wheat'.[5] Glynn (1799–1863) was elected a fellow of the Royal Society of Arts in 1838, and was famous for designing steam engines, particularly naval engines, as well as a machine for draining the marshy fens in Eastern England.

The expertise that Glynn cultivated, and that was documented in the *Transactions*, was a practical and cumulative knowledge that intended to displace the experience of the hand and eye with the language of engineering. The connection between experiment and mathematics would lead to the making of new relations, and of new possibilities. To lift a weight – to change the relations between one material and another – required that a configuration of energy and materials is tested until it fails, and that failure is then treated as a limit condition for further experiments. But that isn't enough, because (as the categories of the *Transactions* indicate) there were some further conditions commonly required to motivate such experiments: 'manufacture', and 'colonies and trade'.

Economics

When you start reading magazines and websites such as *International Cranes and Specialised Transport*, *Cranes and Access*, or *Cranes Today*, you enter a dizzyingly global world. A Shell oil production platform in the Philippines, a partnership between a Belgian and a Chinese company, a flare stack in Saudi Arabia, a bridge replacement in Sydney, a gas turbine in South Africa. This is a world underpinned by engineering, but there are almost no stress equations or experiments here. Instead, we have accounts of particular challenges, because of difficult terrain or weather, and the hardware choices that were made in order to solve these problems. In 2015, the Cambambe hydroelectric power station on the Kwanza River in Angola was having its dam raised by 20 metres. This required two Linden Comansa 21LC750s with a load capacity of 48 tonnes, and one 21LC400 which can carry 18 tonnes.[6] Angola's record of imprisoning anyone who criticized the ruling party – the MPLA – was not mentioned. In the same year, over thirty tower cranes were being used to build a $5 billion 'Olympic' complex in Turkmenistan, which was used for the 2017 Asian Indoor Martial Arts Games. It had seven indoor arenas, hotels, restaurants and an athlete's village together with a 5km monorail to join them together. The personality cult which underpins this dictatorship is not mentioned in the article, though the 350-tonne roof truss of the velodrome merits some attention (Sleight 2015).

It's almost as if the politics – of oil refineries, expensive apartments and dams – becomes imperceptible when seen from a crane. These are engineering challenges stimulated by flows of demand and money. It is the money that allows the engineering to happen, the money that erects cranes and moves steel and concrete. Finance and engineering are not separate, but absolutely conjoined in the sense that no money could be made if the engineering wasn't right, but very little engineering could be done if the money wasn't there. The equations that explain the relationship between load and stress are parasitic on the equations that calculate the daily costs of crane hire, as well as assembly, disassembly, transportation and storage, and the hourly rates and productivity of the human beings who sit in cabs, drive and load trucks and transporters, maintain equipment and sit in offices making calculations about logistics and profitability. There are intersections with other numbers here too, because cranes can only do their work if the wind is not too strong, so it is sensible to ask how many days might they not be productive. Such a calculation will require that a connection be constructed between meteorology (with its alchemy of observations and probabilities) and actuarial science (with its alchemy of observations and probabilities), in order to come up with an insurance cost which is low enough to allow for the possibility of profits but comprehensive enough to ensure that failure doesn't destroy a series of entangled organizations. The numbers all intersect, as they must, in order that a crane can grow.

The language of cranes is a commentary on big construction projects across the world, and on the particular economic circumstances, tax breaks and incentives that might result in the need for cranes. For example, in the July 2015 issue of *International Cranes and Specialised Transport*, the editor bemoans the fact that the UK government has withdrawn incentives from wind power. This is expanded upon in an article later in the magazine in which it is asserted that the change is bad because there will be less need for cranes to erect turbines, and about 3,000 days of crane rental will be lost. In the same editorial, just a paragraph above, the European 'stage V engine emission regulations' due to be implemented in 2019 are bemoaned as 'the destruction of the mobile crane manufacturing industry here in Europe'. Cranes need big engines, and retrofitting them to ensure that exhaust emissions are within tolerance, or buying new machines, will place too big a financial burden on crane hire companies. The environmental contradiction is not remarked upon, perhaps because the logic that ties the stories together is that the encouragement of cranes is the only good. Cranes mean progress, growth, development – and crane money flows when these things happen. The language of cranes is futurist, conjuring a vertical world of skyline urbanism, power transmission and mega-projects.

It is often enough said that the number of tower cranes in a city is an indicator of economic prosperity. There are many crane indexes, and most are produced in order to underpin the urban boosterism which hopes that one crane (the bird that is a symbol of good luck in Asia) will give birth to a whole colony. National and regional crane indices show that they migrate around the world, itinerant labourers selling their services to whoever pays most at the time, then moving on when the money runs out. So certain cities gain temporary reputations as fertile grounds for forests of cranes – Berlin after unification, Moscow after the USSR, Tokyo before the lost decade, Shanghai and Beijing after capitalism grew Chinese characteristics, Dubai after oil, Dublin when the Celtic tiger was out of its cage, and (at the time of writing [2017]) London. The speculative boom in residential property by the Thames has encouraged at least one company to produce a crane survey as a way of both marketing London and selling its consultancy products (Deloitte 2015). Deloitte Touche Tohmatsu Limited is headquartered in New York, and had a revenue of $34.2 billion in 2014. Its New Street Square headquarters in London houses around 10,000 people, and is in a complex of buildings of up to 19 storeys owned by Land Securities. This mixed-use development is worth in excess of £200 million, and generates £32 million a year in rent.[7] Land Securities occupies a nine-storey building a mile away in London, and in 2015 had an income of £2,416 million from controlling 6.9 million square feet of office and retail property in London alone. Money moves cranes, including cranes to build buildings for companies that encourage the developments that require cranes. One of my crane driver interviewees estimated that in 2015, 80 per cent of UK tower cranes were in London. Another said that, on a recent trip down the Thames, he counted 200 cranes on the riverside alone.

Globally, the *International Cranes* share index lists the major manufacturers and consolidates the movements of their shares into a measurement of the highs and lows of the crane market. Bear in mind that these are manufacturers, not rental companies, but the currencies are instructive. Four are priced in Chinese Yuan, three in Japanese Yen, two in Euros, two in US dollars and one is priced in Singapore dollars. As with skyscraper construction in general, the old North Atlantic heartlands have now been largely supplanted by a new global geography around the Pacific. What is happening in Europe and North America is dwarfed by developments in Guangdong and Bangalore. This can be further evidenced by the decline of docks and shipbuilding, with famous old dock cranes – the Armstrong Mitchell in the Arsenale in Venice, Samson and Goliath in Belfast, the Kockums crane in Malmo, Titan in Clydebank – now dissembled or left as rust-porn monuments to industrial history.

The crane manufacturer Zoomlion claims in its advertising that 'The bigger we think, the higher it stands'. Height and scale are here employed as metonymic of ambition, of striving and craning your neck to see what the next challenge might be. But the cranes are mercenaries: they will work for the highest bidder, and what they build is less important than the fact that they must keep building. They must always keep moving, or they will rust and die. The skyline of tower cranes – the exoskeleton of capitalism – shows us upticking towards a high-rise future, but what happens if we zoom in, to see the person in the cab, hands twitching, bladder straining?

Labour

The crane is the fulcrum around which any construction site is anchored, with the turning circle and hook height of the crane describing the limits of the site. The easiest way to paralyze a large construction project is to take over the crane at the beginning of a strike. It ensures no heavy materials can move onto or around the site, and prevents many trades from carrying out their work at all.[8] Other people have occupied cranes too: anti-EU protesters and 'Fathers for Justice' in London, Greenpeace campaigners on a nuclear power station construction site in Finland, migrants in Italy (Oliveri 2014), and South Korean labour activist Kim Jin-suk, who spent 309 days on crane No. 85 at a Busan shipyard in 2011.[9] Thirty-five metres above the ground, she was demanding workers' rights and the reversal of Hanjin Heavy Industries & Construction's plans to lay off around 400 employees. She occupied the same crane as Hanjin union leader Kim Ju-ik, who hanged himself after 129 days of protest against massive layoffs by the same company in 2003. Kim Jin-suk was a 51-year-old former welder. She slept in the crane's cab, used a bucket for a toilet, and dealt with sub-zero temperatures, a typhoon, a heat wave and monsoon rains. After coming down, she gave an interview to a Korean journalist: 'Kim even said she threw up as if like her daily job. Crane was not a stationary house. It was a space which shook incessantly by the wind. At early times of protest, she threw up as if like a seasick all the time.'[10]

In July 2011, more than 7,000 people rallied in support of Kim's sit-in, arriving in a caravan of about 185 'Hope Buses'. In October, she spoke by mobile phone to the Occupy Wall Street protesters in Zuccotti Park:

> Brave citizens of Wall Street, the center of world capitalism and the heart of neoliberalism. This is crane no. 85 Hanjin Heavy Industries and Construction in Busan Korea. I occupied this crane last January 6 and has spent 277 days here since then. [...] You OWS demonstrators who fight at Wall Street, New York actually demonstrate things like these are not limited only to Korea but are pains shared by people all around the world. Although the workers of Hanjin Heavy Industries who fight with me are far away from you, we believe the cause we fight for and the world we want to live in would be the same. A society where labor is respected and human beings come before money. Our dreams are the same.[11]

Being a crane driver is a hard job for ordinary pay: 'The author has for many years had the direction and management of men in considerable numbers. He is convinced that perfect order, strict discipline, and prompt obedience, are imperatively necessary to insure success in the combined effects of many men … ' (Glynn 1849, vi). The job involves boredom and long climbs on freezing ladders, safety and mechanical checks, keeping ladders and work areas clear and not dropping waste from the crane, wearing a rucksack on your front when climbing (not the back), not turning up drunk or using mobile phones, taking rest breaks, having appropriate medical checks and always watching wind and weather conditions (CPA 2008). If the wind gets high, the driver can decide to leave the cab, and allow their cranes to 'weather vane' like Alexander Calder's mobiles, slewing freely to follow the gusts. Crane drivers have to arrive earlier than others on the site, and leave later. Drivers sometimes don't see their co-workers for the entire day, only talking to a few of them on walkie-talkies, and have a reputation on the site for being fat and lazy as they sit 'hunched forward, neck bent, leaning heavily on hands, arms and shoulders, trying to see downwards, looking between the legs and through the floor of the cabin' (Dahm 2015, 17). An UK crane driver activist told me that suicides and depression were high amongst drivers, in part because they have so little human contact. One driver told me that he finds himself 'less inclined as years go by to venture forth into large group settings and have almost no desire to participate in the day to day happenings of the majority of my co-workers. The longer I spend doing this job the greater the isolation feels.' It's a dangerous job too. In September 2006, Jonathon Cloke fell to his death from inside the cab of his London crane when it overloaded and snapped.[12] Isherwood (2010) identified worldwide 86 incidents involving the collapse or major structural failure of a tower crane between 1989 and 2009.

When I talked to drivers, they almost all began by insisting that it was just a job for 'lever pulling monkeys'. As one said on a Facebook site, what they do is 'pick stuff up, put stuff down'. Sometimes they seemed puzzled as to why I would want to talk to them at all, asking them what they did and whether they gave their cranes names.[13] But then they would tell me stories about the 'lunatics' that they knew (because all drivers are, apparently) and the things that they had done and seen. I heard about a crane bucking violently when its load slipped and a cup of coffee ricocheted around the cab, metaphors of boats in rough seas or roller coasters to explain the movements of the cab, views of naked people and sex through windows, and pissing in a bottle so that you didn't come down for break time (because it takes ten minutes to come down from an average crane and the site manager will often pay drivers in extra hours or cash if they don't take their breaks). That means that drivers might cook toasted sandwiches in the cab, and watch DVDs to pass the time. And when they do finally come down, sometimes the world keeps swaying for a while before the seasick driver gets their land legs again.

And then there was something else, towards the end of the interviews. When the composer Donnacha Dennehy was researching for his piece 'Cranes', he visited a school for crane operators on the outskirts of Dublin. Dennehy asked an operator what he enjoyed about his job. The man responded by saying that when he ascended the massive collection of ladders, he left all the troubles of his life down on the ground and could 'watch the whole world go by'.[14] That sense of being 'out of all the silly politics' was common. You see 'how life goes on ... you don't see it normally because you're part of it.' Isolation is sometimes 'a blessing' because it's 'nice and quiet' up there. Sometimes kids notice you, and wave, coming back day after day, but most people just don't see you at all. There is perspective at the top of a crane. As Eva Weber put it, after making her documentary:

> ... in many ways it has been the small observations of the drivers that have really stuck with me: the way people walk differently at certain times in the day, the different way couples look before and after a long and stressful Saturday afternoon shopping trip, or the way office buildings in our financial districts change at night—whereas during the day, mirrored glass keeps the outside world out, you can suddenly see clearly inside at night.[15]

Other creatures use the tower too. Bees sometimes build nests which need to be smoked off before the crane can run. In Australia, green snakes and possums have been spotted on cranes, and birds are common. I was told about magpies, red kites, a peregrine falcon, and in Australia, a sulphur-crested cockatoo. Some drivers live with the birds' nests for months, watching baby crows learn to fly; others destroy the nests before the birds have a chance to lay their eggs in places that might be disturbed by the movement of the crane. And drivers sometimes took pot plants up their cranes – petunias for one – as if they needed to take a piece of earth up with them.

There are other things too. Watching the sun come up and the sun go down over cities and coasts, and seeing storms roll in and the clouds go green with electric fire. Days when you are above the clouds, alone. Drivers would mention such things, but then retreat to something else. Like astronauts or angels, they wouldn't (or couldn't) share what they knew. As a journalist who responded to Eva Weber's film put it, 'I will look with absurd new respect at these men and women, when they return to earth. They will walk into pubs for cold beers like mortals, but they have touched rare serenity' (Ferguson 2008). One driver told me to read Jack Kerouac's 1959 novel *The Dharma Bums* to explain what it was like up there. The story's protagonist spends a summer alone fire watching in a shack at the top of Desolation Peak in Washington State: 'And it was all mine, not another pair of human eyes in the world were looking at this immense cycloramic universe of matter.' And, after months of solitary reflection, as he leaves the shack: 'I turned and knelt on the trail and said "Thank you, shack." Then I added "Blah," with a little grin, because I knew that shack and that mountain would understand what that meant, and turned and went on down the trail back to this world' (2007, 196, 204). Being a crane driver is just a job, but it can never be just a job, any more than a crane can be just a crane.

Aesthetics

The beauty of a crane doesn't only have to be understood as some echo of the natural sublime, an elevation to a landscape that stimulates the deep human interior. The modernists of the early twentieth century were fascinated by the machine age, not the romantic, by the sharp angles of a city and the way in which the speed of a bicycle or train dissolved solidity into endless echoes of movement. The groups themselves were as turbulent as their subject matter – French Cubists and Orphists, British Vorticists, Russian Futurists, Constructivists, Suprematists, Productivists Rayonnists – all insistent that they had the manifesto and methods to capture the modern in ways that others couldn't. In the *Manifesto of Futurist Mechanical Art* from 1922, Pannaggi and Paladini suggest that we

> ... feel mechanically, and we sense that we ourselves are also made of steel, we too are machines, we too have been mechanized by our surroundings. The beauty of transport wagons and the typographic pleasure of solid thick advertising signs, trucks shuddering and trembling of a TRUCK, the fantastic architecture of a construction crane, lucid and cold steels.
>
> *(in Rainey et al. 2009, 272)*

The Italian Futurists, with Filippo Tommaso Marinetti as their impresario, occupied a 'dream-world of trains, planes, submarines and great cities', an attempt to render 'universal dynamism' in painting, poetry, film, architecture (Tisdall and Bozzolla 1996, 33). Work and industry were central to futurism, in a way that they never had been for the Impressionists. An early example, Giacomo Balla's (1904) 'A Worker's Day', is a Pointillist illustration of the play of light on scaffolding and a pile of bricks around a building under construction. Five years later, referencing Bergson's philosophy of flux and movement (which had been translated into Italian in 1909), Umberto Boccioni's painting 'The City Rises' (1910) showed a backdrop of smoking chimneys and houses again surrounded by scaffolding, or in 'States of Mind II: The Farewells' (1911), we see pylons, cranes, gantries, all emerging out of railway station smoke. The cross-hatched silhouette of a girder structures Robert Delaunay's 'Eiffel Tower' series (1909–12) or the painting 'Milan Station' by Carlo Carrà (1910–11). At the same time, architects like Antonio

Sant'Elia and Mario Chiattone were producing line drawings of buildings and imaginary cities, almost all never built, with scale, elevation and the girder motif repeated on bridges, towers and decoration.

Italian Futurism might have ended with the cleansing of war, but its fascination with technology echoed into Soviet post-revolutionary art. Not always cranes, but the disciplined angles of pylons, radio towers, and scaffolding shrouded in smoke or stark against the sky. Kasimir Malevitch's Suprematist phase – see for example 'House Under Construction' (1914–15) – abstracts movement into blocks of colour. Or, perhaps most famously, Vladimir Tatlin's 'Monument to the IIIrd International' (1919–20), an unbuilt tower for Petrograd which was intended to be higher than the Eiffel Tower. A spiral of naked steel and glass, projecting words onto the clouds. Height and metal repeat throughout Soviet art, particularly in terms of the radio tower – Shass-Kobelev's 1925 'Lenin and Electrification' poster, or László Moholy-Nagy's 1928 photograph of a Berlin radio tower. The railway station roof and crane are both featured as backgrounds to muscled workers in Yury Pimenov's 'Give to Heavy Industry' of 1927. A few years later, Iakov Chernikhov's 'Architectural Fantasy: View of the enormous portal cranes with semi-circular corbels' (1932–36), makes gantry cranes into gothic arches in front of a blood-red sky.

Whether in stage sets, photomontage, mobiles, or graphics, much of the art of the first third of the twentieth century was enraptured by Modernism, and its materialization in structures of crosshatched steel. In England, Stephen Spender's 1933 poem 'The Pylons'[16] describes the march of an electricity distribution networks which:

... dwarfs our emerald country by its trek
So tall with prophecy
Dreaming of cities
Where often clouds shall lean their swan-white neck.

The phrase 'pylon poets' (or 'pylon boys') was coined to refer to these younger left-wing poets – Auden, Day Lewis and MacNeice – who turned to skyscrapers, aeroplanes, roads and power stations to celebrate a modern, democratic aesthetic. The pastoral is replaced by something non-human, but to which the future has been granted. In Cecil Day Lewis' poem to Auden, 'Look west, Wystan, lone flyer' (1933), the 'ascetic pylons pass/bringing light to the dark-livers, charged to deal death'. There are shadows of violence here, as there were with the Italian Futurists from the inception, but this is art which, for Day Lewis, points to the future, to 'a new kind of power, like the pylon-carried wires of which Spender writes' (in Purdon 2013, 25). This uncompromising modernism echoed through le Corbusier's architecture, the Russian émigré Louis Lozowick's images of factories and bridges in the US in the 1920s and '30s, the engineer Calder's mobiles, to the science-fiction streamlining of the 1950s, and the Soviet and NASA rocket gantries of the 1960s. The crane is always there at the birth of the new, it assembles the future.

Donnacha Dennehy's (2010) 'Cranes', a piece of jaggedly relentless modern music, was first imagined as a live orchestral performance with the choreographed movement of cranes located at various building sites across the Dublin skyline during the apex of the construction boom.[17] It never happened, because the construction stopped and the cranes took flight. Listening to it now, it is the sound of a future that never happened, an attempt to capture a kaleidoscope of movement, an aesthetics which represents ceaseless mobile relations. Cranes promise, but they are designed to disappear, always seeking something newer. How can we think such mobility?

Ontology

Tim, one of the crane drivers in *City of Cranes*, says that

> When you've got four or five or six cranes together, you've got this wonderful sort of drop in, almost nodding politely to each other and then pulling back and turning round. It's wonderful, and if you are part of it, it's almost like a ballet. But nobody is too arty and if you said 'it's as though we're in a ballet', you most likely get a rude answer over the radio, and fair enough, fair comment. They think 'he's not a ballet dancer, he's a crane driver!'

They are common enough in the Global North, but most people rarely think much about them. Cranes appear in the first episode of the UK TV cartoon 'Mary, Mungo and Midge' in 1969 and in toy and model shops all over the world. We can watch YouTube videos of cranes collapsing, or lunatic free climbers in masks taking selfies as they hang over cities at night (B. Garrett 2014). The James Bond film *Casino Royale* (2006) begins with parkour on cranes, and *Men in Black 3* (2012) has a fight on an Apollo rocket gantry. Yet the crane is almost never a topic in its own right, apart from those who make them or work with them, like Tim, who refuses to dignify his labour with balletic metaphors. Cranes are always in the background, props for the modern urban *mise en scène*, curiously absent from thought despite their ubiquity. The things that they construct are solidly visible, the manifestation of architects' imaginations and the financial desires of developers. Buildings are things, surfaces in space that reflect light and define space. Cranes suggest a different ontology, different lessons to teach us about organization, mobility and process. Perhaps, contra Rorty, we might use them as a 'skyhook' to see things differently (1990, 2).

Looking at a crane, you can see structure. Lines of steel, bracketed and bolted to produce angles which direct lines of force, making some moves possible, and others impossible (if we discount failure, fracture and collapse). Structure, in its simplest mechanical sense, constrains movement. Seeing structure, having structure revealed, allows the viewer to understand what is possible and what is not. We can see the degrees of freedom in the skeleton. So let's think of the crane as a pure structure. Structure can then be conceived as a series of articulations, of joints which allow lines to intersect with planes. When we speak of social structure, such metaphors are rarely made visible, but might be made more apparent when the surfaces are stripped away. Perhaps this is why buildings always look more exciting when they are under construction, when you can see the steel, the floor plates and the sky, and watch the transitions as they take place (Garrett 2014, 87). Once they are clad, they lose their movement and seem to become fixed in place, as if they had always been like that. The structure forgets that it could have been otherwise, becomes an institution, and the cranes that made that possible are gone. Of course this doesn't mean that we should abandon talk of structure – how could we? – but try to build ways of thinking which can preserve its necessarily relational, temporary and mobile nature, in the moment of construction.

Futurists and Constructivists found some beautiful ways of reaching towards this understanding in thinking about an aesthetics which could capture multiplicity. Boccioni was interested in 'those atmospheric planes which bind and intersect things' (1912, 114) and which would become the principle of a new form of sculpture which was predicated on a different ontology:

A piece of Futurist sculpture will contain all the marvelous mathematical and geometrical elements that constitute the objects of our age. And these objects will not be merely placed near or alongside a statue, like explanatory attributes or detached decorative elements, but, following the laws of a new conception of harmony they will be inserted inside the muscular lines of a body. In this way, the cogs of a machine might easily emerge from the armpits of a mechanic, or the lines of a table could cut a reader's head in two, or a book with its fanned-out pages could intersect the reader's stomach.

(Boccioni 1912, 116)

Echoing Bergson, the sculpture is a space/shape brought into existence by other borrowings, or as Varvara Stepanova declared in 1921, 'Technique and industry have confronted art with the problem of construction as an active process and not a contemplative reflection. The "sanctity" of a work as a single entity is destroyed' (in Gray 2012, 289). No wonder that the form of the girder, an assemblage of lines that cuts and joins space, became such an useful way to think about relations, and to try and dethrone the 'bourgeois' fetish of the isolated work of genius. All life could be art, all materials could be understood aesthetically and the modern was distinctive because 'Only the straight line can lead to the primitive purity of a new architectonic structure of masses or sculptural zones' (Boccioni 1912, 119).

The skeletal nakedness of the crane is important because it is an excellent example of the Modernist principle of form being inextricable from function. The aesthetic of a crane is a product of what it is intended to do, in a much purer sense than of the building that it constructs. As we have seen, it is quite possible to see beauty in a crane, but this is not art or ballet or architecture. An analogy with the natural sublime might be a better one, particularly as it is articulated in David Nye's 'technological sublime', which he takes to encompass bridges, dams, skyscrapers, the Apollo moon landing and so on (1994). A mountain does not intend to please, to awe, and neither does the crane. Its aesthetics are a by-product of how it moves and relates to materials, not a matter of its singularity or the 'aesthetic' intentions of its designers. Even the colour of the anti-corrosion paint on the steel, or the shape and location of the cab will have to be justified in terms of engineering or economics.

Consider this in terms of the idea of the heroic agency of the driver which, as we have seen, is something routinely denied by drivers themselves. Physical elevation often metaphorically suggests a greater degree of freedom and power, but (as a high rope access window cleaner put it in an interview with me) he very often just feels 'stuck up there'. Like the driver then, not free, but only able to move in particular planes and lines, depending on the structure. It is, as Tim the crane driver said, a ballet in which certain rhythmic movements are possible, but only certain ones. Consider also that such a position, stuck up there, is temporary, because the modern tower crane can be disassembled, containerized, and constructed in another space with remarkable speed. It is designed to be both solid and ephemeral by turns, a spider's web which can lift masses, and also able to assemble and disassemble itself with the minimum of external intervention. Like a circus,[18] it can unfold itself and reveal a specific set of relations between planes and lines, a particular possibility for movement which wasn't available before. But this isn't a 'self-jacking' ontology, a form of autopoesis (Cooper 2006), because the crane is itself the construction of other relations, borrowings, intersections.

There is more than an echo of Deleuze and Guattari in my formulations here. Also influenced by Bergson, Deleuze and Guattari repeatedly offer an account of planes and lines defining space, refusing an essentialism of things or humans. I can't find any reference to Futurism or Soviet Constructivism in any of their major works (1984, 1988, 1994), but the grammar of expression is very similar. Vladimir Tatlin called for a 'culture of materials', and thought that this radical way of connecting art and life would produce 'a new spatial form: a continually intersecting rhythm of planes whose movements jut into, cleave, embrace, block and skewer space' (Gray 2012, 181). So, in *A Thousand Plateaus* (1988), do Deleuze and Guattari offer accounts of 'planes of consistency', plateaus, strata, territories and many versions of the line, rhizome, 'line of flight', diagram and so on. Later, in *What is Philosophy*, the key idea mutates to the 'plane of immanence' ('a table, plateau or slice' (1994, 35), as the ground from which concepts can grow. Oddly, in the same book, they do repeatedly describe themselves as 'constructivists', defining it as follows: 'Constructivism requires every creation to be a construction on a plane that gives it an autonomous existence' (ibid., 7). This sense of constructivism stresses a world which is made, rather than discovered, but without the central place given to human agency in most of social constructionism. Following Deleuze and Guattari, it is not only us humans who can be understood as causes for the production of 'assemblages', lines and planes of different speeds and viscosities (ibid., 4). For these philosophers, and for the Russian Constructivists, everything is always part of something else, produced by and producing, with its echoes of movement and lines of connection.

Describing Rodchenko and Tatlin's post-revolutionary call for 'Art into life!', a bridge between aesthetics and industry, Camilla Gray says 'The engineer must develop his feeling for materials – through the method of "Material Culture" – and the artist must learn to use the tools of mechanical production' (2012, 284). INKhUK, the Moscow-based post-revolutionary Institute of Artistic Culture, was an attempt to do just this. It insisted that an understanding of making something – which could be in a gallery or a factory – must include three elements: '*faktura* (the process of working material), *tectonika* (tectonics, which is based on the expedient use of industrial materials and which unites the ideological and formal), and *konstrucktsia* (the actual process of putting things together)' (Tupitsyn 1999, 31, also Gray 2012). In this way, the texture of materials, relations between materials and the labour process could be understood as a unity, and expressed in the product as something which was not a commodity fetish, or an expression of bourgeois individualism, capitalist exploitation and so on. In the Constructivist manifesto, Gan called this 'the principle of organization', which Constructivism was formulating, a way of uniting the ideological with the formal (1922, 40).

Setting aside the question of how such production might be institutionalized, this is a remarkable theoretical demand, and one that embeds a complex theory of kaleidoscopic organization. To try and appreciate material properties, relations between materials and their conjoining in a specific form as all necessarily part of the revealing of a thing suggests multiple perspectives in the same sense that much Futurism and Constructivism tried to show the rays, angles, echoes of movement in a running man or a bicycle. This is perhaps what Anton Ehrenzweig (1967) refers to as the 'syncretic' function of art, in that it can help to de-differentiate categories of thought and experience which the adult mind holds separated. The crane, it seems to me, can be a vehicle for expressing this sort of ontology rather nicely, being a provisional arrangement of lines of force and planes of resistance which allow for the balletic movements of mass, money and labour. Addressing the question 'How can Art be Realised', Alexander Calder – the engineer of mobilities – suggests the following:

> Out of different masses, light, heavy, middling—indicated by variations of size or color—directional line—vectors which represent speeds, velocities, accelerations, forces, etc . ...—these directions making between them meaningful angles, and senses, together defining one big conclusion or many.
>
> Spaces, volumes, suggested by the smallest means in contrast to their mass, or even including them, juxtaposed, pierced by vectors, crossed by speeds.
>
> Nothing at all of this is fixed.
>
> Each element able to move, to stir, to oscillate, to come and go in its relationships with the other elements in its universe.
>
> *(Calder 1932)*

Opening up the figure of the crane, like a window as Boccioni says, allows us to see it as a structure which temporarily constructs a set of sociotechnical relations. The social and the material cannot be disentangled here. Like Deleuze and Guattari's 'orchid-wasp' (1988, 11), the crane requires mathematics, the welding of materials, flows of capital and labour, and it can be revealed in different ways through all of these planes too. And this is to say nothing of bees, sulphur-crested cockatoos and electric storms that turn the clouds green.

Whether we can 'see' cranes, or any other assemblage, in such a multiple way is a difficult question, one perhaps limited by our bodies and our imaginations, but perhaps possible with care and attention (Mol 2003). Art is clearly one way to try and do this, a method to produce strange observations, to unfold multiplicities. In David Leavitt's (1986) novel *The Lost Language of Cranes,* we are introduced to a neglected boy who, in the absence of human company, began to imitate the sound and actions of the cranes which he could see from his window. The speech of a crane – its creaks and whirrs – was his only language, and others, for example, a therapist in the book, couldn't learn to speak it, though they tried. So too are planes of immanence organized in a way that allows certain lines of sight and modes of speech. Visibility works like that because there are always ways of seeing which are provided by institutions, disciplines and classifications – whether *International Cranes and Specialised Transport*, a Health and Safety report, a crane index, a place hacker, or Eve Weber's documentary. The intersection of these means that the crane can't be anything at all, because the lines and planes only allow for certain choreographed movements, but it can be many things superimposed at one and the same time. The crane is a manifestation of mathematics, of engineering, of accounting, of construction, a place of work with sausage-roll crumbs on the floor, a place of struggle which tosses in the wind, a harbinger of a world of machines, and an unnoticed source of beauty. It was with the last that this chapter began, but it had to travel through all the others in order to return there again, and see that as if for the first time.

Ideas about organization, understood narrowly, work on a plane which intersects with the concerns of this chapter, but usually only in terms of work and economics. That is because organization theorists usually work in business schools, but there is no necessary reason for that to be the case. This particular concept – organization – doesn't need to dwell in certain buildings and not others, understood as if its heart were resident in labour and finance, but not steel, mathematical calculations of stress, and Russian Constructivism. Thinking with cranes shifts these ideas a little, showing that organizing can be understood in multiple ways, that understanding can be syncretic, and that these lines of sight produce a structure which is a multiple, temporary relation between different materials. Of course, the same work could be done with any other assemblage too, because there's nothing special about cranes, or zoos, or art galleries.

Notes

1 This chapter is based on (2017) 'Tower Cranes and Organization Studies', *Organization Studies* 38/7: 989–1004.
2 Almost no one. See www.vertikal.net/en/news/story/23194/ for a house hanging from a crane in a Karlsruhe art festival.
3 See www.imdb.com/title/tt1387143/ and www.imdb.com/title/tt1336009/, accessed 31 July 2024.
4 Because they are, almost all, men. I was told about some women drivers, but they were rare.
5 www.jstor.org/stable/i40060848, accessed 7/9/15
6 *International Cranes and Specialised Transport*, July 2015: 48–49.
7 www.landsecurities.com/london-portfolio/london-property-portfolio/new-street-square, accessed 17 September 2015.
8 See, for example, www.ucatt.org.uk/construction-sites-facing-standstill-crane-drivers-ballot-industrial-action, accessed 21 July 2015.

9 www.reuters.com/article/2011/07/12/hold-korea-labour-idUSL3E7IB0VR20110 712, and https://koreanstory.wordpress.com/2011/12/03/kim-jin-suk-one-things-that-saved-me-who-even-felt-like-suicidal-was/ accessed 21 July 2015

10 https://koreanstory.wordpress.com/2011/12/03/kim-jin-suk-one-things-that-saved-me-who-even-felt-like-suicidal-was/, written by Hur Jae-hyun, accessed 21 July 2015.

11 https://koreanstory.wordpress.com/2011/10/09/occupy-wall-street-demonstrators-we-are-fighting-the-same-fight/, accessed 31 May 2024.

12 www.gmb.org.uk/newsroom/ten-year-delay-in-battersea-crane-disaster-trial, accessed 8 September 2015.

13 Some of them do, though not most. The names I was told were Jane the Crane, Tinkerbell, and The Goose; together with female names such as Linda Lynne and Jenny.

14 www.wqxr.org/#!/story/67535-donnacha-dennehy/, accessed 17 September 2015.

15 www.documentary.org/feature/meet-filmmakers-eva-weber%E2%80%94-solitary-life-cranes, accessed 12 September 2015.

16 https://allpoetry.com/The-Pylons, accessed 31 July 2024.

17 www.wqxr.org/#!/story/67535-donnacha-dennehy/, accessed 21 July 2015

18 Alexander Calder was also interested in the circus, another temporary and mobile form of organizing. See http://whitney.org/Collection/AlexanderCalder/8336195, accessed 11 November 2015.

PART III

Hierarchy

6
ANGELS

Angels are organized.[1] This chapter surveys their various incarnations, from violent monsters to contemporary spirit guides, paying particular attention to their role in an early legitimation of hierarchy. This is found in the writings of Pseudo-Dionysius, about 1,500 years ago. Despite the fact that he was ordering the world of angels, he suggests both ontological and political reasons for accepting that both celestial and secular organization must equal hierarchy. This is an assumption that is not often contested even today, and the idea of hierarchy is central to theories of organization which justify the managerial prerogative. However, angels have been mutable creatures, and I employ their differences in order to open up this fifth-century common sense. I conclude by suggesting that angelic obedience should be treated with suspicion, and that other sorts of angels, particularly the fallen ones, might lead us away from the tyranny of hierarchy.

Medieval debates about angels translated theological concerns into political legitimations, and contemporary managerialism still operates within the shadow of these assumptions. As in the rest of this book, an understanding of 'organization' can be drawn from a wide range of cultural sources. It is also that interrogating managerial assumptions in this manner can weaken their power as a form of common sense. There is no necessary connection between the former, which merely extends the domain of organization studies, and the latter, which reads critique into the results of such an extension. It is quite possible that some readers will translate fifth-century angelic hierarchy into a lesson concerning proper forms of contemporary governance and order. However, I choose to side with Lucifer, and to position the angels as enemies of a critical project, particularly if the project involves the extension and

DOI: 10.4324/9781032714288-9

celebration of more local and less hierarchical organizational forms (Parker et al. 2007, 2014).

'Organization' is a concept that refers generally to any sort of patterning, a fairly durable set of relations between people and things. Dominant contemporary understandings of organization make this concept almost equivalent to concepts such as management, and hierarchy, and even capitalism. Fournier and Grey (2000) suggest that one of the features of critical work in management studies is 'denaturalisation'. That is to say, when someone suggests that something is inevitable or eternal, it is helpful if the concept can be placed into the contingencies of history. It seems to me that hierarchy is one such concept, and that the story of Pseudo-Dionysius and the angels helps us to denaturalize hierarchy, and think more clearly about what this concept involves. In this chapter I don't offer an alternative theory of organization, but will (at the end) simply point to places where alternatives might be found. My purpose here is to place a particular word back into history, where it belongs. But first, we need to meet the angels.

Monsters

Angels can be found in Judaism (including Kabbalism), Catholicism, Orthodox and Protestant Christianity, Islam, Mormonism and many denominations, sects and cults. Angelic and demonic spirits (*devas* and *asuras*) can be found in Hinduism, and angelic spirits (*devas*) in Buddhism:

> Without committing myself religiously I could conceive of the possibility of there being, in dimensions and worlds other than our own, powers and intelligences outside our present apprehension, and in this sense angels are not to be ruled out as a part of reality – always remembering that *we create what we believe*. Indeed, I am prepared to say that if enough of us believe in angels, then angels exist.
>
> *(Davidson 1971, xii)*

But are they humans, with wings? Ornithanthropus? In the Mervyn Peake novel, *Mr Pye*, the main character oscillates between growing wings and horns, depending on whether he has been good or bad. Both are freakish, 'for after all wings are not the monopoly of the seraphim but equally to be found upon the backs of ducks' (1972, 136).[2] Mr Pye's wings result in strange bulges under his shirt, whilst his horns have to be covered by a hat. Both present him with severe social problems. Whatever the shamans of the contemporary new age might claim, angels are also monstrous.

We might begin with winged Egyptian gods from 3,500 years ago, the Zoroastrian Gods of 600 BCE Persia, and the ancient Greek Eros. The Etruscan and Greek angels of death were winged too, Charun and Thanatos

(Ward and Steeds 2005, 225). Or perhaps we should look towards the Assyrian or Akkadian *Kerubim* (winged bulls) who, according to Theodorus, Bishop of Heraclea in the fourth century, were 'horrible visions of Beasts, which might terrifie Adam from the entrance of paradise' (in Davidson 1971, 86). Lamborn Wilson, borrowing from a variety of Islamic sources, suggests that 'From the soles of his feet to his head, Israfil, the Angel of the Day of Judgment, has hairs and tongues over which are stretched veils'. Mika'il is covered with saffron coloured hairs: 'On each hair he has a million faces and each face a million eyes and a million tongues. Each tongue speaks a million languages and from each eye falls 70,000 tears.' Jibra'il has the sun between his eyes and wings that stretch from the East to the West. The Angel of Death, Azreal, has four faces, four wings and his body is covered with innumerable eyes: 'When one of these eyes closes, a creature dies' (Lamborn Wilson 1980, 35–36)

In the Bible, angels are terrifying too. Perhaps as an ironic joke, 'Fear not!' is usually the first thing that they say to the wide-eyed mortal. The Angel who came to Daniel had a face like lightening, eyes like flaming torches, and spoke with the roar of a crowd (Daniel 10). Ezekiel 1 has a depiction of an angel with four faces like animals, crossed wings, wheels within wheels adorned with eyes, flaming fire and so on. These angels are also mass murderers. In II Kings 19, an angel kills 135,000 Assyrian soldiers in one night, whilst in I Chronicles 21, 70,000 Israelites are slaughtered. In Exodus 12, an angel kills the first-born child of every Egyptian and Israeli family that has not offered a blood sacrifice by midnight. In Matthew 13, we are told that it will be the angels who separate us into those who will be saved, and those to be cast into the furnace of fire. Indeed, in several places in the Bible, we are told that on the Day of Judgement the angels will be causing wailing and gnashing of teeth as they dispose of those who have refused to obey.

The point is that it took a while before these monsters and psychopaths became transformed into gentle superheroes with white wings. Gilles Néret allows us to see this change from about 400 years ago. The 'promoted genies' (such as cherubim and seraphim) can be seen in Christian myth from around the fourth century, but their wings could be blue, green, red, striped, or peacock, and sometimes cherubim were slickly red all over (see Néret 2004 for illustrations). But by the time of Pieter Bruegel the Elder's *The Fall of the Rebel Angels* from 1562, and Frans Floris's painting of the same title from 1600, the rebels are shown as mutants with heads like fish or lions, wings of butterflies, arms like crabs, bellies bursting with eggs. At the top of the picture, the good angels are looking serious and wearing partly white clothing, and their wings are mostly white. The fallen angels can have the wings of bats, as in Gustav Doré's nineteenth-century illustrations of Milton's *Paradise Lost*, but the closer we get to the present, the prettier the good angels get.

Hierarchy

Within the Abrahamic religions, there is a good reason for the angels to be rather stern. It is simply that they are only following orders. Angels (apart from the fallen ones) do not have free will. Made by God, they follow His instructions.[3] They are His representatives, and their existence helps human beings solve a major epistemological problem: how can humans know God? We are small and limited, whilst God is entire and complete. Our being, our substance can only allow us to glimpse the smallest part of Him. If we got any closer to His light of infinite brightness and heat, we would simply shrivel like moths. This is clearly a problem. The usual solution is to suggest that re/presentation is needed to relay His glory. Hence, in the Christian tradition, 'theophany', the showing of God, the symbolization or presence of God in some other thing. This is the moment where difference comes into the world, when representation is needed,[4] and when angels become important. The first Ecumenical Council of Nicea in 325 asserted that angels were part of God's creation, whilst another, in 342, asserted that angels should not be worshipped. This leads to a problem in later angelology. Are angels different from God, or different from Man, or different from both?

For Pseudo-Dionysius, (or Dionysius, or Denys) the Areopagite, in the fifth or early sixth century, the re-presentation of God must be ordered so that relations between things could be properly understood.[5] Angels filled an entire universe of re-presentation, spreading His light downwards but taking a little brilliance off it with each step. At the bottom, humble humans could now enjoy His light without contradiction. Pseudo-Dionysius' work, the *Corpus Areopagiticum*, is first mentioned in 532 CE, but no one knows who wrote it, and what the author's real name was (see Pelikan 1987, Keck 1998, 55). He was possibly a bishop, but whether of Paris, or Antioch, or Athens, is not known. He may have been a Syrian monk, or Peter the Iberian, a Georgian theologian. There is a legend that he was the same Dionysius who was converted by Paul in Athens (Acts 17), and was seen at the death of the Virgin Mary, standing between Gabriel and Michael. Indeed, it was precisely this near-apostolic authority that gave his schema legitimacy within medieval angelology (Keck 1998, 56).

This confusion seems appropriate, for the origins of hierarchy should not be too clear. If origins were not shrouded in mystery, they might be questioned as mere fabulation. Perhaps mindful of such difficulties, even Pseudo-Dionysius does something to cover his tracks by claiming that his teacher, the 'most Holy Hierotheus', who wrote *The Elements of Theology*, inspired most of his ideas. There is no record of such a person, or of such a book, and Luibheid (1987, 69) suggests that this was merely part of the overall fiction, a strategy that often appeared to involve naming other fictional texts, or writing as if this were a letter to someone else. Exactly why Pseudo-Dionysius was concealing his identity, and the provenance of his ideas, is unclear, but when accusations of unorthodoxy were so dangerous to court, anonymity was probably not a bad idea.[6] Even if the cover was blown, the old Hierotheus could be blamed, since they could be claimed to be his ideas in the first place. The displacement of responsibility was embedded from the beginning, which seems appropriate where angels are concerned, since they are only following orders.

The key philosophical problem that Pseudo-Dionysius deals with in writings such as 'The Divine Names' and 'The Mystical Theology' is how to understand and praise 'the name which is above every name', 'the source, and the cause, the number and the order of the one, of number, and of all being' (in Luibheid 1987, 54, 129). How could vulgar symbols capture 'the Cause of all things who is beyond things'? (ibid., 138). How can we describe the indescribable, understand the transcendent? The heresy of idolatry always lurks, in which we worship the symbol, not God. One of Pseudo-Dionysius' strategies to avoid such errors was to proceed by refining language in order that, by dismissing its earthy referents, we could move towards that which cannot be grasped but can be glimpsed. Such a purifying process he describes as climbing higher or clearing aside, but there is another strategy that he puts forward which is to proceed downwards from that which cannot be grasped to its imperfect manifestations on earth. Since God has made the heavenly hierarchies known to us in various ways, these must be ordered theophanies, and this in turn suggests that 'Order and rank here below are a sign of harmonious ordering toward the divine realm.' (ibid., 146).

The two main parts of Pseudo-Dionysius' writings that are of interest to us here are 'The Celestial Hierarchy' and 'The Ecclesiastical Hierarchy'. These are arguments for cultivated men, not superstitions about monsters. The vulgar beliefs of the masses are dismissed as mad fantasies, in which animal-like creatures roam the skies with 'great moos' (ibid., 148). Real knowledge is not for everyone, because not everyone has the subtlety to comprehend the sacred, or the ability to see behind appearances. In fact, it seems, only those people who are already part of the hierarchy could really understand it because 'a hierarchy is a sacred order, a state of understanding and an activity approximating as closely as possible to the divine' (ibid., 153). The whole point of hierarchy is its perfection, its distribution of representations of the divine:

> The goal of a hierarchy, then, is to enable beings to be as like as possible to God and to be at one with him. A hierarchy has God as its leader of all understanding and action. It is forever looking directly at the comeliness of God. A hierarchy bears in itself the mark of God. Hierarchy causes its members to be images of God in all respects, to be clear and spotless mirrors reflecting the glow of primordial light and indeed of God himself. It

ensures that when its members have received this full and divine splendour they can then pass on this light generously and in accordance with God's will to beings further down the scale.

(Luibheid 1987, 154)

There is an interesting logical trick going on here, as well as the legitimation of earthly social order. By claiming that hierarchy is a 'perfect arrangement', it becomes both one thing and many, a form of organizing that is greater than the sum of its parts. The representation problem is not actually solved, but dissolved into a state of affairs where the many (the empirical world) reflects the one (God) through their relations (angels):

> Therefore, when the hierarchic order lays it on some to be purified and on others to do the purifying, on some to receive illumination and on others to cause illumination, on some to be perfected and on others to bring about perfection, each will actually imitate God in the way suitable to whatever role it has.

(Luibheid 1987, 154)

This solution makes organization into the mediating term between perfectionist monism and an atomism that allows humans to be humans. It allows both to be, and the question becomes one of scale, symbolized as vertical elevation, or centrality. The One, despite the fact that it is everything, is positioned at the top of a two- or three-dimensional space. A space that places all other locations in a subordinate position to it. This is not a necessary implication of organization, as a relation between entities, but it is the one chosen.

What Pseudo-Dionysius announces is an arrangement of threes, a number beloved of Neoplatonists. In the first hierarchy we have the thrones, cherubim and seraphim; in the second, the authorities, dominions (or dominations) and powers, and in the third, the angels, archangels, and principalities. Each rank of celestial being has distinct capacities and responsibilities, and these are described with considerable confidence. While he begins by insisting that within each hierarchy there is equality between the three orders, by the time he gets to describing the last order, 'every hierarchy has first, middle and last powers' (Luibheid 1987, 170). Each ranks functions as a messenger for the one above it, and each subordinate is uplifted and held in place by the message that they receive. In 'The Ecclesiastical Hierarchy', Pseudo-Dionysius applies this logic to the powers of the Church on earth and shows how superior and subordinate relationships echo the arrangements of the divine. It also becomes clear that the older term 'hierarch', a high priest or leader (etymologically, *heiros* and *arche*, or holy rule), is being appropriated. Hierarchy is no longer merely about a single charismatic leader, but is a generalised organizational relation in which we are all embedded, whether we like it or not: 'For not everyone is holy and, as scripture affirms, knowledge is not for everyone.' (ibid., 199). The text then goes on to describe, in generous detail, the rites and mysteries proper to different roles. Like secret societies, certain sorts of people say particular things to other sorts of people in particular places, symbols and ointment are used, and there is some singing at times. The three-fold order of heirarchs, priests and deacons is paralleled by different sorts of people seeking purification – catechumens, possessed and penitents. (Though in other places, 'sacred people' and monks are added too.) There are clear divisions of labour, and a ranking of beings that allows us to stretch from the dullest catechumens, who are still being 'incubated' by the Scriptures, to the divine light, via between 15 and 17 orders along the way.

Pseudo-Dionysius was not the first, or the last, to propose some sort of vertical ordering of things, and I am not proposing him as an origin of all ideas about hierarchy. The notion of the visionary ascending to God, negotiating angelic guardians along the way, can also be found in the Kabbalistic *Hekhalot* ('Palaces') from the second century. Both St Ambrose and St Jerome put forward versions of the angelic order in the fourth century. St Augustine speculated on the relative places of animals, humans, angels and God at around the same time as Pseudo-Dionysius. Nonetheless, Pseudo-Dionysius was by far the most influential of these writers. In 787, the second Council of Nicea proclaimed an official 'Dogma of Archangels', mostly based on the *Corpus Areopagiticum*. The earliest Latin translation from the original Greek was made in Paris in 838, with a second following a few years later. Yet his real fame and influence coincides with the birth of the modern European university in the twelfth century (Keck 1998, 50, 75 *passim*). Urbanization and the expanding professional classes had led to the beginnings of specialized religious institutions to teach interpretation, logic and argument. These institutions then became involved in countering various heresies and defending *doxa* against *heterodoxa*. But such deployments of reason also led to an interrogation of the mechanisms of God's order, through natural philosophy, and the search for legitimation of social orders, through angelology and hermeneutics.[7]

Angelology became a way to engage with philosophical debates, and also a method for teaching logic and discipline. As David Keck put it:

Of all God's creatures, human beings are nearest the angels, and angelology thus promises to illuminate anthropology. In the modern world, the impulse to learn about human nature from closely related beings has shifted subjects from seraphim to simians. Whereas modern scientists study the origins of the apes to uncover clues about humanity, medieval theologians investigated angels.

(Keck 1998, 16)

Duns Scotus suggested that angels were denser than God, and that they could independently think and reason. Bonaventure argued that angels were both matter and form. Thomas Aquinas responded by arguing that angels were entirely form, pure intellect, but that they could inhabit human bodies. Though the question of angels and pinheads comes from a later Rabelaisian parody, it does echo Aquinas' question as to whether two angels could occupy the same space (Marshall and Walsham 2006, 1). Questions concerning their agency, substance and free will were central and some serious philosophical and social issues were at stake.

The shift towards university-based philosophy that we see from the twelfth century onwards also supported the idea that angels were gradually being withdrawn from the vulgar miracle work that the masses expected and which had so disgusted Pseudo-Dionysius seven centuries previously. Henry Mayr-Harting nicely termed this the 'aetherialisation' of angels (Marshall and Walsham 2006, 8), but it also had some concrete political implications. One of the most consistent themes in later angelology is the idea that the hierarchy of heaven echoes the proper hierarchy on earth. Someone, in *De Mundo* in the first century BCE, says 'They, all together, singing in harmony and moving round the heaven in their measured dance, unite in one harmony whose cause is one and whose end is one: it is this harmony which entitles the All be called "order" and not disorder' (in Lamborn Wilson 1980, 79). Honorius of Autun, Bonaventure, Bernard of Clairvaux and many others, used these sort of arguments in order to justify a wide range of 'natural' orders. All were hierarchically organized – the levels of spiritual enlightenment that someone must pass through; the relation of man to the natural world; the hierarchy of the Church on earth; the relation of the Church to the State; of Rome to the monastic orders; the organization of monastic orders and so on (Keck 1998, 53 *passim*). Heresies (political, theological, or both) could be put in their place by a form of argument that stressed vertical authority and stability. Mobility and monstrosity were immediately classified as illogical (and dangerous) because, as Aquinas put it 'no creature of a lower order can ever covet the grade of a higher nature, just as an ass does not desire to be a horse: for were it to be so upraised, it would cease to be itself.'[8]

Any symbolization of movement must be highly controlled, and teleological in nature. Jacob, in Genesis 28, dreams of a ladder which reaches to heaven, with (according to *Paradise Lost*) 'angels ascending and descending'. This is an escalator for the messengers, the servants of God, which allows them to visit the earth without themselves being changed. There are also versions of movement that imply human mobility. In Merkabah mysticism, the pious mortal Enoch so pleased God that he was transformed into the angel Metatron (Astel 2005, 154). Matthew 22 suggests that the fallen angels left vacant thrones that can be occupied by the elect among men. St Francis of Assisi is supposed to have been awarded the throne of Lucifer himself

(Lamborn Wilson 1980, 179). Néret even refers to a similar career amongst angels, beginning as singing and dancing cherubs ('chubby aeronauts'), then messengers, then part of the celestial armies (2004, 5).

Visually, from the medieval period onwards, hierarchy became ubiquitous. The soaring front of a cathedral, with niches for each rank of being, and perhaps ladders showing the mechanism of elevation. The illustrations and paintings of near-identical upturned faces in linear rows. Ranks of halos painted gold in horizontal lines. See, for example, Fra Angelico's painting 'Christ Glorified in Heaven', from 1423–24. It contains the prophets on the top row, then a row of male martyrs, then (on the bottom row) the female martyrs (Ward and Steeds 2005, 26). Or, Lorenzo Costa's 'The Adoration of the Shepherds with Archangels' from c.1499, where the full nine orders, holding associated symbols, are arranged vertically along each edge of the painting (Marshall and Walsham 2006, 7). Pseudo-Dionysius' conception of organization had triumphed. Diego Laynez, General of the Jesuits from 1558–1565 expressed the logic in *De Hierarchia, on the Divine Origin of Hierarchy* (Quattrone 2004, 647). Since hierarchy means jurisdiction over everything, any authority that requires jurisdiction must be hierarchically based. Since A equals B, then all B's must be A. As above, so below. God was in His heaven, and all was right with the world.

Popular Orderings

Conceptually, hierarchy is a particular form of organization. The angels have long been implicated in some much more complex forms of organizing, even though it is true to say that the vertical one became dominant after Pseudo-Dionysius. Yet even then, the organization of hierarchy seems to have been mutable. Various writers – John of Damascus, Gregory the Great, Isidore of Seville, Bernard of Clairvaux, Edmund Spenser, Drummond of Hawthornden – proposed different arrangements of the nine, a different nine orders, or even schemas of between seven or twelve orders including 'aeons', 'innocents', 'confessors' 'flames', 'warriors', 'entities', 'seats', 'hosts' and 'lordships' (Davidson 1971, 336 *passim*). And, in case we imagine these as merely alterations in the bureaucratic organogram, the twelfth-century Breviary of St Hildegard, Dante's *Divine Comedy* and Robert Fludd's *History of the Macrocosm* (1617) all translate these orders into Aristotelian concentric circles, or even spheres. For the Jewish mystics, there were seven levels of heaven – clouds and winds; sinners awaiting judgement; Eden; sun, moon and stars; the fallen angels; the radiant angels; and the archangels and ineffable light (Lamborn Wilson 1980, 74–78). For Dante Alighieri, there were nine nested spheres of Paradise, each with its own angel. In the *Paradiso* VIII, he explicitly acknowledges Pseudo-Dionysius, and his Beatrice is a theophany of the Empyrean light, the light of the Primum Mobile.

But these vertical or centralizing maps were only one of the imaginative topologies. In fact, the angels proliferated, both in terms of their different imaginative geographies, and also their connections with the day-to-day matters that concerned common people. As noted above, even though Pseudo-Dionysius and later angelologists were keen to draw a line between popular superstition and true enlightenment, the distinction proved impossible to police. So, in angelological writings, we have many different versions of the identity of the seven archangels; lists of the ruling princes of the nine celestial orders; of the throne angels; and of the 64 wardens of the seven celestial halls (Davidson 1971). This 'internal' proliferation of categories and classifications was related to a dizzying variety of connections between angels and other elements of earthly life. There are governing angels of the seasons, of the zodiac, of the months, of the days, the hours of the day and night; the intelligences or governors of the seven planets; of the cardinal points on the globe and the altitudes of the globe. Add to this angels that bear mystical names, amulet angels, guardian angels, archons and the angels who rule the 28 mansions of the moon. Calvin may have dismissed such writings as 'the vain babblings of idle men' (Davidson 1971, xxiii),[9] but it did nothing to stop angels being dizzyingly good to think with.

This proliferation pre-dates the *Corpus Areopagiticum* which begins to appear like a temporary domestication. For example, Enoch 3 (part of the Pseudepigraphia) identifies 'Ram'amiel, who is in charge of thunder; Ra'asiel, who is in charge of earthquakes; Shalgiel, who is charge of snow', and so on. Each ruling prince of the nine angelic hierarchies has particular responsibilities and capacities. There may be seven archangels, but four are above the rest – Michael, Gabriel, Raphael and Uriel. Each archangel carries certain things, and is associated with particular practices. The seven can also be called the planetary angels (if we delete Uriel but add in Hagiel, Camael, Zadkiel and Cassiel) and have associations with particular elements, metals, numbers, ancient deities, animals, birds, insects, stones, spices, incense, flowers, trees, foods, healing plants, body parts, bodily functions, virtues, professions,[10] activities and keywords. Or, from Kabbalistic literature, there are ten divine energies (*sefirot*) each associated with a particular angel. Things and concepts can also have patron angels, whilst some emotions or desires have assisting angels. There is even an angel for business ventures – Teoael, who happens to be a prince of the Choir of Thrones. In order to get his assistance, write your petition on company letterheaded paper, or include a business card (Melville 2001).

So the hierarchies seemed to float on the surface of a much more ramified and complex will to classify, organize, and order. The angels were not merely 'up there', singing, but 'down here' too. They were in the middle of things, being (as they are now) part of popular culture, an element of the magical resolution provided by charms, superstitions and curses (Keck 1998). No wonder that the universities and the Church needed to elevate the angels away from the masses, and to construct a place for everything, and keep everyone in their place.

War, Surveillance, Seduction

The entanglements between angelic and human organization were not restricted to a relation between Church *doxa* and popular *heterodoxa*. Through the millennium, they become manifested in some specific organized contexts too. Each positions a relation between a hidden celestial order, and the human. In the three examples which I discuss next, the human is more or less subordinate to the celestial, whether watching angels battle it out, being watched for sin, or being watchful of sin.

One of these images is that of the army, which (perhaps since Rome) had been imagined as a hierarchy. Milton's angels are arranged in squadrons, and follow their great commanders (*Paradise Lost*, Book I). They have fluttering banners and are deployed under their hierarchs. The huge battle that takes place in Book VI is a civil war being fought on behalf of mortals. These military and evangelical organizations are clashing in a fight in which we are mere onlookers, civilians. Chapter 5 of Billy Graham's *Angels*, 'Angelic Organization', runs through what Matthew Henry calls their 'offices and employments'. Graham describes Archangel Michael as 'the Prime Minister in God's administration of the universe' (Graham 1976, 54–55). The point is that some sort of organization already exists, and it will defend us in the battle against evil: 'Singly or corporately, angels are for real. They are better organized than were the armies of Alexander the Great, Napoleon or Eisenhower' (ibid., 30). This is the language of an evangelist but, despite all this sound and fury, triumph is guaranteed: 'The Bible declares that righteousness will eventually triumph, Utopia will come to earth, the Kingdom of God will ultimately prevail. In bringing all this about angels will have a prominent part' (ibid., 127) Such guarantees of victory must be comforting for those who know that they are going to win. Like the seventh cavalry, you know that angels will be riding to the rescue. According to some, during the 1914–1918 War, St George and his angels protected the 3rd and 4th Divisions of the British Expeditionary Force from the German First Army during their retreat from Mons. During the 1939–46 War, the British Air Chief Marshall Lord Dowding was supposed to have claimed that angels flew some planes after the pilots had been killed (ibid., 149). The devil may be 'the master-organizer and strategist' (ibid., 133), but it is certain that triumph and victory will go to the angels. Then, we will be able to rest from our 'labours' and 'works' (ibid., 144). But if we are going to win anyway, then why bother with the intervening struggle? Why not sit back and enjoy the show? It is probably for this reason that it is more common for mortals to be implicated, the objects of heavenly organization.

Often, rather than being onlookers of a heavenly battle, we are surveyed by the eyes of angels, watching us as if we were animals in a zoo. This second entanglement is a common trope in films. Powell and Pressburger's 1946 *A Matter of Life and Death* had heaven full of well-coiffeured receptionists in modern offices, and rows of desks. More recently, we have seen solemn people in overcoats, looking over our shoulders, listening to our thoughts, or harassed miracle workers on a mission from above. Nabu, the Babylonian winged god of wisdom (who invented writing) used to write down the decisions about humanity's future each year on the sacred tablets of fate (Ward and Steeds 2005, 33). In the Koran, we have the twin *hafaza*, 'recording angels' – one for the day, the good, and one for the night, the bad – who write down your every act in a book that will be presented at the Day of Judgement. In al-Qazwini's *Wonders of Creation* from 1208, we can see the angels searching through the scrolls of human deeds (Lamborn Wilson 1980, 62).

These are angelic bureaucrats, consulting lists of who is damned and who is saved, as in the orthodox fifteenth-century icon of the Last Judgement from the Novgorod school (in Ward and Steeds 2005, 48). William Blake drew Metatron as The Recording Angel in his illustrations for the *Divine Comedy* (Astel 2005, 155). Or consider the angel in Byron's 1822 viciously satirical poem 'The Vision of Judgment'. Sitting at a black bureau, he had pulled all his wings out to make quills to write down the names of the dead during King George III's reign. Even having a further six angels and twelve saints as clerks didn't help, since they eventually 'threw their pens down in divine disgust' after Waterloo (lines 16–40).[11] Like Walter Benjamin's angel of history, they watch, and record. There is no intervention, and perhaps even a certain impassive despair. Benjamin's angel faces the past, and sees 'one single catastrophe which keeps piling wreckage upon wreckage and hurls it in front of his feet'. At the same time, a storm blows from Paradise, pushing the angel of history backwards 'into the future to which his back is turned, while the pile of debris before him grows skywards. This storm is what we call progress' (Benjamin 1999, 249).[12]

The third entanglement with organization makes us active agents in resisting the strategies of the devil. Here we are not onlookers or objects of panoptic surveillance, but active participants in a complex conspiracy of temptation and fortitude. As Elizabeth Reis (2001) argues, in seventeenth-century Massachusetts, puritans like Cotton Mather and his father Increase Mather (the author of the 1696 *Angelographia*) were continually on their guard against Satan disguising himself as an angel. The Mathers thought that women were particularly vulnerable to the blandishments of the devil. They were susceptible to naive belief and weak of will, when what was required was male strength and moral fibre. Christopher Marlowe's, rather annoying, good and bad 'Angells' in his (c.1588–92) *Doctor Faustus* act to guide, or to tempt:

GOOD ANGELL.   Sweet *Faustus* think of heaven and heavenly things
BAD ANGELL.   No *Faustus* thinks of honour and of wealth
(Act II, scene i)

Power and sex and money and desire swim before our eyes, even though (we know that) this will be a bargain with the devil. Work and the public sphere are the site of many temptations, but those who get sucked into them rarely escape, and end up chained to labour, whipped by demons. Dante, in canto XXI of 'L'Inferno', the first book of the *Divine Comedy*, summons up the metaphor of the Venice Arsenale, the largest form of industrial organization that a fourteenth-century Florentine would have been aware of. He describes the fifth trench of the eighth circle of hell as like a shipbuilder's, just as so many more recent 'gothic' images of work organizations summon dark corridors, fiery furnaces, boiling pitch and the endless labours of Sisyphus. As Milton knew, the good life must be one that escapes the jaws of Mammon, the prince of tempters and demon of avarice:

> … even in Heaven his looks and thoughts
> Were always downward bent, admiring more
> The riches of Heaven's pavement, trodden gold
> Than aught divine or holy.
> *(Paradise Lost* I, 678)[13]

Nowadays, the temptation is the dream of career advancement, the myth sold by the business school. Jean Lhermitte puts it well in his 1963 *True and False Possession*: 'The Prince of Darkness no longer appears as a personage … but disguises himself willingly, even preferably, under the appearance of corporate personalities or institutions' (in Davidson 1971, xiv).

In Glen Duncan's novel *I, Lucifer*, the devil celebrates 'systems', as opposed to individual devilish acts of torture or vandalism. With the system, he reminds his fellow fallen angels that evil can achieve 'a state where despair can flourish with barely any interference from us, when they do it to and for themselves, when that's the way the world is' (Duncan 2002, 145). Then, the inhabitants of hell can lean back and watch, and the angels and the humans will have lost.

Angels Now

Contemporary angels seem to have come closer to the human. They are less like soldiers, bureaucrats, or spies, and more like mysterious friends. But, perhaps to avoid accusations of interference and the violation of our free will, the angels intervene in minor ways, usually just by delivering messages. The origin of the word 'administration' comes from minister, a servant. A ministry was a role, responsibility or mission, or an institution or person who took on such a mission. The angels minister to human beings, they administer the earth: 'They superintend the events of your life and protect the interest of Lord God, always working to promote his plans to bring about His highest will for you' (Graham 1976, 90).

Graham calls angelic communication 'terse'. They often urge haste, and do so with simple and direct commands (ibid., 116). The angel Moroni told Joseph Smith three times where he could find the tablets of the Book of Mormon. In a dream, Gabriel (*Jibra'il*) came to Muhammad in the cave of Hira in about 610 and told him to 'recite!' three times, and when he awoke, the beginnings of the Koran were inscribed upon his heart. Most etymologies of angel involve a reference to the concept or personification of communication. In Sanskrit, *angiras* means spirit, in Persian *angaros* means courier. From there, we get the Greek *aggelos* and the Latin *angelus*, both meaning 'messenger'. In Hebrew, an angel is *mal'ach*, from the Arabic *mal'ak*, which is in turn from *la'aka*, to send on a mission.

Increase Mather knew that Satan could disguise himself as angel, but he also knew that the world was shaped in certain angelic ways (Reis 2001). Angels operated 'behind the curtain', not curing people miraculously, but giving the doctor ideas about how to cure the patient by 'insensible manuduction'. Angels, he said, 'love secrecy in their Administrations'. Reis suggests that seventeenth-century Massachusetts saw a rash of angel sightings which, by the nineteenth century, were becoming more gentle and feminine in appearance. The fearsome monsters had become *putti*, cherubic decoration for paintings, and kindly counsellors dressed in white. Popular imagery connected them with innocent children, pre-Raphaelite radiance and a sentimental notion of comfort. To a certain extent, this had been prefigured by what David Keck calls 'the Christianization of fortune' during the medieval period (Keck 1998, 161–163), an echo of Mayr-Harting's 'aetherialisation'. The people invoked angels for everyday charms and spells, whilst at the same time the angelologists attempted to employ them as categories for interrogating the divine. But the popular ordering of fetishes becomes a threat to those that elevate celestial and intellectual hierarchies. Pseudo-Dionysius himself had complained about the vulgar understandings of his fifth-century populus: 'High-flown shapes could well mislead someone into thinking that the heavenly beings are golden or gleaming men, glamorous, wearing lustrous clothing, giving off flames which cause no harm … ' (in Luibheid 1987, 150). Angels were ideas, not things, and he dismissed 'the sheer crassness of the signs' which showed that too many human beings were willing 'to be lazily satisfied by base images' (ibid.).

It would seem that condemnations of popular angel worship are not at all new, and indeed that the angels of the contemporary New Age are not that new either. Nowadays, the shelves of bookshops and the pages of the internet have plenty of angels, often combining in remarkable ways with crystals, Native American spirit guides, and cultural bric-a-brac from any place and time. These angels leave messages in dreams, they heal, warn, or appear on slippery corners in the middle of rainstorms. They encourage us to treat everyone we meet as if they might be an angel, and to notice when we see a single white feather left rocking in the breeze. Or, on 'World Angel Day' to 'work harmoniously alongside them in their mission to heal the planet' (Astel 2005, 73). Sharon Linnéa, who was a contributing editor to *Angels on Earth* magazine, suggests various theories that might explain an intensification of angelic activity now (Beliefnet 2003, 10–11). Angels might be busier now than they were, which suggests that their activity might go in cycles. That in turn might be because science is revealing cosmic and microscopic mysteries that drive humans to seek further explanations. Or, perhaps we are becoming more receptive to the quiet voices, the messages left that we are often too busy to notice. Or, it might be simply because there is so much evil in the world now that we are seeking help and guidance in order to resist the temptations of the flesh and the violence of humankind.

Linnéa might be right. In a world of Business Schools and Business Angels, Hells Angels and AGM 114L Hellfire air-to-ground missiles, perhaps we do need angels more than ever (Lange 1998). Perhaps when we see the angels 'fleeing with tattered wings before the outrages of modern art' (Néret 2004, 6),[14] some people feel the need to call these nineteenth-century creatures back. These are not the avenging monsters of old, with thousands of eyes and voices like crowds. Like lucky heather or a rabbit's foot, they ask fate to protect us from evil. These are creatures of an age dominated by romantic and therapeutic conceptions of the human, but endlessly threatened by the impersonal violence of the urban, the commercial and the realistic. Edward Burne-Jones put it well when, in a letter to Oscar Wilde, he wrote 'the more materialistic science becomes, the more angels shall I paint' (Graham 1976, 9).[15]

Hard Liberty, or Servile Pomp

The metaphors of angelic organization shift to fit the time of their origin. So let's end with one more. In this, most abstracted, sense of angelic organization it becomes a verb. As St Augustine put it *'angelus est nomen officii'*, 'angel is the name of the office.' It is a function, a movement, a transmission. Not a personage but a way of describing our entanglement in the movements of the world. In the breath of wind, a half-heard whisper, the chance meeting, the ordering and organizing that just happens in us and around us. For Aquinas, these were 'powers' and 'immaterial spirits', 'a succession of contacts of power at diverse places', in time but not in a necessary location. Angels were pure agency, and the question was not 'What is an Angel?' but 'What does an Angel Do?' (Lamborn Wilson 1980, 49). Eight centuries later, this was echoed by Michel Serres, an angelologist at a Parisian university, in an essay on interchangers, intermediaries, and exchange between networks. He describes airports as full of 'angels of steel, carrying angels of flesh and blood, who in turn send angel signals across angel air waves' (1995, 8) The world is a general message-bearing system, and 'angel' is the name for that part of it that is more mobile than the rest. Or Massimo Cacciari, a contemporary Neoplatonist who wishes us to see the angel as that which always escapes expression, of the 'idea in the name' (1994, 48). Of that which escapes from language, but is always necessary for language to begin – a kind of no-place which is always imaginary and which propels communication.

So back to Pseudo-Dionysius. His world was a connected one too, one in which the divine light, angels, human beings and beasts were all a part. His solution to the problem of wholes and parts was that they must be arranged hierarchically. This is not the only solution to his problem. Serres prefers the idea of a network of actants, and Cacciari the mobility and mutability of poststructuralism. All three are modes of organizing, yet the angelic hierarchies are the only ones that can and have been used to justify the proto-bureaucratic life. Serres makes this particularly clear. For him, the messenger should disappear once the message is delivered. Who can tell the message from the messenger? In a network, or in a language for that matter, the two are one. This means that the humble intermediary must always dematerialize, and not get sucked into becoming a self-important machine for manufacturing stable myths (1995, 105). In Serres' network of interchangers:

' ... All hierarchy collapses.'
'And at that point, the machine for fabricating gods (the machine which also produces violence and war) comes to a standstill.'

(ibid., 290)

Most of the time angels *are* known for their obedience, satisfaction with a place in the order of things, piety and chastity (Keck 1998, 118). Angels tend to represent order amidst disorder, the pattern behind the chaos, and a guarantee of the status quo. In his 'The Vision of Judgment', Byron claims, 'for by many stories, and true, we learn the Angels are all Tories' (Byron 1822, lines 206–207).[16] Byron sees them as on the side of conservatism, recording the outrages of power, and washing their hands of any guilt or complicity. During the long hours of ecclesiastical lives, they sing in unison for harmony, unity, living according to the rule, and duty, without wild hatreds or passions. Even Billy Graham seems to be a little impatient with their coolness. He claims Biblical authority for the idea that man is in a 'temporary lower position' than angels, which will be amended once the Kingdom of God has come in its fullness. Man was made higher than the animals, and angels have been commanded to help us because we will be higher than them after the resurrection (Graham 1976, 43): 'Someday man will be as perfect as angels are now' (ibid., 47). Man struggles, and will experience salvation, faith and God, and have an experience that angels can never possess, but 'no angel can be an evangelist' (ibid., 106). Even if we might not agree with Graham that he is better than the angels, we can recognize his irritation at their condescension. In the science-fiction writer Theodore Sturgeon's short story 'It Opens the Sky', their composure becomes deeply annoying. Angels are sanctimonious creatures who 'Just went around smiling and being helpful and reminding people to be kind to one another.' (1978, 112) When they look at you with those big, open, compassionate eyes, they deserve a punch.

The really terrible thing about all this, the thing that makes you want to shake them, is that they *were* offered a choice. According to Aquinas, at the moment of their creation, all the angels were offered liberty. Two-thirds chose to become servants of God and to sing praise to Him until the end of their days. Beings with wings that gave them the freedom to become a bird – to soar over the earth, looping the loop and becoming part of networks, multitudes, alternatives – chose to become servants. Milton tells us that one-third chose freedom:

> … preferring
> Hard liberty before the easy yoke
> Of servile pomp.
> (*Paradise Lost* II, 255–257)

Once Lucifer and the others had made their choice, had chosen will and the overthrowing of established order, there was no way back to the 'tyranny of heaven':

> Suppose He should relent
> And publish grace to all, on promise made
> Of new subjection; with what eyes could we
> Stand in His presence humble, and receive
> Strict laws imposed, to celebrate His throne
> With warbled hymns, and to His Godhead sing
> Forced hallelujahs, while he lordly sits
> Our envied sovereign, and his altar breathes
> Ambrosial odours and ambrosial flowers,
> Our servile offerings?
> (*Paradise Lost* II, 237–46)

Of course, the hierarchical angels reply that Satan is proud, and bent on our destruction. In the Koran, Iblis (Satan) refuses to bow before a being made from clay. On his banishment, he tells the creator that he will deceive and exterminate these low creatures. Such refusal to bow when told to is jealousy, arrogance, and even (in a pre-Foucauldian twist) a further form of slavery:

> This is servitude:
> To serve the unwise, or him who hath rebelled
> Against his worthier – as thine now serve thee,
> Thyself not free, but to thyself enthralled;
> (The Koran, Book VI, 179–181)

But they would say that, wouldn't they? To justify their place in the order of things, and avoid 'His wrath, which He calls justice' (Book II, 1733). Because the hierarchical angels are advocates for secular and celestial sclerosis, for the great chain of being and the order of things. The point of hierarchy is to stop movement, or at the very least, slow it and make it predictable. It is to chain the universe with something that ties all being together, and ensures that the only mobility is that which is already determined at the moment of creation by the first mover. No wonder the popular and polymorphous angels were treated with suspicion, and why Serres' and Cacciari's angels are endless movements, not obedient employees. Glen Duncan's Lucifer understands this problem in a way that Pseudo-Dionysius never could – 'for an angel there is only one true freedom, and that, I'm honestly sad to say, is freedom from God' (Duncan 2002, 210).

The precondition for freedom is a consciousness that things could be otherwise, that this form of organizing could be disorganized. The myth of the Areopagite, in its incarnations of stone, paint and institution, tells us that things are eternally the same. Pseudo-Dionysius is not the sole origin of this version of organization, though certainly an important relay, but his version of angelic organization has spent a millennium struggling with the popular angels. In my view, this struggle is still continuing, even though the ontology of angels is no longer the central terrain, and it is now Western managerialism as taught in business schools, as well as many other churches, attempting to hold the high ground. Unsurprisingly, those who benefit from hierarchy are busy naturalizing it, and claiming some sort of inevitability to the function, cadre and discipline of management that supports it. There *are* other accounts and practices of organization that assume that hierarchy is not inevitable – anarchism, feminism, forms of environmentalism and communitarianism (Marshall 1993, Ferree and Martin 1995, Naess 1989, Lovink and Scholz 2007, Parker et al. 2014). There are histories of rebellion and popular orderings, a multitude of intentional communities, and many, many utopias that imagine worlds in which power is not concentrated at the top of a chain of beings (Parker et al. 2007). There is not *one* alternative to Pseudo-Dionysius's cosmology, but many.

In Thomas More's *Utopia*, there is a type of person who 'rather than live in wretched poverty at home, volunteers for slavery in Utopia' (1965, 102). That is what organization means to them. A steady job, shops with food in them, and a police force that enforces the law. This has its attractions, and anyone who studies organization will understand the importance of certain sorts of predictability and rule following. Lucifer would rather 'reign in hell than serve in heaven' (*Paradise Lost* I, 263). That is what angelic organization means to him. It means preferring disobedience and disorder to the boredom of condescending angels, to the inevitability of hierarchy, the asymmetry of power, and the machine that endlessly manufactures false Gods. As Kurt Vonnegut beautifully observes, 'There is no reason why good cannot triumph as often as evil. The triumph of anything is a matter of organization. If there are such things as angels, I hope that they are organized along the lines of the Mafia' (Kurt Vonnegut, in Griffiths 1980, 107). Organization is never one thing, whatever 'the most Holy Hierotheus' might claim.

Notes

1 This chapter is based on (2009) 'Angelic Organization: Hierarchy and the Tyranny of Heaven', *Organization Studies* 30/11: 1281–1299.
2 In A.S. Byatt's *Angels and Insects*, one of the characters suggests that angels would need a breastbone protruding by several feet to counterbalance the wings, and another remembers her brother commenting that 'angels are only a clumsy form of poultry' (1993, 202). My friend Peter Armstrong calculated that the average angel would have a wing loading of about 35lb per square foot, about the same as a WW2 Spitfire. This would require a takeoff speed of about 110 mph, which means they would have to be able to run quite quickly.
3 I will follow convention here, and assume that God is a male, and that he is insecure enough to demand capitalization. The two assumptions may be related.
4 Just why God needed to set representation going is unclear. Some accounts might suggest that he wanted to be known, others that he was simply a control freak who desired undiluted adulation, ad nauseam, ad infinitum. That's why he filled the universe with '301, 655, 722 extramundane brown-nosers for – He's – a – jolly – good – fellowing Him in deafening celestial harmony' (Duncan 2002, 9).
5 I am not alone in mentioning Pseudo-Dionysius here. See Burrell 1997, 68, and particularly Kornberger et al. 2006, both also attempts to historicize the theory of organizations.
6 This is a strategy employed by many later authors, including many who wrote utopias. For example, see Hamilton and Parker 2016.
7 And, perhaps, a few centuries later, to Cartesian ideas about a hierarchy of knowing through reason which would be capable of resisting the mystifications of an evil demon, and placing man in relation to the natural world (Jones 2006).
8 https://aquinas.cc/la/en/~ST.I.Q63.A3.C, accessed 31 July 2004.

9 It is worth noting that the classifications of demons in demonology are just as complex. Medieval 'Grimoires', such as that written by Bishop Pierre Binsfield, often contain descriptions of demons of each deadly sin, of different layers of the earth and air, of hierarchies, of months, of different forms and so on.

10 For academics and writers, the angel is probably Raphael, who represents communication and science. You are also encouraged to eat celery, and pay attention to the number eight, and monkeys.

11 https://petercochran.wordpress.com/wp-content/uploads/2009/03/the_vision_of_judgement3.pdf, accessed 31 July 2024.

12 Though, as Maeseneer points out, the function of Benjamin's angel is ambivalent. He may have begun with the notion that the angel symbolized the necessary violence of revolution, an angel of destruction (2003a, 513–516), which later mutates into an angel of witness (2003b, 378).

13 In De Plancy's *Dictionnaire Infernal* (1825–26), Mammon is said to be hell's ambassador to England, the most industrialized country in the world at the time (Davidson 1971, 182).

14 Compare the antique angels in Néret 2004 with the contemporary devils in Néret 2003 for some proof of this.

15 It is worth noting that (in addition to the ape) another figure enters the picture here too: the alien. What Maeseneer calls the 'phantasmagoric anthropology' (2003b, 383) that sustained angelology has, to some extent, relocated to UFOlogy. See Appleyard 2006.

16 https://petercochran.wordpress.com/wp-content/uploads/2009/03/the_vision_of_judgement3.pdf, accessed 31 July 2024.

7
SKYSCRAPERS

In this chapter I show how, use this word to show how a particular artefact – the skyscraper – is both a noun and a verb.[1] In this case, the noun refers to a cultural symbol and the verb to a capitalist project. The former alerts us to what something 'means', the latter to a logic which gathers together people and materials into a temporary arrangement which generates value. Concentrating on organization as a mediating term, I can show the symmetry of cultural and economic forms of explanation for the existence of tall buildings.

In 2009, the Burj Khalifa in Dubai became, at 828 metres, the tallest human structure ever constructed. This building marked a step change in height. The tallest structure ever built by that time was the Warsaw Radio Mast which collapsed in 1991 and was 646 metres high. The Burj is still a lot taller than anything else but the time of writing [2015], the Jeddah Tower in Saudi Arabia, is once again under construction. It is proposed to top out at one kilometre high. Why are these structures built? Explanations in terms of 'symbolic power' (Acuto 2010) seem to underplay the ways in which skyscrapers have been projects tied to rental incomes, urban boosterism and national economic strategies. Yet it is also difficult to see the tall building as merely a machine for making the land pay, when its materialization is often so excessive, so extreme in its technology and scale.

If we go back to the beginnings of the skyscraper, we can see how even then they were seen to symbolize economic aspiration through elevation. Lewis Mumford, in his essay 'America and Alfred Stieglitz' (Frank et al. 1934), claims that 'sky-scrapers' were named after the topmost sail on a ship.[2] Presumably, the first thing you would see over the horizon was the tip of the skysail, or sky-scraper, just as the tips of the buildings would be the first parts

DOI: 10.4324/9781032714288-10

of Manhattan seen from the sea. The term was first applied to architecture in 1883 by John Moser in a piece entitled 'American Architectural Form of the Future'. In it, he says 'This form of sky-scraper gives that peculiar refined, independent, self-contained, daring, bold, heaven-reaching, erratic, piratic, Quixotic, American thought … ' (in Landau and Condit 1996, x). The 1870 eight-storey Equitable Life Assurance Society Building in New York is usually argued to be the first skyscraper, so by the time Moser was writing, there were already many tall buildings in New York and Chicago, and other large US cities. Alfred Stieglitz was one of the photographers of the early twentieth century who catalogued the rise of tall buildings with a similar awe, but Mumford himself had no time for skyscrapers. They defrauded people of 'space and light and sun, turning the streets into deep chasms' and annihilated 'whatever stood in the path of profit' (in Marqusee 1988, 160). Just as the skyscraper has been thought to be the architectural expression of the commanding heights of modernity, so has it also been thought to be an example of greed on an inhuman scale.

Very often, skyscrapers are treated as merely advertisements for ego; thieves of light and air and energy; representations of hierarchy and exclusion; and (of course) penis substitutes. A great deal of the writing on skyscrapers has used them as illustrations in cultural criticism. For these authors, skyscrapers need to be brought down to size, to be made modest and to harmonize with the human scale of the human city. Sometimes this is tied to a critique of capital, or the city, but more often to a denunciation of scale. Like Versailles, the tall building may be awe inspiring, but it is also vulgar, immodest and un-necessary. We could point out, as the architectural critic Deyan Sudjic does, that the architect of the World Trade Center – Minoru Yamasaki – also designed the gigantic Pruitt-Igoe housing project in St Louis (Sudjic 2006, 301). Charles Jencks famously claimed that its demolition in 1972 marked the end of architectural modernism, whilst others have noted that certain notions of rational social planning also died in its long, dark, piss-smelling corridors (Dale and Burrell 2008, 292). Like so many of the stumpy residential blocks across the world which have provided mass housing for migrants or a decanter for slum clearance, this is a version of the modern city which engineers its working class into towers with broken lifts.[3]

It might be the case that tall buildings are not always shiny and exciting, but still I can't help being swept up by the romance of the skyscraper as a defining feature of modern urban life. I pore over my glossy coffee-table books of New York, and enjoy the sheer climb, the dizzying peaks. Imagining the drop from steel beam to pavement, whilst the nerveless Mohawk construction workers in flat caps eat their black-and-white lunches and look at the camera. The IKEA posters of midtown at night; the countless opening shots of films which the helicopter pans in over Manhattan, and the evil villains who look over Gotham from the fiftieth floor. And now the baroque orientalism of the towers in Dubai, Taiwan, Kuala Lumpur and Shanghai, built by migrant labour and Western companies, and soaring into clear blue skies. They are all beautiful. All beautiful and terrifying at the same time. In part, this is the sublime terror of the abyss and the peak, of elevation and descent. It is also the sense of being diminished by something on an entirely inhuman scale, with the possibility that a small squashy body is reduced to insect-like insignificance in the face of such mass. From King Kong to the falling man, height can be given sickening sense by the splat on the sidewalk.

Jon Goss has argued that what he calls 'an architectural geography', needed to be attentive to the multiple meanings of buildings, to the fact that they are 'multifunctional objects rather than reflective facades' (1988, 392). He suggested that buildings could be seen in at least four ways – as cultural artefact, sign, object of value and spatial system. McNeill (2005) does something similar when he asks 'Which discipline owns the skyscraper?' These might seem to be questions which appear remote from studies of organization, but it seem to me that the concept of organization is actually rather crucial. The common division between culture and economy means that there is a tendency to focus on *either* symbolic meanings *or* the economics of generating value. It seems to me that understanding the skyscraper as a thing which symbolizes *and* as an example of a process which is made possible because of a particular set of economic relations allows us to transcend this rather easy dualism. John Dewey suggested that 'It is no linguistic accident that "building", "construction", "work" designate both a process and its finished product. Without the meaning of the verb that of the noun remains blank' (1980, 51). The skyscraper is an organization of non-human and human materials and it is also an organizing process for making money. This is a common enough distinction in terms of the entity and process view of the social world, and it has found application in studies of organization too.[4] Here I suggest that we can adopt a similar view of the dichotomy between culture and economy and suggest, along with Dewey, that one remains blank without the other.

Despite being in search of a certain kind of symmetry in which 'culture' and 'economy' are linked through 'organization', we have to begin somewhere. I will begin with culture, looking at the common responses to height and the skyscraper, whether sublime, anti-modernist, or celebratory. I then move on to show that the tall building is an organized economic object too. Many critics have seen the skyscraper as merely a *sign* of capitalist modernity, but I will argue that this is to be dazzled by the facade. Skyscrapers were, at the times and places of their origins, machines for making money in large cities, and a whole host of material and social technologies developed in order to maximize the amount of profit that could be generated from a small piece of land. Using the work of architectural historians, I will suggest that this sort of approach also allows us to see tall buildings as processes which involve a complex division of labour that allowed for speedy and efficient forms of construction (and demolition) in cities with high land values. I end with some thoughts on the politics of cultural representation, and on the ways in which 'organization' can be used as a term which makes it harder to forget that culture is economy, and economies are always cultural.

The Meaning of Big Things

Deyan Sudjic's *The Edifice Complex* (2006) argues that most big buildings reflect the desires of a little man, or his fawning acolytes. Hitler's neo-classical Berlin was intended to ensure that future generations would not end up admiring 'the department stores of a few Jews as the mightiest works of our era, and the hotels of a few corporations as the characteristic expression of the culture of our times' (Hitler, in Sudjic 2006, 37). Hussein, Stalin, Mitterand, Mussolini and Trump are all similarly condemned for their externalization of insecurity in the form of monumental bad taste. Tall buildings, with a few exceptions, are condemned as not being primarily about architecture, but 'an assertion of political will in steel, marble and glass' (ibid., 318). The very idea of building tall is dismissed as 'ludicrously childish' and even economically irrational. Sudjic is sure of his tastes, and presumably also certain about the sort of politics that attaches to such aesthetic choices. This account asserts that skyscrapers are about egos, whether corporate or state (King 2004, 10), or an element in a cultural battle between old and new money (Rubin 1979), or old and new cities (Acuto 2010) and it is difficult therefore to see them as other than symbol.

In his essay 'The Eiffel Tower', Roland Barthes tells us that Maupassant often lunched in the restaurant in the tower because it was the only place in Paris where you couldn't see it (in Leach 1997, 172). Barthes himself is much less interested in such sniffy judgements, and instead concerned to note the various ways in which it functioned as a signifier for the city. The tower is, he says, useless, and is remarkably open to mythical meanings. Like all tall structures it is 'an object that sees, a glance which is seen' (ibid., 173). It gathers sight to it, but also allows for a certain kind of viewing:

> ... the Tower makes the city into a kind of nature; it constitutes the swarming of men into a landscape [...] The bird's-eye view, which each visitor to the Tower can assume in an instant for his own, gives us the world to *read* and not only to perceive; this is why it corresponds to a new sensibility of vision [...] the bird's-eye view, on the contrary, represented by our romantic writers as if they had anticipated both the construction of the Tower and the birth of aviation, permits us to transcend sensation and see things *in their structure*.
>
> *(Leach 1997, 175)*

One structure permits the visibility of another. No longer in the middle of things, the viewer can now link points of visibility, and connect and disconnect points of experience. This is an abstracted vision: 'one can feel oneself cut off from the world and yet the owner of that world' (Leach 1997, 180).

Barthes' nod towards the European romantics seems important here, and also the importance of a certain sort of gaze. The idea of a 'view', was something that began to be initially articulated primarily as a perspective over nature, not culture. The sixteenth-century Belvedere was a piece of architecture which provided a view over the countryside, just as grand estates were often organized around views of the landscape beyond. By the eighteenth century, the educated vocabulary of nature was beginning to include elements of danger too. Crashing waves, dizzying cliffs, and deep abysses became part of what Edmund Burke and others were terming the sublime. Burke's *Philosophical Enquiry into the Origin of our Ideas of the Sublime and Beautiful* of 1757 defined a very influential view of the natural sublime:

> The passion caused by the great and sublime in *nature* when those causes operate most powerfully, is Astonishment, and astonishment is that state of the soul, in which all its motions are suspended, with some degree of horror. In this case the mind is so entirely filled with its object that it cannot entertain any other, not by consequence reason on that object which employs it.
>
> *(Burke 1990, 53)*

If beauty is small, smooth, polished, light and delicate, then the sublime is vast, rugged, dark, gloomy, massive and solid (Burke 1990, 113). The sublime produces an effect of 'delightful horror, a sort of tranquillity tinged with terror' (ibid., 123). This response can be produced by human creations too, such as buildings, though Burke is clear to point out that this does not mean excessive height or length, but a 'generous deceit' which can 'effect the noblest designs' (ibid., 70). A century later, as this form of understanding becomes more common, the cultural critic John Ruskin is perfectly prepared to claim that the soaring vaults and spires of Gothic churches could be understood as sublime, and that they had improving effects because they revealed truths about labour and life which were eternal (Ruskin 1985, 77 *passim*).

So the combination of the view, the idea of the sublime, together with rapid urbanization provides for a sensibility in which elevation over a city can also become a pleasurable experience. The 'Panorama', a circular painting, invented by the Scottish painter Robert Barker in 1793, was initially used to depict the classicism of the city of Edinburgh, but paintings of views over urban landscapes often also begin to show us the industrial metropolis, factory chimney and so on (Nye 1994, 109). There are also technological developments implicated here. Mark Dorrian (2006) draws attention to the views and photographs that later become possible from the hot air balloon, whether tethered or floating, and the Ferris wheel, first exhibited in Chicago in 1893. David Nye suggests that the US in the nineteenth century was particularly receptive to viewing this monumental conquering of nature. His 'American Technological Sublime' embraces dams, bridges, railways, electrification, the Apollo programme and skyscrapers as sites of tourist interest and popular amazement (Nye 1994, 87 *passim*; 2005). The tall building in the city both reverses and echoes Burke. Rather than being awed by the scale and power of nature, we are awed by *human* creations. They dwarf us, and we wonder at their ingenuity, and at the superhuman forces that have made them.

But there is another twist to what Nye calls the 'geometrical sublime'. Kant wished to argue that the magnitude and violence of the sublime exceeds our capacity for embodied understanding, but also that simultaneously we feel a sense that our minds *can* intellectually grasp such scale. The Kantian argument is that phenomena which exceed our corporeal senses also show us that our disembodied reason actually exceeds phenomena, that humans can be more than shuddering awestruck creatures (Shaw 2006, 80–83). There is an echo of this in Nye's suggestion that the skyscraper makes possible an Olympian gaze across a city (1994, 96; 2005). Using early twentieth-century magazine adverts and novels as his texts, and building on Barthes' analysis, Nye notes that the view from the skyscraper is a view from, and to, capitalism. It is the gaze of the 'Captain of Industry' that we are given, and that allows us to map the city from above. The maps that we find in the observation decks of tall buildings encourage us to do precisely this. For those down below, it is difficult to see the skyscraper when you are close to it. Further away, it is more visible, perhaps at the moment when you are no longer visible to it as anything other than texture in the landscape. Unless, and this is crucial, you have a similar elevation, like de Certeau looking down from the 110th floor of the World Trade Center, in which case you can look across the rooftops towards the other towers too. People and cars become insects, and you can see the patterns they make as a text to be read, as you are 'lifted out of the city's grasp', leaving the mass behind (de Certeau 1984, 92).

Against the Skyscraper

This exploration of the aesthetics of scale is often what so many others have found disquieting about the tall building. Long before the skyscraper, the Prussian architect Karl Friedrich Schinkel toured industrial Britain in 1826 observing Manchester mills that were taller than the length of the royal palace in Berlin (Darley 2003, 30). These shapeless, blackened gothic monstrosities, with their belching chimneys, made the scale of the city a horrible thing. It is difficult, in early criticisms of the skyscraper, to detach specific complaints from a general condemnation of the urban, or of the conditions for alienated labour under capitalism, or of modernity itself. The first period of skyscraper building in lower Manhattan in the 1870s produced much discussion about congestion, the deprivation of light and air, and proposals for height limitation. By the 1890s, there were serious concerns about the dissipation of foul and noxious air, or the 'sweat' of the city. In 1894 the *Record and Guide* worried that

> ... if the whole commercial quarter were built up with high buildings it would be a very terrible region for all but the occupants of the topmost stories, a region of Cimmerian gloom ... The tenants who now have pure air and a wide outlook would face other tenants across a well.
>
> *(in Landau and Condit 1996, 111)*

These 'hygienic' condemnations were paralleled by many who saw the skyscrapers as uncaring capitalism made stone. Henry James, returning to New York in 1904, condemned the ugliness of 'the thousand glassy eyes of these giants of the mere market' (in Marqusee 1988, 81). The Spanish poet Federico Garcia Lorca bemoaned the 'geometry and anguish' of this 'extra-human architecture' (ibid., 162), and US architect Frank Lloyd-Wright the 'false, cruel ambition [which] is painting haphazard, jagged, pretentious, feudal sky-lines trying to relieve it and make it more humane by lying about its purpose' (ibid., 165). For the most part, these were European condemnations of modern industrialism. A city like New York was understood in terms of the materialization of mass and motives that were inhuman in their implications, particularly if compared with older European cities with their supposed modesty and human scale. The German critical theorist Ernst Bloch, for example, suggested that modern city dwellers live a 'termite existence in box houses' whilst 'monstrous, schematically rigid skyscrapers project out of a raging sea of lacquered tin' (in Leach 1997, 45). Seemingly ignoring the working-class slums and tenements that surrounded the core of most industrial cities, whether US or European, the US skyscraper becomes an emblem of heartless modernity. Like the workers in expressionist films like *Metropolis* (1927), who are reduced to the lock-step of labour, the towers ingest and excrete the mass of humanity whilst the executives look down from above.

This sort of anti-modernism is perhaps the most common way in which the skyscraper has been used for cultural criticism. Robert Jungk's essay 'The Church and the Skyscraper' (1954, 159 *passim*) begins with the destruction of St Nicholas Church in Manhattan, and its inevitable replacement with a 21-storey office block. The efficiencies of organization and profitability are captured in the character of 'Mr White Collar', the efficiency engineer, who is watching people using the lifts in a new building in order to determine maximum throughput and minimum waiting times: 'Thus I came to know the time-taker who reckons in seconds and minutes in the place where only two years earlier the joys of eternity were being preached' (ibid., 174). A similar suspicion of the modern, though with much more conservative political inflections, was contained in the Prince of Wales' influential condemnation of the Canary Wharf tower as somehow un-English. This is a theme that dates back to at least a century previously (Landau and Condit 1996, 285), and positions tall buildings (apart from the church spire) as against tradition, and lacking a human scale (Prince of Wales 1989, 54). His contrast between Wren's spires as painted by Canaletto and the post-1960s tower blocks that then dwarfed St Paul's Cathedral evokes a powerful sense of a lost city, and the triumph of utilitarian values that erase a millennia of history.

There is an odd paradox here, because many of these critics would bemoan the loss of authentic individualism which the mass building supposedly erases, at the same time as they would lament the loss of collective identity which results from the anomie and alienation of modern life. Both individual and group are at stake here. The 'pylon poet' W.H. Auden, in his poem 'September 1st, 1939',[5] describes a New York which is Stalinist in its crushing of difference:

> Where blind skyscrapers use
> Their full height to proclaim
> The strength of Collective Man,
> Each language pours its vain
> Competitive excuse,
> But who can live for long
> In an euphoric dream;
> Out of the mirror they stare,
> Imperialism's face
> And the international wrong.

Collectivism shouts down the individual, but produces an urban order which is shallow and hypocritical, not genuinely collective. Neither identity or community can be secured in the face of such massive lumps of ideology. Christopher Isherwood, who travelled with Auden to New York, is more explicit about his fears: 'the Red Indian island with its appalling towers [...] You could feel it vibrating with the tension of the nervous New World aggressively flaunting its rude steel nudity [...] We promise nothing. Here you will be on your own' (in Pye 1993, 20). Behind the facade, there is the lonely crowd, the organization man, and the pretend mobility of the elevator and the corner office.

So skyscrapers have often been understood as an emblem of a damaged modernity. They destroy the authentic human and the communities that they might be rooted in. Their elevation and decoration badly conceals their coldly commercial intentions, and their masculine urge to dominate. Now, after 9/11, this diagnosis has gained a strange intensity. Martin, an European character (possibly with leftwing sympathies), in Don DeLillo's novel *Falling Man*, puts it well: 'Weren't the towers built as fantasies of wealth and power that would later become fantasies of destruction? You build a thing like that so that you can see it come down. The provocation is obvious [...] You are saying, Here it is, bring it down.' (2007, 116; see also Darnton 2011, 245).

For these commentators, the skyscraper is a symbol, a metaphor. The tall building is an entity which points to a problem, but its economic logic is effectively made invisible. We can't see the process because the object gets in the way. If we look at writers who were more enthusiastic about the skyscraper, we can begin to see an opening for understanding how and why this symbol was constructed.

Capitalist Modernism

Rather than horror, the eruptions of Chicago and New York in the late nineteenth century began to create a new image of the city, a city of towers, endlessly photographed from a distance, and then circulated around the world as postcards of 'an imagined city of the future' (King 2004, Moudry 2005, 10). This was a bar chart of masses in relation to each other, viewed from the air, or from over the river. From the early twentieth century onwards, futurists such as Antonio Sant'Elia inspired illustrators like Hugh Ferriss to imagine *The Metropolis of Tomorrow*, published as a book in 1929. Both drew cities of soaring spires connected by bridges over rivers of traffic, visualized in the film *Metropolis* and the scene settings of *Just Imagine*, a musical from 1930 (Bingham et al. 2004, Wells 2005).

The aesthetic struggle for verticality was articulated by up-and-coming architects as a certain sort of honesty. Partly in response to the dominance of Beaux Arts classicism, and perhaps mindful of the limited legitimacy that tall buildings had, the dominant model for early tall buildings was generally one that stressed horizontal banding, usually with a three-part base, column and capital decoration. Louis Sullivan, an influential architect and writer of the turn of the century, suggested a modernized version of this form, but with a greater stress on verticality, and (for him) a certain democratic transparency too (Landau and Condit 1996, 185; Dupré 1996, 21). Yet the architecture of individual buildings seems to have been less important in the popular imagination of the time than the new idea of the 'sky-line' (McNeill 2005, 46), with sublime metaphors becoming routinely adopted. For a commentator in *Scribner's* in 1899, skyscrapers were

> … symbols of modern capital, perhaps, and its far-reaching possibilities, or they may remind you, in their massive grouping, of a cluster of mountains, with their bright peaks glistening in the sun far above the dark shadows of the valleys in which the streams of business flow, down to the wharves and so out over the world.
>
> *(in Landau and Condit 1996, 277)*

Elevation could also become a sign of progress, of striving. As Edgar Saltus said in 1905, 'It will be demonstrable that as buildings ascend so do ideas. It is mental progress that skyscrapers engender' (in Frongia 2005, 220–221). For many of these commentators, there is a sense that these buildings represent a shameless statement of national character, as if commerce (and the United States) was no longer embarrassed about its activities (Rubin 1979, 342). Proud, in both senses of the word, and a concrete representation of a masculine sense of beauty.

Yet the battle for verticality was soon to become more than an attempt to stretch classical architecture. For 'international style' modernists such as Alfred Barr in 1932, 'capricious façade ornament' such as Sullivan's only represented the 'architectural taste of real estate speculators, renting agents and mortgage brokers!' (in Hitchcock and Johnson 1966, 14). Denying the influence that capital should have on *real* architects, Barr stresses discipline, restraint, and an avoidance of the aesthetic chaos of having skyscrapers built in, say, Gothic, Aztec, or Romanesque styles. Hitchcock and Johnson, in the book that Barr prefaces, wish for an authentic relation between structure and surface. Steel cage buildings can be light and tall, vertical without the clutter of masonry or a cornice. But verticality itself was not a virtue either, simply because it was a commercial response to the zoning and set-back laws which were intended to allow light down to the streets. Neither verticality or horizontality were principles in themselves, the point being that the architect should become an engineer of space, 'protected from all aesthetics' and 'pseudo-style' (Hitchcock and Johnson 1966, 67).

Johnson's modernism (he was later the co-architect of the high modern Seagram Building in Manhattan) echoed with a new sensibility in which shining factory chimneys and soaring grain elevators were being held up as icons of function (Guillen 2008). Le Corbusier's 'Contemporary City' of widely spaced 60-storey towers dates from 1922, but even more radical was his 1935 plan to demolish parts of elderly cramped Paris and replace it with a new 'Radiant City'. The celebration of both demolition and elevation appeared to combine capitalist creative destruction with an idea of the architect as visionary. As he says in 1936, upon arriving in New York:

> Monday morning, when my ship stopped at Quarantine, I saw a fantastic, almost mystic city rising up in the mist. But the ship moves forward and the apparition is transformed into an image of incredible brutality and savagery. Here is certainly the most prominent manifestation of the power of modern times. This brutality and this savagery do not displease me. It is thus that great enterprises begin, by strength.
>
> *(in Marqusee 1988, 16)*

Le Corbusier's dream did not die. It was resurrected in Frank Lloyd Wright's mile-high 'Illinois Sky City' in 1956; Norman Foster's 1993 plan for the M Tower, a 170-storey self-sufficient city two kilometres into Tokyo Bay; and now, the endless proposals for super-tall buildings in just about every Asian and Gulf state. Even old London Town now has its 310m Shard.

For Henry Cameron, one of the single-minded architects in Ayn Rand's 1943 novel *The Fountainhead*, vertical buildings should not conceal their elevation by pretending to be something else:

> While architects cursed, wondering how to make a twenty-story building look like an old brick mansion, while they used every horizontal device available in order to cheat it of its height, shrink it down to tradition, hide the shame of its steel, make it small, safe and ancient – Henry Cameron designed skyscrapers in straight, vertical lines, flaunting their steel and height.
>
> *(Rand 1993, 44)*

The individual, like the building, must stand straight and be themselves, not hiding behind convention, but rising 'as arrows of steel shooting upward without weight or limit'. Howard Roark, an architect who learns much from Cameron, but faces many obstacles, eventually designs the Wynand Building, a 'long streak slashed through space': 'They say the heart of the earth is made of fire. It is held imprisoned and silent. But at times it breaks through the clay, the iron, the granite, and shoots out to freedom. Then it becomes a thing like this' (Rand 1993, 692).

Or, as Ezra Pound wrote on seeing New York at night, 'we have pulled down the stars to our will' (in Lindner 2006, 5). The tall building becomes a celebration of the power of man,[6] whether the collective energies of a city or state, or the individual force of an architect or industrialist. These are buildings that inspire thoughts of elevation, and a certain sort of unconditional prose is needed to express such emotions: 'No matter where they are built, how they are financed, or what they look like, the daring heights achieved by each new generation of skyscrapers excite the mind and heart as Icarus once did, pulling us dangerously and thrillingly upward and into the future' (Dupré 1996, 119).

Such celebrations certainly embed capitalism into their understanding of tall buildings, but they still make the building into a symbol. They suggest that the skyscraper is the result of organizing and economy, but again tell us little about how and why it was made, again leaving the building as a noun with certain ascribed meanings. In the next section, I want to show how both the 'nostalgic anti-modernist' and 'capitalist modernist' accounts are made possible by suggesting that the skyscraper does not merely *symbolize* modern organizations, but is itself a materialization of modern organizing. Skyscrapers can be symbols, and they may provoke the sublime, or horror and joy, but they are not simply built to be symbols, and their building is a complex process of organizing.

Building a Building[7]

The city of New York was founded by mercantile capitalism in the form of the Dutch West India Company. For much of its history, it has been a haven for novel forms of economic activity, whether merchants and traders, or pirates and Mafiosi. The city has long been a site for capital accumulation, for speculation and development (Harvey 1985), and is an extraordinary example of these processes made into stone (Fainstein 2001, Darton 2011, Sorkin and Zukin 2012) This, it seems to me, should encourage us to understand the birth of the skyscraper in more organizational and economic terms. Rather than ending by being repelled or awed by their cultural or semiotic imputations, it is possible to understand these buildings themselves as forms of industrial capitalism. In that sense, they are testaments to the complexities of the division of labour and the logic of capital accumulation. When Pye describes Manhattan as 'an engineer's diagram, a fixed, hard-angled thing' (1993, 257) we can understand him as not being merely metaphorical. The construction and maintenance of a skyscraper requires extraordinarily complex forms of labour, and the scale and height of buildings can be read as a bar-chart of land-values.

Skyscrapers do not merely metaphorize modern organizations, they *are* forms of modern organizing. After 9/11, the air was full of office stationery, 'contracts, resumés blowing by, intact snatches of business, quick in the wind' (DeLillo 2007, 4). An office tower, from the inside, is a workplace, 'a banal cocoon for water-coolers, dress down Fridays and leaving parties' (Sudjic 2006, 305). Firms such as banks, real estate brokers, architects, engineers, interior design consultants, accountants, venture capitalists and construction firms inhabit the very towers that they gain profits from building. Musing about what a tall building represents often misses the calculations about rental income, expenditure and profit. When the 700,000 square metres of office space contained within the Twin Towers was lost, real estate brokers were immediately calculating the loss of rents, but seeing a good market for displaced tenants. It was noted that the disaster had happened at an auspicious time because the collapse of dot-coms nine months previously had left much empty space in Manhattan (Dale and Burrell 2008, 288–289).

It is obvious that this sort of rental income analysis would stay clear of the sort of judgements that those who would celebrate or condemn skyscrapers usually trade in. Mona Domosh (1992, 72) suggested a reading of the skyscrapers of lower Manhattan as the expression of corporate culture. Citing some pop management writers, she suggests that the culture of an organization is manifested in its building. By this, she appears to mean that the skyscraper can be a giant billboard for the owners and top managers of an organization. But whilst a few buildings were clearly engineered for marketing a particular corporation (Moudry 2005, 130), to treat all skyscrapers as if they were merely facades built by CEOs is one dimensional. So too is the suggestion that the building has one evident meaning, as when Jon Goss (oddly) claims that 'the towering office block with its reflective skin signifies a powerful anonymous authority' (1992, 162). It might, but (as he points out in his earlier piece) cleaners, managers, town planners, architects, engineers, pizza delivery drivers and property speculators are unlikely to read the same structure in the same way (1988, 398; also McNeill 2005, 43). In addition, the majority of US skyscrapers were (and are still) constructed as speculative rental properties by groups of investors (Willis 1995). They were rarely built by, and occupied by, single corporations, with the majority being leased to a large number of small businesses and professional services firms.

Importantly, the early story of the rise of the skyscraper is also the rise of the office building, and of the rise of the office itself. Such structures are predicated on the generation and storage of files, of paperwork, of the bureaucratic lifeworld which only came into existence in the private sector in the second half of the nineteenth century. Most office buildings prior to the 1850s were simply converted dwellings (Landau and Condit 1996, 5). The beginnings of a rationalization of organization, as a verb, also meant the rationalization of space though open-plan arrangements, typewriters, office chairs with castors, pneumatic tubes, telephones and paper-storage technologies.[8] So the growth of the skyscraper is predicated on the growth of the bureaucratic organization, but this did not mean that the big corporation was actually the dominant player in building them. In the 'first' skyscraper, the Equitable Life Assurance Society Building only occupied two floors of the seven (Landau and Condit 1996, 68), because the rest was intended for rental.[9] Of the 55 storeys of the New York Woolworth Building, in 1913 the Woolworth company only occupied two, and there were over 600 other small businesses with offices there (ibid., 148). The names of skyscrapers are certainly sometimes the names of their principal tenants, but often are not, and even when they are, these names can change.[10]

In fact, the Woolworth Building, in both financing and the expense and personalizing of its decoration, is rather an untypical skyscraper. In 1900, Cass Gilbert, the architect of what the newspapers called a 'cathedral of commerce', defined a skyscraper as 'a machine that makes the land pay' (Willis 1995, 19). To which it might be added, that it makes the air pay too. Frank Woolworth had gained a huge pile of cash by paying low wages to employees in order that they sell cheap goods to poor people (Watts 2005, 195). Huge turnover in 684 stores, low mark-up and effective distribution systems meant that Woolworth had money he could invest with the expectation of return. Whilst ego may have played a part in the decoration, as well it being 'a gigantic sign board' (Nye 1994, 93), the building was built for rent. 'Making the land pay' is the key to understanding why early skyscrapers were constructed, and not merely the standard story about competition between the egoistic robber barons who wanted to build the highest structure. Using the Woolworth, Chrysler and Empire State buildings to explain (away) the skyscraper, mistakes an effect for a cause, and ignores the huge majority of tall buildings that made the new city skyline.

In her historical study of skyscrapers in New York and Chicago, Carol Willis (1995) refuses either the story about the Great Architect, or corporation, and instead concentrates on rental values as the key determinant of skyscraper form. She points out that in the professional literature for the builders of tall buildings, contractors, owners, engineers and many architects were not concerned with style, but with economics. This meant that income was the key issue, and all decisions were made in order to maximize return on investment. Architects, like Louis Sullivan, might have claimed to be disinterested in such matters but Willis appears to see this as a claim about professional identity, not practice. For example, George Hill, writing in the *Architectural Record* in 1904, puts the matter very simply indeed:

> The writer wishes to state once and for all, and as strongly as it can be put, that the only measure of success of an office building is the average net return from rentals for a period of, say, fifteen years. Everything put into the building that is unnecessary, every cubic foot that is used for purely ornamental purposes beyond that needed to express its use and to make it harmonize with others of its class, is a waste – is, to put it in plain English, perverting some one's money.
>
> *(in Willis 1995, 15)*

Plain English indeed, and the coincidence between the rise of 'form follows function' modernism, and the interests of capital then becomes rather useful on both sides.

But, Willis is clear, if something is built to generate rents, then the facade and lobby will be important too. In contemporary language, the more 'branded' the space, the higher the rents are likely to be. But 'return' is the key. Starting from plot size, shape and location, this means that calculations about floor space, ceiling height, distance from natural light, costs of heating, number and positioning of elevators and so on are necessarily calculations about return on capital invested. The application of scientific management and time-and-motion techniques to office space was not only a question of the rationalization of the worker, but also an attempt to rationalize the space that each worker would use. The more people, the more offices, the more return. Typical early office plans, with demarcations for window access, secretarial cubicles, typing pools and so on embedded gender and class hierarchies in terms of an economy of space. Light courts, and H-, E- or U-shaped plans meant that offices would be no more than 20–25 feet from windows (Willis 1995, 81). But when lighting technology improved, buildings could become even more lucrative, because lighting can be artificial in the core. Again, it seems no accident that this happens at the same time as 'modernism' begins to displace 'classicism' in skyscraper design. The functionality of massing then harmonizes with the interests of capital. Even the eventual passing of the zoning and set-back laws in New York in 1916 can be understood in this manner. The massive and vertical Equitable Building, finished in 1915, is often cited as the cause of the zoning laws. However, the Equitable had also generated 1.2 million square feet of rentable space, stealing sunlight and tenants from nearby buildings. The passing of the zoning laws provided for different areas of the city and different assessments of the amount of air that could be filled depending on the width of the street and the size of the plot. There had been concern about the 'hygienic' implications of tall buildings for 45 years, but it was only when their very proximity began to be in danger of damaging property values that key interests swung behind the legislation and produced the 'set-back' skyscraper (Landau and Condit 1996, 395).

So the Empire State Building appears like a spire in order that it could be built at all, not so that it looked beautiful. What we might call 'aesthetics' was important, but only insofar as it advertises the rental space, or gets around restrictions placed by authorities and planners. Indeed, all the early plans for the Empire State were '*entirely financial, not architectural*. The different schemes were described only in numbers – stories, cubic feet, operating costs, and projected income' (Willis 1995, 95, emphasis in original). It was eventually completed in 18 months from the first sketches, and shaped by an initial assumption of 12.6 per cent return on capital: 'Rather than interpreting corporate skyscrapers simply as *representations* of big business, we need to understand them also as *businesses themselves*' (ibid., 153, emphasis in original).

The buildings are temporary sites for the reproduction of capital, not ends in themselves. Skyscraper cities are temporary, 'a provisional city' as Le Corbusier once styled New York (Page 2005, 181), with creative destruction happening continually as taller or more productive buildings replace older ones. The Equitable Life Assurance Building now exists only in photographs and plans.[11] In 1897, the slim and striking 19-storey Gillender Building was completed in New York, but it was demolished in 1910 to make way for the 39-storey Bankers Trust Building (Willis 1995, 41; Landau and Condit 1996, 249). Its 13-year life seems tragic, but New York on fast forward shows little sentimentality. The Gillender had itself been built on the site of the Union Building, which lasted less than 50 years. Even the demolition of the Gillender proceeded with speed, the whole structure disappearing in 45 days, and the new structure being ready for rent in 23 months. But even more famous buildings are not immune, and the tower crane allowed for this cycle of disorganization and organization to happen even more rapidly. The iconic 47-storey Singer Tower in New York, the tallest in the world in 1908, was demolished in 1968, and still holds the record for the highest building ever demolished by its owners (Landau and Condit 1996, 361). As Lietzmann puts it, 'every pile of rubble turns into humus for a forest of new spires' (in Wolf 1980, no p.).

Architects do not 'build' skyscrapers, and neither do corporations. First, they are imagined as financial instruments by investors and accountants. Then they are imagined as structures by architects and engineers. Simultaneously the building, as verb, begins. Land is bought, many contracts are signed, surveys are made, and clearances and permissions negotiated. Demolition companies and wreckers crush and tear at whatever was on the land already, and a stream of trucks negotiates city streets to take rubble away for disposal on the edge of town. Then down in what will be foundations and sub-basements, piles are sunk and steel and concrete meshed together. More trucks arrive, bringing different machines, girders, bolts, cables, windows, plumbing and elevators. Connected to all of these items are factories and warehouses some distance from the tower, all tied into production and delivery schedules of their own from their own suppliers. Plans, charts, schedules, models, diagrams construct the building in advance of materials, and time the flows of people and materials from place to place, floor to floor. Each single piece of steel is designed, fabricated and delivered at a particular time to fit into the building as it grows. They are connected together by people who work cranes, heat rivets, check the plans, tighten bolts, and weld joints. Later, people pour concrete, and smooth concrete, and polish concrete. Then panels and windows are attached to the steel, and insulation attached to the panels, and walls attached to the insulation. Later again, people run ducts and cables, fit windows, install toilets, hang doors, paint walls, place signs and bring in furniture and plants. Other people, perhaps the Mafia,[12] collect money for making sure that nothing goes wrong, while inspectors and trade union officials visit to make sure that nothing has gone wrong. Even before the skyscraper is open for business, it has been an example of extraordinarily complex organization.

This can, again, be tied back to the interests of capital accumulation. The control and scheduling of labour through the technologies of project and operations management, and the coordination of time schedules are necessary in order that large structures can be constructed in time periods that shorten interest payments on large debts. The quicker the build, the quicker people start paying rent, so forms of complex coordination were absolutely necessary as part of a business plan. The role of General Contractor, the first being the George Fuller Company of Chicago in 1882, became a way for investors to externalize the relations between speed and price by embedding them in contracts (Landau and Condit 1996, 179). Just as bricklaying was being subjected to time-and-motion studies by Frank Gilbreth, so were all aspects of 'The Modern Building Organization' being subject to greater systematization and control. On the Empire State Building, in order to achieve a floor of brickwork per day, the bricks were delivered to the bricklayer by a system of hoists which meant that no one on site handled them until the bricklayer put them in the wall (Nye 1994, 101). Even architectural and drafting practices grew in scale and developed hierarchies and divisions of labour for producing different sorts of drawings, and managing relations with engineers and fabricators, such as Cass Gilbert's practice in New York in the 1890s. Indeed, Gilbert called the Broadway Chambers Building, constructed in four months, 'a triumph of organization' (in Fenske 2005, 24, 27). So the skyscraper is a social and material technology that developed in tandem with financial instruments that allowed for large interest payments on huge debts, underpinned by the assumption of future rents.

Seeing the skyscraper as a machine that makes the land pay doesn't necessarily suggest that the cultural celebration or suspicion of the tall building is irrelevant, simply that such buildings are not just symbols. They are treated as such, with many commentators seeming to suggest that they are meaningless as anything other than symbols, since they make no economic sense (Nye 1994, 88; Sudjic 2006, Acuto 2010 for example). In contrast, I think that they can also be understood as forms of organization themselves and that they are driven upwards by speculations about capital accumulation. But that doesn't also stop them from being adopted as symbols, as Claude Bragdon did in the *Architectural Record* in 1909:

> The tall office building, our most characteristic architectural product is a symbol of our commercial civilization. Its steel framework, strong, yet economical of metal, held together at all points by thousands of rivets, finds a parallel in our highly developed industrial and economic system,

maintained by the labour of obscure and commonplace individuals, each one a rivet in the social structure.

(in Landau and Condit 1996, 377)

Bragdon is right. These buildings are contingent on organizational arrangements, but his functionalist gloss is doing a lot of symbolic work too. Skyscrapers, in their US incarnations, are capitalist organizations, but they can also be used to symbolize the aspiration or arrogance of such organizations. The former is a question of historical record, if architectural historians are to be believed (Willis 1995, Landau and Condit 1996), whilst the latter is a question of politics. So when Willis says 'Skyscrapers are the ultimate architecture of capitalism' (Willis 1995, 181), this is not just a claim about what they mean, but what they do. Or, in reverse, it is not until the symbolic politics is moved to one side that the economic and organizational relationships can be seen more clearly.

Topping Out

It is easy to think about height as something necessarily associated with power and hierarchy. The great chain of being that leads to God and the angels is not so far from the Chief Executive in the office on the hundredth floor (Dale and Burrell 2008, 50). And once elevation is fixed in steel and stone, and mobility happens in little cages, then it is hard not to imagine that we are witnessing the petrification of power. Either we cringe before its magnificence from the pavement, or we glory in our far-sightedness from the penthouse – 'Olympian or Orwellian, depending on how you look at it' (Huxtable, in McNeill 2005, 52). The symbols matter, because the skyscraper is an entity that meaning can be attached to, but this is only half of the story. It is also an example of organizing driven by processes of capital accumulation, a verb which reaches into the sky into order to make the land pay. Culture and economy are intertwined, and one is blank without the other. There is no pure market logic, because judgements will always attach to the artefacts produced for the purposes of making money and thereby influence how the money can be made. The speculations of speculative capital are never merely utilitarian, but also produce aesthetic statements, with attached ethical judgements too.

Since elevation is an advantage in both battle and theology, it seems evident that skyscrapers must often symbolize the domination of a few whilst the many live in the shadows. These inequalities are underlined by the manifest problems with high buildings. Sudjic, King, Dale and Burrell and a good many good people see windows creaking and groaning and falling out. They see set-backs littered with dead birds, and pedestrians thrown off their feet by downdrafts. They see ostentation, corporate verticality and buildings built by men. It is fair to say that many of the heroic readings of skyscrapers assume a certain gender, class and ethnic position (Lindner 2006, 18 *passim*), and that they tend not to mention the secretaries and cleaners. I have sympathies with these commentators, but their largely symbolic analysis ends up with an oddly one-dimensional analysis of tall buildings. Too much emphasis on 'corporate verticality' does a great deal to hide the actual processes which lead to the construction of the skyscraper (Willis 1995). There was a clear economic logic to the skyscraper boom in New York and Chicago, and it was based on speculators attempting to maximize rental income from many small professional firms. The corporate tower is the exception, not the rule, and even that was built to make money, not just to show power in stone. Further, the processes of finance, design, construction and demolition are clearly related to forms of the division of labour that were aimed at maximizing capital. Such an analysis of capitalism and organization is often overlooked by those who prefer to pursue the symbol as if it were a noun.

Of course, as the skyscraper moves, so does its logic. As King (2004), McNeill (2005), Acuto (2010) and others have noted, the dissemination of the skyscraper across the US and wider world was often influenced by the idea of a downtown like Manhattan. The Stalinist 'Seven Sisters' in Moscow, built between 1947 and 1953, were not built to reflect land values, but to emulate a particular form of urbanism. More recently, the destruction of the old and sprouting of tall buildings in Asian cities is certainly related to the possibility of accumulation, but in advance of a relationship between density and price. The flats, offices and shops in the super-tall Burj Khalifa have been rented to the super-rich, whilst the building has been constructed cheaply and quickly by poorly paid migrant labour working in largely deregulated conditions for 24 hours a day. This tower is both a process for making money, and the peak of a skyline which symbolizes the new Dubai. In both cases, it is an example of organization.

It doesn't really matter which 'discipline owns the skyscraper' (McNeill 2005, 41), as long as the division of labour recognizes this necessary relation between noun and verb which can help us draw together the cultural and the economic. 'Organization' can function here as a mediating term, one which allows us to see cultural representation and economy as necessarily entangled. Cultural representations attach symbolic value to nouns, whilst the economy is a process for generating value. To account for the skyscraper, we require a symmetrical form of explanation which takes both into account and marginalizes neither. The concept 'organization', because of its ambiguity, can be a mediating concept to help us think about the construction of meanings and the construction of things, and not only a term which is used in a discipline which studies organizations. The theoretical symmetry is to try and see it as both noun and verb, as a symbol of the 'organization of production' and an example of the 'production of organization' (Cooper and

Burrell 1988, 106). It is hard to see an entity like a building as in process, even though glass flows and buildings fall, but the Burj Khalifa was not always there, and it will not always be there.

When we encounter it, the skyscraper is material. It is capital made durable, made solid in ways that conjoin Burke's 'astonishment' and 'horror'. However we 'read' the skyscraper, and however we theorize its production, it is the sheer scale of the 'thing' that we are confronted with, and that demands explanation. Le Corbusier captures this paradox nicely. Writing of New York: 'It is a titanic mineral display, a prismatic stratification shot through with an infinite number of lights from top to bottom, in depth, in a violent silhouette like a fever chart beside a sickbed' (in Wolf 1980, no p. no.).

The skyscraper is pathological and breathtaking at the same moment, just as it allows you to look down and look up. Kant, at the beginning of Part One of *The Critique of Judgement* suggests that you don't have to like the world that produced something in order to find the thing itself beautiful (Kant 1951, 38). Judgements of beauty, of the sublime, should be disinterested about such causes and interests. For myself, the world of power and money that produces the skyscraper is not one I like very much, but the buildings themselves always make me stop and stare.

Notes

1 This chapter is based on (2015) 'Vertical Capitalism: Skyscrapers and Organization' *Culture and Organization* 21/3: 217–234.
2 Though Landau and Condit (1996, ix) add that its earliest known occurrence was as the name of a horse that won the Epsom Derby in 1789. During the nineteenth century, it was also used as a word for a hat, a tall man, and a high ball in baseball or cricket. McNeill suggests that other words were used for tall buildings too – cloud-supporter, cloudscraper and skysweeper (2005, 49).
3 This also opens the possibility of an analysis that does not begin with capitalist office blocks in New York and Chicago. On the 'residential high-rise', see Jacobs 2006, Jacobs et al 2007.
4 See Cooper and Law 1995 for an example; Hernes and Matlis 2010, Helin et al. 2014 and Langley and Tsoukas 2016 for reviews
5 https://poets.org/poem/september-1-1939, accessed 31 July 2024.
6 Gender intentional.
7 See the 1933 Mickey Mouse cartoon of the same name.
8 There is also a parallel story about the gendering of work, technology and space in the new office. See Fine 2005, Schleier 2005, and Moudry 2005, 133. It is possible to argue that, by about 1920, the majority of workers in skyscrapers were women.
9 Though others would argue that Chicago's Home Insurance Building of 1885 is actually the first (Dupré 1996, 15). It depends on what you mean by a skyscraper.
10 In New York alone, the RCA Building has become GE, Pan Am is now MetLife and the AT&T Building is now the Sony Tower. In Chicago, the Sears Tower is now the Willis Tower. And so on.

11 As does the Home Insurance Building.
12 Sabbagh (1989, 186, 195) is explicit about Mafia involvement in the building of Worldwide Plaza, also in New York, in the late 1980s. Given their involvement in unions and construction, it would be surprising if this were not also another part of 'making the land pay'.

8

SUPER FLAT

The Japanese artist Takashi Murakami produces a range of cultural objects – paintings and sculptures, but also 'commercial' products such as little plastic figures, mouse mats, T-shirts and key chains.[1] His work is broadly inspired by the Japanese animation and comic book traditions of *anime* and *manga* – highly coloured cartoons of fantasy figures which often exhibit a big-eyed cute (*kawaii*) menace – and is often generally referred to as an *otaku* aesthetic. His work, like that of Andy Warhol, Jeff Koons, Damien Hirst and many other 'pop' artists, operates to blur the distinctions between 'high art' and popular culture (Bankowsky et al. 2009), as well as in his case between the West and the rest. Murakami describes some of his work as 'super flat', and I take this to be a description of both the quality of the highly coloured, glossy, computer-generated surfaces of the objects he makes, but also of an approach to cultural forms. There is only surface, and any claims about depth or elevation are dismissed as illusory pretensions, held in place by the operations of power and a sensibility that trades on some elderly normative assumptions about the aesthetic.

Probably the most famous of Murakami's characters is Mr DOB,[2] a hypercoloured mutant Mickey Mouse with a crazed grin. Mr DOB's big eyes shine as he cavorts with smiling flowers, pandas, mushrooms and jellyfish. Sometimes he has sharp teeth and slides through bad acid-trip backgrounds. DOB can be anything – a sculpture, balloon, painting, sticker, bath towel, video, plastic toy. He is happy, sad, scary and shocked. He is reproduced on expensive paintings, cheaper prints, and cuddly toys – serially produced and customized for different market niches. Mr DOB is only part of Murakami's output. His resin sculpture 'My Lonesome Cowboy', a naked and fully erect

DOI: 10.4324/9781032714288-11

kawaii figure with a lasso of spunk around his head sold at Sotheby's in 2008 for $15.2 million dollars. Murakami also does work for Louis Vuitton, the luxury goods manufacturer; as well as organizing GEISAI, a biannual arts fair that features other Japanese artists and teen J-Pop stars. The candy-coloured sex and violence of 'toon world, the global art market, and the gyrating 120 beats per minute video on a flat plasma screen. It's all the same. As disposable and as important as a Mr DOB *shokugan* – a 'snack toy'.

The superflat ontology and politics that Murakami trades in seems to me to be related to other ideas about lateral relations – the generalized symmetry between people and things that philosophers of the material have promoted, as well as the many attempts to dethrone 'high' culture, and celebrate the everyday that we find in cultural studies and social theory (Deleuze and Guattari 1984, Latour 2005, Barad 2007). It seems to me that it is also related to ideas about hierarchy in organization. In general terms, we seem to find it difficult to express flat relations, perhaps feeling that the flows of cause and power expressed in vertical relations – top/bottom, surface/depth, superstructure/base – somehow explain the world more fully. Like Bhaskar's (1978) realist device of a 'stratified ontology' which explains social phenomena in terms of underlying mechanisms, it is as if we see the lateral as merely descriptive, a mapping of a terrain, whilst the vertical captures necessary causal truths that explain why the visible is laid out in the way that it is. Indeed, for some realists, to call an ontology 'flat' is to suggest that it has no explanatory power (Reed 1997). And so it is, relentlessly, with questions of organization. From bureaucratic organograms to expressions of the transcendent power of leaders, our dominant conceptions of organization appear to be constituted as if elevation necessarily provided vision, and that only rare and precious creatures can breathe the air of the executive suite at the top of the skyscraper. Power, it seems, only works properly when it is piled on top of itself, and the higher the pile gets, the more effective the power is.

In this chapter, I will explore these ideas by responding in a meandering way to Murakami's project. If organizations are constituted culturally, and culture can be understood in some super-flat ways, then what does this do to our conceptions of organizing? Murakami's work encourages us to question our hierarchies – to treat cartoons, toys and pornographic sculptures as art, and to treat his mass production as a challenge to the 'white-cube' gallery. Such flattening might well be helpful for political projects which push radically democratic forms of decision making (Lovink and Scholz 2007) but, just as importantly, it might also encourage us to see organizations in different ways, with power as an effect of particular organizational arrangements, rather than the reason why all organizing inevitably has to be hierarchical. It might be that this sort of anti-art provides a way to think beyond a culture which sanctifies power as the inevitability of obedience to hierarchy. So what happens when all judgements have been suspended, and everything is as good as everything else? Is it possible, or even desirable, to have super-flat forms of organizing?

Flat Culture

One way to locate Murakami is through the frame of 'Business Art'. His Tokyo-based Kaikai Kiki Co. Ltd studio and production facility, like Andy Warhol's Factory, is both art and business. In 2011, when I was writing the first version of this chapter, he employed fifty people in Tokyo and a further twenty in an office in New York. The organization curates art exhibitions and sells stuffed *kawaii* toys, works on brand goods, makes music videos and always refuses the separations between high art and low commerce. In 2010, Kaikai and Kiki (also both cartoon characters themselves) became gigantic balloons for the Macy's Thanksgiving Day parade in New York. Murakami is certainly not the only artist to have proposed that art, money and work are intimately layered together (Molesworth 2003, Siegal and Mattick 2004), but he is perhaps one of the most challenging contemporary examples, simply because of the number of fields that he has now become involved in. Murakami continually shifts. When the Japanese TV star Kase Taishuu lost the legal right to use his image and name after a dispute with the producers of his show, Murakami hired four actors to be him until the Yakuza – heavily involved in Japanese media – objected because it was damaging their profits (Siegal and Mattick 2004, 62–65). He routinely employs other people to make his work, and PR consultants to help him with his media image. Google his name and there are lots of images of Murakami smiling. A round impenetrable smile, repeated at exhibitions across the world. Like his cartoon flowers, tessellated together and grinning so hard that the image is emptied, and becomes blankly manic:

> Thus, according to this alternative value system, Murakami is no 'sell-out' as would be said of an artist in the West; the white-cube art production, luxury fashion brand consulting and Kaikai Kiki merchandising are all equally weighted in his radical cultural maelstrom.
>
> *(Gingeras 2009, 80)*

The Kaikai Kiki Co. Ltd doubtless has a structure of some sort, with a division of labour and someone who makes sure that the hundred employees on three sites get paid and the art supplies cupboard is refilled every week. It might be a flexible structure of the sort that creative industries are said to have, but it will be a structure nonetheless. It would be difficult to imagine how a Mr DOB *shokugan* could be imagined, made and placed in a snack packet without some intricate arrangements of people and things to ensure that the stuff arrived in the right places at just the right time:

> In New York and Tokyo, highly trained Kaikai KiKi employees work under the supervision of Takashi Murakami to produce cutting-edge, innovative artworks [...] Kaikai Kiki paintings are painstakingly rendered by hand, using computer rendering technology and advanced printing techniques as guides. After a training of at least 1 month, each staff must, as an initiation test, complete a small painting of a mushroom to be critiqued by Murakami.

This is a description of an organized world, one in which there are employees who are 'supervised' by an authority which establishes the rules governing labour and technology in a particular time and place. The employee must pass the tests set by the authority, and the implicit assumption here is that if your mushroom painting fails to meet a standard determined by a particular individual, you will no longer be an employees. As we all know, employees are like mushrooms. Kept in the dark and fed shit.

In the 'Super Flat Manifesto', Murakami compares his thesis about two dimensionality to the process of producing graphic art:

> One way to imagine super flatness is to think of the moment when, in creating a desktop graphic for your computer, you merge a number of distinct layers into one. Though it is not a terribly clear example, the feeling I get is a sense of reality that is very nearly a physical sensation.
>
> *(Murakami 2000, 5)*

'A sense of *reality*?' As if the real were flat, and there is a kind of vertigo in no longer seeing it as layered? As Murakami explains in his essay 'A Theory of Super Flat Japanese Art' (2000, 9–25), for a long time Japan has produced art forms which emphasize surface. Other art might be concerned with depth and perspective, such as that which develops in Italy in the fifteenth century (Berger 1972, Azuma 2000), but he claims that Japanese art is planar. There is no optical illusion of a viewer, with the world unfolding away to a vanishing point in front of them, but an image to be scanned. Further, the technical means to produce this image are clear on the surface of the work. In a drawing of a plum tree, or Mount Fuji, there is no attempt to fool us into thinking that we are looking at a plum tree, or Mount Fuji. This flatness then extends, Murakami argues, into a cultural flatness too. It is difficult to express the singular idea of 'art' in Japanese, and to distinguish it from technique, craft, or learning. The Western idea of 'art' was imported in the late nineteenth century, and an understanding of what counts as 'art' is inextricably associated with particular non-Japanese forms and the markets they since created. Since that time, the popularity of pottery, sculpture, or Japanese painting, or Western painting, or Japanese versions of Western painting styles have fluctuated depending on fashion and economics.

So if Japanese art tends to flatness, and the distinctions between 'art' and its other are unstable, it follows that Godzilla is equivalent to Kurosawa. It might sound like a radical cultural relativism to those schooled in Western aesthetics, but for Murakami's Japan this is no more than expressing a truth about perspectives and markets: 'Art is the supreme incarnation of luxury entertainment' (Murakami 2011). Things are worth what you might pay for them, and of taste there is no disputing. His book treats *anime*, teen J-pop, classical Japanese drawings and paintings as equivalents. The 'Western' moral economy that celebrates age and craft skill, and is suspicious of market penetration and mechanical reproduction, is irrelevant here, and Murakami presents a variety of cultural goods with equal care. Video game screenshots, photographs of varying quality, pop song lyrics, enamelled screens and detailed embroideries, cartoon panels and dance instruction drawings are laminated next to erotic resin sculptures of teenagers with big eyes and delicate prints of the fading pink petals of a lotus flower. The market makes these things flat, exchangeable with one another, and he wants to ensure that the work of Japanese artists (such as those working within Kaikai Kiki) has a market. Flatness, in that sense, has another connotation – being just as good as the West. In Murakami's floating world, everything moves relative to everything else. There are no foundations, no places we can stand in order to ground a hierarchy in which this is better than that.

Thomas Friedman's pro-globalization book *The World is Flat* (2005) seems to echo Murakami rather neatly. The relentless predicate of the book is that everything can be exchanged and value is a matter of markets. Friedman's thesis is that the application of information and transportation technologies to multiple markets has made the global economy into a level playing field. Anyone can sell anything anywhere, and geography and history no longer matter that much. Though Friedman wants to warn his fellow Americans that they need to develop skills to prevent themselves from being washed away by this tsunami, his message is not protectionist. Just as Murakami sweeps into Manhattan, so will 'Globalization 3.0' do away with elderly ideas about the competitive advantage of nations. The market corrodes established hierarchies, and makes everyone the same. We can all exchange value, and move people and things without friction across the surface of the world in jets and shipping containers. All hierarchies are temporary, all rules, laws and institutions are provisional, all that was solid melts into air. Murakami, in response to being told that one of his works was printed upside down in a newspaper article responded that 'it didn't matter much' (Azuma 2000, 147). Perhaps this super flatness is the 'postmodern' condition, a relentless creative destruction that bulldozes everything in its path.

The Fear of Flatness

But what happens when all the world is flat, and all value is reduced to exchange? In Robert Bolt's play *A Man for All Seasons*, Thomas More has faith in institutions, including the King who eventually martyred him. He worries about the consequences of flatness:

MORE: What would you do? Cut a great road through the law to get after the Devil?

ROPER: I'd cut down every law in England to do that!

MORE: Oh? And when the last law was down, and the Devil turned round on you – where would you hide, Roper, the laws being all flat? This country's planted thick with laws from coast to coast – man's laws, not God's – and if you cut them down [...] d'you really think you could stand upright in the winds that would blow then?

(Bolt 1960, 39)

It seems fitting that this Tudor cleric with such faith in the sheltering capacities of organization should be the author of *Utopia* (1516), a thought experiment which has given its name to an entire genre. Murakami and Friedman's celebrations of flatness seem to be the cultural and economic equivalent of the great wind that so troubles More, because what will be left after such a bonfire of the certainties?

In his essay 'The Bottom Line on Planet One', the cultural critic Dick Hebdige invited us into a different sort of thought experiment. He asks us to imagine two worlds based on different principles. Planet One has 'a priestly class of scribes' who 'determine the rules of rhetoric and grammar, draw the lines between disciplines, proscribe and prescribe the form and content of all (legitimate) discourse and control the flow of knowledge to the people' (Hebdige 1988, 158). Thanks to the activities of these mandarins, this is a world with depth, as signs are made to signify for other signs, and with history, as signs are made to tell stories. Planet One is our world, a world in which cultural distinction is made through authority relations, and maps of social distinctions can be constructed that locate people and things in more or less predictable relations (Bourdieu 1984). Planet Two, on the other hand, is a world where

... the vertical axis has collapsed and the organization of sense is horizontal (i.e., this world is a flat world). There are no scribes or priests or engravers here. Instead knowledge is assembled and dispensed to the public by a motley gang of bricoleurs, ironists, designers, publicists, image consultants, *hommes et femmes fatales*, market researchers, pirates, adventurers, *flâneurs* and dandies.

(Bourdieu 1984, 159)

First published in 1985 in an art photography magazine, Hebdige's 1988 essay explores a similar sense of flatness, a world of kaleidoscopic configurations which need no authorization to be what they are and in which the fluctuations of the patterns cannot be called history – in a teleological sense – but merely tell of endlessly shifting difference.

Hebdige was writing as a response to the British style magazine *The Face*, which was at that time an example of the image-driven glossy collision of ideas which was then called 'postmodernism' but is now just culture. Interviews with pop stars, fragments from fashionable intellectuals (Derrida, Foucault, Deleuze ...), pictures of clothes and buildings, ethnographies of sub-cultures, political gestures, ironic nods to old styles and coverage of opera, starvation somewhere and adverts for anything that might sell to the inhabitants of Planet Two. Because everything in *The Face* is for sale, it's just a question of how you consume as you drift across the shiny surfaces of words and things. What makes Hebdige's essay really interesting is that, for a commentator who has done so much to celebrate treating popular culture as every bit as important as high culture (1979), and who studied at the Birmingham Centre for Contemporary Cultural Studies, Hebdige appears to be nostalgic for Planet One:

> To stare into the blank, flat *Face* is to look into a world where your actual presence is unnecessary, where nothing adds up to much *anything* anymore, where you live to be alive. Because flatness is the friend of death and death is the great leveller. That's the bottom line on Planet Two.'
>
> *(Hebdige 1988, 161)*

Though he is sceptical of the epistemology of Planet One, one in which it is assumed that the elect can see through appearances to a reality which lies behind and beyond, Hebdige baulks at the ethical-political implications of such flatness. Since there is no topology to Planet Two, he fears skidding off the surface, becoming paper thin, and floating in space not knowing which way is up.

2D v. 3D

There seems to be a problem here. Murakami wants to flatten things, because he sees the hierarchies that exist as arbitrary. His logic is based on a hostility to cultural and historical hierarchies, which he sees as complicit in the dismissal of Japan, Japanese art, and Japanese popular culture. This is a programme of cutting things down to size, a radical democratization of questions of judgement which uses Friedman's market equivalence as its means to place Mr DOB alongside Mickey Mouse, and *otaku* in the elite white-cube galleries of The West.

Hebdige is troubled by this flattening, because he wants to be able to celebrate and condemn, to engage with warm people rather than the one-dimensional ciphers of the market. He seems sympathetic to a politics of symbolic redistribution, but worries about what flatness does to judgement. His sentimental humanism demands purchase on the surface of Planet Two, as he continues to insist that everything is not the same, and some things are better than others. If everything is flattened by the market, then how do we organize ourselves around things that matter? This seems to be a normative demand for judgement to be recognized as what humans *should* do:

> Whatever Baudrillard or *The Tatler* or Saatchi and Saatchi, and Swatch have to say about it, I shall go on reminding myself that this earth is round not flat, that there will never be an end to judgement, that the ghosts will go on gathering at the bitter line which separates truth from lies, justice from injustice, Chile, Biafra and all the other avoidable disasters from all of us, whose order is built on their chaos. And that, I suppose, is the bottom line on Planet One.
>
> *(Hebdige 1988, 176)*

It seems we have a reassertion of some sort of hierarchy against flatness here, but it has been flatness that appears to have been fashionable for some time. Nietzsche announced the 'transvaluation of all values' over a century ago (2007), and many of the posts which have been staked since are an attack on the idea that some grounds for judgement are more elevated than others. Those who sit at the top of the church, state, university, art gallery, or corporation have no more right to determine right than those who don't, so drag the angels down and storm the universities. But, Hebdige reminds us, if everyone is the same, then are there no grounds for decision, for preferring Beethoven to Taylor Swift, or democracy to fascism. Everything is permitted, everything is for sale. If we are looking for some grounds to prefer flatness to hierarchy, then this needs to be addressed, because (unless we are happy to give up on institutions altogether) we need to decide how decisions are made in order that we can make worlds to live in together. These are organizational matters, questions of distribution and legitimacy which cannot be solved by simply insisting that everything is treated as equivalent, however attractive such rhetorical declarations of horizontalism and prefiguration might sound.

Flatness and Hierarchy

Is organizing necessarily hierarchical? Let's begin by noting that we don't *need* to imagine the intricacies of institutions as vertical matters, like a Super Mario platform game where an employee jumps up to a new level and collects some gold coins. This is a habit, one that is difficult to break perhaps, but it is not a necessary condition of organization. It is quite possible to think about organization as a distribution of capacities, each node or element performing some function which is different from others. We do not need to assume the argument from the fictional Hierotheus that the universe is ordered from God downwards. The great chain of being might have been an influential template for thought, but it is quite possible now to think about organizations as systems, with functions distributed across a network, in the way that they are in the human body or a computer, for example. Indeed, the Christmas tree organization has a rather fairy-story verticality to it, assuming as it does that there is only one sort of power and you will find it in the pointy top. In the place under the skyscraping peak of the organization, enclosed in an office somewhere so that it doesn't leak out. Indeed, if we want to trouble stories of hierarchy, then it's a good idea to start off by noting just what a bizarre story the organization chart tells. If someone suggests that it is 'idealistic' to want to explore alternatives to hierarchy, does that mean that the organogram is a realistic depiction? All it really charts are the imagined distributions of tasks and rewards. It ignores 'informal' elements of organizing (all those that are not 'formalized') and is a truly fantastic representation of the empirical.

If instead we were to take the organization chart, lay it flat, and then redistribute or explode it like a circuit board, engineering diagram, maze, or mandala, the imagined geography of hierarchy becomes clearer. A flat depiction of a division of labour doesn't necessarily assume that some bits are more important than others, or that some parts can see the whole. Flatness has a democracy to it too. It dispenses with the idea that some are more equal than others, and consequently that some are special and deserve parking spaces and shiny suits. Flatness doesn't dispense with the idea of organization, of the patterning which is an effect of the dispersal and arrangement of people and things. Neither would flatland organizers be troubled by the idea that some bits might coordinate, or relay, or occupy a centre, node, or steering position of some kind. Such questions are technical matters about how particular things get done, and how certain sorts of powers are allocated to different parts. What the reduction to surface plan does is to suggest that *hierarchy* is not necessarily embedded into organizing in the way that we might assume is inevitable. The change of perspective re-orders what we see, and encourages us to think in different ways.

On the other hand, describing things as ontologically flat doesn't make them politically flat, because it can all too often simply ignore existing sedimentations of power. This is the problem with Friedman's view from the New York Times Building, across a world in which many people don't have access to telephones, let alone the internet and shipping containers. His assertions about the way that things are reflect fifty years of post-industrial futurology in which bureaucracy is replaced by the project, the matrix and the virtual. Take the example of the word 'network'. This word has been applied to transportation, media, biology, technology, mathematics and human societies. In its essence, it suggests a non-hierarchical web of connections (or ties) between organizations and/or people and/or objects. Such a web would have communication nodes but no controlling centre. In principal, unlike a hierarchy, the network does not need centralized direction, and could still operate even if parts of it were not functioning. It thus has something in common with 'cellular' or 'bottom-up' methods of organizing. However, the metaphor is an elastic one, since some 'nodes' can be conceptualized as more important than others (in terms of establishing rules for the rest of the network), and some connections can be seen to be more important than others (if their information is particularly valued). In other words, things called 'networks' can easily begin to look like hierarchies if there is a great deal of distinction between the elements of the network. Further, since networks have been thought as being 'weak' or 'strong', then it is possible to imagine a hierarchy of networks, or even (in the most conventional case) the word 'network' functioning a little like the term 'informal structure' in relation to the formal structures of organizations. The utilitarian use of the term 'networking' appears to have this meaning, by people who really want to make sure that they climb up a hierarchy.

The non-hierarchical potential of the word has been degraded considerably. At its most general, it has even been used (by Manuel Castells 2000, or Boltanski and Chiapello 2005 for example) as a general description of an information society – just the sort of social order that Friedman is describing. However, since this 'network society' contains forms of organization and economy that are clearly hierarchical and exclusionary, it is difficult to see what distinctiveness the word has in this context. Like so many 'new' organizational forms over the last fifty years, the managers and their gurus are still the ones insisting that others be flexible. Claims about the world being flat – informalization, empowerment, the wisdom of crowds, postmodernism, post-bureaucratic organization – should not be treated as empirical statements or ontological claims but as advertising slogans. Indeed, almost always they should be treated with extreme caution because the person who claims that we are all in the same boat usually isn't: 'Treating hierarchy as if it does not exist offers wonderful support to those at the top of the hierarchy' (Bratton 1989, 1499).

Hierarchy denial can be a form of ideology, a sort of myopia experienced by those whose elevation allows them to see no detail of the everyday lives experienced down there on the ground. So we cannot wish political hierarchies away with fashionable words, but neither should we assume that hierarchy is a *necessary* organizational form. Other worlds are possible. That is to say, there are plenty of places where we can often empirically document hierarchies, but this doesn't mean that all organizing *must* (and therefore should) be hierarchical. To assume the latter would be to fall into the

Functionalist Fallacy 101, that the social phenomena that do exist must exist, and that radical social change is merely idealism. The question that remains is whether there are ways of thinking which can preserve the possibility of different and non-hierarchical forms, but without losing a sense of organizing as the engineering of relative powers.

Dimensions of Organizing

Let's begin by thinking about hierarchy and super flat as being equally two-dimensional accounts of organizing. Whether flattening distinctions, or constructing them, the oscillation takes place between the horizontal and the vertical when neither can possibly be stable states. First, the vertical organogram tends not to express horizontal relations, even though it has been empirically established since at least the 1950s' 'dysfunctions-of-bureaucracy' literature that the informal is what allows the formal to exist at all. James Scott notes that the organization chart is the public or official transcript of some sort of institution in which all members are joined only by vertical relations, and ultimately only given unity 'by the lord, patron or master, *who represents the only link joining them*' (1990: 62, emphasis in original). This is a form of picturing the social which ignores so much else that connects and divides people. The informal organization is then relegated to being what Scott calls a 'hidden transcript', a kind of residue which is only of interest insofar as it assists or blocks the schemes of those 'higher up' the organization. So we might say that an emphasis on hierarchy is a way of seeing, which ignores the lateral nature of much of what actually happens in organizations – the self management, informality, sub-cultures and so on – in favour of an account which justifies the elevation of those who provide it. No wonder that the schools which teach management also tend to teach the inevitability of hierarchy.

Second, though the impulse to push over the Christmas tree is understandable enough from those with commitments to equality, a flat picture of organizing does fail to capture its political topology in a very convincing way. It tends to be a normative description, one motivated by certain commitments which I happen to agree with, but which (as Hebdige noted) end up describing a world which is just as glossily unrealistic. Complex forms of organizing do have centres of power. For example, as Pamela Lee (2007) suggests, it is vector graphics programmes like Adobe Illustrator which have allowed Murakami to produce scalable images that can be reproduced on and as a wide range of products from Macy's parade balloons to a key chain. Adobe allows for stretchable surfaces, and hence for both customized high-end products and cheap serial production. So Mr DOB represents a form of branded commodity which has partly been made possible by the technology provided by a global software company with headquarters in San Jose, California, a turnover in 2009 of $2.946 billion and 8,715 employees.[3] This particular version of mechanical reproduction is using post-Fordist production methods to sell into luxury markets willing to pay for a Louis Vuitton accessory, others willing to pay a few yen for a snack toy, as well as millionaires and museums who will bid on art works worth $15.2 million. Louis Vuitton is part of the LVMH group, the world's largest producer of luxury goods with a turnover of €20.3 billion in 2010. I'm with Hebdige here. This doesn't seem like a very flat world to me, and saying that organizing is flat doesn't make it so.

The problem might be the Manichean nature of the set up – either hierarchy or super flat – when the ontology and politics of organizing is always more complex than that. Indeed, there is no particular reason to assume that a particular claim about the ontology of organizing commits you to a politics which necessarily supports or questions political hierarchies. Those who assert that the world is flat might be doing so in order to ensure that you buy whatever it is that they are selling, and those who insist on hierarchy might be imagining organizations that more effectively distribute resources for reasons of social justice. The shape of the world is not so simple that one dimension can be celebrated over another.

Post Hierarchy

There is an odd convergence between the pro-market claims of Murakami and Friedman, and the long-standing suspicion of hierarchy that we find in a wide series of anti-authoritarian positions. Both viewpoints appear to be trading on some notion of human freedoms and an opposition to constraint. For Friedman, the ceaseless waves of innovation are inevitable, and his objections are not to hierarchy as such, but rather to the idea that any particular hierarchy could last. Like a bourgeois merchant, he objects to the feudal and the bureaucratic, but only in order that he can get his own pile. Murakami, it seems to me, is a similar case, with his seductive attempts at equalizing cultural value being largely plays *within* a market system, and being both predicated and justified on the same grounds which that system provides. If you sell more product, you deserve more profit, and to claim anything else is rather old-fashioned. So these are not objections to hierarchy in general, or in principal.

However, from another point of view, there are plenty of good reasons why hierarchy itself should be regarded with suspicion. Gibson Burrell quotes the novelist Julian Barnes claiming that 'after death the heart assumes the shape of a pyramid' (in Burrell 1993, 66) As Barnes appears to be implying, the bureaucratic organization appears petrified, rather than alive. Decades of writing on organizations have suggested that its immutable hierarchies produce bureaucratic personalities, banal conformists who follow orders, solidify rituals and spend lifetimes striving for the favour of their superiors (Whyte 1961, Bauman 1989). Symbolically, it very often seems that hierarchy is conservative and arboreal whilst radicalism is flat, lateral and rhizomatic. The tower must be pulled down and the new world built prefiguratively:

> The diverse factions which gather in the Post identify the centralised source of this oppressive power variously as the Word/the Enlightenment Project/European Rationalism/the Party/the Law of the Father/the Phallus as (absent) guarantor of imaginary coherence. In other words, the project is a multi-faceted attack on the authority/authorship dyad which is seen to hover like the ghost of the Father behind all First World discourse guaranteeing truth, hierarchy and the order of things.
>
> *(Hebdige 1988, 163)*

There are lots of capitals in these sentences, lots of ironic implications, but many forms of intentional community, alternative organization, anti-capitalist movement and utopia are informed by some sense of organization as distributed and democratic, as pushing against the capitals. Hierarchical assumptions, whether institutionalized in political parties, states, capitalist organizations, or particular human relations, have been subjected to consistent suspicion. Radicals tend to assert that the work of organizing can and should proceed through the autonomous yet coordinated activities of the organizers. This could be an imagined state of social order in an utopian sense; or the operationalization of a normative political philosophy like anarchism, socialism, environmentalism, postcolonialism, or feminism; a technological practice in the case of open source, creative commons and copyleft ideas; or a specific and located form of intentional community or cooperative. In all these cases, there are deep and practical commitments to direct democracy and engagement, as forms of life that need to be worked at in order to sustain them. If hierarchy is a form of the petrifaction of power, as many of these alternative organizers would agree, then it needs to be continually addressed, reflected upon, and challenged in order that it can be resisted (Bookchin 1982, 62 *passim*; Blaug 1999).

But, this does *not* mean that the result of these reflections are necessarily normatively flat forms of organizing. Indeed, Murakami's version of flatness is a wilful myth, precisely because his practice actually requires that the cultural hierarchies are there in the background. There would be nothing interesting about Mr DOB in an art gallery if art galleries and cartoon characters were normally part of the same world. If *otaku* was equivalent to Leonardo, Murakami would have less distinctiveness. It is the fact that they are not that makes Murakami interesting, and provides his work with a market value. Murakami isn't flattening but social climbing. In order to make sense of his practice, it needs to be understood as incongruous against some sort of backdrop. Murakami's seeming commitment to cultural equity is laudable only if we view it as the sort of flatness which Friedman describes. As an artist of floating values, he will sell into whatever markets are available, and that includes the hyper-rich consumers who can afford a superluxury Louis Vuitton handbag for more money than most people on the planet earn in a year. Murakami is a contemporary version of what Hebdige fears: a fluid movement of capital across the surface of the world assembled and dispensed to the public by a motley gang of *bricoleurs*, ironists, designers and so on. There are no rules, only choices, and the only commitments that make any sense are those of Friedman's free market, of which Murakami's art market is a small example.

It does seem important to question hierarchy in the way that Murakami does, but not to thereby suggest that two-dimensional flatness can or should replace two-dimensional verticality. To borrow some terms from Deleuze and Guattari, but refuse the politics which has often been imputed, arboreal and rhizomatic accounts are not in opposition to one another (1988, 3 *passim*). This is a practical fact of organizing, and simple dualisms are in danger of obscuring it. Many 'alternative' forms of organizing do have hierarchies, but they are rarely naturalized or assumed to be inevitable. In two hundred years of radical thought, we have a vibrant variety of accounts concerning how and whether individuals or groups should coordinate the life and labour of others. Added to that are questions concerning the length of tenure, the span and limitation of responsibilities, differential rewards, the processes of consultation and democratic participation, and grounds for legitimacy (Marshall 1993, Ferree and Martin 1995, Lovink and Scholz 2007, Parker et al. 2007, Parker et al. 2014). The literature on alternative ways of thinking about organizing is huge, but rarely recognized within business schools that teach the inevitability of management. These are three-dimensional issues, practical issues, and they demand that organizing is conceptualized as taking place in space and not in a single plane, whether vertical or horizontal. Opposing hierarchy with flatness does not recognize the ways in which arboreal forms of organizing work well for trees, and rhizomes produce sprouts which push upwards. Simple oppositions rarely capture empirical complexities, or the ethical political questions that are raised by any form of organizing that wants to get things done *and* also reflect on the means by which things are done. As Matt Wilson puts it in the title of his book of reflections on anarchism, the goal should be to have rules without rulers (2014).

If institutions are power made durable, then the question is not whether hierarchy can be opposed with flatness, but whether and how institutions can keep de-institutionalizing themselves, can stay in movement. Judgements will happen, Hebdige is right, but the hierarchy of Planet One can represent judgement turned to stone. Decisions will be made, hierarchies will grow as power congeals for a while and produces certain sort of arrangements and effects. But that doesn't mean that hierarchy is the equilibrium state of organizing. Order can exist without hierarchies being permanent. Positioning a theory of organizing, or a political practice, against the *inevitability* of hierarchy does not imply that everything becomes equivalent and we end up in Mr DOB's world. This flattening which is predicated on the market runs the danger of reducing incommensurable values to one common coin, and effacing other sorts of value superpositions altogether. In other words, there is no reason why hierarchy itself cannot serve a value, without it thereby becoming an universal principal.

Edwin Abbot's mathematical romance *Flatland* (1884/1992), first published in 1884, tells the story of a square and his two-dimensional universe. The Flatlanders are a narrow and conservative bunch, with severe traditions and judgements about the rectitude of the angles of their fellows. For male Flatlanders, the more sides the better, with circles being the most perfect. The working class are triangles, with equilateral triangles being the most respectable, whilst women are very dangerous and pointed needles who can easily kill by accident and require firm control. Despite their flat world, the Flatlanders have clear hierarchies and classes, enforced by violent authority, and no doubts that theirs is the only sensible world that should and could exist. When our protagonist sees 'Lineland' (one dimension) and 'Spaceland' (three dimensions), he begins to reflect on the relativity of customs and assumptions that he had always assumed inviolable. Of course he is assumed to be mad or seditious by the rulers of Flatland, and writes to us from prison. Generally assumed to be a satire on Victorian morality, as well as a neat primer in the mathematics of dimensions, *Flatland* does not present flatness as a virtue and shows that hierarchy can exist even there.

Spinning *Flatland* on its side to make it a vertical plane allows us to see that the problem that I set myself is two dimensionality, not flatness as such. Claiming that the earth is flat, or that we are part of a great chain of being, or that the social world has a stratified ontology, simply refuses to acknowledge the complexity of the *politics* of organizing. The tree is not bad, and the rhizome is not good, and both actually spread in three dimensions. Opposing hierarchy with flatness is like opposing the X axis with the Y axis, and such a definitively Cartesian gesture is unlikely to produce any convincing accounts of the world, or ways of acting on that world. Better to be clear about what sort of organizations are wished for, what sort of utopias can be imagined, and work towards those, than claim a warrant in preferring one dimension to another. Mr DOB has helped me think through what flatness means, but his politics are as thin as a coin. Alternative organizers have been concerned with these issues for hundreds of years, and their accounts of organizing are driven by ethical-political commitments, not a marketing strategy or naturalized ontological myths.

Notes

1 This chapter is based on (2015), 'Superflat: Hierarchy, Culture and Dimensions of Organizing', in T. Diefenbach and R. Todnem By (eds), *Reinventing Hierarchy and Bureaucracy Research in the Sociology of Organizations*, Vol. 35 (pp. 229–247). Bradford: Emerald.
2 In Azuma's essay in the *Super Flat* book (2000), the words 'DOB' and 'Super Flat' are rendered in Western characters in the Japanese text. I assume this is significant.
3 www.adobe.com/aboutadobe/pressroom/pdfs/fastfacts.pdf, accessed 18 March 2011.

PART IV
Visibility

9

GOTHIC

The Goths, like the Vandals and the Huns, were nomadic tribes who brought the classical era of European history to an end.[1] Where the Greeks and Romans had established learning and order, these central European hordes swept in and celebrated a mobile form of anarchic violence. After them was a thousand-year-long age of darkness, where the lamps of civilization flickered in only a few places. No wonder the Goths have a bad name.

This chapter is a small attempt to rehabilitate the Goths and the descendants who now claim their title. Though early gothic was colourful, since the eighteenth century, the term has come to mean a form of darkness, and in its mobile transmutations, has celebrated various forms of disorder and transgression, claiming the darker sides of Western culture. The seething desires of the unconscious, the night, the serial killer or sexual deviant, blood, loneliness, becoming animal or alien, the monstrous mob, the graveyard and the ruin. As many commentators have suggested (Botting 1996, Davenport-Hines 1998, Grunenberg 1997), for more than two hundred years, gothic has taken contemporary fears and made them its own. Here I will scratch at the specific conjunction between gothic and representations of industry and organization. It seems to me that we can trace a stream of imagery that presents the urban world of work in ways that are heavily indebted to the gothic. I think that this represents a powerful form of cultural critique through representation. Organizational gothic is one way of resisting sanitized visions of a brave new world, and it has haunted the culture of organization for many years.

My wider point is to solicit certain forms of representation and conjoin them with a critique of contemporary forms of market managerialism. It seems to me that accounting frauds, anti-corporate protests, movements

DOI: 10.4324/9781032714288-13

for business ethics and social responsibility, and the growth of critical management studies all point to a sustained political and ethical suspicion of large-scale forms of organizing. What I want to add is a cultural dimension, one based on an appreciation of the ways in which 'gothic' representations have become common ways of imagining our lives at work. I have explored this elsewhere in terms of the ubiquity of visions of the grey bureaucrat, the heartless corporation and the corrupt executive (Parker 2002b), but here I want to explore the genealogy of these ideas as an enduring criticism of the modern world. Later, I will also consider whether invoking the gothic is *necessarily* a critical move, and also the status of a cultural criticism of organizations more generally.

Darkness

In perhaps its most consistent meaning, the gothic is that which diverges from Rome. If Rome represents the centre, order, visibility and civilization then it is the Goths who demand something other. In cultural terms, the label was first applied during the later Renaissance as a derogatory one to buildings that departed from the golden age of symmetry and proportion. Giorgio Vasari (1511–74), an Italian painter, architect and writer, noted that there 'arose new architects who after the manner of their barbarous nations erected buildings in that style which we call Gothic'. Slightly later, John Evelyn (1620–1706), an English diarist, wrote that 'ancient Greek and Roman architecture answered all the perfections required in a faultless and accomplished building' but the Goths 'introduced in their stead a certain fantastical and licentious manner of building: congestions of heavy, dark, melancholy, monkish piles, without any just proportion, use or beauty' (both cited in Cram 1909).

But if the gothic was here employed as a negative term that served to elevate certain classical virtues, its reincarnation in the middle of the eighteenth century reversed the assessment. By the time of John Ruskin's 1853 essay 'The Nature of Gothic', the 'fallen Roman, in the utmost impotence of his luxury, and insolence of his guilt' (1985, 80) has become the antithesis of virtue and authenticity. The corruption and sterility of neo-classicism provides the justification for an increasing celebration of the medieval, whether it be a conservative lament for feudal orders or a radical celebration of craft guilds. This later version of the gothic as a colourful celebration of nature and artifice seems to begin at about the same time that notions of the 'sublime' and 'picturesque' become central to reorganizing a relationship between the urban and the rural, the past and the present. The idea that wild and unruly nature was a source of beauty and awe would not have made much sense to those who spent their lives struggling with the earth, and in that regard, it is hardly surprising that the educated and elite members of a newly stratified society began to celebrate that which they had achieved some distance from. Tiring of the ordering that characterized neo-classical aesthetics, the rigid patterns of hedges and proper orders of column, the idea grows that yawning chasms, ruins and volcanoes could provoke reactions which were more than simply pleasing.

One hundred years before Ruskin, Edmund Burke's *A Philosophical Enquiry into the Origin of Our Ideas of the Sublime and Beautiful* (1757) had provided the aesthetic rationale for willingly exposing oneself to the awe-fulness of nature – its vastness, darkness and danger. It is because, Burke suggests, these phenomena remind us of our mortality and insignificance that exposure to the sublime provokes such strong emotions. Salvator Rosa's (1615–73) images of the Bay of Naples lit by Vesuvius and craggy Neapolitan landscapes populated by witches and bandits had already been brought back to Northern Europe as Grand Tour mementos. Withered trees and storms began to establish a new grammar for extreme experiences that were supposed to broaden the mind. By the middle of the eighteenth century, Alexander Pope, Horace Walpole, William Kent and others had began to establish irregularity and artifice as principles upon which nature could be represented in design (Davenport-Hines 1998). An increasing number of landscapes employed shell grottoes, hermits, obelisks and ruins to stage an emotionally dramatic movement from one prospect to another. The melancholy of decay also inspired the castellations and towers of houses and follies. One of Pope's engravings for his 1745 *Essay on Man* depicts a sea of derelict monuments, including a broken pediment inscribed '*Roma Aeterna*' – eternal Rome. Rather than timeless order, it was now melancholy, mortality and human insignificance that organised a new aesthetic.

At the beginning of Walpole's novel *The Castle of Otranto* in 1764, a gigantic helmet falls into the castle courtyard and kills the only heir just prior to his marriage. The intricate events that follow provide much of the imagery of the haunted house that has been so central to gothic ever since – ghosts, prophecies, murder and lust. Whilst Walpole's rather camp playfulness began to be made more formulaic in the writings of novelists like Ann Radcliffe, William Beckford and Matthew Lewis, it also feeds on some much darker forms of social criticism that emerge from the late eighteenth century onwards. Piranesi's prints of imaginary prison interiors (the *Carceri*), Goya's illustrations of the horrors of war, and the Marquis de Sade's incarcerated explorations of sexual desire and freedom all shared a deep pessimism (or realism) about the human condition. In many of these books, we also find evil lurking in the representatives of the Roman Catholic Church, perhaps the global institution of its time and 'widely regarded as [a] sinister machine of cruel controls' (Davenport-Hines 1998, 224). The arrogance of order and the cruelties of power haunted those Europeans who lived through religious wars and the age of revolutions. A darker gothic sensibility seems to part company from medievalism and romanticism, and terms that had been synonyms, the picturesque and the grotesque, were increasingly distinguished (Hollington 1984, 23).

Fred Botting has suggested that the gothic is concerned with excess and transgression, the 'negative, irrational, immoral and fantastic'. He is also clear that the figures of the gothic have been mutable, reflecting the fears of the age that they grow from. So, the desolate mountain becomes the haunted house, which in turn becomes the labyrinthine city or factory. The evil aristocrat or monk becomes the mad scientist or Machiavellian capitalist (1996, 2). It seems to be a genre which is continually concerned to celebrate that which is secreted away and oppose that which is deemed natural: 'It negates. It denies. It buries in shadow that which had been brightly lit, and brings into the light that which had been repressed' (McGrath 1997, 156).

Yet, unlike more reasoned and illuminating forms of critique, the gothic suggests no tidy solution. There is no way out of the haunted house, the vampire never really dies, and the skeletal hand will always reach out of the earth to grasp your ankle just as you think you have got away. But we shouldn't understand the monstrous merely in terms of golems, blood-suckers and doppelgangers, as if modern gothic were merely about transgressive bodies, because the gothic is also a way to represent social relations and institutions. In the form that it has taken from the nineteenth century onwards, the gothic has been profoundly concerned to show the darkness hiding in the light, to pursue a form of social criticism through cultural re-presentation.

Industry

The emergence of the 'sublime' and the 'picturesque' began to make nature into an object of a new form of aesthetic interest. However, in another sense, it also began to secure a new vocabulary within which urbanization and industrialization could be represented. The dramas of light and shade explored by Rosa had been applied to industrial subjects by Joseph Wright of Derby (Hetherington 1997, 109), and it is easy enough to see how echoes of hell could be forged from the smoke and fire of William Blake's 'dark satanic mills'. In a sense then, one element of the emerging critique of industrialism was to connect the manufactory and the city to established ideas from mythology (for examples, see Chapple 1970, 93). If Eden was the pastoral idyll, then the growing industrial towns were far from green and pleasant – *The Nether World* of George Gissing's 1889 novel. But, perhaps most importantly, they were founded on new social relationships which questioned an older order. Much of nineteenth-century gothic takes key figures in this new landscape and plays with the ambivalences that they contain.

The three key texts that provide so much of this imagery can illustrate this well enough. Mary Shelley's *Frankenstein* (1818), Robert Louis Stevenson's

Strange Case of Dr Jekyll and Mr Hyde (1886), and Bram Stoker's *Dracula* (1897) are all novels set in the contemporary – told through letters, reports, diary entries and so on – but yet contain abnormalities that lurch through the text. In *Frankenstein*, the arrogance of science is exposed in a sorcerer's apprentice fable that illustrates hubris creating an external nemesis. In *Dr Jekyll and Mr Hyde*, Stevenson reworks older stories of possession and werewolves into a tale of scientifically induced nemesis from within. Finally, in *Dracula*, the forces of reason and civilisation are pitted against something entirely unworldly that merges anxieties about class, sexuality, religion, human and animal bodies and even death itself.

There are, of course, plenty of other ways to read these stories, but the key theme I want to bring out is the massive tension they produce between their 'realism', being credible stories about modern people, and the eruption of horrific fantasy into the everyday. Of particular relevance here is the scientist or professional as a modern type who produces (Frankenstein), embodies (Dr Jekyll) or counters (Van Helsing) threats to order. These books are populated by doctors, lawyers and scientists, the emergent Victorian middle classes whose orderings did so much to create the modern world. Whether attacked by the disdainful aristocratic Count Dracula or the 'stunted proletarian monster' Mr Hyde (Davenport-Hines 1998, 312), the position of the professional classes is far from secure. So, if eighteenth-century gothic was medieval, nineteenth-century gothic used darker aesthetic mechanisms in order to insist that the battle between science and superstition has not been settled, and perhaps never can be.

Perhaps 'superstition' is too loose and pejorative a word in these contexts. What these novels establish is the possibility that a wide range of 'Others' could be deployed to interrogate the present. Merely taking these three novels as exemplars, we have oppositions between food/blood, scientist/aristocrat, Western Europe/Eastern Europe, science/alchemy, human/animal, life/death, day/night, Christianity/paganism, reproduction/consumption in which the former term (perhaps the 'settled' term) is exceeded or inverted by the latter. I will say some more about this (rather structuralist) understanding of gothic later, but for now I just want to note the power of gothic imagery as a way of condensing a certain moral censure. In summoning the image of Dracula, Frankenstein's monster, or Mr Hyde, we can re-describe a person, thing, or relation. Indeed, terms like 'vampyre' and 'blood sucker' had been used as derogatory alternatives to 'sharper', 'userer' and 'stockjobber' since the early eighteenth century at least (Davenport-Hines 1998, 239). So when Karl Marx, writing before Stoker, uses various rhetorical flourishes in the *Eighteenth Brumaire*, *Grundrisse*, the inaugural address to the First International, and *Capital* (Godfrey et al. 2004) to apply the metaphor of vampirism to the bourgeois order, he is relying on an already fairly well-established convention: 'Capital is dead labour which, vampire-like, lives only by sucking living labour, and lives the more, the more labour it sucks' (Marx 1976, 342).[2] In suggesting that capital is like a vampire, Marx perverts capitalism by equating the vitality of capitalist production with the sickening consumption of the parasite. The moral economy of value that Marx despised is re-described in terms that force the reader into some kind of imaginative leap. Whether they accept the implicit proposition that he makes is another matter, but Marx's metaphorical strategy is clear enough:

> [S]ome of the most gruesomely archaic echoes of fairy-tale, legend, myth and folklore crop up in the wholly unexpected environment of the modern factory system, stock exchange, and parliamentary chamber: ghosts, vampires, ghouls, werewolves, alchemists, and reanimated corpses continue to haunt the bourgeois world, for all its sober and sceptical virtues.
>
> *(Baldick 1987, 121)*

These ideas and characters do not exhaust the gothic. Indeed, I think they are merely the tip of an imaginative iceberg that throws a cold light on the modern world. In nineteenth-century gothic, it is all too often the city itself that plays this role – a grim city populated by institutions of various degrees of cruelty – prisons, workhouses, schools, factories and laboratories. Take Charles Dickens, for example, an author who might not have been understood as gothic, but certainly continues what Hollington (1984) has termed 'the grotesque tradition'. In many of his novels, he employs extreme characterization and chiaroscuro description to present the city and its denizens as polluted by money, whilst the simplicity and authenticity of the country lies elsewhere. Country folk are corrupted (*Great Expectations*) or easily hoodwinked (*Oliver Twist*) by the baleful influence of London, whilst Dickens continually expresses mock naivety about the motives of those populating various self-congratulatory yet cruel institutions. In his *Bleak House* of 1853, travelling to the 'iron country' involves leaving 'fresh green woods' behind and entering somewhere with 'coalpits and ashes, high chimneys and red bricks, blighted verdure, scorching fires and a heavy never-lightening cloud of smoke' (Dickens 1853/1993, 695). Rouncewells' factory is described in similar terms:

> ... a great perplexity of iron lying about, in every stage, and in a vast variety of shapes; in bars, in wedges, in sheets; in tanks, in boilers, in axles, in wheels, in cogs, in cranks, in rails; twisted and wrenched into eccentric and perverse forms, as separate parts of machinery; mountains of it broken up, and rusty in its age; distant furnaces of it glowing and bubbling in its youth; bright fireworks of it showering about, under the

blows of the steam hammer; red-hot iron, white-hot iron, cold-black iron; an iron taste, an iron smell, and a Babel of iron sounds.'

(Dickens 1853/1993, 696)

In Dickens' most celebrated 'industrial novel', *Hard Times*, he portrays Coketown as 'a town of machinery and tall chimneys, out of which interminable serpents of smoke trailed themselves for ever and ever' and factories which were 'vast piles of building full of windows where there was a rattling and a trembling all day long, and where the piston of the steam-engine worked monotonously up and down like the head of an elephant in a state of melancholy madness' (Dickens 1854/1994, 19). In perhaps his clearest anti-bureaucratic satire, *Little Dorrit* of 1857, we are introduced to the 'Circumlocution Office', an arm of government with the motto 'How not to do it'. Its particular expertise was in ensuring that any matters that were referred to it 'never reappeared in the light of day. Boards sat on them, secretaries minuted upon them, commissioners gabbled about them, clerks registered, entered, checked, and ticked them off, and they melted away.' (Dickens 1857/1954, 106) The novel's protagonist is passed from office to office, through endless corridors and piles of forms that ensure that nothing is ever done:

> "May I enquire how I can obtain official information as to the real state of the case?"
>
> "It is competent," said Mr. Barnacle, "to any member of the – Public," mentioning that obscure body with reluctance, as his natural enemy, "to memorialise the Circumlocution Department. Such formalities as are required to be observed in so doing, may be known on application to the proper branch of that Department."
>
> "Which is the proper branch?"
>
> "I must refer you," returned Mr Barnacle, ringing the bell, "to the Department itself for a formal answer to that inquiry."
>
> *(Dickens 1857/1954, 112)*

But the 'industrial novel' is not, of course, limited to Dickens. Elizabeth Gaskell's 1855 *North and South*, dramatizes the ugly town of Milton in the northern county of Darkshire and its contrast with the rural idyll of Helstone in similar ways. The first intimation of Milton that Margaret Hale sees is a 'deep lead-coloured cloud hanging over the horizon' (Gaskell 1855/1995, 60), and, in her new house, 'thick fog crept up to the very windows, and was driven into every open door in choking white wreaths of unwholesome mist' (66). She meets Thornton, a local industrialist whose 'mill loomed high [...] casting a shadow down from its many stories, which darkened the summer evening before its time' (159), whilst all around 'the chimneys smoked, the ceaseless roar and mighty beat, and dizzying whirl of machinery, struggled and strove perpetually' (407).

In Emile Zola's *Germinal* of 1885/1954, we find similar metaphors at work, though this time they are being used to describe a mine rather than a townscape. Village Two Hundred and Forty is surrounded by decaying factories, and the Le Voreux mine is the last major employer for its desperate citizenry. It is continually described as a monstrosity that swallows men. The pump of the mine is 'like the breath of an insatiable ogre [...] this god, crouching and replete, to whom ten thousand starving men were offering up their flesh' (1885/1954, 80). The mental and physical suffering and disease caused by mining are described in hideous detail, and the lengthy winter strike that occupies most of the novel results in starvation, mob violence and the eventual destruction of the mine, which collapses into itself just as so many gothic mansions do at the end of the tale: 'The evil beast, crouching in its hollow, sated with human flesh, had drawn its last long heavy breath [...] Soon the crater filled up and the place that had been Le Voreux was a muddy lake, like those lakes beneath which lie evil cities destroyed by God' (ibid., 452–453).

In these novels, the organization is rarely treated as a problem in itself but provides a scene for broader complaints. Instead, the industrial and the urban are co-implicated as the causes of a degradation in both ethical sensibilities and aesthetic experience, and this is expressed through imagery of the manufactory and the city as grotesque places populated by stunted characters. Clearly this emerging anti-aesthetic is shared by the iconic gothic novels that all express a suspicion of the modern and, perhaps most importantly, employ a more or less explicit representational form of criticism. Just as empire and industry marched onwards to the future to the sound of a chorus of self-congratulatory approval, so did 'gothic's antagonism to the possibility of human progress' (Davenport-Hines 1998, 276) provide a counterpoint, reminding readers that darkness and pain were also being manufactured.

Organization

It is not really until the early twentieth century that organizations themselves begin to become represented as sites of darkness. Echoing the older image of the haunted house, we begin to see images of organizations as labyrinths with endless corridors and locked doors hiding evil secrets. Or, as the places where monsters are fabricated, and people themselves become monstrous. This is, in part, a shift from exteriors to interiors, from the dirty city street to the cramped office or nightmare factory. As good place as any to begin is with Max Weber's deeply ambivalent 1905 description of the 'conditions of machine production which today determine the lives of all individuals who are born into this mechanism' (1930, 181). This is the 'iron cage' (ibid.) of bureaucratic administration in which the 'professional bureaucrat is chained to his activity by his entire material and ideal existence. In the great majority of cases, he is only a single cog in an ever-moving mechanism which prescribes to him an essentially fixed route of march' (in Gerth and Mills 1948, 228. Such mechanistic descriptions echoed through twentieth-century politics and culture, articulating an intimate combination of ruthless efficiency and moral impoverishment.

Perhaps with Piranesi's *Carceri* in mind, the vocabulary of German expressionism in film from the 1920s onwards gives stunning visual illustration to Weber's terrors. Given post-war inflation, unemployment and war reparations, Davenport-Hines suggests that 'All human institutions were thus discredited in Weimar Germany [...] It was a ripe period for goths, although gothic could not be medieval and knightly in a period of sordid squabbles over percentages' (Davenport-Hines 1998, 327) In Fritz Lang's (1926) film *Metropolis*, 'the gloomy city is divided between a class of industrially engineered human slaves forced to live a subterranean existence maintaining the awesome machines powering the city, and the rich who enjoy the luxuriously decadent pleasures of the world above' (Botting 1996, 166) A key element of the imagery is that of workers being appendages of giant machines:

> Dressed from throat to ankle in dark blue, men walk to their shifts with hanging fists and hanging heads. Row upon row, they shuffle into elevators taking them into the city's machine rooms. These machine rooms are places of roaring furnaces, heat-spitting walls, the odour of oil, and dark machines like crouching animals far below the streets.
>
> *(Tolliver and Coleman 2001, 44)*

The industrial troglodytes are contrasted with the glorious indifference of the suited managerial classes in the city above, enjoying drinks in wood-panelled offices in skyscrapers. The towering masses of the cityscape are the new gothic castles and the monsters are now machines.

The visual imagery of *Metropolis*, as well as films like René Clair's *A Nous La Liberté* (1932) and Chaplin's *Modern Times* (1936), may well reflect a Weberian diagnosis but there is another important influence too. As McGrath has argued, 'psychoanalysis has in this century fulfilled the traditional function of gothic literature' (1997, 156). After all, the expressionist film set is also a landscape of the mind, in which the suspension of disbelief allows for fantasy to mutate everyday features of the modern so that they become threatening phantoms. In fantastic fiction, whether these are real terrors or imaginary ones is not particularly important: 'Freud's remarkable achievement is to have taken the props and passions of terror Gothic – hero-villain, heroine, terrible place, haunting – and to have relocated them inside the self' (Edmundson, cited in Davenport-Hines 1998, 325).

There is no better source for this than the fiction of Franz Kafka, particularly his posthumous novels *The Trial* (1925/1953) and *The Castle* (1926/1957). In both novels, the narrator is K – a bank manager in *The Trial* and a land surveyor in *The Castle*. The former tells the story of K's arrest, trial and eventual execution for a crime which is never specified, the latter of K's attempts to discover why he has been brought to a village beneath a towering castle to perform a task which no one seems to want him to do. In each case, the ordered certainties of a smug professional are gradually stripped away as the logic of the organization – 'a rigid obedience to and execution of their duty' (Kafka 1926/1957, 245) – exposes him to a series of increasingly bizarre humiliations. K is often sweating in low corridors, waiting in passages and being interviewed in chambers at the top of narrow staircases, the victim of a confusion or conspiracy which no one completely understands:

> The ranks of officials in this judiciary system mounted endlessly, so that not even adepts could survey the hierarchy as a whole. And the proceedings of the courts were generally kept secret from subordinate officials, consequently they could hardly ever quite follow in their further progress the cases on which they had worked; any particular case thus appeared in their circle of jurisdiction often without knowing whence it came, and passed from it they knew not whither.
>
> *(Kafka 1925/1953, 133)*

K's eventual assassins in *The Trial* are two 'pallid and plump' gentlemen (1925/1953, 245), in frock coats and top hats who bow politely but say nothing. They don't know why they have been sent to administer 'justice', any more than K does.

In Kafka's world, cruelty is a bureaucratic matter, and the affairs of little people are of no consequence to those who merely carry out orders. Even misunderstandings are orders, after all. From *The Castle*:

> In such a large governmental office as the Count's, it may occasionally happen that one department ordains this, another that; neither knows of the other, and though the supreme control is absolutely efficient, it comes by its nature too late, and so every now and then a trifling miscalculation arises.
>
> *(1926/1957, 62)*

The person who is telling K this, the Superintendent, has a cabinet full of unfiled papers, and more piles of papers in the shed. Yet, because 'it is a working principle of the Head Bureau that the very possibility of error must be ruled out of account' (1926/1957, 66) the 'Control Officials', and those who control them, rarely intervene in such trivial matters. Indeed, even communicating with the Castle is a random matter, since there is so much important business to be transacted that the telephone is randomly switched between extensions.

Kafka's visions have since become archetypes, and the *Catch-22* type of organizational logic that he parodies has now made his name into an adjective. In an important sense, 'Kafkaesque' captures twentieth-century organizational gothic very nicely indeed. Darkly fantastic representations of work and organizations can be found in ever greater numbers as the twentieth century develops, for example, such as Karel Capek's 1922 play *R.U.R* – 'Rossum's Universal Robots', Yevgeny Zamayatin's explicitly Taylorist 'OneState' of *We* (1924), Aldous Huxley's *Brave New World* (1932) and George Orwell's *1984* (1948). These visions variously dramatized the contrasts between industrial robber barons and mechanized worker slaves, the growth of scientific management and the bureaucratized violence of everyday life.

In the 1950s and '60s, organizational gothic seemed to be rather eclipsed. Perhaps the contradictions of capitalism were no longer as stark, or the industrialized agony of the killing fields of the Second World War was just too painful to consider, but the dominant message seems to be one of the organization as a site for romance and upward social mobility.[3] However, Mervyn Peake's Gormenghast trilogy (*Titus Groan* (1946/1983), *Gormenghast* (1950) and *Titus Alone* (1959)) is an important exception. Peake's Dickensian characters inhabit a gigantic sprawling castle that is run according to ancient ritual instructions contained in dusty volumes containing

> ... the activities to be performed hour by hour during the day by his lordship. The exact times; the garments to be worn for each occasion and the symbolic gestures to be used. Diagrams facing the left hand page gave particulars of the routes by which his lordship should approach the various scenes of operation [...] Had he been of a fair skin, or had he been heavier than he was, had his eyes been green, blue or brown instead of black, then, automatically another set of archaic regulations would have appeared ...
> *(Peake 1946/1983, 66)*

Madness and bureaucracy become closely intertwined in a rambling story of intrigue and rebellion that, by the third novel, sees Titus the 77th Earl of Gormenghast escape to a city of strange and wonderful technological marvels, of shimmering metal and glass buildings. Yet this is also a city with smoking factory buildings, flying surveillance drones, a Kafkaesque court and prison system and, like *Metropolis*, an entire culture of outcasts and fugitives beneath the city itself in the 'Under-River'. Whether the institutions are feudal or modern, it seems Titus can find no road to freedom, no place outside the sets of rules that constitute organized lives.

The Monster Wakes

Gormenghast apart, it isn't really until the 1970s that organizational gothic begins to re-emerge in a more generalized sense. Grunenberg claims that contemporary gothic is driven by 'an increasing weariness about the alienating power of technology and its disastrous social consequences', and adds 'The Draculas of today are the greedy corporations, automation, corrupt parties and politicians who deliberately erode the foundations of the welfare state' (Grunenberg 1997, 197). It seems to me that some very common motifs in fantastic fiction over the last three decades have been the figure of the corporate tycoon conspiring at the top of their skyscraper; the organization as a place where monsters are spawned; and the visualization of work as incarceration.

So when Dracula is relocated to London in the Hammer film *The Satanic Rites of Dracula* (1974), he is disguised as D.D. Denham, a reclusive property developer with a corporate tower who is secretly plotting to unleash a fatal virus upon the world. And when Damien, the anti-Christ, returns in *Omen 3: The Final Conflict* (1981), he is a thirty-something CEO of a huge multinational corporation, Thorn Industries, who lusts for control of the world. Pretty much the same figure of the corporate megalomaniac reappears in a whole host of other films – perhaps most splendidly in *Batman Returns* (1992) as the magnate Max Shreck (named after the actor who played the vampire *Nosferatu*). In all these examples, and many more, the image of the well-dressed and dastardly chief executive looking out over the city from their tower is a powerful continuation of gothic and melodramatic imagery. Indeed, such ideas are now pastiched in comedy films like *Austin Powers: International Man of Mystery* (1997), in which Dr Evil's henchman, Number Two, is portrayed as a corporate man with an eye-patch and a briefcase who has built Virtucon into a global business. After Dr Evil's rather old-fashioned attempt to blackmail world governments with a nuclear device has failed, Number Two turns to him and says:

> I spent thirty years of my life turning this two-bit evil empire into a world class multinational. I was going to have a cover story in *Forbes*. But you, like an idiot, wanted to take over the world. But you don't realise there is no world anymore – it's only corporations.

It seems that the easiest stereotype for a scriptwriter who wants to construct a villain is to conjure with wealth, class and gender and then embody them within the figure of the corporate executive. The melodramatic villain[4] no longer ties the innocent victim to the railway tracks, but throws her from his corner office.

Central to fantastic fiction films and novels are references to some part of the state or the military-industrial complex that has, because of greed, ambition, or paranoia, invested in a dark conspiracy of money and power. In Rollerball (1975), for example, the hero 'Jonathan' is lectured by a senior corporate executive when he refuses to be retired from an exceptionally violent gladiatorial game which provides a circus for happy consumers. And, in a series of examples, the corporation produces or protects a monster that either rampages or rebels against its creators – the Tyrell Corporation in the *Blade Runner* films; the Weyland-Yutani Corp in the *Alien* films; Cyberdyne Systems in the *Terminator* films; and Omni Consumer Products in the *Robocop* films.

Indeed, this pervasive fog of organizational paranoia is constitutive of the many 'trust no one' conspiracy narratives of the *X-Files*, or films like *Conspiracy Theory* (1997), *The Game* (1997) and *Enemy of the State* (1998). Organizations, these texts repeatedly claim, are dark places where secrecy lurks behind closed doors and men in black are listening to every conversation (Parish and Parker 2001). In a reversal of much of the post-Second World War organizational consensus, but a return to the narratives of *1984* and *Brave New World*, 'the technocrats are now the bad guys and the good guys are the reactionaries' (Franklin 1990, 25). Images of rows of desks, endless corridors and insane bosses abound in *Brazil* (1985) where torture and repression are bureaucratized through the 'Ministry of Information'; *Joe and the Volcano* (1990) in which Tom Hanks' character seeks salvation from a grey dehumanized job, and *Being John Malkovich* (1999), where our hero works on the 7½th floor with a ceiling that makes him have to stoop continuously. In these films, expressionist gothic is used to visualize the distorted lifeworld of the corporation, and the haunted house has mutated into a steel skyscraper. Though not all anti-organizational representations draw on gothic imagery, many of them do – a law firm run by Satan in *The Devil's Advocate* (1997) as well as the TV series *Angel*; the 'Denmark Corporation' in a remake of *Hamlet* (2000); and the Green Goblin in *Spider-Man* (2002), who is actually the CEO of Osborne Industries. Perhaps archetypally, in the cartoon series *The Simpsons*, we have the etiolated Mr Burns, the evil capitalist who lives in a looming mansion with his fawning acolyte and plots against his employees and the residents of Springfield (Rhodes 2001).

The evil villain twirling his moustache and plotting, the labyrinthine haunted house hiding secrets, the monster produced by mad science: all of these are now stock characters and settings, familiar to children and easily written into almost any piece of fantastic fiction. The corporation is taken to be their most credible site. Questions of motive are then simply assumed, because 'everybody knows' that corporations are motivational structures of greed, power and envy, machines for generating profits, pollution and collateral damage. So, at the very moment when global capitalism seems to be at its most triumphalist, when there appears to be no alternative, and the ideology of market managerialism reaches down from the corporate tower into the crevices of the management of everyday life, careers and relationships, there is a simultaneous, and largely unremarked, 'common sense' that claims exactly the opposite.

Culture, Criticism

A powerful gothic sensibility stalks our age. Many authors have suggested as much, cataloguing 'horror, madness, monstrosity, death, disease, terror, evil, and weird sexuality' (Grunenberg 1997, 210), as these themes are played out in contemporary sub-cultures, fiction, film and art (Latham 2002). The activist group Earth First! tells us of a monster that

> ... gobbles whole mountains and forests, drinks rivers dry, spews toxic waste, and enslaves whole populations. It has all the rights of a citizen, but few of the limitations. It can cross national borders as if they were cobwebs. It is immortal, and can therefore amass wealth and power beyond the capabilities of mere mortals [...] We are talking about the CORPORATION.
>
> *(in Starr 2000, 87)*

Yet, as this chapter has shown, gothic representations of industry and organization[5] have been a pervasive feature of societies in the Global North for at least 150 years. My use of the word 'gothic' is not at all precise here, and I suppose I am really referring to some family resemblances between horror, the grotesque and melodrama – all genres that employ distortion and myth in order to achieve dramatic effects. It seems to me that this monstrous collection of texts represents a lengthy form of cultural struggle against the hegemony of a modern organized world. Following a cultural Marxism in the most general of terms, we can see these expressions as instances of contestation. Not the only ones, because there are plenty of examples of cultural contestation that are clearly not primarily gothic (comedic portrayals of management as stupid,[6] or romantic accounts of the freedoms that lie outside the work organization, for example), and plenty of struggles that are not primarily cultural (trade union recognition, or anti-corporate protests).

But what does it mean to suggest that 'organizational gothic' is an example of cultural struggle? On the one hand, it is obvious enough that explicit gothic metaphors have played an important role as an imaginative resource for re-description. In referring to 'Frankenstein foods' to condemn genetic manipulation, or describing people as 'Jekyll and Hyde' characters, we are employing common clichés that rely on a metaphorical exchange between two domains. So when two academics want to reframe knowledge management as the transfusion of vital fluids, they title their chapter 'Organisational Gothic' precisely to contrast the bright-eyed utilitarianism of the knowledge managers with the seduction and coercion of the foul-breathed vampire. For Garrick and Clegg, in the learning organization, the 'individual souls in the corporation that learn are those replenished by being sucked dry and recruited as brides and grooms to the new organisational Draculas' (Garrick and Clegg 2000, 154). Or when Pelzer and Pelzer assert that 'organisations create fear, dread, helplessness', that they are self-created prisons, a 'threatening fact taking away our personalities, sucking life out of our bodies and brains without touching the surface of our skin' (1996, 19), they rely on the same melodramatic grammar. In structural terms, the collision between a signifier for some form of horror and another domain (in this case, the work organization) causes the latter to be infected or, let us say, rethought. A commonly accepted, perhaps hegemonic, image is articulated in a different form. Whether this is the city as hell, the vampire metaphors in Marx, Weber's organization-machines, or the CEO being revealed as the devil, it is the same operation at work.

However, to claim that this is necessarily a heroic form of criticism, in which the modern is *always* exceeded or inverted by the gothic, is to de-historicize both words and the movements that might happen between them. When Kenneth Gergen wrote in 1992 about the differences between romantic, modernist and postmodernist versions of organization, he doubtless would not have anticipated that the term 'postmodernism' (or 'post-modernism') would often become a conventional way of celebrating the endless exchanges of capitalist globalization, and not the unsettling that he anticipated (Gergen 1992). In the same manner, gothic imagery can itself become 'settled' or 'unsettling' depending on the context. Disorganizing, revalorizing closeted terms, soliciting the other, exceeding and inverting are all operations given meaning by a particular context, not having some transcendental or immanent meaning in themselves (Parker 2002a). It would be naïve to treat gothic as it were necessarily always a great refusal which can and should be solicited by those who are excited by the romance of resistance. Gothic ideas are the stuff of common cliché, and just as corporations can be described as the new Draculas, so can elected governments, or universities, or social workers. Gothic can be sold as a form of authenticity for middle-class teenagers seeking community, or filmmakers seeking box office receipts, or nostalgics who wish to condemn versions of progress through science or urbanization, or progressives who see the rural past as a haunt of irrational fears, or domesticators who wish to subdue the monsters from the Id, or punk academics selling rebellion for money. The point is that, as Botting (1996) argues, the gothic is mutable and it can be (and has been) employed for all these purposes and more. So in suggesting that the gothic can function as a form of representational critique, I am pointing at its power to denaturalize at one moment, but must also remember that it can itself naturalize as it becomes cliché – a metaphor that first shocks[7] and then becomes an excuse for not thinking. A (post-) Fordism of the intellect. Any colour you like, as long as it is black.

Nonetheless, there is something curiously powerful about this particular set of metaphors, because even whilst they decay into cliché, they remain marked by such extremity. The images of horror, grotesquerie and melodrama that have haunted this chapter seem to have a certain power, since once you have re-imagined the corporate tower as the castle on the hill, it is difficult to shake off that sense of unease. As Franco Moretti comments, an older literature of terror 'presents society – whether the feudal idyll of *Frankenstein* or the Victorian England of *Dracula* – as a great corporation: whoever breaks its bonds is done for' (Moretti 1983, 107) Nowadays, escaping from the great corporation might be just exactly what you need to do in order to survive. The message might be that you should stick to the path and stay out of the woods in case the wolf gets you, or that the wolf is already waiting for you at work. Or worse, that you look in the mirror of the washroom at work through yellowing eyes to discover that your eyebrows are thickening. Moretti describes horror as a 'literature of dialectical relations, in which the opposites, instead of separating and entering into conflict, exist in function of one another, reinforce one other'. But this is not, he claims, the mere functioning of ideology – generating the mists that obscure monsters:

> The more a work frightens, the more it edifies. The more it humiliates, the more it uplifts. The more it hides, the more it gives the illusion of revealing. It is a fear one *needs*: the price one pays for coming contentedly to terms with a social body based on irrationality and menace. Who says it is escapist?
>
> *(Moretti 1983, 108)*

And here is a curious twist. If we do not treat culture as escapism, as an epiphenomenon of structure, then it can become both a topic and a resource for critique. If we treat the gothic, and specifically gothic organization, as being an element in this 'literature of dialectical relations', then we have a way of grasping historical embeddedness more fully. Dialectics (if not understood too rigidly) explores the changing relation between opposing propositions, and the interconnectedness of supposedly separate terms. In general terms, it therefore presumes a relationality which suggests that individual and context, particularity and generality are necessarily made in conjunction. In philosophical and political terms, this adds up to questioning any approach which assumes an escapist separation between the romantic subject and their object of enquiry, or between the knower and the known. These, Baldick suggests, are precisely the limitations of realism, and in fact the only way in which the 'monstrous dynamics of the modern' (1987, 198) can be apprehended are through the historically embedded techniques of estrangement that gothic has employed with such regularity. The reason that 'realists' like Dickens, Marx, Zola and Weber turn to monstrous metaphors is precisely because the 'conjuring powers available in language' (Smith 2001, 51) can reveal through re-description, can unveil by veiling. At any given historical moment, the products of culture can label injustice in dramatic forms that can in turn provide resources that are good to think with.

Gothic criticism of organizations will not save anyone from the corporate beast, but it is a symptom of the times. Those critical of market managerialism may well employ such metaphors in their own attempts to sponsor change, to be (for a time, for our time) new Goths who oppose the ordered cruelties of a new Rome. As Ricardo Blaug (1999) illustrated in his paper on the defeat of the well-organized XXth Roman legion by a swift and invisible gothic tribe in AD 9, 'hierarchism' causes a form of blindness to other organizational forms. In a parallel way, we could suggest that too much reliance on structural struggles inspires a kind of blindness to cultural struggles, and the tactics that they might employ. Not that either can be separated, since they are dialectically related and co-produced, but it seems obvious enough that seeing things differently might be a precursor to doing things differently. Which is, in a conclusively anti-gothic spirit, to end with revolutionary romanticism and a futile hope that the dead hand of capital doesn't reach from the grave I am digging for it.

Notes

1   This chapter is based on (2005) 'Organizational Gothic', *Culture and Organization* 11/3: 153–166.
2   To which might be added the relation between economics and desire. For a vein of speculation which has employed an admixture of Marxism and psychoanalysis, see Moretti 1983, Baldick 1987, Gelder 1994, and Brown 1997. Godfrey et al. 2004 usefully open an Althusserian gap between 'ideological' and 'scientific' readings of the vampires in Marx. This chapter is primarily concerned with the former, theirs with the latter.
3   See Parker (2002b) for more on this.
4   A villain with a pedigree in melodramatic theatre and literature throughout the nineteenth century. For example, Alec D'Urberville, from Thomas Hardy's *Tess of the D'Urbervilles* (1891). Alec is a typical moustached Victorian rake, a rich and morally corrupt seducer whose claim to the d'Urberville name is completely false.
5   And perhaps not only 'Western', though the ethnocentricity of this paper is clear enough. See Parish (2000) and Smith (2001) on occult capitalism in Ghana and Nigeria respectively.

6 Which certainly links to older notions of the grotesque, and the carnivalesque laughter that turns the world upside down (see Bakhtin 1984, Rhodes 2001).

7 Smith (2001, 50) makes a connection between this and Brecht's 'alienation effect'. The point being that such an effect cannot rely on the same strategy every time if it is to shock an audience out of its existing state of consciousness.

10
SECRET SOCIETIES

It is often enough said that the contemporary world is dominated by formal organizations.[1] It should not surprise us then that ours is also an age of organizational conspiracies, such as in Dan Brown's *Da Vinci Code*, an extraordinarily popular account of a secret society which concealed the fact that Jesus Christ had children. His protagonist, Langdon, does not believe in coincidence:

> As someone who had spent his life exploring the hidden interconnectivity of disparate emblems and ideologies, Langdon viewed the world as a web of profoundly intertwined histories and events. The connections may be invisible, he often preached to his symbology classes at Harvard, but they are always there, buried just beneath the surface.

So there is plenty of interest in conspiracies, but the specifically *organizational* aspect of this feature of our culture is less often remarked upon.

We can assume that organizations are the causes of many of the things that happen in our world. We see a building or a crane with a neon sign on the top, a doorway with a brass plate, a van with a logo on the side. A letter on headed paper arrives, someone in a uniform does something that a voice on a telephone said that they would do, or we buy a product in a box that tells us who manufactured it and gives an address in Texas or Hong Kong. These organizations tell us that they exist, indeed they often insist that they exist, using the full spectrum of the marketing mix to ensure that we cannot miss them. But paralleling this hyper-visibility is another set of organizations; ones that we believe exist, but know little about: national and international criminal networks; associations of the wealthy and powerful who meet in

DOI: 10.4324/9781032714288-14

hotels once a year; fraternities that own properties in cities across the world; religious sects and cults, and shadowy organizations which are historically documented, but whose aims and purpose are unclear. We might add to this list the national and international security apparatus of the state, because they are almost always entangled in such landscapes as well.

In their very helpful review of 'organizational secrecy', Costas and Grey suggest that it involves topics which 'lurk marginally in the shadows of organization studies, almost as secrets in themselves' (2014, 19). They insist that an 'informational' approach to secrecy needs to be augmented with an understanding of secrecy as a social process. I agree, and here want to build on these ideas by exploring an area which they deliberately exclude, concentrating as they do on 'secrets within non-secret organizations' (ibid., 2). So this is not a chapter about secrecy in conventional organizations, though it has implications for that, and neither is it about non-secret organizations that have as their business the acquiring of information by nefarious means – spy agencies, industrial espionage and the like (Grey 2012). Rather, I will be concentrating on the 'secret society' – a term which I am going to treat as synonymous with 'secret organization' – because I think that this category of institutions helps us think about some general properties of organizing. My argument is that organizations like the Masons, Opus Dei, and the Skull and Bones are important because of the light that they throw on the formal organizations that constitute the world around us. Unusual forms of organizing – angelic choirs, circuses, zoos – as well as the Order of the Peacock Angel, the Holy Vehm, and the Decided Ones of Jupiter the Thunderer (Daraul 1965) can be used to help us see conventional forms of organization differently.

The theoretical concern that motivates me is fairly simple. How do we know that something is an organization? Stohl and Stohl ask the same question of a 'clandestine' organization, in their case al Qaeda. As they suggest, despite the endless incantations of its name, 'the communicative and material constitution of al Qaeda, *the organization*, remains an enigma.' (Stohl and Stohl 2011, 1201, emphasis in original). This presents them with some interesting ontological problems, particularly since they are convinced that organizations are produced as systems of communication. Stohl and Stohl quite rightly conclude that there is almost always an assumption about trying to make things visible in organizational research, whether the data are numbers, texts, or conversations. The evidence we use is usually of the empirical kind, the equivalent of looking for the neon sign. But none of these things are the organization. We can never see the organization, but only catch fragmentary signs of its presence. Even when we visit a building that 'contains' an organization, we don't see 'it' – we see a display of materials associated with it. By definition, the successfully secret society would leave no such evidence, which means that all the organizations I mention here have accidentally or deliberately failed in their attempts to be invisible. They have left traces of their existence and we, like Dan Brown's suspicious detective who does not believe in coincidence, then look for connections buried below the surface.

The secret society allows us to pose questions about the epistemology and ontology of organizing. Much business-school research has tended to assume that organizations are visible and transparent (Erickson 1979, 122), but I will instead propose that much about organizing is actually invisible or opaque. Ideas from hermeneutics, psychoanalysis and studies of culture, resistance and informal organization all suggest that the organization is a gothic haunted house, not a brightly lit machine. I will begin with a consideration of the characteristics of historical and contemporary organizational conspiracies, and then move on to elaborate what sort of 'facts' need to be claimed about a secret society to bring it into existence. After a section on the politics of contemporary organizational conspiracies, I conclude with some speculations on what the example of the secret society can tell us about the epistemological strategies pursued by organizational researchers, and the radical doubt that they might need to cultivate. In conclusion, I suggest that all organizations share many characteristics with secret societies, and that understanding invisibility and opacity should make researchers rather more paranoid.

Conspiracy Theory and Organization

Karl Popper, in his 1945 *The Open Society and its Enemies*, was scathing about what he called 'the conspiracy theory of society', and located it as a mistaken attempt to personalize the impersonal forces and coincidences that structure our lives:

> The gods are abandoned. But their place is filled by powerful men or groups – sinister pressure groups whose wickedness is responsible for all the evils we suffer from – such as the Learned Elders of Zion, or the monopolists, or the capitalists, or the imperialists.
>
> *(Popper 2002, 352–353)*

Like Richard Hofstadter's condemnation of the 'paranoid style' of politics (1966), and Carl Sagan's diagnosis of a 'demon haunted world', in which 'significance junkies' obsessively search for evidence of wrongdoing (1996), it is common for post-war intellectuals to dismiss contemporary conspiracy theories as a form of paranoia (Ronson 2001). That being said, plots and schemes are as old as recorded history, with disguises, assassinations and coups being regular features of the ancient world. So too are ideas about heretical sects, subversives and religious or ethnic groups organizing against the public or hiding secrets from the masses (Cohn 1970). However, it is not until the early modern world that the idea of enduring formal organizations which hide their existence became a common part of culture. It is noteworthy that this is at the same time that the first corporate charters are beginning to be granted by the state. There are echoes of this in the *Sociedad Anónima*, *Société Anonyme*, *Società Anonima* and many other variants in North Western Europe – 'societies of the nameless' with purposes which transcend individuals. So when Adam Smith suggests in 1776 that when tradesmen meet 'the conversation ends in a conspiracy against the public', he is telling us something rather important about the relationship between secrets and organizing. Perhaps it is no accident that the 'Unlawful Societies Act' was passed in the UK 23 years later, a statute that outlawed any groups that swore oaths of secrecy, with the exception of the Freemasons. It was not repealed until 1967.

The ubiquity of formal organizations in contemporary conspiracy theory is evident, and has occasionally been remarked on by commentators (Parker 2001). However, it tends to be seen as an epiphenomenon of a general tendency, such as the way that the target of conspiracies has become 'evil elites' and not scapegoated 'evil others' (Campion-Vincent 2003, 2004). It is widely agreed that the dominant optic of conspiracy has shifted from being focused downwards – elites worrying about the masses – or laterally – the masses gathering against some particular minority – and is now focused upwards. It is the common people who are now trying to identify conspiracies within the elite, a phenomenon which both Peter Knight and Mark Fenster suggest reflects a wider crisis of the legitimacy of authority (Knight 2000, Fenster 2008). This is not to say that attempts by the powerful to identify 'the enemy within' or outbreaks of popular aggression against strangers have ended, but that many people now have an *X Files* attitude to explanations provided by the powerful – 'trust no one.' Investigative journalists and hardline conspiracists who assume that the world is a tissue of secrets and lies (Ronson 2001, Millegan 2004, Southwell 2005) share this hermeneutic of suspicion. I find these accounts of shifts in conspiracy logic pretty convincing, but my concern here is more specific, in the sense that I want to look in more detail at the secret organizations themselves, treating them as the imaginary engines of conspiracy.

The social theorist Georg Simmel wrote a typically dense essay on secrecy in the early 1900s, and a central concern for him was the 'secret society' as an example of the general problem of the individual wanting to be both different and the same (1906). As a first move, Simmel wants to insist that pure transparency (knowledge) or opacity (ignorance) are not possible in social relations, and that the question is not whether secrecy exists, but how much and why. His use of the secret society as an example is important because he uses the features of that particular organizational form as an ideal type of more general social processes involving the marking of boundaries and the shaping of identities. As Simmel, Jung and others have noted (Costas and Grey 2014), secrecy has many charms. It is a marker of belonging, a statement about privilege and status, a claim to possession of a mystery:

> To associate with other like-minded people in small, purposeful groups is for the great majority of men and women a source of profound psychological satisfaction. Exclusiveness will add to the pleasure of being several, but at one, and secrecy will intensify it almost to ecstasy.
>
> *(Aldous Huxley, in Marx and Muschert 2009, 225)*

If we accept that one of the general social processes going on here concerns *secretus*, in the sense of exclusion and separation, then a structural analysis would suggest that the opposite process is also likely to be invested with social significance too. Uncovering, revealing, exposing, are likely to matter in a context in which hiding has social value. And this is precisely what we see in contemporary representations of organizations. The plots of a huge number of films, TV shows, comic books and so on concern the role of organizations in conspiracies of different kinds, and very often the question of the ontology of the organization itself is at issue, as the protagonists attempt to discover its nature and scale. For example, the notion that there is some sort of power behind the scenes is played out quite literally in the film, *The Adjustment Bureau* (2011) based on Philip K. Dick's 1954 short story, 'Adjustment Team'.[2] Characters step through an unassuming door and behind the scenes of the world to see besuited employees arranging matters according to a specified plan. And if someone does discover this deep structure to the world, the organization will then distract them by making their bus late (in this film), or make them forget what they have seen (in the *Men in Black* films, and Dr Who's suited enemy 'The Silence'), or kill them (in countless films in which the hero has to run around a lot and can't trust anyone).

In this world, 'plot' – and the ambiguity of the word is helpful here – is predicated on the exposure and mapping of connections, and much of the time those connections are institutionalized, named as a shadowy organization which must be exposed – 'SPECTRE' in James Bond, 'Hydra' in Marvel Comics, DC Comics 'League of Assassins' and so on. In cyberpunk fiction, there is a continual reminder of what William Gibson has called 'invisible lines up to hidden levels of influence' (in Czarniawska 2011, 33), and this is echoed in popular writing on organized crime in which the distinction between evil organization and legitimate business organization dissolves. Mark Lombardi's fantastically detailed drawings of the connections between the powerful and their businesses inscribe a network of invisible order (Grayson et al. 2006, 88). Accounts of secretive offshore shell companies which discreetly avoid tax and publicity through chains of mailbox addresses and holding companies are revealed in art and political economy (Cameron 2014, Shaxon 2011).

Internet and telecommunications frauds are carried out by entities such as the Russian 'Business Network', which operates in different countries with different names (SBT Telecom Network, Nevcon Ltd, 76Service), the South American 'Superzonda', or the worldwide 'ShadowCrew' (Goodman 2011, Berinato 2011, 220). Add to this the business activities of Latin American cartels, Mafia groups, Russian and Balkan Mafiyas, English 'firms' or 'gangs', Hells Angels, Asian Yakuza and Triads, Caribbean Yardies and Posses, Prison and Barrio gangs, street collectives such as Mara Salvatrucha and you have a landscape of organizations with no office, no address, and which tend to leave few traces (Gilman et al. 2011, Parker 2012).

This is a hall of mirrors, with corporate offices appearing normal from the street, but secret lifts taking you down to an underground lair; organizations working parasitically within others; large businesses having hidden interests in lots of other firms, and, of course, everyone is buying off the police and the politicians. Iain Banks, in one of his final novels, wrote about 'The Concern' or 'l'Expédience', an organization which might itself be fragmented into cliques and hierarchies with different agendas, and perhaps opposed by 'a sort of anti-Concern, some equally worlds-spanning shadow organization opposed to everything we do' (Banks 2009, 187):

> We knew there were various levels and classes of executives within l'Expédience with, at the apparent pinnacle of this structure, the Central Council itself, composed of people who knew all there was to know about the Concern's provenance, extent, operational methods and aims – and some of us were of the opinion – always perverse, in mine – that there might be one central authority figure at the head of all this tiered knowledge and power, a kind of organizational autocrat to whom everybody else was obliged to defer. But for all we knew that final, single, near-godlike Emperor of the realities – if he or she did exist – was little better than a foot soldier in a still greater grouping of other Concerns and meta-Concerns ... .
>
> *(Banks 2009, 246)*

The secret society, as a social form which Simmel saw as exemplifying general features of everyday personal interaction, should also be understood as part of a social imaginary in which secrecy and organization are inextricably intertwined. This is not a world of clearly bounded and legitimate organizations, but of crime, conspiracy and paranoia. The intentions of organizations are unclear, who is 'inside' seems vague and shifting, and even their very existence is in question. So when Michael Bradley, in his *Secret Societies Handbook*, asserts that there are 6 million Freemasons, in 100,000 lodges (Bradley 2005, 52), it is difficult to know whether he is right, and how (given what he says about their secrecy) he would know. That the Freemasons exist seems clear enough, but the organization itself has consistently claimed that there is no overarching Grand Lodge, since each local Lodge is sovereign. So where do his numbers come from, and why should we believe Bradley anyway, who appears from his other publications to believe that Jews are descended from Neanderthals and are more aggressive than Cro Magnons? The problem of evidence is clear enough, and this is to use the example of a formal and well-documented organization in a building with its name on the front. If we ask similar questions about Opus Dei, the Templars, the Bilderberg Group, the Yakuza, or the Trilateral Commission, then the epistemological problems multiply.

Structures of Secrecy

Books like Bradley's do tell us something about just how the secret society is described. All these descriptions have interesting similarities, and collectively they tell us something about what needs to be said to suggest that an organization exists at all. For example, according to a retired US intelligence officer, al Qaeda[3] possessed

> … a standing army; it has a treasury and a consistent source of revenue; it has a permanent civil service; it has an intelligence collection and analysis cadre; it even runs a rudimentary welfare program for its fighters, and their relatives and associates. It has a recognizable hierarchy of officials; it makes alliances with other states; it promulgates laws, which it enforces ruthlessly; it declares wars.
>
> *(Bobbit 2002, 820)*

Whether this is true will be as hard to establish as the worldwide number of Masons, but as Stohl and Stohl (2011) and Schoeneborn and Scherer (2012) show, the fact that it was asserted consistently for ten years made it true. The organization was talked into solid existence through a kind of mimicry, an insistence that despite the lack of clarity about people, places, money, routines and so on, that it simply does exist. So what needs to be said in order to make an organization real?

My 'evidence' here comes from a whole series of texts, some popular and some academic, which concern secret societies. What interests me here is not whether these are 'true' or 'false' accounts in themselves, but rather what they tell us about how such truths might be established. So, for example, a common feature of any secret society is the idea that it has existed for some time. The Italian Carbonari claimed descent from the cult of Mithra, the Gnostics and the Templars (Daraul 1965, 90; Harding 2005, 46). The Freemason's origins are said to be found at the time of the building of the Temple of Solomon, or in ancient Egypt with the construction of the pyramids. Various documents have been found claiming to be descriptions of the Rosicrucians from the early seventeenth century onwards (Daraul 1965, 170; Bradley 2005, 122; Harding 2005, 120), even though concrete evidence about the existence of an actual secret society appears to post-date them. Claiming duration is thus a way of claiming solidity, so the publication of the *Fama Fraternitas of the Meritorious Order of the Rosy Cross* in 1614 provides a warrant for the existence of the organization. Or, as another example, the London coroner William Wynn Westcott was said to have received a document from a fellow Mason, who had himself found it in a bookshop. The document described five Masonic rituals in coded fragments, and an attached letter suggested that more could be discovered by contacting *Sapiens Dominabitur Astris* at the *Licht, Leibe und Leben* branch of the German Rosicrucians. This was the origin story of the Isis-Urania Temple of The Hermetic Order of the Golden Dawn founded in 1888 at 17 Fitzroy Street, London (Bradley 2005, 58).

If duration is one criteria, then another is the idea that entrance to the organization must be marked by ritual. This seems fairly universal, and most societies seem to have some sort of purification and promise at their heart. Ancient Phrygian accounts of Mithraic cults required drinking wine from a cymbal and eating bread from a drum (Daraul 1965, 68), just as early industrial craft guilds employed complex initiations involving wine, a crucifix, torches, a tablecloth, special roles and costumes, questions and answers and so on (Hobsbawm 1965, 150 *passim*). The Triads are said to have a six- or seven-hour ritual involving a 'mountain of knives', a fruit seller and a sacrificed cockerel, among other things (Booth 1991, 36). Part of the Entered Apprentice oath for Freemasons is:

> I most solemnly and sincerely promise and swear, that I will always hail, ever conceal, and never reveal, any of the arts, parts or points of the hidden mysteries of ancient Freemasonry [...] under no less a penalty than that of having my throat cut across, my tongue torn out by its roots, and buried in the rough sand of the sea at low water mark ... .
>
> *(Bradley 2005, 55)*

Second-degree Masons risk having their hearts ripped out, whilst third-degree Masons will have their bowels burned to cinders (Streeter 2008, 76). The oaths and speeches are often constructed in a self-consciously ancient or legal language, such as the Ku Klux Klan's 'solemnly pledge, promise and swear' and the Triads 'Thirty Six Oaths' (Bradley 2005, 77; Booth 1991, 193). Perhaps in an echo of the requirement for duration, the language needs to sound as if it has been echoing down the centuries too.

The internal structure and role of the organization is often remarkably detailed, in an almost parodic echo of formal organizations. According to the *Dossier Secrets d'Henri Lobineau*, the Priory of Zion comprised of 1,093 members, each in seven grades of membership, with the numbers in each grade determined by multiples of three (Cox 2004, 50). The Templars had knights, sergeants, chaplains and servants, a model adopted from the Cistercians and later adopted by the Freemasons (Bradley 2005, 71). There are seven different Operating Thetan levels for the Scientologists. The Bavarian Illuminati had three levels of initiation – the Nursery, containing the degrees of Novice, Minerval and Illuminatus Minor; the Masonic, containing Illuminatus Major and Illuminatus Dirigens, and the Mysteries, containing Lesser and Greater Mysteries. Each of the latter were also divided into two – the Presbyter and Prince, and Magus and Rex (Streeter 2008, 103). The structure of the Golden Dawn consisted of ten or eleven degrees of membership depending on which account is to be trusted (Bradley 2005, 59; Streeter 2008, 136). They were based on the degrees of the Sephiroth from the Kabbala, and were divided into three orders, which moved members from the Neophyte to the Ipsissumus.

This is not merely an enumeration of names, but also a description of hierarchy with initiation rituals to enter a higher level. In a marvellous echo of Weber, and of Pseudo-Dionysius, the highest level of the KKK was a Grand Wizard ruling an Invisible Empire, then a Grand Dragon ruling a Realm, a Grand Titan over a Dominion, Grand Giant a Province, and finally Grand Cyclops managing a Den (Harding 2005, 100). Forms of naming might also reflect a division of labour. The Garduna, Holy Warriors of Spain, divided their members into *chivatos* (initiates), *floreadores* (fighters), *ponteadores* (swordsmen), *capataz* (bosses) and the *Hermano Mayor* (grand master). Women were known as *cobertas* (covers), *serenas* (sirens) and *fuelles* (bellows), depending on what part they played in ambushes or assassinations (Daraul 1965, 99; Harding 2005, 65). Divisions of labour are also divisions of knowledge. For the Assassins (*hashshasin*) of twelfth-century Syria, at each level of initiation they were told that what they had learnt at the lower level was false (Streeter 2008, 242). They also operated a cellular arrangement (Bradley 2005, 14) in order to ensure that few or no people had a full picture of the organization. The secrecy of any society also appears to become even more intense as we move to higher levels, with vague accounts of the three Ordines who are at the top of the Illuminati (Harding 2005, 111) and 'Secret Chiefs' or 'Tibetan Masters' – 'cosmic moral guardians' who run the world and perhaps the universe (Streeter 2008, 137).

Within the genre of secret societies, the descriptions of everyday activity are notable by their absence. There are no accounts of routines and rules, of the dull nine-to-five of the office life, but many descriptions of the extraordinary, the taboo. So we have accounts of the ecstatic dancing and flagellation of the Skoptsi ('Castrated') of Russia (Daraul 1965, 79); the repeated initiations of the Cult of Mithra (Harding 2005, 54 *passim*); the triple incisions of the Odin Brotherhood; the cannibalism of the West African 'Leopard Men', and the mortification of the flash using a whip or cilice for members of Opus Dei (Allen 2005). Uniforms might also be important during rituals, such as the white hoods of the KKK or the aprons of the Masons, and there are also accounts of places which are particularly associated with the society, such as 'The Tomb', the home of the Skull and Bones society at Yale University, or the campground at Bohemian Grove in California (Millegan 2004).

However, by their very nature, material evidence of secret societies is scarce. The revelation of locations, membership, dress and so on is prevented by ensuring that information is only shared by others within the organization, by means of password routines, secret handshakes and codes. The Bavarian Illuminati of the late eighteenth century adopted classical Roman and Greek names, and codenames for their headquarters. Messages were written in codes, the months were renamed, and dates of years were changed to the Parsee calendar (Streeter 2008, 103). The Triads are said to communicate by the 'manner in which a cigarette is taken from a packet; the way in which a tea-cup or chopsticks are held; the way money is offered in payment; the manner of holding a pen … ' (Booth 1991, 38). The organization will only be visible to those who already know the codes. Levitt and Dubner illustrate this nicely with the story of Stetson Kennedy helping to break the KKK by leaking passwords, names and plans to radio shows 'making precious knowledge into ammunition for mockery' (Levitt and Dubner 2006, 50–59). For example, when the show *Adventures of Superman* broadcast a description of the KKK as a secret society with the password routine 'Do you know Mr Ayak' and 'Yes, and I also know Mr Akai',[4] then the actual passwords became worth nothing. A similar example is the publication of Scientology materials on the internet, such as the account of how the Thetans were removed from their home planet and sent to Teegeeack (which is Earth), and how the 'body Thetans' cause humans problems to this day (Streeter 2008, 202 *passim*). Members had to pay for these materials in order to become one of the elect, so having them freely available means that it was harder to sell what L. Ron Hubbard (the founder of Scientology) called the 'mystery sandwich'.

This summary of the characteristics of various secret societies tells us what sort of evidence appears to be required in order to specify something as an organization. Because of their clandestine nature, as Stohl and Stohl point out, the organization leaves less sign of its presence (2011). What the popular literature on secret societies shows us is what sort of phenomena we assume to be traces of organization – temporal duration, a barrier between inside and outside, internal structure and a division of labour, roles, rules, materials, rituals, codes and so on. Not all of these are necessary, because the existence of organization can be imputed on the basis of just a few, but at least some of them are needed for the account to be persuasive. In many ways, 'the secret society becomes a structural image of the very world to which it has placed itself in contrast and opposition' (Hazelrigg 1969, 325; see also Erickson 1981). That is to say, the secret society seems to have the same sort of features as the non-secret organization, which suggests that the reverse might be true as well. Do what seem to be clearly visible forms of organizing share features with the secret society? Before exploring the epistemological and ontological issues that this question raises, I first want to consider the politics of organized secrecy. The sort of judgements that are made about secret societies are rather similar to social science in general, and it is important to see this clearly before we proceed.

Conspiracy Politics

In theory, a secret society could exist to either protect *or* subvert the dominant order. In the German *Bundesroman* of the nineteenth century, beginning with Schiller's 'Ghost-Seer' (1787–89), we have many accounts of heroes uncovering plots by both evil Jesuits bent on world domination, or lofty nobles preserving humanist values in a corrupt world (Ziolkowski 2013). Political judgements about the activities of any given society can only be made within a particular context, and with reference to some evaluation of the merits of existing social arrangements. So, for example, the Freemasons were persecuted for being a Jewish organization by Italian, German and Spanish Fascists, and as a Zionist organization in Saddam Hussein's Iraq. They are seen as a capitalist organization in communist countries, as devil worshippers for some Christian groups, and as an 'old boys network' for many people who have concerns about nepotism (Streeter 2008, 80–82). Yet there is also a suggestion that progressive ideas were being disseminated by Freemasons in France prior to the revolution, as well as evidence that Freemasonry was a mechanism for the organization of resistance to Spanish imperialism in South America in the early nineteenth century (Streeter 2008 91–94). The same organization appears to mean different things, unless we decide that it isn't the same organization.

We can find evidence of secret societies that have supported leftist revolutionary causes – the Cerce Social and *Conjuration des Égaux* during the French Revolution. The 1799 Unlawful Societies Act was intended to ban supposedly seditious groups such as the London Corresponding Society and the United Britons, as well as proto-trade unions such as the Tolpuddle Martyrs. It was followed by the Irish Unlawful Oaths Act (1823) aimed at both Catholic and Protestant Societies. There are also plenty of examples of groups supporting revolutions from the right – the Ordo Novi Templi, Thule Society and Higher Armanen Order in early twentieth-century Germany, and which influenced German fascists and private armies (Cantor 1970, 125 *passim*), or Opus Dei in Franco's Spain (Allen 2005, 56 *passim*). Claims concerning who organizes and for what purpose are always political. In the

US in the 1950s, the John Birch Society claimed that the Illuminati were the precursors of communism, and accused Marxists of merely propagating Illuminati propaganda in order to bring about the New World Order. In all of these cases, the clandestine organization can be understood as a minority who aim at destabilizing the status quo. Secrecy is then

> ... a tactic used by those who don't have the resources or numbers to accomplish their goals through the methods of ordinary politics [...] secrecy is an equaliser: it's one of the few tools that allow the little guy to contend with the power structures of society. What the ruling class doesn't know about is a lot harder for them to trample!
>
> *(Michael Greer, in Streeter 2008, 248)*

Depending on who is looking, this might be understood as heroism or treason, but both share a sense that 'secret societies protect heretical ideas' (Streeter 2008, 249; Cohn 1970). It follows then that the identification of the covert organization is a matter of locating members, documenting practices, finding meeting places and so on.

Yet the dominant contemporary form of conspiracy thinking makes the organization of secrecy into a much more diffuse matter, since it involves powerful groups who are intent on keeping the world as it is, or want to change it to their advantage. The 'enemy within' are now the private and state organizations which govern us, and use ideology to persuade us that we are really free. As Marx and Muschert put it:

> What if Simmel made a visit to a contemporary supermarket and was greeted with his own image on a video monitor, heard advertising on a loudspeaker, provided a discount card to the checkout clerk, and received personalized (or at least "profilized" messages on the sales receipt promising future discounts?
>
> *(Marx and Muschert 2009, 226)*

The contemporary world is not what it seems. Organizations continually tell us that they are doing things for particular reasons (because they care about customers, pandas, the planet), when we know that this is at best an evasion, at worst a lie. Our experience encourages paranoia, because the intensity of customer service, marketing, political communication and the spatial organization of supermarkets and airport gift shops can leave us in no doubt that we are the subjects of manipulation. For anyone to assume otherwise would be naivety, or madness.

The very idea of the secret society can be understood as an intensification of ordinary experience, a form of popular critique embedded within popular culture (Campion-Vincent 2004, 111 *passim*; Fenster 2008). Consider Michael Bradley, writing about Yale University's 'Order of Skull and Bones':

Some would argue further that globalization, materialism and the permissive society is another way that the Bonesmen are successfully ushering in a New World Order by breaking down the family unit – the single biggest obstacle to totalitarian mind control – while being seen publicly to be struggling to protect it. The most visible and vocal protectors of morality are the very people who are working behind the scenes to destroy it.

(Bradley 2005, 109)

At its heart, this is a suggestion that contemporary capitalism, of the sort practiced by the sort of people who join elite university societies, damages social relations. Of course, to say that the world is run by a few in the interests of a few is a criticism which could be voiced by the majority of contemporary social scientists too, whether their arguments concern equality, income, wealth, education, globalization, or whatever. So a conspiracy theory, such as a well-documented one which involves Roberto Calvi, the P2 Masonic lodge, the Vatican's Banco Ambrosiano, the Mafia, the CIA and their 'Gladio' operation to counter communist influence, is merely a specific example of some commonly understood general *organizational* processes.

My point is that organizational conspiracies are ordinary, and that contemporary conspiracy theory is about organizations. There are plenty of radicals who make connections between corporations, the World Bank, World Trade Organization and so on. These are John Pilger's *New Rulers of the World* (2002), a group of interests hidden because as, Noam Chomsky suggests, democratic societies practice 'thought control' (1989) and practice Klein's 'shock doctrine (2008). So when a conspiracist like Michael Streeter names the Council on Foreign Relations, the Royal Institute of International Affairs, the Trilateral Commission, and the Bilderberg Group (Streeter 2008), he is identifying some credible agents with comprehensible motives:

I now believe that Western history needs to be completely rewritten to tell the hidden story behind our true economic and political global hierarchy. The more I have researched, the more alarming my discoveries have been [...] I have woken up to the possibility that we are not free, that we do not control our destinies, and that we are the puppets, not the masters.'

(Bradley 2005, 9–10)

The metaphor of puppets is also one used in Peter Berger's *Invitation to Sociology* (1966, 199) in order to explain the importance of social forces, and consequently the importance of sociology. The idea that the world happens behind our backs is, in much social science, given names like 'realism', 'functionalism' and 'structuralism', all dignified words for the same sort of imputation. But as Jon Ronson shows nicely, in his book of adventures with David Icke, Islamic fundamentalists and the Klu Klux Klan, 'their' logic is pretty much the same as 'ours' (Ronson 2001).

The shift from top-down to bottom-up versions of paranoia also seems to be a shift in the epistemological warrant required. The descriptions of older secret societies are catalogues of bounded organizations with distinctive features and they are identified as organizations in just the same way that any non-secret organization would be – rules, roles, entry criteria, duration and so on. However, if we look at contemporary conspiracy theory, the descriptions are less specific, but propose greater power and reach. The very ontology of powerful forces – structures, systems, networks – seems to exceed simple descriptions of single institutions, and become a field of enmeshed organizations, a dark net of secrecy, a relational web which captures everything.

In Search of Organization

In 1564, Cosimo I de' Medici, the ruler of Florence, commissioned a one kilometre-long covered and enclosed corridor. The Vasari Corridor stretches from the Uffizi to the Pitti Palace, and the small round windows in the corridor were called 'Cosimo's eyes' from which the people of Florence could be spied upon. The founder of this banking dynasty, Giovanni di Bicci de' Medici, had as his motto 'always keep out of the public eye' (Hibbert 1979). Contemporary power is no different, and the injunctions to invisibility are amplified when the business requires concealment.

The Mafia, for example, is an organization that attempts not to leave any traces, and that covers its tracks (Parker 2012). As the gangster Henry Hill remembered, 'we paid cash for everything. This way, there were no records or credit card receipts' (2004, 35). After the arrest of the Mafia Don Bernardo 'Tractor' Provenzano in 2006, many tiny scraps of paper – '*pizzini*' – were discovered in his clothing which referred to his various business associates by number. He was Number 1, and the numbering went up to 163. According to Longrigg and McMahon (2006), 'the ghost of Corleone' never used mobile phones, and 'believed in keeping the organization out of sight, the better to do business'. The Mafia attempts to leave no footprints, no noises. Many members deny that the organization exists at all. Don Calò Vizzini, a Sicilian Mafiosi, was interviewed by a newspaper journalist in the 1950s:

Don Calò: The fact is that every society needs a category of person whose task it is to sort out situations when they get complicated. Generally these people are representatives of the state. But in places where the state doesn't exist, or is not strong enough, there are private individuals who ... '

Interviewer: 'Mafia?'

Don Calò: 'The Mafia? Does the Mafia really exist?'

(Dickie 2004, 253)

Let us take that at face value. Perhaps Don Calò was asking an important ontological question about organizations in general. We imagine they exist, because they constantly tell us that they do, but what is an organization but a moving flux of people and things? This certainly seems to fit with ideas about the death of bureaucracy and the growth of a network society. Indeed, from the 1980s onwards, much of the literature on post-Fordism and the 'Third Italy' – the clusters of small firms which developed in the 1970s and 1980s in the central and northeast regions – stressed that the success of industrial districts was about semi-visible informality, not the gigantic apparatus of the contemporary corporation. The sort of words and phrases that attempted to capture this rotated around the idea of a network of family-run firms, hence 'cohesion', 'inter-firm linkages', 'trust', 'cooperation' and so on. In this post-bureaucratic world, written contracts were rare, but senses of loyalty and interdependence with other organizations were high. Sterling notes that the Mafia also entered into partnership arrangements with the Camorra from Naples, the Calabrian 'Ndrangheta, the Hells Angels, various US-based Latino gangs, the Chinese Triads, Caribbean gangs and so on (Sterling 1991, 386). As Gilman and colleagues' (2011) edited collection on criminal globalization demonstrates, these are networks that are durable and powerful, but that leave only suspicions and whispers.

This is further illustration of what Stohl and Stohl call the 'fragmentary materiality' of clandestine organizations. We seek evidence of their existence, but in the knowledge that such evidence will be hard to find, and those traces that we do find might have been placed there by agencies who wish to distract us from discovering the truth. How we evaluate evidence then becomes crucial: ' "What an organization is" always depends on who is speaking *in its name, on its behalf,* or *for it*' (Stohl and Stohl 2011, 1207; original emphasis).

One of the problems in claiming to know about secret societies is that we might doubt the evidence of their existence. This is the case of the High Priesthood of Thebes, or the Elders of Zion for example, which are both dismissed by authorities on the matter (Harding 2005, 81; Streeter 2008, 149). However, after a chapter on 'False Cults and Societies', Arkon Daraul follows it with a chapter on the High Priesthood of Thebes claiming that their 1785 anonymous pamphlet is 'plausible' (Daraul 1965, 115). There is plenty of evidence that secret societies are sometimes invented or elaborated upon in order to suggest that there is a conspiracy of some kind, such as

Jews, or Muslims in the case of various more recent conspiracies. Or the same thing might change its name continually – what we now call the Triads being variously termed 'the White Lotus Society', *Hupeh*, *Shansi*, 'the Cudgels', 'the Boxers', 'the Big Swords', 'the Red Fists' and so on since the late eighteenth century (Booth 1991, Harding 2005, 139). Or even what we think are separate organizations are actually entangled. The eighteenth degree of the Scottish Rite of Masonry is known as the Knight of the Rose Croix (Streeter 2008, 115). Surely this shows that the Rosicrucians and the Masons are working together?

In Book One of *The Meditations*, Descartes considers the possibility that his perceptions of the world are being systematically distorted:

> I shall then suppose, not that God who is supremely good and the fountain of truth, but some evil genius not less powerful than deceitful, has employed his whole energies in deceiving me; I shall consider that the heavens, the earth, colours, figures, sound, and all other external things are nought but the illusions and dreams of which this genius has availed himself in order to lay traps for my credulity [...] I may at least do what is in my power and with firm purpose avoid giving credence to any false thing, or being imposed upon by this arch deceiver, however powerful and deceptive he may be.[5]

Descartes' move here is intended to ensure that he is not being played for a fool by an agency with greater powers than his, and social scientists have been seduced by such Gnosticism ever since. The idea that the world we see is not all that there is, and that a demiurge seeks to mislead us, is common to any form of thought which seeks to understand hidden systems, ideologies, discourses, hegemonies (Rossbach 1996). In the present age, such a caution is more apposite than ever. There are plenty of people who want us to believe things, and who have stealthy and viral technologies to nudge us in the directions that they intend. Anyone who believes that contemporary organizations are transparent hasn't been paying much attention.

In an odd misstep, or perhaps a joke, Simmel suggests early on in his essay that larger organizations are now more transparent than they were – 'able to act with complete integrity in marketing their goods' – and that smaller business people will catch up with this modern way of doing business eventually:

> So soon as the methods of doing business among small traders, and those of the middle class, have reached a similar degree of perfection, the exaggerations and actual falsifications, in advertising and recommending goods, which are today in general not resented in those kinds of businesses,

will fall under the same ethical condemnation which is now passed in the business circles just referred to.

(Simmel 1906, 447)

Later in the essay, he suggests that the same is happening with the state, with individuals gaining privacy just as 'politics, administration, justice have lost their secrecy and inaccessibility' (Simmel 1906, 469). There is a sense in which he (like Mauss and Jung) regards secret societies as somehow prior to formal public organization, a simpler and more primal form of association.[6] Yet the overall argument in his essay suggests that secrecy is not something that can be replaced by transparency, as if it were possible to imagine relations between people in which all parties knew everything (Vattimo 1992). Simmel fails to apply the lessons of the secret society to organizing more generally, in part because he assumes that authoritarian societies produced secret societies as an arena of freedom (Hazelrigg 1969). This progressive account prevents him applying his insights to modern organizing, even though there are plenty of suggestions in his essay that organizations themselves produce secrecy because people enjoy being in cabals, and because hierarchy is predicated on what we would now call 'information asymmetry'.

If we strip away this assumption that there is a move towards public openness, we might use Simmel's ideas to suggest that organization always produces both secrecy and transparency. Further – following hints in Birchall (2011), Horn (2011) and Costas and Grey (2014) – I want to suggest that this is related to the formal operations that produce entities that we recognise as organizations. *Secretus* begins with separation, with a setting apart that marks different social spaces. Such boundaries are constitutive of organizing, and of organizations. The boundary, the seam that divides and joins (Cooper 1989), is one that must be marked by ritual and symbol, by descriptions of how what happens inside is different to what happens outside, because these are the traces that we look for when seeking evidence for the existence of an organization, such as a secret society. This would be a reasonable assumption to make for someone like Simmel, with his concern for the relationship between wholes and parts, collectives and individuals. However, in the present age, even if we do not find such evidence, it does not mean that organization is not present. Simmel can also be read now as a poststructuralist, always insisting that one category makes another, and that any terms can only be understood in relation (Cooper 2010). In this way, it becomes possible to assert that the boundary between 'inside' and 'outside' is an epistemological one too, a filter which prevents certain information from becoming visible. In that sense, there is a logical similarity between a contemporary anti-corporate position and the idea that secret elites are running the world. Both assume that Descartes' demiurge is capable of manipulating the traces of organizing, of making us see what 'they' want us to see. Secrecy and organization are structurally linked, but the contemporary dominance of formal organizations has made secrecy into an epistemological condition for all of us, not an occasional choice for some to wear robes and chant in darkened rooms.

Social science, whether seeking accounts of structures of formality or of processes of informality, tends to assume that what is being investigated is in principal amenable to investigation. Whether using science, phenomenology, or hermeneutics, there is a narrow path to truth. However, if we see the world of organizations through the optic of the secret society, such an assumption becomes questionable because we are immediately in danger of being deceived, and there is no one person or agency who we can trust to show us truth. This is a diagnosis about method which is a consequence of what it means to live in an organized world. As the sci-fi author William Gibson puts it, intelligence and security are the opposite of advertising and marketing (Gibson 2007, 208), though we might add that the spy and the spin doctor are both engaged in the management of secrecy. There are two ways in which we might understand the implications of this. The first is a political assumption about epistemology, in the sense that contemporary conspiracy theory assumes that organizations – including the state – are agents involved in deception at every level. We can understand this in terms of ordinary matters such as marketing claims for products and services, corporate social responsibility statements, or justifications for high levels of pay. It is not a big leap to then suggest that corporations are conspiring with politicians, or that states engage in false flag and black propaganda operations. Such assertions reflect judgements about distributions of power and suggest a sceptical stance with regard to the accounts that any organization provides.

The second implication reflects an ontology which shapes an epistemology, in the sense that the secret society forces us to think about what it means to claim that something is an organization. As we have seen, the traces of secret societies are faint and require decoding. Like Robert Langdon, we need to assume that the connections may be invisible, but they are always there, buried just beneath the surface. They involve histories and events told by unreliable witnesses which may, or may not, intimate the presence of something we can claim to be a cause, and then name. When we claim, as is often the case, that this or that organization did something, or that the world is now dominated by organizations, it is easy to forget that we have never seen one. We see people, uniforms, organization charts, buildings with neon signs. It is easy enough to make the mistake of assuming that what is visible to us *is* an organization, rather than fragments, hints and suggestions. Because an organization is never visible, and much evidence of it is deliberately kept secret from us. Our social science often tells us to look for structures or agents, and it often encourages scepticism, but it rarely encourages the sort of consistent paranoia which is associated with contemporary organizational conspiracy theories. Perhaps we need an epistemology which is less complacent, and more suspicious of the accounts provided by organizations. As Schoeneborn and Scherer (2012) suggested, al Qaeda was marked by some sort of relation between extreme visibility and extreme invisibility, and I think that this might be an assumption that is more generalizable than a terrorist cell. Because if we start from the idea that ours is a society of secrets, populated by secret societies which masquerade as formal organizations, then a paranoid epistemology is the only rational response.

Notes

1 This chapter is based on (2016) 'Secret Societies: Intimations of Organization', *Organization Studies* 37/1: 99–113.
2 In *Orbit Science Fiction*, September–October 1954, No. 4.
3 At the time of writing this, I was assuming here that it was an organization distinct from ISIS, ISIL, or 'The Islamic State', which emerged into public consciousness in 2014.
4 Standing for 'Are you a Klansman', and 'A Klansman am I'.
5 https://yale.learningu.org/download/041e9642-df02-4eed-a89570e472df2ca4/H2665_ Descartes%27%20Meditations.pdf, accessed 31 July 2024.
6 Mauss's writings in this area seem to have influenced Georges Bataille to found his secret society, 'Acephale', which allegedly met in the woods and read Nietzsche and de Sade.

11

JAMES BOND

As we have already seen, it is common within studies of popular culture and organization, to observe that management and work are generally presented negatively, and that this is a form of the 'critique within culture'.[1] Cartoons, TV comedies, pop songs, science fiction and other texts have been enrolled as examples of satire, subversion, suspicion and so on, and which show management as evil, organizations as places which crush the soul, and work as something to be escaped from. Such an analysis reflects the sort of politicization of the mundane, of mass culture, which was a common strategy for early cultural studies, particularly that associated with the Birmingham 'Centre for Contemporary Cultural Studies' (CCCS) from the 1970s onwards (Hall and Jefferson 1976, Willis 1977, Hall et al. 1980).

Whilst not questioning the general tone here, it does miss some nuances.[2] A huge number of fictional representations of working lives don't fall easily into this framing, and this is often because they are concerned with occupations that are broadly understood to be socially admirable, and with jobs that are often understood to involve dramatic events. This covers medical dramas, police procedurals, films and TV series about firefighters, mountain or coastal rescue services, lawyers, coroners, forensic psychologists and so on. Much of the time, the drama of the events supports a plot which illustrates the danger or complexity of the task at hand and the bravery and intelligence of those involved. Not always, of course, because there is also an occasional subplot which involves greed, corruption, or stupidity from someone who is working for the organization concerned (usually a manager), and a requirement on the part of the hero to deal with the wrongdoers to achieve the virtuous ends which the organization strives for.

DOI: 10.4324/9781032714288-15

These sort of conspiracy subplots are most common in depictions of the police and criminal justice, very common in detective narratives, and perhaps dominant within another related genre, that of the spy or secret agent who must go 'rogue' to achieve their goal. The most famous secret agent in the world is James Bond, the subject of many novels since 1953 onwards, and many films since 1962 onwards. One might expect that Bond would be an example of someone who breaks the rules of the organization in order to achieve its goals but, on reading the novels, it seems to me that the early Bond can be understood in a different way, as an 'organization man' (Whyte 1961). Bond is rather different from many of the spies and detectives who follow him from the late 1960s onwards in that he is an obedient employee. He is certainly an autonomous professional, a project worker granted a great deal of freedom over his work, but (in the novels) he very rarely makes any explicit or implicit criticism of his employers, and the threats he deals with are all external to the organization. Though Bond does begin to change as the films go on, in the novels and short stories published between 1953 and 1966, he is a model employee.

In *Diamonds are Forever*, published the same year as *The Organization Man*, Bond suggests that he couldn't marry a woman because he is already married to a man: 'Name begins with M. I'd have to divorce him before I tried marrying a woman' (DF, 194).[3] Bond and his boss are both loyal organization men, often opposed to other evil organizations – notably SMERSH and SPECTRE – but most of the time Fleming does not use this as a reason to characterize them as grey-flannel 'yes men'. In the novels, learning difficult skills, following rules, being an obedient worker are all presented as elements in a noble vocation. Within this form of thriller, 'one knows that eventually, through heroic effort, right will prevail and order will be restored' (Neuse 1982, 304). It seems to me that the 1950s Bond is a character who offers what Phil Cohen (1972/1997, 94), then a member of the CCCS, called a 'magical resolution' to the tensions between collectivism and individualism, which were later to become so stark in representations of spies and detectives, and of the world of work more generally. Comparing the novels to the Bond and other spy films allows us to see the contrast between the forms of obedience we find in the 1950s Bond – ironically working for an organization which is centrally concerned with conspiracies – with the thoroughgoing scepticism about organizations and their motives which begins in the 1960s and continues to the present day.

I think that the representations of organizations that we find in popular culture are useful ways of examining the changes and fractures in understandings of work and authority. Bond has changed a lot in sixty years. He begins as an obedient worker but nowadays has become an employee who is often critical of the means and ends of the organization that he works for, even to the extent of going 'rogue' to fulfil his mission. This, it seems to me, tells us something rather important about the ways in which work and organizations were understood in the 1950s, and then how they changed from the late 1960s onwards (Parker 2002b, 140 *passim*). Given our contemporary schizophrenia about the pleasures and horrors of work, trying to understand an era when organizations and employment were presented in some rather different ways shows how difficult it might be now to give our manager the affection, loyalty and obedience that Bond gives to his. I have a strange sense that much contemporary management theory and practice still assumes that it addresses the supposedly gullible and faithful 1950s employee, and that might explain why it so often produces cynicism and withdrawal.

It is worth emphasizing that I am not making claims about the actual practices of espionage organizations in the UK during that period (Hennessy 2003, Grey 2012), though it is clear that Fleming did base much of the content of the novels on his own experiences during the Second World War (Chancellor 2005, 26 *passim*). This chapter is about the representation of work within popular culture during a particular period so that we can understand just how much they have altered over the past half-century. I begin with some thoughts on theories of popular culture and ideas about organization, before moving on to discuss the Bond phenomenon and some of the ways in which it has been understood by cultural theorists. I then look at what the novels suggest about understandings of work and organizations in the 1950s before comparing that period to later Bonds. This involves thinking through some of the ways in which an understanding of historical context is crucial to thinking through the production and consumption of any text, whether about work and organizations, or anything else. I conclude with some thoughts on the impossibility of the Bond novels being written in the present age, a time when the boss has an MBA and the organization's motives are anything but noble.

Popular Culture and Work

The discipline of Management has become separated from the humanities and, more recently, from much of the social sciences too (Colby et al. 2011, Steyaert et al. 2016). Indeed, it could be argued that the invention and consolidation of any new discipline requires that it distinguishes itself – in terms of methodologies, terminology and social networks – from other disciplines, in order that it can claim novelty and carve out a place within the contemporary university. Concepts from sociology, anthropology, cultural studies and so on have become alien within the business school and, if imported, have often been simplified considerably. As we saw in Chapter 2, this is the case with the concept of 'culture', a central one in much thinking on the humanities and social sciences for two centuries. Until recently, the primary engagement between the disciplines of management and the study of culture was through the study of 'organizational culture' from the 1980s onwards (Parker 2000). Interesting though this work was, it effectively treated culture as if it were a set of shared beliefs held in an organizational container, and largely avoided discussions of how a local culture might be shaped by a more general anthropological sense of culture. At the other extreme, Hofstede's (1991) work on national cultures assumed a similarly shared set of values, but this time within the container of the nation state. Further, when the term 'culture' was employed within organization and management theory, it was also often assumed that the key respondents were managers, and that the lived culture of workers, or of culture more generally, was of little interest. Not exclusively, because there was some work which did take a more anthropological view of culture (Smircich 1983, Frost et al. 1991, Czarniawska 1992), but the dominant perspective on culture contained a strong emphasis on managers as the makers of meaning.

This was a view of culture which had long been eclipsed in other parts of the university. For the thinkers associated with CCCS in the 1970s, the study of culture was a search for the ways which dominant, preferred, or hegemonic meanings were always in contest with other understandings – those produced and consumed by the working class, women, ethnic minorities and so on (Hall and Jefferson 1976, Willis 1977, Hebdige 1979, Hall et al. 1980). This approach had two important consequences. One was to pay attention to the way in which 'readings' of cultural texts should not assume that the meaning of a text is immanent within it, and therefore to be offering readings that are sensitive to difference and contradiction. The second was to shift attention to texts that were previously considered to be of little interest because they originated within mass or (more positively) popular culture. 'High' cultural texts – literature, classical music, fine art – were eschewed in favour of pop music, magazines, street fashion and so on. This was a shift from an epistemological definition of culture, as Matthew Arnold's 'the best that had been thought and said', to an anthropological definition of culture, as the lived ways of life of a people (Williams 1976). So far so good, but the institutionalization of cultural studies from the 1980s onwards tended to produce an account of culture which mostly investigated leisure rather than work. The focus was on consumption rather than production, on culture as a category that did not include the economy. The work of popular culture, and the popular culture of work, was falling into a gap between two disciplines.

As we have seen, it was not until the 2000s that writers located in organization and management began to systematically explore the ways in which popular culture represented management, organization and the economy. The dominant assumption in this sort of work has been that cultural representations reflect social tensions, and do not merely ventriloquize shared meanings. However, in searching for various forms of 'critique in culture', there hasn't been a great deal of attention to the historical specificities of cultural production and consumption within particular eras. To put it simply, the popular culture of work has often been read as if the TV cartoon *The Simpsons*, the film *9 to 5*, or a pop song about working for the weekend all had meanings which could be harvested from the text by an attentive academic. Questions concerning the ambiguity of readings, the responses of different audiences, or historical changes in production and consumption have rarely been addressed, and it is this that I want to do with Bond.

James Bond

It seems pretty clear to me that there isn't one Bond. There are twelve novels and two short-story collections by Ian Fleming, but he died in 1964 and in the following half-century, Bond has appeared in every manifestation of popular culture. The first post-Fleming novel was *Colonel Sun*, written pseudonymously by Kingsley Amis and published in 1968. Since then, eight other authors have written 29 other authorized novels, or novelizations of films. There are also young Bond novels, three novels about his secretary Moneypenny, many short stories and countless books about the Bond universe, or various aspects of it (such as the 1997 collection of bridge-related stories, *Your Deal Mr Bond*) as well as books on the cars, posters, music and so on. There are also two TV adaptations and one cartoon series, at least six radio adaptations, 52 comic-strip series in English, and hundreds of comics about Bond and Bond Junior in English, Swedish, Spanish, Japanese, Dutch and so on. There are also a lot of video games, as well as board games, jigsaw puzzles, shoes, dolls, trading cards, lunch boxes, alarm clocks, toy cars, guns, briefcases, pyjamas, watches, model kits and rear-view spy glasses.[4] All this is before even mentioning the 24 'official' films and two unofficial ones, the oldest and one of the highest-grossing film series in cinema history.[5]

Given the multiplicity of cultural texts here, it simply isn't possible to say what Bond represents or means without being specific about which Bond is being referred to. The Bond of Ian Fleming's 1953 novel *Casino Royale* is only distantly related to the Bond of the 2021 film *No Time to Die*. There are certain similarities, but the differences are just as instructive. In an odd sense, we have a sort of longitudinal dataset here – a set of texts spread over nearly sixty years in which certain variables have been kept constant – a secret agent, M, sex and violence, and an evil opponent – but their treatment has altered considerably. The secretary who was largely invisible in the early novels becomes a sign of frustrated desire or maternal affection in the later novels and films, and finally a special agent in her own right in the most recent films. The racial and national stereotypes that are used to characterize the villains in the early books gives way to conspiracies which involve corporations, organized crime and terrorists. SMERSH, the imagined Soviet spy organization, is replaced in the novels by SPECTRE (Special Executive for Counter-intelligence, Terrorism, Revenge and Extortion) from *Thunderball* (1961) onwards, and from the first film – *Doctor No* (1962). In the novels, the conspiracies tend to be aimed at Britain; in the films, the targets are often American, or global. Also, and most importantly, M changes from being the object of Bond's adoration and loyalty, to someone whose motives and character are sometimes in question.

As an illustration of the topics and methods of contemporary cultural studies and the ways that they are employed within the humanities in general, work on Bond is fairly typical. There is a great deal of literature from the 1970s onwards,[6] and it tends to focus on gender, imperialism and consumption, as well as demonstrating certain methods for addressing cultural texts. In terms of the latter, Umberto Eco's 1979 essay 'Narrative Structures in Fleming' is exemplary in demonstrating what a structuralist semiotic reading of the novels might look like, showing how the stories reprise certain structures, character types and plot arrangements. For Eco, Bond is a text to be analysed in order to demonstrate certain formal techniques, but a great deal of the subsequent writing on Bond is concerned to establish Fleming/Bond's role in the production of problematic representations, not just texts to be analysed. So, we have readings which are concerned with the misogynistic and often violent representations of women; masculine anxieties about technology, the body and power; Fleming's profoundly snobbish accounts of consumption, class and etiquette; the tourist gaze and the beginning of international air travel; the casually racist stereotypes of anyone who isn't white and British; a British Cold War ideology combined with a desperate attempt to recapture the powers of Empire and so on (Cawelti and Rosenberg 1987, South and Held 2006, Winder 2006, Chapman 2007, Lindner 2009). These analyses are often fascinating, but (Chapman apart) they rarely take Bond's historicity very seriously, and even more rarely consider Bond as an employee. Putting it simply, I don't think that we would find the 1950s Bond credible anymore, in part because he is such an obedient organization man.

Before I continue, it's worth noting that novels and films are not the same. The intricacies of plot and character that a 200-page novel can build cannot be replicated in a 100-minute film, and the 'action' film genre is defined by certain visual effects and sequences which to some extent also determine plot and character. It is difficult not to present a spectacular Bond in a popular film, a form of cultural production that avoids banality and stillness. However, it seems to me that for certain purposes we can treat the technology of representation (novel or film) as a container for its contents, as what Latour calls an intermediary rather than a mediator (2005, 40). This isn't an argument that will always be convincing, but with the Bond corpus, we have sixty years of representations of one particular form of work, and it is the changes of representation over time that I want to focus on, so I will bracket the shaping effects of the different technologies which have been employed to describe Bond's world.

Novels and Work

It is easy to forget that the Bond novels are about work. Not in the same world-weary way as later spy fiction – such as that by Len Deighton, Grahame Greene, or John le Carré (Cawelti and Rosenberg 1987, Denning 1987, 35, 101; Neuse 1982) – but Bond is clearly working. He arrives at 'that deadly office building near Regent's Park' (CR, 5), 'the gaunt high building' (LD, 11) to experience 'the grudging warmth of the hissing gas fire in his office' LD, 35). *Thunderball* begins with him complaining about 'More than a month of paper-work – ticking off his number on stupid dockets, scribbling minutes that got spikier as the weeks passed, and snapping down the telephone when some harmless section officer tried to argue with him. And then his secretary had gone down with the flu and he had been given a silly, and, worse, ugly bitch from the pool who called him "sir" and spoke to him primly through a mouth of fruit stones. And now it was another Monday morning' (T, 2). The novels contain realistic signed and dated memos and appendices (CR, 8 *passim*), and they often begin with paperwork and corridors and offices. We learn that Bond is paid £1,500 a year, 'the salary of a Principal Officer in the Civil Service', as well as an extra £1,000 tax free. He goes on missions two or three times a year, and has office hours between ten and six (M, 8). In the novels, we meet some of his colleagues – the annoying Armourer, Major Boothroyd; the officious Paymaster Captain Troop; Bill Tanner, the amiable Chief of Staff, and of course M, whom we will return to shortly.

One of the ways in which Bond's work is represented as boring is because it is full of women – the 'desirable Miss Moneypenny' (LLD, 12; G, 50), Loelia Ponsonby and Mary Goodnight, his two secretaries and various other unnamed women who 'carry the files, operate the decoders, oversee the paperwork, screen the appointments, and supply the canteen services which keep the institution running. Headquarters hums with efficient women … ' (Bold 2009, 207). At his Chelsea flat is May Maxwell, his loyal and elderly Scottish housekeeper. Though some of these women are desirable, in a casual way, they are all safe and sensible. For Bond, this means boredom, and perhaps even capture, since (as M tells him) women 'hang on your gun-arm' (RL, 105). So, the novels often begin with tedium – with 'The Soft Life' (RL, 95) of being stuck at a desk, but the real story begins when Bond is rescued by an exciting mission that usually sees him catching a plane from 'London Airport' to somewhere exotic the next day.

He is still working then of course, having been given a tough 'job' by M. Sometimes he is also pretending to be a member of a different organization, a salesman for 'Universal Exports',[7] the cover employed by the Service. And it is then that he comes up against other organizations, sometimes commercial fronts for the villains, but usually bankrolled by SMERSH and SPECTRE. Both are again represented through realistic memoranda, and frequent hints at the complex forms of secrecy which underpin their plans. The opening chapters of *From Russia with Love* show us the SMERSH bureaucracy, the 'cold, brilliant efficiency of the Soviet machine' (RL, 21). In *Thunderball*, SPECTRE announces its intentions by means of a particularly wordy extortion threat that reads like it had been repeatedly edited by company lawyers.

The villains themselves are always physically monstrous, foreign, not sexually normal, cruel and greedy but each has 'exceptional inventive and organizational qualities which help him to acquire immense wealth' (Eco 1979/2009, 40 *passim*; see also Amis 1965, 65). Crucially, it is their ability to scheme which makes them somehow inhuman, as if such cool rationality were itself enough to provoke suspicion. It seems that 'the size and sophistication of the various criminal organizations mirror the size and sophistication of their criminal conspiracies'. There is often a secret base, 'a space to accommodate not only the ranks of sub-villains, thugs, saboteurs, and assassins, but also the string of torture-chambers, holding cells, laboratories, and nerve centres' (Lindner 2009, 82). Indeed, the sub-villains themselves exemplify the pathology of obedience, with their ant-like dedication to the cause[8].

Bond's organization is different. The Service values more than mere adherence to the plan. It fights against the cerebral and amoral machinations of the enemy with character – bravery, steadfastness and pluck:

> To the typical qualities of the Villain are opposed the Bond characteristics, particularly Loyalty to the Service, Anglo-Saxon Moderation opposed to the excess of the half-breeds, the selection of Discomfort and the acceptance of Sacrifice opposed to the ostentatious Luxury of the enemy, the genial improvisation (Chance) opposed to the cold Planning which it defeats … .
> *(Eco 1979/2009, 43)*

Eco's point is echoed by General Vozdvishensky of SMERSH when he considers the motivations of British spies, and the paradox of their excellence:

> 'Their agents are good. They pay them little money – only a thousand or two thousand roubles a month – but they serve with devotion […] They are rarely awarded a decoration until they retire. And yet these men and women continue to do this dangerous work. It is curious. It is perhaps the Public School and University tradition. The love of adventure. But still it is odd that they play this game so well, for they are not natural conspirators.
> *(RL, 42)*

Bond, and the rest of them, seem to succeed despite the lack of formal rewards and punishments within the organization. Instead they have 'character', a form of intrinsic motivation which is more valuable than the explicitly strategized clockwork of the enemy's schemes.

The character of M is important here, because it is through M that Bond's relationship to the Service is most clearly revealed: 'There was a creak from M's chair and Bond looked across the table at the man who held a great deal of his affection and all his loyalty and obedience. The grey eyes looked back at him thoughtfully. M took the pipe out of his mouth' (DF, 13). In the books, M is generally the unquestioned object of Bond's admiration, a shrewd father-figure with a background in the Navy who continually plays with his pipe: 'M's face was suddenly friendly. It wasn't friendly often. James Bond felt a quick warmth of affection for this man who had ordered his destiny for so long, but whom he knew so little' (LT, 27).

Kingsley Amis, in his *James Bond Dossier*, parodies Bond's observation of M's 'shrewd, healthy, hard, frosty, damnably clear eyes' (1965, 74). Amis tells us that, in the twelve books, M's 'demeanour or voice is described as abrupt, angry (three times), brutal, cold (seven times), curt, dry (five), frosty (two), gruff (seven), hard (three), impatient (seven), irritable (two), moody, severe, sharp (two), short (four), sour (two), stern and testy (five) ... ' (ibid., 75). M is hard to please, and refuses sentimentality, but Bond is always waiting for his call in order to escape from the soft life. He obeys M, sometimes cursing and resentful, but always does what he asks. Even when M, in the short story 'For Your Eyes Only' (1960), gives him an obviously off-the-books assignment to avenge the murder of one of M's friends, Bond obeys.

Obedience to M is a duty, a personal compulsion that reflects 'a certain moral force, an obstinate fidelity to the job – at the command of M, always present as a warning' (Eco 1979/2009, 37). Bond does serve the organization, the 'Service', but his allegiance is an intentional stubbornness, a choice to accept and live by certain rules: 'It's a confusing business but if it's one's profession, one does what one's told' (CR, 59). The novels present a world of obedience to organizations, both good ones and bad ones. The only difference appears to be whether that obedience is chosen for honourable reasons. In *You Only Live Twice*, after describing the Japanese practice of ON, or 'face', Dikko Henderson, Bond's local guide, says, 'Got it? It's not really as mysterious as it sounds. Much the same routine as operates in big corporations, like ICI or Shell, or in the Services, except with them the ladder stops at the Board of Directors or the Chiefs of Staff' (LT, 39).

James Chapman suggests that we can understand Bond as a 'middle-grade civil servant' (2007, 29, borrowing a line from Kingsley Amis 1965, 11). He is a skilled and trained professional who makes calculated choices, and follows an ethic of duty. This supposedly contrasts with the ruthless bureaucrats of SMERSH and SPECTRE, mere tools within authority structures. In *From*

Russia with Love, Bond admires the joyful enthusiasm of his Turkish contact Kerim Darko, and contrasts him to the deracinated planners of SMERSH. Perhaps, he thinks, 'the right man was better than the right machine' (RL, 154).

Fleming's Bond is conventional, and the political views he expresses are those of a *Daily Mail* middle Englander railing against the 'permissive mushiness of Welfare England' (Landa 2006, 91). In *You Only Live Twice* (1964), Tiger Tanaka, a Japanese secret service agent, drunkenly rants about the Suez Crisis of 1956, and then goes on to complain to Bond that

> ... your governments have shown themselves successively incapable of ruling and have handed over the country to the trade unions, who appear to be dedicated to the principle of doing less and less work for more money. This feather-bedding, this shirking of an honest day's work, is sapping at ever-increasing speed the moral fibre of the British, a quality the world once so much admired.
>
> *(LT, 80)*

Bond roars with laughter, and suggests that Tanaka write a letter to *The Times*. In the books, Bond is no freethinker, no 1930s dilettante secret agent driven by ideas of justice, but neither is he a sociopath who dispenses judgement. Kingsley Amis contrasts him to a contemporaneous literary creation, Mickey Spillane's Mike Hammer, a violent American PI. In *One Lonely Night* (1951), Hammer muses, 'I lived to kill because my soul was a hardened thing that revelled in the thought of taking the blood of the bastards who made murder their business ... I was the evil that opposed other evil, leaving the good and the meek in the middle to live and inherit the earth!' (quoted in Amis 1965, 29). Most of the time, Bond simply lacks such imagination, leaving it to the villains, in this case Blofeld, to characterize him best of all.

> You are a common thug, a blunt instrument wielded by dolts in high places. Having done what you are told to do, out of some mistaken idea of duty or patriotism, you satisfy your brutish instincts with alcohol, nicotine and sex while waiting to be dispatched on the next misbegotten foray.
>
> *(LT, 192)*

Bond does (very occasionally) reflect, in *Casino Royale* (134 *passim*) for example, but such introspection is rare. After some mournful bed-bound self-doubt following a bruising encounter with the villain Le Chiffre, he is chastised by his colleague Mathis and told – 'don't let me down and become human yourself. We would lose such a wonderful machine' (CR, 139). The culmination of this first novel, with the death of his treacherous lover at the hands of SMERSH, clearly marks the end of his doubts about his occupation. It is a position he often enough restates, in *Moonraker*, for example: 'There must be no regrets. No false sentiment. He must play the role which she expected of him. The tough man of the world. The Secret Agent. The man who was only a silhouette' (M, 246).

After the Novels

Fifty years of films, and all the other cultural products, tend to conceal the novels nowadays, and in any case, the Bond we know has gradually changed, becoming more an action hero and less a self-effacing public servant. Moneypenny – with the cups and saucers kept in her office – flirts more and more desperately in the earlier films (Brabazon 2009, Stock 2009) and then later transforms into a secret agent in her own right. M becomes an increasingly 'fuddy-duddy Establishment figure', less threatening and more blustering (Bennett and Woollacott 1987, 34). His office is staged with framed paintings of tall sailing ships, a model of a ship in a glass cabinet, replica cannons, busts of historical figures, thick green curtains, a globe, and old telescope and antique maps (Stock 2009, 252). When M is finally played by a woman in 1995, her office is marked by a '90s modernism – black leather chairs and vertical blinds, as well as a much more combative relationship with Bond.

These markers of social change are interesting, but the most important difference between the novels and the films is the extent to which Bond finds himself at odds with the Service itself. He comes late to this position because cops and detectives had often become outlaws and vigilantes from the early 1970s onwards (Sparks 1996, 353; Chapman 2007, 129, 211). Beginning perhaps with *Dirty Harry* (1971), the dominant motif is that the law enforcer has to break the rules of the organization in order to bring justice to the lawless. *Dirty Harry* was followed by four sequels, and its themes were echoed in other film series like *Death Wish, Lethal Weapon, Die Hard,* Jason Bourne films and so on. These are anti-organization films, narratives in which conspiracies mean that the institutions of law and justice cannot be trusted, that bosses let you down and nothing is what it seems: 'Many of these films seem to imply a failure of politics as such: there is a vacuum, into which the hero must step, motivated not by profession, duty or patriotism but rather by his purely personal and familial bonds, or by a still more basic instinct for survival ... ' (Sparks 1996, 356).

Though Bond did threaten resignation in the 1969 *On Her Majesty's Secret Service* (an echo of some musings in the novel), it is not until *The Living Daylights* of 1987 that he refuses to kill someone, before eventually going rogue in the 1989 *License to Kill*. Clearly getting a taste for his new-found independence, in *Die Another Day* (2002), he is suspended, then reinstated, with the same again happening in SPECTRE (2015).

The film Bond, slowly and hesitantly, becomes the 'lawless hero' who raises some very contemporary questions about the relationship between

'law' and 'justice', between 'institutions' and 'freedom' (Forster 2006, 126).
Yet his roots are in a different time, and reflect some different assumptions.
The Bond books occupy an unusual period, one in which the activities of the
business organization seem to have been regarded as relatively benign. This
contrasts with representations from before the Second World War, a world
of films like *Metropolis* and *Modern Times*, of organizational gothic like *The
Castle* and *Brave New World* and sparkling-eyed criminals who steal from
the rich (Parker 2002b, 136–140, 2012, 113 *passim*). As Penzler puts it:

> The impoverished multitudes blamed the actions of Wall Street brokers,
> bankers, big businessmen and factory owners for their plight, so what
> could be more attractive than to see someone break into their posh
> apartments and crack their safes, or nick the diamond necklaces from the
> fat necks of their bloated wives?
>
> *(Penzler 2008, xi)*

Using Eric Amber and Graham Greene's spy fiction from the 1930s as his
illustrations, Michael Denning shows how business was often used as the
origin of the problem that the amateur sleuth needs to solve: 'Cator and
Bliss', 'Pan-Eurasian Petroleum' and the 'Eurasian Credit Trust' for Ambler,
and 'Midland Steel' and the 'Beneditch Colliery Company' for Greene
(Denning 1987, 74 *passim*). In the 1950s, Fleming appears to be writing
during a moment in which such criticisms had become rather muted, a world
in which the organization was a backdrop for romance in films, or the source
of material wealth and scientific expertise (Parker 2002b, 140–142). Work
might be boring, and there might be stupid bosses and irritating colleagues,
but the legitimacy of the organization itself was not in doubt. The system had
worked, and the armies and factories of the Allies had defeated the fiendish
schemes of the enemy.

Denning suggests, borrowing some ideas from Frederic Jameson, that it
isn't until the 1970s that capitalism once again becomes 'figurable' in the
person of the multinational corporation. At that point, 'capitalism becomes
objectified and dramatized as an actor and as a subject of history with an
allegorical intensity and simplicity that had not been the case since the 1930s'
(Denning 1987, 74). Simultaneously, representations of work then become
much more ambivalent, with threats just as likely to come from within the
organization as outside it. The spy novels from this later period, such as those
by John le Carré, Len Deighton, and Grahame Greene again, become 'cover
stories of white-collar work, of the organization man' (ibid. 1987, 117).
Denning quotes Greene, speaking of his 1978 novel *The Human Factor*:

> My ambition after the war was to write a novel of espionage free from
> the conventions of violence, which has not, in spite of James Bond, been

a feature of the British Secret Service. I wanted to present the Service unromantically as a way of life, men going daily to the office to earn their pensions, the background much like any other profession – whether the bank clerk or the business director – an undangerous routine, and within each character the more important private life.

(Denning 1987, 130)

The novel itself is a story of betrayal, of secrecy and paranoia within the organization. Within the spy genre, these themes become dominant from the 1970s onwards, with le Carré's George Smiley series being perhaps the best example (Cawelti and Rosenberg 1987, 156 *passim*). This is what Neuse, following Palmer (1979), calls the transition from 'thriller' to 'negative thriller'. If the protagonist in the former overcomes obstacles to maintain the organizational status quo, then the latter recognizes that 'the hero's own organizational system is an impediment to the resolution of the conspiracy' (Neuse 1982, 297). Bond's loyalty to M's clear blue eyes really does begin to look anachronistic compared to 'the deeper, more critical tale where the real enemy is the organization itself, the organization that never keeps faith, the organization that betrays its own men' (Denning 1987, 140). This, it seems to me, is the world that we live in now, a world in which management and organization are understood to be the generators of conspiracy, not the solution.

Figuring Work

Drew Moniot, in 1976, outlined a broadly functionalist explanation for the first decade of Bond films, suggesting that what he called 'formula' culture has similarities with other rituals which allow for a structure for excitement, suspense and release. The highly choreographed arrangement of events in the films allows for a temporary and fantastic resolution of the frustrations and tensions of everyday life (Moniot 1976, 29). So far this looks like an argument based on assumptions about social integration, but Moniot then adds something rather more interesting. He notes that the films also concern themselves with the 'Corporate State', with the crime syndicates which hide behind the facades of factory and office complexes: – *Goldfinger*'s 'Auric Enterprises' (1964), the 'Osato Chemical Corporation' in *You Only Live Twice* (1967), the 'Institute of Physiological Research' in *On Her Majesty's Secret Service* (1969) and the Willard Whyte empire in *Diamonds are Forever* (1971). In the first film, *Dr No* (1962), Julius No's bauxite mine is 'but a microcosm of the organization, syndicate, call it what you will' which aims at 'ultimate control, complete, all powerful, of the world … and beyond'. Behind the corporate-industrial, Moniot suggests, lies evil and greed (ibid., 30). And the Bond of the films also works for an organization like this,

Universal Exports, with its unassuming exterior, and an interior of desks, files, secretaries, bureaucracy and a boss figure in his office: 'The structure of both organizations is that of the Corporate State. The difference lies not in the structure of the system but rather in the ultimate objectives and the means employed in attaining those objectives' (ibid., 31). Moniot concludes that Bond's job is to get rid of pathological characters, not to change the system itself. It's a message is a comforting and conservative one, that 'the existing social system could still be cleaned up rather than being discarded' (ibid., 32).

Moniot's argument interests me because of what it misses out – the novels. In fact, there are very few named corporations in the novels themselves, but more and more in the films. As well as Moniot's examples, we can add 'Stromberg Shipping' in the 1977 *Spy Who Loved Me*, 'Zorin Industries' in *View to a Kill* (1985), the 'Carver Media Group Network' in *Tomorrow Never Dies* (1997), 'King Industries' in *The World is not Enough* (1999) and so on. Chapman is unconvinced by Moniot's presentation of the anti-corporate Bond, suggesting that the idea of the individual against a machine-like organization was not new in the 1960s, and mentions Chaplin's *Modern Times* (1936) as an example (Chapman 2007, 97). Chapman is right of course, but his example comes from an earlier time. What Moniot's analysis of the films allows us to distinguish is that the Bond novels come from a very particular period, one in which the machine organization (SMERSH, SPECTRE) was seen to be an external threat, whilst the 'home' organization was a force for good. It is not until the films in the 1960s that the corporation begins to be 'figured' as a potential threat in the Bond Universe at all, and even then it can be countered by the daring of one loyal man supported by a professional team.

The other part of Moniot's analysis suggests that the films supply a fantastic resolution to the tensions of everyday life. His suggestions largely stay at the level of the individual gratifications that might be gained from being a spectator of a Bond-formula film, but a more social analysis of cultural texts is perfectly possible too. Phil Cohen (1972/1997) suggested that culture could be understood as an imaginative response to social tensions and contradictions. This is a development of anthropologist Claude Lévi-Strauss's definition of myth in pre-industrial societies, as a form of thought which 'progresses from the awareness of oppositions towards their resolution' (Lévi-Strauss 1963, 224). It is latent, in the sense that the participants in such imaginings do not *necessarily* connect their fantasies with the social conditions that generated them. But then, by definition, the meaning of fantasy cannot be manifest. If its cause and aim were clear to all who produced and consumed it, it would no longer be fantastic. So Cohen's point is something to do with a certain sort of fantasy, but not a fantasy in the sense of ungrounded escapism, a castle in the air. Rather than running away, this was a fantasy that took everyday materials and reworked them into some sort of account that helped resolve them. Not solve them, because that would require social structural change, but to imagine a situation in which the injuries no longer hurt for a while.

The word 'magical' is important here, in the sense that it suggests a method for overcoming obstacles or contradictions by deploying powers and devices not commonly found in everyday experience. Fleming himself referred to his books as 'fairy tales for grown-ups' (Chancellor 2005, 100). Michael Denning (also a onetime member of CCCS) suggests that this element of the fantastic is a way in which we might understand the attraction of the spy genre as a whole. It is a 'cover story', a form of ideology which serves to glamourize ordinary white-collar work: 'the magical nature of the secret agent functions both as a wish-fulfilment, returning agency to a largely meaningless kind of work, and as an explanation of that work, a recognition of one's own lack of power' (Denning 1987, 35).

Denning wants us to think about the people who read spy fiction and suggests that it is largely the professional classes. So this is white-collar workers reading about white-collar work, or what Julian Symons has called a 'perfect pipe-dream figure for organization man' (in Denning 1987, 93). Spy fiction matters because

> … its focus on the world of espionage does not necessarily make it about spies. Rather the intelligence community serves as a shadowy figure for the social world of late capitalism where the opacities that surround human agency are cut through by projecting an essentially magical figure, the secret agent.
>
> *(Denning 1987, 29)*

The early British spies – Sapper's Bulldog Drummond, Buchan's Richard Hannay and so on – were gentlemen amateurs, bored with the routine of office and club. They escaped to spying as plucky improvisers who would set right particular wrongs. Bond, on the other hand, is a professional. He is trained by the organization, is subject to authority and orders, and suffers all the petty indignities that any office worker experiences. The only sense in which he continues an earlier amateur tradition is in his consumption habits, for particular cigarettes, suits, food, travel and so on. He is, as Landa suggests (2006) an 'aristocratic bourgeois', a character with aristocratic tastes and a bourgeois lifestyle.

The Bond of the novels is a splendid example of Cohen's magical resolution, in the sense of a character who is riven with contradictions (Cawelti and Rosenberg 1987, 154). He allows the professional to display amateur traits, to be cool and calculating at the same time as being passionately loyal and patriotic. For the male heterosexual reader, Bond can be a recognizable white-collar worker who idly fancies his secretary, but at the same time is a dangerous and sexually predatory rake who travels the world. Bond is both an obedient employee who does what he is told and an autonomous adventurer. The resolution is even captured in the phrase 'licensed to kill'. Bond is licensed, by some legitimate authority. He is not allowed to kill anyone, under any circumstances, and so is not a mere murderer, a psychopath. His killings are 'jobs', clearly justified in memos, licensed as necessary by a man with clear blue eyes. David Frum, writing about the cultural contradictions of the 1950s, suggests that 'Bond is simultaneously an organization man and an individualist. Above all, he can do wrong for a greater good without losing his moral bearings' (cited in Forster 2006, 124). The 00 section dispenses with legal procedure, allows Bond to kill people when other private citizens can't, and at the same time allows him ethical immunity. The law is somehow suspended, placed in a state of exception which allows it to both exist and disappear at the same time.

The Bond novels are not a simple vehicle for the communication of shared meanings, but a symptom of the anxieties of a particular time, particularly those about work;

> These stories permit the recognition of contradictions at the same time as they establish conventional ways of managing and resolving those contradictions. Thus a study of popular narratives has a purchase which the study of other recreations may not – for these narratives are not only *of* the culture but are *about* the culture.
>
> *(Denning 1987, 24; emphasis in the original)*

The novels came out at a time when a world war was barely two decades in the past, in a period when Britain's empire was crumbling, its industries were collapsing, and its 'great power' status was becoming a bitter joke (Winder 2006, 102). In a nice irony, after the Suez debacle, the then-PM Anthony Eden decided to have a holiday and ended up staying in 'Goldeneye', Fleming's home in Jamaica. He resigned a few months after his return, a symbol of the post-Imperial despair and longing that Fleming had crystallized in the magical figure of the secret agent. Bond's social attitudes, his casual racism and superhuman ability to defeat external threats can be contrasted with a Britain that was becoming an irrelevance; 'Bond in fact became in the 1960s pretty much the only British national capable of damaging anybody at all' (Winder 2006, 196).

Bond Now

Kingsley Amis was a fan of popular narratives, particularly science fiction. He was keen to defend Bond against the many who, from the late 1950s onwards, were accusing Fleming of writing fictions which were immoral, and even sadistic. The reviewers have never much liked Bond. Amis accepts

Bond's vices, but also points to his virtues: 'Some things are regarded as good: loyalty, fortitude, a sense of responsibility, a readiness to regard one's safety, even one's life, as less important than the major interests of one's organization and one's country' (Amis 1965, 85). This is a remarkably traditional set of characteristics for a killer, indeed a list which (perhaps sacrifice of life excepted) many professional employees would be happy to endorse as necessary for the performance of their occupation. Amis clearly finds Bond's 'concern to do his job, devotion to M and trust in M's judgment, personal obstinacy, plus finally the vaguest patriotism' much more attractive than the 'anguished cynicism and torpid cynicism respectively of Messrs le Carré and Deighton' (ibid. 94).

However, at the time of writing. Bond is not doing well. The last incumbent, Daniel Craig, reportedly said that he would 'rather slash [his] wrists' than make a fifth Bond film. He did of course, presumably because the contract was binding, or the money too good. The franchise continues to make money, though less than it used to, because cinema fantasy is now dominated by superheroes, conspiracy thrillers and science fiction. Bond can only become a contemporary action hero if he rejects being an organization man, if he refuses to obey M and believe in the rightness of the British Secret Service. Bond's gender and ethnicity are even more troubling for 'a character who was a cardboard throwback even in the 1960s ... a wall-eyed, traumatised thug, a protagonist who is two-dimensional precisely because he is empty inside' (Penny 2015, 31, see also Sparks 1996).[9] Yet, whatever the critics might say, and have been saying for half a century, the potential for magical resolution is still there;

> The dilemma of James Bond is a pantomime version of the dilemma facing most men who grew up watching the films and wondering what it would be like to be that guy, whom everybody seems to love not in spite of the awful things he does but because of them. In real life, anyone who behaved even slightly like James Bond would be ostracised, arrested, or both.
>
> *(Penny 2015, 31)*

As she knows, Laurie Penny is writing sixty years after the first Bond novel and her argument, like mine, is an attempt to historicize Bond. It seems to me that if we want to understand any cultural text, we need to situate it within particular moments of production and reception. If we try to set aside the differences between novels and films, then it becomes clear that the meaning of Bond has changed, and that it will continue to change. As Pierre Macherey rather beautifully observes, understanding culture involves understanding the conditions of its production and also its history: 'everything which has been collected on it, become attached to it – like shells on a rock by the seashore forming a whole incrustation' (in Woollocott 2009, 117). So reading Bond now is different to reading Bond then, something that needs to be remembered in the analysis of any cultural text, whether about organizations and management or anything else.

Ours is a world in which corporations and governments are assumed to lie, in which conspiracy and secrecy go hand-in-hand, and anxiety and insecurity are common experiences of working life. Representations of work are always shadowed by such assumptions, with even 'good' occupations – doctors, the police – often are entangled in Machiavellian plots. The Bond of the novels reminds us of a time when formal organizations might have been imagined to be sites for some sort of authenticity and salvation, even those organizations that were centrally involved in conspiracies. The characters and plots show us that the Service will save us from the evil schemers of SMERSH and SPECTRE, and that men at desks can also be men of action. It's a moment that is difficult to recover now, when even Bond goes rogue and doesn't shave on occasion.[10] George Smiley's 'Circus' captures the labyrinthine gothic of contemporary organizations rather more effectively. Indeed, his author, John le Carré, makes this into a timeless diagnosis of the human condition:

> I think all of us live partly in a clandestine situation. In relation to our bosses, our families, our wives, our children, we frequently affect attitudes to which we subscribe perhaps intellectually but not emotionally. We hardly know ourselves – nine-tenths of ourselves are below the level of the water [...] So the figure of the spy does seem to me to be almost infinitely capable of exploitation for purposes of articulating all sorts of submerged things in our society.
>
> *(in Bruccoli and Baughman 2004, 36)*

Fleming, in Bond's mock obituary at the end of *You Only Live Twice*, allows M to allude to the 'series of popular books ... written by a personal friend and former colleague' as 'high-flown and romanticized caricatures of episodes in the career of an outstanding public servant' (LT, 202). It's a self-effacing dismissal of the popular, the romantic, as if culture had very little to say about the sorts of lives that people actually live in organizations. I don't agree. I think that we can learn much from popular books, and popular culture generally, and in the case of Bond, what we catch is a glimpse into a moment in British understandings of the organization man and the redemptive possibilities of work. The relationship between Bond and M, between loyal employee and gruff but kindly father-figure, is simply no longer credible, and this is a conclusion which is both realistic and tragic.

Notes

1 This chapter is based on (2018) 'Employing James Bond', *Journal of Management Inquiry* 27/2: 178–189.

2 Another nuance that I don't explore in this chapter is the positive representation of belonging and criminal organizations, see Parker 2012.

3 The Bond novels I have cited are all the 2004 Penguin Classics editions. The key is as follows, CR – *Casino Royale* (1953), DF – *Diamonds are Forever* (1956), DN – *Dr No* (1957), G – *Goldfinger* (1959), LLD – *Live and Let Die* (1954), LT – *You Only Live Twice* (1964), M – *Moonraker* (1955), RL – *From Russia with Love* (1957), T – *Thunderball* (1961).

4 Moniot quotes someone calling this the 'Bondanza', and gives more examples of early merchandise (Moniot 1976, 26). See also Chapman 2007, 92.

5 And this is also without mentioning the way that Bond explicitly or implicitly functions as a reference point or counter point in other literary spy fictions, such as that by Frederick Forsyth, Desmond Bagley and Len Deighton; other spy films and TV series such as the Harry Palmer, George Smiley or Jason Bourne; parodies such as the Flint, Matt Helm, Austin Powers and Johnny English film series; TV shows such as *The Avengers*, *The Man from U.N.C.L.E.* and so on (see Moniot 1976).

6 Much of it being characterized by weak Bond-related puns for titles, subheadings, or concluding sentences.

7 Changed to the 'Transworld Consortium' in *The Man with the Golden Gun* (1965). Peter Hennessy notes that there was a secret committee charged to investigate the possibility and consequences of nuclear attack on Britain in 1950. It was titled the 'Imports Research Committee' (2003: xix).

8 For some thoughts on the HR implications of being a henchman for a supervillain, see Winder 2006, 232, and several scenes in the 1997 parody *Austin Powers: International Man of Mystery*.

9 Oddly, Fleming himself referred to Bond as a 'cardboard booby' (Chancellor 2005, 101).

10 Land et al. (2014) make the convincing argument that the 'rogue' (their example is the trader) is a figure who marks the grey zone within which behaviour is no longer either good or bad. Adapting their argument, I suggest that the appearance of the rogue marks a legitimation crisis for the organization, so the rogue lawman brings the law into question.

PART V

Movement

12

SHIPPING CONTAINERS

In 2009–10, the Polish artist Miroslaw Balka constructed a gigantic box for the Turbine Hall in the Tate Modern Gallery London and called it 'How It Is'. A metal ramp leading up to a metal box containing blackness. 13 by 13 by 30 metres, on 2 metre high stilts. 390 square metres of nothing reflecting the steel frame of a five-storey hall of nothing which used to be a power station on the banks of the Thames. The comments of those who wrote about it suggested that it was a gas chamber, a cattle truck, a place to hold the stalking shadows of those who had already gone in. It was a sensory deprivation tank producing claustrophobia, holding the unknown, making people disappear. It was Balka's reference to concentration camps and the industrialization of the world. It was art, because it was in the Tate, but it was just a metal box. A box that could swallow you, contain you, and cover you in darkness.

Roberto Saviano's extraordinary book about the Camorra crime families of Naples begins with a section on the port. The Bausan and Flavio Giola docks had about 150,000 shipping containers per year moving though in the mid-2000s:

Everything that exists passes through here. Through the port of Naples. There's not a product, fabric, piece of plastic, toy, hammer, shoe, screwdriver, bolt, video game, jacket, pair of pants, drill or watch that doesn't come through here. The port of Naples is an open wound. The end point for the interminable voyage that merchandise makes. Ships enter the gulf and come to the dock like babies to the breast, except that they're

DOI: 10.4324/9781032714288-17

here to be milked, not fed. The port of Naples is the hole in the earth out of which what's made in China comes.

(Saviano 2008, 4)

Saviano describes one container breaking free of its crane, lurching wildly in the air as the doors break open and the frozen bodies of Chinese women, men and children fall down onto the concrete where they break on the ground. They were identifiable only by tags around their necks, migrant workers who had died in Italy and wished to be buried back in China. After being stuffed back into their container, they went on their way. Containers can contain anything.

Both these stories are about containers, but somehow not contained by them. The dimensions of the box are not sufficient to explain what the box does. The paradox of the shipping container is that its standardization is commonly argued to have led to the rationalization of global trade, but it has also allowed for the production of art, crime, housing and the repatriation of dead migrant labour. The story of the mundane intermodal container is one of capitalism and control but also the production of excess and danger. Containers, as a mobility-system (Urry 2007), can produce complex and paradoxical effects. As materials, they are in a moving relation with heterogeneous and multiple spaces, always being entangled in trajectories that make new relations. As Doreen Massey claims of space – 'it is always in the process of being made. It is never finished, never closed.' (2005, 9). So it is, I would claim, with the container. Its sameness makes difference, its security manufactures danger and its plenty produces emptiness. That is to say, a simple account of the economics and technology of the container can't manage to capture so much of the other baggage that the container carries.

This chapter[1] uses the container to show how economics produces culture, and vice versa, again demonstrating that any form of organization always simultaneously disorganizes (Cooper 1986). Mobility systems are never one dimensional, never super flat, but always complex entanglements of 'physical, informational, virtual and imaginative forms' (Hannam et al. 2006). I want to demonstrate this through a mode of writing which partly captures an object, but then unfolds it to multiple possibilities. Thinking is a form of containerization too, and I want to open the cabinet as much as possible. Beginning with the standard account of the importance of containerization, I then undo it by a focus on the aporias, or contradictions, which the container has produced. This involves attending to the huge number of ways in which the container has come to mean and be something else – a house, a bomb, a quiet stillness, an artwork. Their seeming sameness conceals huge differences. Concerns about security have produced paranoia, the plenty they promise is predicated on emptiness, and the economic rationalism they symbolize has mutated into a huge range of cultural representations. Finally, I consider just what sort of 'container theory' might be required to understand the container as a box which can't be boxed. An account of rationalization, standardization and economics can never explain our fear of darkness, or just why someone would pay for their frozen body to be shipped back to China. Neither can it account for the complex ways in which one mobility system has moved ports to new moorings, as well as opening the possibility of filling art galleries, and academic books.

8x8x20/40

The most widely travelled story about containers goes like this. In 1937, Malcom McLean was waiting for his truck to be unloaded at a New Jersey pier, when he realized it would be more efficient to load the entire truck body onto the ship. McLean went on to found a shipping container line, and the dimensions of the box went on to reconfigure the world. Lorries, ships, ports, cranes, trains, products and people all become tessellated into a system which we now call globalization. But Marc Levinson, in his definitive history of the container (2006), claims that this Archimedean moment never happened. There is no evidence for it, and plenty of examples of containerized transport in many different countries before 1937. He thinks that McLean just needed to tell a story when someone asked him where the idea came, but that innovation rarely begins like this, with a single idea in someone's head. Nonetheless, Levinson agrees that McLean was centrally responsible for the dissemination of containerization. This was because he was a businessman who saw that the problem was efficient movement of materials. It wasn't a problem about owning ships, or driving lorries, or making dockers work harder, or ports getting bigger, but just about the organization of mobility, of moving stuff from here to there. As Philips-Birt put it when the system was still in its infancy:

> … the logic and inherent virtue of the container system, and its economic merit, can only be derived from the through-transport concept involving pure container ships with the terminal arrangements reaching far inland. The revolution so caused is initially one of organization rather than naval architecture.'
>
> *(Philips-Birt 1970, 87)*

Everything else was secondary to organization – to the equations of speed, weight and money. Everything else would fall into line.

It was on 26 April 1956, according to all the books on containerization (Broeze 2002, Cudahy 2006, Donovan and Bonney 2006, Levinson 2006) that the modern world began to become organized in a different way. Malcom McLean's converted tanker *Ideal-X* sailed from Newark, New

Jersey with 58 aluminium truck bodies on board. In the next fifty years, space and time begin to reconfigure because many things can be made anywhere, and things can be made from things that come from all over the place. Established ports are either rebuilt or decline if they don't have the land, frontage, cranes and transport links to ensure rapid movement of containers. The congested waterfronts of New York, London and Baltimore emptied, and then many (like Albert Dock in Liverpool) are gradually turned into expensive flats and offices for knowledge and creative industries with art galleries next door. New ports remake the economic geography of nations and regions, and factories move to national and global locations where they can take maximum advantage of declining transport costs and the new markets which are opening up. Manufacturing doesn't need to happen near the port anymore, and the port doesn't need to be anywhere in particular as long as they have space and links to the container mobility system, such as the movement from London Docks to Felixstowe in Suffolk in the late 1960s. Operations research and Enterprise Resource Planning systems solve supply-chain scheduling problems and mean that the movements of things and money can be tightly coordinated (Neilson and Rossiter 2010, Holmes 2011), even down to the way that containers are packed, and the order in which they are placed on and taken off ships. According to Holmes, in 2005, Wal-Mart imported 350,000 containers to the US, almost 30,000 tons of material a day. Factories and big box retailers are now able to construct just-in-time systems and keep their inventory costs down, leading to the increasing interdependence of logistics and manufacturing organizations and global supply chains which make assembly into a stage of production which can take place wherever is most profitable.

The reorganizations which produced the modern container port were not merely about ensuring that boxes were the same size. They also involved reconfiguring dock communities, and particularly the labour practices which had ensured predictable levels of employment and income in an industry which had unpredictable labour demands, a solidaristic culture and was beloved of industrial sociologists (Hill 1976, Turnbull and Wass 1994). Trade unions representing longshoremen, stevedores and dockers were often powerful, and they policed local bargaining arrangements as well as custom and practice. Agreements about men per pallet, men per hatch,[2] or the use of technology were defended because these were arguments about jobs, and also about families and communities. Most of the work involved hauling cargo with hooks and muscle, and since the cargo came in all shapes, sizes and weights, loading and unloading mixed ships was a complex and time-consuming operation. In 1954, the *SS Warrior* cargo ship travelling from Brooklyn to Bremerhaven contained 194,582 separate items – itemized as cases, cartons, bags, boxes, bundles, packages, pieces, drums, cans, barrels, crates, reels and so on (Levinson 2006, 33). Moving all these items was dangerous and physically exhausting, and various over-manning practices were justified on the grounds that rest was both deserved and required for the sake of safety. For example, in Liverpool, the 'welt' ensured that half of a gang was absent for a while (perhaps in a nearby pub) whilst the other half worked (ibid., 28). Stealing was also rife, with a long-standing sense of entitlement to goods which were easily moved out of the dock gates and sold on in the local (and usually poor) communities.

In addition, moving items from one mode of transport to another often came up against labour regulations which controlled the movement of materials – such as the New York 'public loader' system which essentially meant that particular piers could only be worked by certain union-backed associations, and that there were set rates for moving different sorts of cargo (Levinson 2006, 77–78). The enforcement of these arrangements was through union solidarity often enough backed by violence and organized crime. To make matters more complex for the shippers, various national and international institutions and arrangements also policed the competition and prices. Transport by road, rail and ship was often regulated by state bodies such as the US Interstate Commerce Commission to ensure that prices did not undercut each other too much, and that profits and employment remained stable. Cartels called 'conferences' established the terms of trade for international shipping, based on contracts which ensured that shippers only used conference vessels, or ran the risk of never being carried at all.

All these issues converged on the problem of the box itself. In the late 1950s, a container could mean many things. European models tended to be wooden crates about 4 feet tall, whilst the US Army used 'Conex' boxes 6 feet 10½ inches high:

> The Marine Steel Corporation, a New York manufacturer, advertised no fewer than 30 different models, from a 15-foot-long steel box with doors on the side to a steel frame container with plywood sides, 4½ feet wide, made to ship "five-and-dime" merchandise to Central America.
>
> (*Levinson 2006, 127*)

To make matters more complex, some containers had hooks on the top for cranes, some had slots in the bottom for forklifts, and there was no agreed system for stacking boxes or calculations about the weight they could hold either inside or as part of a stack. There was also no agreement on construction materials, rebating door hinges, or the design of hooks or spreaders.[3] This meant that cranes, boats, trains and trucks were also not standardized, and there was every possibility that the contents of a container would be need to be unloaded and stuffed into a new box to continue its onward journey. In which case, the shippers reasoned, what was the point of putting them into containers in the first place?

A host of organizations debated these issues from 1958 onwards (Levinson 2006, 127 *passim*). In the US, the Maritime Administration had established two committees, but was in regulatory competition with the American Standards Association. The ASA had created Materials Handling Sectional Committee 5, which in turn set up various subcommittees. Each different committee was being lobbied by companies which had already invested in ships with container cells of a particular dimension, or cranes capable of raising certain weights. Then the National Defense Transportation Association entered the debate, representing military cargo interests. After three years of discussions and changes of policy, 8x8 was agreed for height and width, with standard lengths of 10, 20, 30 and 40 feet. At this point, the problem became bigger, with the International Standards Organization (ISO) getting involved. The ISO Technical Committee 104 established three working groups and debated lifting and locking devices, many of which had already been patented by various shipping lines and container manufacturers. A decision on these was reached by 1965, followed by debates about maximum loads and stresses, consideration of end walls for rail cars, deck lashings, government subsidies for non-standard container ships, air containers and so on. By 1970, after 13 years of wrangling, and given considerable impetus by the US military wanting to move massive amounts of equipment to Vietnam, the ISO published the final draft of its standardized container specifications.

Since then, the dominant account goes, despite resistance from the dock communities, bankruptcies for companies which had invested in the wrong size technology, and huge spending on dock refurbishment which didn't always pay off, the containers swept all the market imperfections aside. The Twenty-foot Equivalent Unit (TEU) becomes a standard. The traditional labour arrangements just disappear as the dockers hang up their hooks when ships no longer call at their silent ports and instead pass by, square shapes on the horizon. The costs of transport continue to fall as a proportion of the product, including the costs of insurance, since commodities are no longer being stolen and damaged as often. States withdraw from the regulation of national and international transportation, and in some cases begin to withdraw from port ownership too. The conferences simply collapse as new shipping lines invest billions of dollars in huge new ships. The market is dominated by big conglomerates and big ships, such as the *MV Mærsk Mc-Kinney Møller*, which can move over 18,000 TEU. Mærsk now owns Malcom McLean's old company, Sea-Land, and there are no US firms in the top ten container shipping operators or builders. The biggest ship is now *MSC Irina*, built and owned in China, with a capacity of 24,346 TEU. These are barely ships any more, just big metal boxes for holding some of the 65 million containers in use, sliding without friction through a deregulated world.

This story of containerization is supposedly an account of the rationalization and standardization of the world. Globalization trades on the interchangeability of people, parts and processes. For market liberals like Thomas Friedman, this is an account of how the world was made flat, so that things could move more easily (2005). Most container movements are of 'intermediate goods' on their way to be assembled into something else, or disassembled in the rubbish dumps of the Global South. The competitive advantage of nations is no longer about proximity to the sea, natural resources, or climate, but costs of labour, rents for factories, government policies and transport links. China, Singapore, Korea, Japan become the new global hubs for trade, while the smaller ports of the Atlantic grow nettles and cranes rust. In 2009, six out of the ten busiest container ports were in China, with the largest post outside Asia being Rotterdam, in tenth place. The largest port was Singapore, which moved nearly 26 million TEU that year,[4] out of a global total of something like 465 million movements.

Waste is reduced, business is re-engineered and nautical sentiment gives way to calculations about speed. In Singapore, NYK Lines can now move a container from one ship to another in an hour (Cook and Oleniuk 2007, 141). So this is the dominant version of the history of the container, and it fits nicely with other accounts of the free market, the use of technology, and the importance of rationalized organization. It is an entirely unsurprising morality tale – roll back the frontiers of the state, automate or liquidate, and let management have the right to manage. It is a picture of a world in which standardization has reconfigured time and space, and profit is the only criteria for material and social organization. McLean's first container company – Pan-Atlantic – was managed by his sister Clara, who occupied a desk in the middle of the open-plan office in a converted warehouse in Newark:

> She knew who had come in late. She decorated the office: managers who were promoted into glass fronted offices of their own found that she had selected the furnishings for them, right down to the art. "If you put a picture or a calendar on the wall, you got a note from Clara the next morning," one recalled. She set the rules: coffee nowhere but the coffee room, no personal phone calls, desks cleared every night. She personally reviewed every single time card and approved every hire.
>
> *(Levinson 2006, 59)*

Clara has now been replaced by algorithms, but this obsession with control continues.

Four Aporias

Levinson, in his 350-page study of transport and innovation, is oddly dismissive about the container itself. 'What is it about the container that is so important? Surely not the thing itself. A soulless aluminium or steel box held together with welds and rivets, with a wooden floor and two enormous doors at one end: the standard container has all the romance of a tin can' (Levinson 2006, 1). To me, this seems too definitive a dismissal, because the container itself cannot be ignored so quickly. 'The thing itself', as Levinson nicely echoes, has actually become important in a huge variety of ways which can only be reduced to economics through an analysis which ignores much else. The container has come to mean and be very many different things, and has become entangled in many different relations. The story of containerization as standardization told by Levinson et al. is belied by all the ways in which the container cannot itself be contained.

In this section, I want to show how features of the intermodal container produce their opposites, just as steel produces rust, so does the can become uncanny. The container overflows or involutes and in doing so begins to trouble the neatness of a story that positions it as neatly stacked in an account of movement and exchange. Any form of organizing produces disorganization. The explication of the point in this particular case merely requires an attention to connections, and a curiosity about the wide variety of ways in which containers have been used to do something other than move products around in the ways determined by logistics programmes. Ideas about sameness, security, plenty and the logic of economics can be demonstrated to be empirically contested by difference, danger, emptiness and cultural mediation. This allows us to understand the box as a node from which 'there are always connections yet to be made, juxtapositions yet to flower into interaction [...] relations which may or may not be accomplished' (Massey 2005, 11). Let's begin with the very idea of standardization which is central to the Levinson et al. story.

Sameness and Difference

The key to the seamless tessellation of boxes was that they should come in standardized sizes, with uniform methods of construction and locking mechanisms which would allow them to be stacked. There are now many global standards which ensure that coordination between organizations and technologies can happen so the example of containers is not an unique one. Like the time standardization necessary for national railways (May and Thrift 2001), or the ISO 9000 quality management standard (Brunsson and Jacobsson 2002), the account here assumes that advanced mobility is predicated on eradicating difference. Yet the odd thing is that, in the containerization example, standardization doesn't actually appear to have happened, despite fifty years' work at the project.

For a start, containers are actually rather a small percentage of international trade. According to Roland (2007), two-thirds of the global economy is in services not things, and even out of those things the vast majority of cargoes are bulk. Indeed, only 8 per cent of shipping is containerized, and the fastest growing area of freight is by air, not ship, truck, or train. In empirical terms, the ubiquity of the metal box can easily be overstated, as can the idea that it has conquered time and space since, according to Roland, most countries still do most of their trade with their neighbours. We can also question the idea that containers are the most efficient way of moving the 3 per cent of global trade which is containerized. As Levinson himself acknowledges, the boxes might be the same size, but that doesn't stop there being different optimum sizes of load depending on market demands in particular places, or the physical obduracy of materials (2006, 129). Not everything fits neatly into 8x8x40. Making boxes for rubber ducks, motor bikes, models of container trucks and garden furniture usually involves making different sizes of boxes, and often enough placing those boxes into different size boxes and stacking them in different orientations and heights. This means that containers are rarely 'full', in the sense of there being no more space inside or outside the boxes in the box. Dockers with hooks would pride themselves on their skill in stuffing odd-shaped articles into unusual spaces, but this required that the pieces were heterogeneous to begin with. In fact, much empty space is being moved around by containers, space which is hidden by the tessellation of the boxes in the port and on the ship, but is there nonetheless. Unlike real Chinese boxes, these ones don't nest into each other that well.

It might be precisely because of the obduracy of materials that, when investigated, the 8x8x40 story doesn't really work that well as an empirical claim either. The TEU is not actually a consistent measure of space or cargo, more an approximation of the footprint of the box. Neither does it make any reference to other features of the container, which can be collapsible, a frame holding a gas bottle or tank, contain a generator, be insulated, open-top bulktainer for loose cargo, refrigerated, open sided for loading large pallets, ventilated, garmentainers for hanging clothing and so on. In addition, there are actually many different sizes of container in common use.[5] One of the oddities in Cook and Oleniuk's 2007 glossy book on the journeys of an NYK container appears on page 25, where we see a labourer 'cross-docking' from a 40-foot container to a 53-foot US truck trailer. Malcom McLean's dream of a liftable truck body seems not to have happened in the US, with 48- and 53-foot trucking containers still being standard. There are also alternative heights of container, with 'hi-cube' units at 9 feet 6 inches and 10 feet 6 inches, and 'half-height' containers at 4 feet 3 inches. It gets even more complex than this though, because some 'standard' containers are actually two inches wider to accommodate Euro-pallets, or the Australian RACE containers which accommodate Australia Standard Pallets. Further, the 45-foot-wide hi-cube shortsea container is becoming common in Europe, partly because it can be given legs to become a 'swap body' unit which can be moved between trucks without needing a crane. In the last decade, this has led to the European Intermodal Loading Unit initiative, the subject of an European Commission consultation paper in 2003 which attempted to deal with different sorts of locally specific transport logistics, such as canal barges, and more lately has led to two 'Marco Polo' initiatives intended to produce specifically European standards.[6]

The existence of different types and sizes of containers, and different regional standards, combined with the problems of making materials fit into boxes, begins to make the Levinson et al. story feel rather partial. The fact that all these measurements are made in imperial rather than metric makes the account of standardization even less convincing, given that the latter has a perfectly accepted unit of length which since 1960 has been internationally agreed under the *Systeme International d'Unites*. It might be that the older term 'Americanization' is actually more useful here, since that is the only major nation not to routinely use SI units. It works as an origin story if we add reference to the 1960s US and their military-industrial interests in Vietnam. Only then can we begin to see what 'standardization' actually means in the context of containers. This is a mobility system which has locally specific origins, and varies in detail across the globe.

But even then, so much escapes, largely because not only are many of these boxes different, but they are also put to a dizzying variety of uses. As materials, they seem to proliferate, producing variety, not similarity. When Malcolm McLean's Sea-Land company began routes to Puerto Rico in the late 1950s, they often 'lost' containers. This was because, identified as no more than boxes, they would be appropriated 'to be converted into shops, storage sheds, or homes' (Levinson 2006, 71). In the last fifty years, the flows of global trade now mean that some parts of the world have far too many boxes. Rather than being mobile, these are boxes which are quiet and still, waiting for a cargo which rarely arrives (Neilson and Rossiter 2010). Deficits of containers in China are caused by stockpiles in Oakland or Liverpool. Depending on the price of steel, it is often cheaper for exporting countries to make new containers than it is to ship the empty ones back again. So, like bits of global driftwood, they pile up and rust in the quieter parts of the world.

Supposedly predicated on continuous movement, they are given new life by being still, or moving episodically and outside the container mobility system. This has led to a huge variety of innovations with the use of containers for housing, office space, pop-up events and so on. The use of containers as riverside or dockland housing is probably the most common example, with a wide variety of developments now using the box frame in various combinations and heights. Using ideas which are similar to Le Corbusier's 'Dom-ino' boxes which could be multiplied in various combination, or Moshe Safdie's 'Habitat 67' project in Montreal, the container becomes an architectural component.

Its steel frame can be cut, welded, or stacked. Sides, floors and ceilings can be stripped, sliced, or clad. Windows and doors can be inserted, pitched roofs and verandas attached (Slawik et al. 2010). Examples are London's 'Container City' work/live developments, a theatre in South Korea, or minimal accommodation for students and migrant workers in the Philippines. The huge 'Seventh Kilometre' market near Odessa in the Ukraine, and the 'Four Tigers' market in Budapest are mostly made from containers. Brothels and prisons have been made from containers too (Broeze 2002, 273). The portable metal box becomes the Electric Hotel moving theatre, or a wide variety of mobile shops, art galleries, shopping malls, restaurants and cafes. Cost and mobility has also made it a good solution for rapid-build housing after a crisis – such as the work done at Auburn and Arkansas Universities after the Hurricane Katrina crisis in New Orleans,[7] or emergency health centres and kitchens.

Unsurprisingly, given the importance of the container to the logistics of Vietnam, the ISO container is now widely used in military contexts. The US military used containers to hold detainees in Afghanistan and at Camp Delta in Guantánamo Bay, as well as for a wide variety of other transport and storage solutions. In mid-2011, there were over 10,000 containers being employed for a wide variety of purposes in Camp Bastion, the city-sized British base in the Afghanistan desert. One was even used as a Pizza Hut franchise (Hopkins 2011). A buried shipping container also works well as an underground bunker, or even a hidden greenhouse for drugs. In 2008, police in Sussex, England, discovered eight subterranean containers joined by passageways and connected to a generator for light and heat.[8] There are similar reports from Canada, New Zealand and Australia.

Containers and container ships can also be re-imagined as pirate prizes too, such as the 74 attacked in 2010, out of a total of 445 actual or attempted acts of piracy that year (ICC 2011, 14). One of the exemplifications of what it means to escape from territorialized control, the pirate forces an intersection with an entirely different economy of movement and ownership (Neilson and Rossiter 2010, Parker 2012). Sometimes the pirates steal cash or property from the ship and crew, including breaking into containers; on other occasions, they attempt to hold the ship, cargo and crew to ransom, such as the *Albedo*, a Malaysian container ship with 23 crew which was hijacked off Somalia in November 2010. The last hostages weren't released until 2014. There is even an attempt to use the box itself as a commercially available weapon. The Club-K container missile system is outwardly a standard 40-foot container, but contains a hydraulic platform which allows it to launch four cruise missiles. It could be sent, undetected, on a truck, ship or train, and used to carry out pre-emptive strikes.[9] Rather ironic, since an early selling point of containerization was greater security.

Security and Danger

The first containers crossing the Atlantic in the 1960s were filled with military goods on the way to Europe, and whiskey on the way back. Distillers were particularly keen on bottling in the US, because of the huge levels of theft from the docks. Cases went missing, whilst entire stainless-steel tanks of whiskey were harder to steal (Levinson 2006, 165). In theory then, once the container was sealed – in the factory or transport depot – it wouldn't be opened again until it arrived wherever it was going to be used. There would be no damage or pilfering, and customers would be happier and insurance costs would be lower. Yet such an emphasis on the security of the container has also made them into objects which bring threats.

Sealing the container brings with it opacity, and the possibility of hiding things that you don't want others to see:

> According to the Italian Customs Agency, 60 percent of the goods arriving in Naples escape official customs inspection, 20 percent of the bills of entry go unchecked, and fifty thousand shipments are contraband, 99 percent of them from China – all for an estimated 200 million euros in evaded taxes each semester.
>
> *(Saviano 2008, 7)*

This means products that haven't had tax paid on them, or are stamped 'Made in Italy' but come from Bangladesh, that don't meet safety standards, or have fake designer labels. In Naples, Saviano explains, the Camorra are collectively referred to as 'the system', and it is the business interests of the clans, particularly in the manufacture and distribution of clothing, which provides the contents for containers as part of the global capitalist system (Saviano 2008, 38). There is no clear distinction between the legitimate and the illegitimate here. The territory of the port allows both to coexist, because no one can know what is in all those boxes, where they really came from and where they are really going to.

Even if you opened the container, you will most likely be met by a wall of cardboard boxes, and behind them, who knows? Since a large port will be dealing with 10,000 containers a day, checking the contents of all these boxes would require huge numbers of inspectors, or huge delays, neither of which are going to be popular with the people paying the bills. When Saviano was writing his book, 1.5 million containers moved through the port of Naples every year, many loaded with 1.6 million tons of Chinese merchandise. That was 171 containers per hour, in a port that only came 36th largest on the world rankings in 2009. According to Saviano, another million tons of unregistered materials passed though as well, much of it disguised by the fact that multiple containers are given the same tracking number (Saviano 2008, 7).

Of course this isn't merely about fake designer labels, but also moving cigarettes, alcohol, drugs, guns and people. Many of these items can be hidden in the products, or at the back of the container behind a wall of legitimate products, or between the cladding of the container and the steel skin. For immigrants, those that Martin calls 'desperate passengers' involved in a 'violent mobility' (2011), concealment usually just involves the construction of a rudimentary room with an air supply of some kind. According to Broeze (2002, 259), Chinese 'snakehead' gangs have made this into a one billion dollar industry, with the 5,000 US-bound customers per year being charged up to $60,000 per head. Many die on route, but in Gioia Tauro, in the Bay of Naples, a container stowaway was discovered in 2001 who has now assumed legendary status. Now called 'Container Bob', he had a well-appointed room within the container which contained a bed, toilet and heater, as well as phones, a computer and various security passes for US airports. He had travelled from Port Said, but disappeared after being bailed, further adding to conspiracy theories about who he was and what he was intending to do in the US (Cohen 2005, 19).

Such fears of what containers might bring don't stop at migrants, fake brands and drugs. Stephen Cohen, in a thoroughly post-9/11 working paper titled 'Boom Boxes' describes them as 'the poor-man's missiles' (Cohen 2005, 3).[10] He speculates about the dangers of importing supplies for terrorists, the possibility of a small dirty bomb spreading radiation across New York City, the spread of biotoxins and chemical weapons across the US on trucks and trains, as well as the destruction that could be caused by an ordinary bomb near a major target. For Cohen, the problem of counterfeit goods – which he estimates as between 5 to 7 per cent of world trade – indicates just how difficult it would to stop a determined terrorist from visiting horror on an US city. He cites an ABC documentary in which depleted uranium was smuggled into the port of Los Angeles simply by not declaring the box's contents (ibid., 18). The aporia is clear enough. The very efficiencies which have made the box such an effective instrument of international trade have also made it into a major threat to national security. Any attempt to increase security – auditing personnel involved in loading and transporting to any US port wherever they are in the world; in-port and in-box surveillance using radiation detectors; X-rays of boxes; electronic and auditable documentation; GPS box tracking – runs the danger of being an 'autoimmune' reaction which might destroy international trade (ibid., 10). In neoliberal terms, ensuring the best security would be a market failure which is analogous to the unions and cartels which existed before the box swept them away. In this way, the limits of the 'geography of calculation' (Thrift 2005) is exposed. Making all dangers visible would produce time-space frictions which in themselves damaged capitalist interests (Neilson and Rossiter 2010).

Another category of threats are environmental. The huge increase in shipping volumes has resulted in an increase in pollution – directly in terms of the diesel exhaust fumes which count for twice as much CO^2 as air travel[11] – but also volatile compounds which are produced during tank venting and the poisonous anti-fouling agent Tributyltin. The development of new ports has meant that they have expanded along shorelines, sometimes into local nature reserves. The increasing size of ships also means that there is need for constant dredging which again damages local ecosystems, and provokes a need for places to dispose of dredged material, causing further problems (Broeze 2002, 267). Containers also carry their own biosecurity issues, with documented cases of mosquitoes travelling in boxes, as well as other non-native species which become classified as invasive weeds. Even when still and silent, the boxes bring dangers. One million containers go out of service every year (ibid., 270) and the ship-decommissioning beaches in Pakistan, Bangladesh and India are some of the most dangerous and polluted places to work in the world (ibid., 266).

About 10,000 containers fall off ships every year too. In 1992, three containers containing about 30,000 bath toys were lost at sea. Rubber ducks bleached white from the sun and the salt were being found on English shores in 2007, after following the lonely ocean currents for 15 years (Hohn 2011). There are similar (but possibly apocryphal) stories about 34,000 ice hockey gloves being washed up on beaches, and containers full of left-footed Nike trainers (the right ones being in a different can, to prevent pilfering). In January 2007, the *MSC Napoli* was beached near Sidmouth in Cornwall after being damaged in a storm. One hundred and three containers fell into the sea, with many floating onto the beach at the holiday resort of Branscombe where they were forcibly opened and salvaged by hundreds of people.[12] Motorbikes, perfume, children's nappies and car parts were taken away before the police closed the beach. However, by then items from the *Napoli* had followed trajectories along a long stretch of the south coast of England, and attempts to claim that scavenging was a criminal offence did little to discourage enthusiastic beachcombers who wished to enjoy the cornucopia.

Plenty and Emptiness

The end point of all this movement is people paying money for things to eat, to wear, to play with. This is the gravitational force which drags containers across the world, full of the stuff which fills the shelves which feed the consumerism of the Global North. The promise of a manufactured Cockaygne is here because 'inside those containers are our new things, and they are pristine in the darkness, still encased in plastic and cardboard, our sealed and unblemished toys, electronics, white goods, clothes' (Farley and Symmons Roberts 2011, 49). These boxes are treasure chests, packed with the dreams that we work and steal for. No wonder that Farley and Symmons Roberts think of container depots as 'places of beauty and mystery', where uniformity hides the huge surfeit of a billion cubic metres of stuff on the move. All the containers are pretty much the same, apart from different pastel colours of rust and a (supposedly) distinct ISO 6346 reporting number, but inside there could be anything.

At the same time, and in the same places where all this excess is stored is an emptiness, a still place with few or no people in view (Neilson and Rossiter 2010, 51). Compare a bustling street scene from the Liverpool docks with the placeless towering container cities which are constructed on the tarmac before they are taken apart and sent to St Etienne and Stoke-on-Trent. Big grey sheds with big car parks in what Farley and Symmons Roberts call the 'edgelands'. The container has made the edgelands – an undefined place which is neither city nor country – into a somewhere where things are assembled, stored, moved from and to. One of the Liverpool dockers who didn't lose his job moved into driving a container crane, said how lonely his new job was – 'all the fun had gone.'[13] Streets and workplaces full of smelly people, pubs full of drunken men, scams and fiddles and union solidarity all replaced by the episodic whine of motors in silent acres of waiting steel.

Only twenty people are needed to take 3,000 containers, with 100,000 tons of product from Hong Kong to Germany (Levinson 2006, 4). The ships are barely ships, with few watery curves, being instead 'a floating cubist sculpture in muted Kandinsky tones' (Gibson 2007, 264). As the ships get bigger and bigger, so do they become even emptier of people. In 1970, Douglas Philips-Birt quoted a 1967 article in *The Times* about 'tanker sickness':

> As tankers get bigger and crews decrease, the problem of loneliness increases. The officers and men tend to lose touch with reality – sometimes suffering the agonising biological fears of the prisoner of war – and a general melancholy sets in, which occasionally lands the victim of these unnatural surroundings in a straight-jacket.
>
> *(Philips-Birt 1970, 78)*

He goes on to explore the possibility of remote-control 'Zombie' ships, which will steer on with 'icy computer minds' even though there is no one left to steer.

When they reach port, a few people in machines – high up in Constructivist cranes – take about three minutes to move a box like an absurd Lego brick onto a transporter to move it into a storage location. The transporters take the containers to rolling stacker cranes, where they rest for awhile six high, before being collected by a truck. Digital algorithms control the mechanical machines – reading the bar codes, calculating movement instructions and tracking the speed and paths of ships, trains and trucks. Humans are barely visible as we watch 'these complex, almost autonomous creatures, operated (or not) by something fleshy in their interior' (Hatherley 2011, 29). As Owen Hatherley notes, the promise of automation was that we would be able to watch the machines working as we fished in the afternoon and philosophized in the evening, rather than engaging in servile service industry work with fewer rights and less bargaining power. Driving into the container port of Southampton, he sees the piles of boxes full of imported goods on one side of the road and the blind fascias of the gigantic WestQuay shopping centre on the other. He muses on the possibility of using the boxes for transportation, shopping and living all at once, 'the cruise ships of the twenty-first century' (ibid., 29, 44).

Perhaps the boxes are empty, and the shopping centre losing money. The manager of Felixstowe docks in the documentary *The Box That Changed Britain* estimated that half of the containers that leave the docks are empty. A trade gap could be interpreted quite literally. Sending 'light' containers means sending empty ones, transporting space back to some places where it can be filled again. During a recession, there is an oversupply of containers, which means when demand reduces, the ships are laid up, slow steamed, or only charge operating costs, effectively transporting cargo for free – as happened on the Europe-Asia routes in 2009 and then again during COVID-19. The production lines, the ships, the cargo cranes, the shopping malls have to continue moving, even if more slowly. As quite a few authors have noted recently, there is a relation here between movement and stillness (Bissell 2007, Bissell and Fuller 2010). Containers are often still, waiting for the next operation. They are an example of what Gillian Fuller, writing about airports, has called a 'store>forward' distribution architecture, in which waiting is a prerequisite for mobility (2009). When stacked on docks, in depots, or on mobile platforms such as ships and trains, they are part of a hybrid network in which immobility is just as important as mobility. The emptiness of their surroundings, and their episodic movement, are just as constitutive of this system as the mobile plenty which they bring to the supermarket shelves.

Economics and Culture

The representation of things in motion – landscapes, people, machines – is part of the idea of the modern world. *Around the World in Forty Feet* is a book of photographs which tracks 200 days and over 122,000 kilometres in the life of box number NYKU 596079-1 as it travels from Shenzhen in China to Yokohama in Japan (Cook and Oleniuk 2007). Along the way, it calls at Hong Kong, Los Angeles, Singapore, Surabaya, Jakarta, Milton Keynes, Greenock, Southampton, Bangkok, Lacm Chabang, Sydney, Adelaide, Singapore (again), Amsterdam, Ludwigshafen, Rotterdam, New Jersey, Springfield, Santos, São José Dos Campos, Minas Gerais and Durban.

Its cargoes include radio alarm clocks, raw cotton, electric pianos, whiskey, microwave ovens, white wine, pharmaceuticals, resin and coffee. The book was produced by the Nippon Yusen Kaisha Line, a major container shipper, and the photos document a world of full-colour work and movement. People in hats with different-coloured skin concentrate, pressing buttons, talking on phones, or staring at the horizon. The backdrops of Mount Fuji or the Suez Canal slide past on the glossy paper, a series of images which make movement frictionless and global trade into a coffee-table book.[14]

It's quite a beautiful volume, though aimed primarily at NYK shareholders, employees and shippers, and perhaps better understood as a form of marketing rather than a form of expressive culture. Of course the two are inseparable. Graeme McAulay's 2010 documentary *The Box that Changed Britain* begins with people who drive to sit on the seashore watching the big boats coming in and out of Felixstowe,[15] anoraks who see aesthetic qualities in the trajectories of these quiet giants, coming in from Rotterdam or on their way to China. And inside these containers might be the cars and equipment for Formula One racing teams, the Cirque du Soleil, the stage and lighting for the next AC/DC tour, or horses for the Olympics in containers turfed with real grass (Broeze 2002, 258). Not only does the container contain culture, it is culture – cut, folded and welded into architecture; market stalls, or an underground grow-up for drugs.

William Gibson, in a novel which has a container at its centre, has one of his characters say, 'Artists or the military. That's something that tends to happen with new technologies generally: the most interesting applications turn up on the battlefield, or in a gallery' (Gibson 2007, 66). If he is correct, then it shouldn't surprise us that Balka's box at Tate Modern in London should show the container as something more than an outcome of the need to supply soldiers in Vietnam, but this is by no means an isolated example. Rotterdam's 1997 World Port Festival featured the 'World's Largest Chess Game', with containers as pieces (Broeze 2002, 258). Since 2001, the port city of Kaohsiung in Taiwan has held a biennial 'Container Arts Festival'. The Italian ContainerArt group has also held many shows since 2005, initially in Italy, but more lately in a variety of cities across the globe. From simply using containers to exhibit artists in unusual locations, ContainerArt has moved to the construction of temporary museums. Ronald Facchinetti, ContainerArt's founder, likes the idea of being isolated within an austere container, somewhere in a city you don't normally visit, and faced with the 'beauty inside' of aesthetic experience.

In this sense, the container is just that, a box which can be anywhere and contain anything, such as Tom Wolseley's travelling container show CABIN/ET in 2009, which was both a cabin on board a ship and a cabinet of curiosities brought from elsewhere to here. A very different sense came from Clare Bayley's claustrophobic play 'The Container', performed at the Young

Vic in London in 2009, and reflecting on the human cargo that containers often carry.[16] In 2010, the Lisbon-based P28 group established a show called 'Contentores', in which various artists used the backdrop of the industrial River Tagus to exhibit art in and with cans. The 2011 show reflected on location, migration and displacement, and was put together at almost no cost because two shipping companies provided and moved the containers. There were exhibits both in containers and with containers, stacked or used as a frame for the port beyond.[17]

Perhaps the most sustained attempt to come to grips with the cultural meaning of the container has been a research and art project at the University of California Santa Barbara.[18] In association with a container rental and sales company, the Institute for Research in the Arts worked on a variety of projects in 2005–07, including a competition to create affordable, mobile and sustainable housing; an exhibition using the container to display work concerned with cheap products and cheap labour; two mobile galleries involving local schools and communities; a course taught across cultural studies and the history of art, and a conference on the interdisciplinary study of containers – 'The Traveling Box: Containers as the Global Icon of Our Era', hosted by UCSB's Interdisciplinary Humanities Centre in 2007.

The idea that containers have themselves become a global icon is something that can be documented much more widely than 'the arts'. Media representations of the box often now use its edgelands instead of the alleyways of the city. The back alleys in which Starsky and Hutch used to crash through piles of boxes and wrestle on fire escapes have now been augmented with a new playground for chases and threats. The towering avenues of containerland provide a cheap site for filmmakers to imagine stunts, but also to play shell games with the hostages, weapons, or bodies which might be found within. In the *X Files* series 5 episode 11 'Kill Switch', co-written by William Gibson, a container with a mess of computers and cables in it is blown up with a flowering explosion which contrasts beautifully with the vorticist angles of the piled boxes. In season 7 of *24*, bio-chemical weapons are moved around in a shipping container, and at the end of the 2004 film *I Robot*, the ranks of empty containers on the dry shore of Lake Michigan become a new city for robots.

It's not just thrillers of course. *The Wire* series 2, set in the dying docks of Baltimore, has beautiful shots of still and silent salt-bleached and rusted containers surrounded by weeds and set amongst the dispirited communities which used to work the port. Nowadays, they make a little extra by making containers disappear from surveillance for some organized criminals who are willing to pay a lot more then their employers do. Frank Sobotka, boss of the union local, does illegal things but is basically a decent man:

> He gets in bed with gangsters to do right by men who maybe stole a case of Scotch and a TV set now and again – sometimes a container of appliances

– but who nonetheless have mortgages and car payments and remember a way of life that went back before their great-grandfathers' day.

(Alvarez 2009, 127)

The story begins when one day they find 'thirteen dead girls in a can' – prostitutes shipped over to work in the US who have suffocated when the air pipe on top of the container was crushed, presumably by being stacked. David Simon, creator of *The Wire*, described series 2 as a wake for the 'death of work', charting a Baltimore surrounded by rusting piers, abandoned breweries and the carcass of the Bethlehem Steel shipyard (Alvarez 2009, 125). As Frank sees it, automation has all but killed these places and the people who made them live: 'Down here it's still "Who's your old man?", till you get kids of your own then it's "Who's your son?" But after the horror movie I seen today – piers full of robots! – my kid will be lucky if he's even punching numbers five years from now' (ibid., 127). He is trapped here, nostalgic for another world in which things were made and used, and not merely moved from somewhere else. A world in which place and things mattered, and not mobility – 'We used to make shit in this country, build shit. Now we just put our hand in the next guy's pocket.'

What I have called these four 'aporias' of containerization seem to show that the simple account of mobility and globalization doesn't work very well. Containers are varied in size and function, dangerous, empty, still, and symbolically rich *as well as* being elements in a mobility system which is predicated on standardization. This is necessarily a relational claim about people and things, and one that entangles territories, technologies and im/mobilities (Hannam et al. 2006). The container becomes more than just a steel box, a symbol and a ground for forms of cultural production which mediate on the present in a startling variety of ways. So what sorts of thinking are needed to explore the container like this?

Container Theory

One of the difficult problems for the legal acceptance of the container was whether it should be treated as one thing or many. For the purposes of tax, freight billing, insurance claims, loading and stuffing, a variety of parties wished to claim that it was either one item – and should be dealt with as such – or a box for many items – which should be dealt with separately. For example, dispute focused around the meaning of the word 'package', which in US law has particular importance, and attempts were made to resolve this question by considering the description on the bill of lading; the functional possibilities of separate transport, the identity of the person or persons who stuffed the container and their role within the process as manufacturer, shipper, or carrier (Wilson 1988, 190–193). Metaphorically, this is the very problem of the container. It appears as one thing, stacked in a particular account of a world in which market economics combines with sameness and security to produce plenty. But when you look at the container in more detail, it fragments into a multiplicity of things, it becomes mobile and intermodal, with a host of relations which are disparate and often contradictory. Xeno-tainers, strange boxes containing strange people and things.

The box can't easily be boxed: 'The ultimate meaning of containerisation must therefore be seen not only in its remarkable contribution to the growth of the world economy and to globalisation but also in its role in the creation of the forces that are arising in sharp opposition to these very phenomena' (Broeze 2002, 277). In some sense, it is not a thing but a blankness – something which disguises other things and which provides multiple possibilities. Its explicit function is to enclose trade and exclose market imperfections, but it has become entangled with many mobilities and moorings. This clearly leads to questioning the tessellated story of technological determinism which most of the accounts rely upon in some way or other (Broeze 2002, Cudahy 2006, Donovan and Bonney 2006, Levinson 2006). Admittedly, Broeze and Levinson's books are more circumspect, both preferring to suggest that containers made certain things possible, but that they are used for other purposes too. Yet the key problem remains. Did containers cause globalization? Roland (2007) thinks that determinist arguments should be treated with suspicion. If we want to understand containerization, it isn't enough to imagine it solely as a particular mobile arrangement of materials which causes a progressive change in economic relations. That is one account, but we would also need to add in political and structural explanations involving neoliberal deregulation and the attack on unions, increased global capital flows, post-colonial economic relations, accelerating over-consumption in the Global North, and the global supply of labour. All these, but also information and communications technologies, jet travel, motorways, and refrigeration.

So we can make arguments here about the raw complexity of causes and effects, but there are some rather dialectical implications in the example of containers too. Allan Sekula, a photographer with a particular fascination with the sea, seems to regard it as a place where possibility and constraint are often related. It is a place for mercantile relations of trade and the imperial violence of war, but also the resistance of piracy, and an imaginary for freedom. So too with the ship:

> Deleuze has argued that the Melvillean ship constitutes the meeting point of order and disorder, of control and chaos. Viewed schematically, the ship is a model of order, of containment. Viewed phenomenologically, it is a labyrinth, threatening madness, claustrophobia, blindness, drowning.

The first vantage is that of the captain, the second is that of the crew. And yet the captain is human, and prone, like Ahab, to descend into chaos, just as the crew is capable [...] of rising to the level of autonomous collective command. The ship, then, can be said to be both a 'heterotopia,' that is 'a space without a place that is [...] closed in on itself and at the same time is given over to the infinity of the sea' (Foucault), and a great contested instrument of power, the very model of the war machine.

(Sekula 1991, 107)

There is a relationality here which refuses to allow one thing to mean one thing, and to question the idea that the world could be reduced to a single story told by anyone. Perhaps it should not surprise that containers can express such aporias, such dialectical tensions, because that is what a relational and mobile analysis will tend to do: show how the same produces difference, security produces danger, plenty produces emptiness, and economy makes culture. Foucault's 'heterotopic' ships are 'the great instrument of economic development' and 'simultaneously the greatest reserve of the imagination' (1986, 27). Just as James Scott insists that the 'hidden transcripts' of a culture tell us something about the resistance which exists in 'nonstate' spaces (1990, 1998, 187), so can we suggest that the story of the container cannot be summarized as being 'about' one theme. Questioning categories requires attention to varied details, and a scepticism concerning simple accounts of what things are and what they can do. To say that something is complex is a starting point, but complexity doesn't capture the relationality which appears to allow the box to often mean and be the opposite of what the dominant account claims.

I think these tensions can be seen in the box's materiality, its status as steel and paint and rust, rather than the frictionless conquering of time and space. They are not same-sized shiny busy boxes always on the move, but varied, always decaying, and just as often static and peeling. The container is itself an 'intermediate good', always becoming something else. Indeed, it takes much work to keep them on the move, hence the constant washing, fumigation, repainting and repairs which take place in specialist facilities near large ports (Cook and Oleniuk 2007, 41, 207). It takes work to keep the dominant account moving too, and all the while the obduracy of materials disorganizes and reorganizes through the traces of previous cargoes, the rusting of steel, and the collisions of wind and waves. The appropriation of containers, whether by Puerto Rican shop owners, artists, cannabis farmers, pirates, Chinese migrants, architects, a Pizza Hut franchise owner in Camp Bastion, or my old neighbours Mike and Mandy in Stoke-on-Trent who have one in their garden to store all the things they can't fit in their house, is not epiphenomenal to the dominant account, but illustrations of these many different ways in which the container can be manifested.

When comparing the neatness of Levinson et al. with the messy story I have told here, it seems that an idea of space as relational, multiple and in process (Massey 2005) also applies to materials. The transient matter of the container moves space and reconfigures space, yet is also itself changed as its mobilities and immobilities spread across the planet. What counts as organization, and what counts as disorganization, depends on how we look; otherwise how could we account for Mike and Mandy's container, rusting at the bottom of their garden, filled with Chinese fireworks and old computers?

Notes

1 This chapter is based on (2013) 'Containerization: Moving Things and Boxing Ideas', *Mobilities* 8/3: 368–387.
2 Men, of course.
3 The jaws on a crane which clamp to the container in order to lift it.
4 http://en.wikipedia.org/w/index.php?oldid=443408658, accessed August 2011.
5 http://en.wikpedia.org/w/index.php?title=Intermodal_container&printable=yes, accessed August 2011.
6 http://europa.eu/legislation_summaries/transport/intermodaliy_transeuropean_n etworks/index_en.htm, accessed December 2011.
7 See the 'Container Bay' section of www.fabprefab.com for a fairly comprehensive list, and www.ihc.ucsb.edu/containers/boxconference_schedule.html and associated video for details of the housing initiatives, accessed July 2011.
8 http://news.bbc.co.uk/1/hi/england/sussex/7320358.stm, accessed August 2011.
9 www.telegraph.co.uk/news/worldnews/europe/russia/7632543/A-Cruise-missile-in-a-shipping-box-on-sale-to-rogue-bidders.html, accessed June 2011.
10 See also Willis and Ortiz 2004.
11 That is about 5 per cent of the total, see www.guardian.co.uk/environment/2007/mar/03/travelsenvironmentalimpact.transportintheuk, accessed September 2011.
12 See https://followtheblog.org/category/melanie-jackson/ for more details about the art and writing that followed the event, accessed 31 July 2024.
13 www.bbc.co.uk/iplayer/episode/b00scpzn/The_Box_That_Changed_Britain/, accessed September 2011.
14 The same project was repeated the following year by the BBC, this time following NYKU 821050-6 using GPS tracking technology to update a website. However, it suffered technical problems, and the GPS tracking ceased in April 2009.
15 www.bbc.co.uk/iplayer/episode/b00scpzn/The_Box_That_Changed_Britain/, accessed September 2011.
16 See also Ursula Biemann's video 'Contained Mobility', in Holmes 2011.
17 See www.containerart.org/eng, and www.contentoresp28.com, both accessed August 2011.
18 www.ucira.ucsb.edu/ucira-container-project/, accessed August 2011.

13

ROCKETS

In 1968, James Edwin Webb, the ex-administrator of NASA, delivered a series of McKinsey Foundation lectures at the Graduate School of Business, Columbia University, which were published under the title *Space Age Management* the next year (Webb 1969), but before the moon landing of July 1969.[1] According to Klerkx (2004, 155) the book was kept near the desk of Sean O'Keefe, the NASA administrator from 2001–2005. At that time, 'Space Age' was a prefix that was being applied to everything. Effectively, it meant something like 'modern', with connotations of being streamlined, efficient and fashionable. The coupling of 'Space Age' and 'management' combines this modernity with a technocratic sense of order. The Space Age was an age of mass organization, of pills instead of meals, of new products that saved time, of factories and offices and launch pads connected by freeways and telephones. It was a world of harmonious organization, managed by wise and well-qualified elders who would eradicate the problems that beset humanity in its earthbound dark ages. The paradox, for Jim Webb, was how to retain the advantages of this technocracy without losing democracy. After all, there would be no point in winning the space race against the Soviets if the form of social organization that enabled this was effectively reproducing the centralized repression of communism.

I will engage with Webb's paradox in two ways. One, by exploring the sense in which the Space Age was necessarily the age of management. In order to achieve Kennedy's goal, huge numbers of people, things and places needed to be made coordinated and controllable. In 1966, NASA directly employed 36,000 people, with another 360,000 people working for 20,000 contractors and 200 universities in 80 countries (Bizony 2006, 79; Johnson 2002, 5) The total cost, at that time, for the Apollo programme was $24 billion, 90 per

DOI: 10.4324/9781032714288-18

cent of which ended up in the private sector. This meant accounting for people and things, chains of command, scheduled meetings with determinate agendas, as well as plans, graphs, reports and deadlines. The moon landing was a triumph of organization, of project management and control of a complex socio-technical system. It was also a huge exercise in New Deal economics, with a wide variety of state subsidies being channelled through NASA to aerospace corporations, universities, local regions and so on. The contradiction between the myth of individualism and the free market, and the centralized technocracy did not go unnoticed, and meant that Webb and others needed to make constant reference to a dead president and a new frontier, in order to keep NASA's funding rolling in.

More than this though, there is a further question about the ends of organization. Going to the moon made little rational sense. It was criticized then and since as a monumental distraction from the problems of the earth, a subsidy for the military-industrial complex, and (in cultural terms) a white, middle-class, male fantasy, in which heroes ride rockets whilst the rest of the world looks on in awe (De Groot 2007, Dickens and Ormrod 2007, Parker 2007). Without dismissing these criticisms, Apollo was also one of the iconic moments of the twentieth century, and one that inspired feelings of awe that still resonate for many, including me. It has also encouraged many people to make connections between science, fiction, and possibility that were substantially at odds with the political and financial interests that were key to driving the programme (Mailer 1971, Nye 1994, Jameson 2005, Parker 2009, Shukaitis 2009). Given its Cold War roots, and its managerialist methods, how did Apollo produce something so incomprehensibly strange, and excessive?

I first look at the forms of organization that made the Space Age possible, and some of the political paradoxes that needed to be negotiated. I then go on to think about NASA as a mundane work organization, one in which (most of the time) people did jobs for money, and large companies made profits. Finally, I move to considering the way in which organization is necessary in order to produce an event that exceeds it, that suggests the sublime, and opens up possibilities that have not yet been imagined. *Space Age Management* is an account of how something astonishing was made, but it never approaches its object, its end, because it does not have the language to do so. It seems to me that, symmetrically, the only way that we can understand how that transcendent event happened is as the outcome of Space Age management, and of the political and administrative contexts that made it possible.

New Deal Administration

James Webb was, from 1962–1968, the Chief Administrator who understood that making things happen required politics. Webb had experience in Big Oil and Big Aerospace, as well as various posts in a series of administrations, including being Director of the Bureau of the Budget under Truman. According to most sources, Webb's real skill was in Washington, where he bamboozled politicians with jobs, universities with research money, and journalists with wholesome stories and an unstoppable torrent of words. He also kept a direct line to two presidents, ensuring that their interests didn't diverge too much from his, and spent a considerable amount of time organizing and reorganizing different lines of communication, job descriptions and spans of control, restlessly trying to find an organizational form that would be both stable and dynamic (Lambright 1995, Bizony 2006). The lessons for 'management' in *Space Age Management* are less about 'managing employees', and more often about managing other executives, as well as politicians. Webb's line is essentially a Machiavellian one. If you wish to keep a big organization going, you need to ensure that your friends are close and your enemies even closer. But beyond the tactical pragmatism, Webb is also selling a 'new deal' and 'big government' line. He wanted NASA to be an example of large-scale intervention that required 'rapid advances in so many disciplines – engineering, physics, astronomy, mathematics, economics, political science, psychology, public administration – the whole list of the physical, behavioural and social sciences' (Webb 1969, x). He wanted the space programme to change the United States.

This is a long way from the idea that space investment merely resulted in Teflon and pens that can write upside-down. Webb wants to claim that his Keynesian approach to spreading gigantic NASA contracts around the private and public sectors was not merely political pragmatism, but also an example of large-scale social engineering which by 1966 had resulted in 420,000 people owing their jobs to the organization. It is this, rather than any sniff of the sublime, or starry-eyed belief in exploring frontiers, that provides his rationale for spending so many billions of dollars. Webb is clear that much of what NASA did had nothing to do directly with the moon landing, but was basic science and engineering aimed at developing long-term national capacity. Unmanned probes, new materials, better missiles, but also a knowledge of the sort of large-scale administration upon which all these sort of projects depended. Not very far in the background here is a response to one of the most perplexing questions left by Apollo – 'if we can put a man on the moon, why can't we … ?' And whether the question ends with education, poverty, housing, healthcare, or whatever, Webb suggests that big projects from big government are the answer. There are approximately 2.5 million solder joints in the Saturn V launch vehicle. It weighs the same as 19 Boeing 707 jets, or heavier than a naval destroyer.

But aggregations of resources and power, like giant rockets, need sophisticated control systems that can deal with turbulent conditions, and provide the sort of 'dynamic equilibrium' required to keep it moving forward

(Webb 1969, 11). So whilst Webb has to appreciate the importance of a certain sort of bureaucratization in order to achieve coordination of a large number of people and things, he is continually also aware of the dangers of command and control, in terms of political authoritarianism: 'Otherwise we might well destroy the values we are trying hardest to preserve and promote' (ibid., 15). Getting to the moon first will be pointless if it merely demonstrated that the Russians were right, so 'freedom' needs to be both a means and an end: 'Goals that depend on undesirable systems are undesirable goals' (ibid., 27). 'Bigness', whilst often needed to create great nations and great events, is also something to be feared, something that needs to be treated with a certain suspicion. But, suspicion or not, Webb has enough faith in science and research to suggest that much can be learned for the future by comparing NASA with other large forms of organization and innovation. The railroads, US Steel, General Motors, Du Pont Chemical and others are compared with huge state-sponsored projects, particularly that paragon of demand-side intervention, the Tennessee Valley Authority. These comparisons are not systematic, though certainly insightful, but it is the wartime organization of the state which is most useful in understanding Webb's perspective on what the state can do.

Comparing NASA to the War Production Board, the Manhattan Engineering District Project and the Office of Price Administration allows Webb to show the modern state as necessarily entangled with the private and public sectors. During the war, the partial control of large corporations, and the direction of universities, was effectively ceded to state bureaucracies whilst the state printed money and attempted to control demand and supply. In 1958, in the middle of the Cold War, this was the institutional history which administrators like Webb understood, while at the same time the more perceptive amongst them also understood that demonstrating the virtues of freedom and the market through state control was a rather contradictory project. Webb, and NASA, were the culmination of an understanding of government interventionism that begins with Roosevelt, runs through Truman and Kennedy, and ends with Johnson's 'Great Society' initiatives. Even Eisenhower, the cold warrior in the middle who reluctantly began the agency, was explicitly and famously suspicious of the ways in which the 'military-industrial complex' could influence state policy. This was a generation of politicians who were shaped by the deep suspicion of business that led to New Deal progressivism in the 1930s, but also the distrust of state control and the suppression of liberties that were at the heart of the Cold War interpretation of what the US was fighting for.

This has some interesting consequences for Webb's account of liberty within the workplace. He knows Taylor, Weber, and Fayol, as well as 'the newer doctrine of the behavioural or participative school' (Webb 1969, 65), but is most impressed by the new sciences of systems, with their emphasis on operations, forecasting, and quantitative methods. And here the paradox once again surfaces. Webb wants clear limitations on the freedom of the many, because participation in goal setting simply isn't feasible or desirable for them, at the same time as the freedom of the few is to be enhanced and recognized as a special skill that must be discovered and nurtured and which he calls 'leadership'.[2] So we have computers and systemic control for middle management and below, but 'the art of administration' for those at the top, because the computer might become 'the master of the systems disciple rather than an useful tool in his hands' (ibid., 67–68). Later on, he suggests that 'executives' (not managers now) should not be constrained by defined areas of responsibility and control, or centralisation, or plans and objectives.[3] Neither do such people need to be 'psychologically coddled' in the way that the participative school suggests (ibid., 136). These executives, Webb's peers (and by implication the author himself) are not the sort of vulnerable children who need to be looked after by personnel managers, or given instructions by their superiors.

The elitism here is underpinned and legitimised by an assumption of 'public responsibility'. Whether the leaders are politicians, administrators, university presidents, or CEOs, they all share the burden for their society, their nation. This means that it isn't enough for any leader, particularly a business manager, to limit themselves to looking after their own organization. Their views 'must be expanded to include school dropouts, crime rates, the prevalence of poverty, the number of university graduate students, effectiveness of government policies, incidence of group violence, and even indexes of the nation's willingness to act like a great power on the international scene.' (Webb 1969, 76) There is a systemic view of the social at work here which echoes the systems view of the complex organization, and adds a certain moralism. Organizational self-interest is not enough and, by implication, market mechanisms do not necessarily produce the greatest good for the greatest number. For example, the Office of Price Administration prevented profiteering, and protected both consumer and taxpayer. The view of society as in some sort of dynamic balance, or equilibrium, also suggests that there will need to be continual vigilance about the unintended consequences of large organizations and new technologies. Like Plato's philosopher kings, or the 'voluntary nobility' who govern H.G. Wells' *Modern Utopia* (1903/ 2005), Webb's executive class see everything, and understand everything, and assume their responsibility is to look after the common people.

Reading *Space Age Management* gives you the impression of a man who is more interested in management than space. Like Eisenhower, Kennedy and Nixon (though perhaps not Johnson), there is no particular sense of Apollo being interesting in itself, but only as a form of politics by other means. And the means were organizational, led by 'men of rare abilities' (Webb 1969, 169). Or, as Bizony expresses it, Webb believed in a 'perfectible society, led by selfless philosopher-kings' (2006, 68). Webb left NASA in 1968, worn down by continual budget cuts due to the increasing costs of Vietnam, and bruised by the damaging enquiry into NASA's relationship with North American Aviation after the Apollo 1 launch-pad fire that killed three astronauts in 1967 (Bizony 2006, 154; De Groot 2007, 212 *passim*). Ultimately, Webb's vision of great leaders shouldering great burdens required an agreement concerning what the aims of the social system were. As De Groot acidly concludes, 'only in outer space could consensus be reached', simply because the rest of the great society projects – education, housing, healthcare – were too contentious (2007, 259). In the background to Webb's lectures was the Tet Offensive, the My Lai massacre, the Soviet invasion of Czechoslovakia, the assassinations of Martin Luther King and Robert Kennedy, student protests and Olympic athletes making Black Power salutes on the podium. Even an administrator as gifted as Webb couldn't solve all those problems.

NASA/Work

Hannah Arendt's The Human Condition (1958/1998) begins with the launch of Sputnik, and the dream of the 'automation' of work. Both, she thinks, are linked to a certain mythic liberation from the earth. Though Arendt doesn't pursue the point, the launching of rockets actually required the automation of human work in a much more profound sense too. This wasn't the sort of automation that left people free to do whatever they wanted to, but that channelled labour in the name of a common goal. One version of the Space Age was certainly a golden age of leisure, as the machines made your dinner in streamlined kitchens, but another was the elaboration of forms of work that were increasingly monitored and controlled. People had been cogs in the machine since industrialization, but the machine was now capturing more and more kinds of people.

Standing in front of a 1960s office building, posed for the camera, are five rows of white men in dark suits and dark ties. They are all attentive, some wear thick glasses, or have handkerchiefs protruding from breast pockets, and all have short tidy hair. They could be insurance salesman, but this is actually the 8th NASA Management Conference, held at the Ames Research Center in 1963 (Levine 1982). In many ways, this image of NASA is a more representative one than that of the flame-wreathed Apollo-Saturn, or the reflective visor of the astronaut. For most people, most of the time, the space programme was a workplace with offices, meetings and coffee machines. People wore suits, and spent Sundays mowing the lawn or washing the car. For the vast majority, they weren't even directly employed by NASA, but by a whole network of large corporations and small companies who were contractors or subcontractors on some part of NASA's ramified network. The point is that the space programme was, most of the time, a mundane experience of labour. It was design specifications, wiring harnesses, weekly reports and the possibility of promotion and a higher salary.[4] In the Saturn Apollo launch vehicle, there are 2 million working parts. The engines of the first stage burn 3,500 gallons of fuel per second and develop a thrust equivalent to 543 fighter jets.

Even those who were ostensibly doing something rather exciting were, most of the time, involved in something rather ordinary. Reading biographies and autobiographies of astronauts involves reading an account of paid work – even if the accounts are often sanitized, and the narratives concentrate on the few hours and days of moon landings and spacewalks. Joining the key events together are meetings, offices, bosses and co-workers. Car parking and cafeterias are mentioned, and sometimes there are criticisms of management, suppressed jealousy about colleagues, and complaints about the pay and conditions (Scott and Leonov 2004, Hansen 2005).[5] Even the physical settings seem more like the grubby present than the shining future. Gene Krantz, Mission Control for many of the major flights, describes getting to his station on the Apollo 11 landing shift:

> The coat rack is overly full. It swings like a pendulum and it threatens to tip over as I hang up my sport coat. The trip to the flight director console is like walking through a minefield, dodging books, lunches and the spaghetti of headset cords. The room smells of cigarettes, with an overlay of pizza, stale sandwiches, full wastebaskets, and coffee that has burned onto the hot plates.
>
> *(Krantz 2000, 278)*

This is where 'Flight' and 'Capcom' sat, communicating in a mysterious code, punctuated with beeps, across the crackling silence of space. Around them, the ordinary stains and piles of any workplace accumulate, and the cleaners curse in their cupboards.

Krantz rarely saw Webb, and describes him as living in a different world – Washington (Krantz 2000, 211). He is absent from virtually all the astronaut biographies too – just a shadow whose name they know, and who shook their hand once. Yet Webb's account of the systems approach to management did fairly accurately describe the progressive bureaucratization of manager, scientist and engineer as NASA grew. This didn't mean that there were car-parking spaces or that the wastebaskets were emptied often enough, but that, as Stephen Johnson shows, 'integrated control' became more and more pervasive. He bullishly calls this 'a bureaucracy for innovation', and defines systems management as 'a set of organizational structures and processes to rapidly produce a novel but dependable technological artifact within a predictable budget' (Johnson 2002, 4, 17). Though the technology might have been innovatory, the organizational form essentially depended on Weber and

Taylor plus computers. What was novel about NASA, according to Johnson, wasn't scale, but heterogeneity. Electrical power systems, skyscrapers and railways were gigantic enterprises too, but NASA required bringing millions of different people and components into alignment, unlike the repetitions required for the mass production of scale. So NASA organization attempted to control for any form of deviation, whether in work processes, electrical currents, or the interaction between complex systems. This meant that everything needed to be documented, and made visible. So heterogeneous engineering didn't produce autonomous workers, but an even greater requirement for managerial control. As a NASA saying goes – 'In God we trust, all others bring data' (in Boin 2006, 259).

The early years of the organization were largely predicated on the US Air Force's Cold War assumption that 'we have to buy time with money' (Douglas, in Johnson 2002, 41), but the largesse didn't last long. By as early as the end of 1963, NASA's budget was under tight scrutiny, and accounting measures became a necessary part of systems management, in order to prevent the sort of cost inflation on projects that began to look a lot like Second World War profiteering. Oversight committees could no longer be guaranteed to support huge expenditures that produced rockets that blew up on the launch pad, unmanned probes that crashed, and endless delays to schedules. At this point, Johnson suggests, the dominance of Air Force weapons entrepreneurs and scientists gives way to managers and design engineers (2002, 213 *passim*). This was, in organizational terms, a decisive move away from the military roots of NASA, and from the research ambitions of scientists. Instead, managers attempted to maximize organizational efficiency and minimize cost whilst engineers focused on technological reliability and predictability. The more speculative and comparatively loose forms of organization favoured by scientists, research engineers and military officers wanting weapons systems by yesterday gives way to an expanded authority for occupations that emphasize control. It is these groups that then define an organization based around Gantt charts, project milestones, flow charts, critical path analysis and costings for all the people and things being fed into the organization. This is a viral organization too, because it demands that these forms of control will be adopted in the organizations that it signs contracts with. As part of the strategy of 'contractor penetration', NASA people could audit what was going in on Boeing, Grumman Aviation, and even the Elgin National Watch Company.

In a way, NASA became all these organizations, and they all became NASA if they wanted to keep lucrative contracts. This meant that manufacturing workers far away from the Cape or Mission Control became exposed to systemic forms of audit and quality control, as well as a series of 'cultural' interventions. Those working on NASA projects were identified by being given badges or certificates, and sometimes even toolboxes painted

Air Force blue with the workers name on it (Johnson 2002, 126). Visits from heroic astronauts were also common, partly to sprinkle space dust on the factory floor, but perhaps also to ensure that workers would be more careful with their welding if they could see whose life depended on it. The astronaut embodied NASA, and this is true not merely in an symbolic sense. Armstrong and the others were thoroughly penetrated by the organization, both manufactured by it and also defined by a particular form of obedience, the ideal employee. The spaceman is not a swashbuckler, lonesome cowboy, or courteous knight – not the sort of masculine hero that dominated US popular culture in the 1950s. Barthes, in a short essay on 'The Jet Man', notes that this sort of hero 'is defined less by his courage than by his weight, his diets, and his habits (temperance, frugality, continence)' and his mythology manifests 'the plasticity of the flesh, its submission to collective ends' (Barthes 1957/2000, 72). The astronaut has been trained to be an organization man (Whyte 1961), a component of the machine. Without the complex systems of people and things, the launch and landing would simply not happen, and the heroism could not be engineered either. What we might admire cannot be separated from the assemblage.

As Marina Benjamin comments, the astronauts were the ultimate product of Webb's *Space Age Management* – 'both systems components and end-of-line commodities [...] model citizens of the new technology' (Benjamin 2004, 70). Just as the workers on the factory floor were subject to total quality control, and the middle managers and engineers coordinated their flow charts, so did the astronaut become rewarded for steely denial and emotional absolute zero. Norman Mailer's stunning account of Apollo 11, *A Fire on the Moon*, is punctuated with growling distaste at what he hears at the news conferences. For Mailer, the 'heart of all astronaut talk, like the heart of all bureaucratic talk, was a jargon that could easily be converted to computer programming' (1971, 28). This was the essence of depersonalization, in which one sentence could be spoken by anyone, and acronyms, abbreviations and circumlocutions are used to construct a precision which avoided talking about infinity, fear and death. Perhaps as a way for them to contain such matters, 'their time on the ground was conventional, practical, technical, hard-working, and in the centre of the suburban middle class' (ibid., 47). Sill wrestling with his ambivalence with what Apollo might mean, he muses on the night before the landing:

Who indeed can understand the psychology of astronauts? Let us try to comprehend how men can be so bold yet inhabit such insulations of cliché. As they sleep, we are forced to think again about the mysteries of make-up in those men who are technicians and heroes, robots and saints, adventurers and cogs of the machine.

(Mailer 1971, 287)

Looking now at the Technicolor photographs of the Apollo astronauts, we can see men with careful hair and v-neck sweaters, whilst the Saturn V towers in the Florida sunshine as a backdrop. They look not dissimilar to the managers on the steps of the Ames Research Centre, or probably the managers who ran the factory that made the sweaters.

For all sorts of NASA employees, whether factory worker, flight controller, or astronaut, these were jobs. For all, they were also jobs with a high degree of control, and very little responsible autonomy. NASA, as a work organization, seems to be structured around this dialectic 'between adventure and boredom' (Jameson 2008, 173). Jameson was writing about how films represent space travel, but his observations could be said to apply to space work on earth too. The vast majority of the work that went into Apollo was boring, repetitive, and carried out on factory floors, or in offices that smelled of pizza. Even the astronauts had little time to reflect, most parts of their days being filled with checklists and routines (Hersch 2009), and all the while a manager looked over their shoulder, ensuring that the timeline was met. *Space Age Management*, and systems engineering, meant that NASA work was audited heterogeneous engineering, controlled and programmed. Everything was supposed to be boring, because boredom meant no surprises, and hence the possibility of the adventure in some sense rested on its denial.

Organizing Space

Exploring the heavens has often required organization. Aristotle organized the geocentric universe as a series of interlocking spheres, with the furthest away from the earth being those closest to perfection. As we have seen, medieval cosmologies echoed this in their accounts of angelic hierarchy, and the assumption of a necessary hierarchy on earth which reflected the natural ordering of the universe – as above, so below (Dickens and Ormrod 2007). It was as if the vast emptiness of the skies, the darkness above, could only be thought by filling it with some sort of cognitive machinery that made the unknowable good to think with, and made stars into constellations, signs centred on the earth. At the opposite end of the millennium, it does also seem that ordering was necessary for Apollo too, but in a much more material sense. The Command Module has more than 400 switches, dials and fuses, and more than 2 million parts, not counting wires and skeletal components. The Lunar Module is made from more than 1,101,000 parts, and it took 92,207 engineering drawings to make it. A chain of organization led a quarter of a million miles from the Sea of Tranquillity, and this greatest escape of all entangled half a million people in its net. Key to this was management, as a dominant organizational logic which made such action at a distance visible on earth. Management is a specific form of organization, one that privileges a particular occupational group, and a hierarchical power relationship. Management as such is a relatively recent invention, and the use of the term on the cover of Webb's book reflects some fairly well recognized occupational shifts in large organizations in the post-war USA (Johnson 2002, Jacques 1996).

So if we treat management (as occupation and activity) as a specific instance of organization, we can begin to see how, in order for Armstrong and Aldrin to spend two-and-a-half hours collecting rocks a quarter of a million miles away, large parts of the world needed to be reordered. That ordering, that organization, meant that millions of people and things needed to be brought into alignment, and required that managers and engineers developed systems for controlling the times and spaces where these people and things were, and weren't. So metal, super-cold gases, pay cheques and flesh needed to be brought together and held apart, and even that coordination had to be made visible, in the shape of tables of numbers, minutes of meetings and flow charts:

> The really significant fallout from the strains, traumas, and endless experimentation of Project Apollo has been of a sociological rather than a technological nature; techniques for directing the massed scores of thousands of minds in a close-knit, mutually enhancive combination of government, university and private industry.
>
> *(T. Alexander, in 1969, cited in Johnson 2002, 115)*

Alexander is very perceptive here, in that the space race is just as interesting and important for what it did on the earth, and not just the moon, but I want to suggest that this is a theoretical statement, and not only a 'sociological' one.

Apollo, as Webb knew, is one of those events that can be set alongside other monumental achievements that involved the massed scores of minds and bodies. In that sense, it is no different to building the pyramids, the Great Wall of China, or the construction of the Burj Khalifa. All of these can be thought of as feats of organization which involved some form of complex coordination. In terms of Actor Network Theory, or the sociology of translation, matter on and off the earth was made manageable by placing actors and actants into some sort of temporary relation (Latour 2005, Czarniawska and Hernes 2005). But unlike the materials assembled in the other examples, which are slowly crumbling, the moon landing was largely an event, a moment of ordering that – despite the co-implication of huge numbers of people and things – has left little of material significance behind. To put this another way, the archeological record for Apollo will be slim, because so much of what made it matter was consumed in the event and what was brought back is only given significance by its part in the event. You would not know a moon rock if you saw one, unless it was labelled and in a vitrine.

I think this tells us something rather interesting about organization, and its relation to Space Age management. Apollo cannot only be imagined as an example of 'freedom' or 'escape', whether in political or theoretical terms. Despite the sight of an astronaut bouncing on the moon at one-sixth G being a liberation from gravity, the exploration of a new frontier, humanity leaving the cradle and so on (Parker 2007), it is clear that this could not have happened without very significant constraints being assembled. In political terms, and as Webb was well aware, what William Proxmire disparagingly referred to as 'corporate socialism' in November 1963 was necessary in order to channel huge resources (Bizony 2006, 121).[6] This was state interventionism on a massive scale, not an example of the freedom of the pioneer, 'lighting out for the territory' (Klerkx 2004, 336). At the same time, the organizations that were involved in the project gradually became more managed too, and the networks of organizations more densely interconnected. All sorts of other organizations also ramified from this network, selling breakfast cereals and frying pans. Even the Mafia got in on the act, managing to gain an interest in the vending-machine contracts at North American Aviation – a fact that did not help Jim Webb when it began to circulate in the post-Apollo 1 launch-pad fire enquiry (Bizony 2006, 188). For the mission to work, materials needed to be in certain places – ensuring that oxygen was in backpacks, water in spigots, and reactants in engines. One form of material in the wrong place at the wrong time, such as a wrench left in a machine, or not in place, such as the missing item on a checklist, could ensure that the whole network collapsed. Or, to put it in a less humanist way, that the network was 'reordered' in ways that could be fatal to many of the human elements involved.

In theoretical terms, this assembling of constraint involved the construction of a heterogeneous network of people and things in some sort of relation. There is symmetry here, not at all unlike the symmetries of angels and celestial spheres. The structuring of space requires the structuring of earth, and space ends up being organized in ways that reflect the interests of the key players on earth. Because this was organization on such a huge scale, or because the parties involved – big aerospace and big government – were already networks based on certain principles, it is hardly surprising that the form of organization that emerged was one which relied on market rhetoric, but did everything in its power to ensure that markets did not disrupt the predictability of flows, particularly flows of cash. The strategy of 'contractor penetration' by NASA meant 'NASA penetration' by contractors, and the inseparability of the two networks (Klerkx 2004, 164). Capitalism and nation-state socialism were necessarily entangled on the way to the moon. It helped that this was also a form of organization that grew from a genealogy of military understandings of necessary obedience and national duty, and consequently that constructed rules that ensured that deviance was excluded (Dickens and Ormrod 2007,

MacDonald 2007). NASA placed managers, and managerialist politicians, at the centre of how the organization understand itself (Johnson 2002).

The great chain that put boot prints on the moon was shaped by capitalism, the military and management. Some sort of organization was always going to be necessary, simply to ensure that success and survival were not random events, but did it have to be of this form? Were the stories of something else, something radically Other, always necessarily compromised by these entanglements with the powers and principalities of the earth?

The End

The first thing that Armstrong and Aldrin did on the moon was to eat a meal of beef and potatoes, butterscotch pudding, brownies and grape punch. Then they spent two hours and 31 minutes walking 250 metres on the moon. The end of Apollo seems trivial compared to the means. A few rocks, some photos, a litter of urine bags, trampled dust and a collapsed flag. The final end of Apollo came only two-and-a-half years later, with Apollo 17. No one has been back, and eight of the astronauts who stood on the moon are now dead, as of 2024. This is now a science-fiction future fading into the past. In a sense, the Space Age was the end of the age of industry, its steaming roaring metal now replaced by the marketing of information, miniaturization, and communication (Parker 2008). But it certainly wasn't the end of management. Indeed we could explain the ends in terms of the management means, as James Webb does. He, like Kennedy, wasn't really interested in space, but in what the state could do if enough organizations and resources were pointing in the right direction (Klerkx 2004, 134 *passim*). Apollo was intended to be a demonstration of this point, but I think it demonstrated something else too. The endless lists of amazing facts and big numbers are incredible enough in themselves, but for me the real seduction is untouched by such 'believe it or not' lists. The paradox was ultimately not about the state versus the market, but that NASA's complex organization intimated something else, something entirely other, something that could result from organization but never be explained by it.

In his book *American Technological Sublime*, David Nye writes about railroads, bridges and skyscrapers as examples of the sublime response that can be created by awesome forms of industrial engineering (1994). Or, to be more precise, he is writing about a particularly American sense of these as modern collective projects that are worthy of being tourist attractions in their own right. If the classical sublime was concerned with the emotions produced by peaks and storms, then this modern sublime is concerned with great energies, heights and distances. Precisely the sort of incredible facts that have I have sprinkled in this chapter. Nye devotes half a chapter to Apollo, and nicely demonstrates its aesthetic affinity with the atomic bomb, the World's Fair and the electrified cityscape. They were illustrations of the control of power, and of the power that can result from control, from being the most technologically advanced nation on the planet. Still, I think that Apollo exceeds all of these descriptions. The moon landing is certainly parasitic on power and technology, and the Apollo-Saturn vehicle the size of a small skyscraper. As I have shown above, it is also the end point of a hugely ramified and complex network of people, things and controls that shape the earth in order to make space possible. But all this does not contain Apollo, does not organize and manage its meaning for everyone, even for boys who 'like huddling in gangs and knowing the exact time'.[7]

Italo Calvino's *Invisible Cities* tells of one that rests on the earth only by long flamingo legs, whilst the city itself is high above the clouds:

> There are three hypotheses about the inhabitants of Baucis: that they hate the earth; that they respect it so much they avoid all contact; that they love it as it was before they existed and with spyglasses and telescopes aimed downward they never tire of examining it, leaf by leaf, stone by stone, ant by ant, contemplating with fascination their own absence.
>
> *(Calvino 1974, 77)*

Space is this absence in a much more profound sense. The absence of human organization, and the absence of any value that might mark an enduring difference between flesh and moon dust. This is entropy, the absence of organization, of order. The astronauts were fascinated by the earth, and took endless photographs of it, as it receded and then grew through their triple glazed portholes. Outside was vacuum and very little, almost nothing. Certainly nothing that could be inscribed with the varieties of humanism that made the flight possible, and allowed an astronaut to look misty eyed with wonder at their 'home'. Frederic Jameson says something similar, with reference to 'science fiction' films, noting the difficulty of representing space when it is so easy to 'paradoxically abandon space for the earthbound world of competition, government funding, male bonding, patriotism, science, bureaucracy, and technological innovation' (Jameson 2008, 183). In order to fit space into a plot – manifest destiny, market managerialism, humanism – the emptiness of space needs to be ignored in order to become the stage set for a story. That is why Webb's book is really about the age of management, and space is never given any space at all.

In Andrew Smith's touching book about the remaining moon walkers, he suggests two rather interesting, and perhaps contradictory, ideas. One is that his book was motivated by a single question, the question that everyone has always wanted to ask Armstrong – 'what was it like?' Embedded in that question is the idea that there must be something else, something we don't yet know, despite the millions of words that have been spent on Apollo since. Perhaps a glint in his eye, or some reassurance about infinity, from the man who was there, then, and could blot out the earth with his thumb. But what could he say to us, this man who 'never admits surprise' (Smith 2005, 349), the product of management that was designed to fill space with organization, and reduce chaos to prediction within normal parameters. The very person who might open the Otherness that the Apollo programme had as its end is incapable, because of its means, to tell us about anything but engineering. His is the language of management, and the calculus of the engineer, all packed in the obedient body of a military man.

William Burroughs captured the paradox nicely:

> Dr Paine of the Space Center in Houston says: "This flight was a triumph for the squares of this world who aren't ashamed to say a prayer now and then." Is this the great adventure of space? Are these men going to take the step into regions literally unthinkable in verbal terms? To travel in space you must leave the old verbal garbage behind: God talk, country talk, mother talk, love talk, party talk. You must learn to exist with no religion, no country, no allies. You must learn to live alone in silence. Anyone who prays in space is not there.
>
> *(Burroughs 1999, 320)*

No self- respecting NASA manager would have given this drug-addled homosexual the time of day, so he hadn't got a prayer of getting into space anyway. He and his like never will, unless the Space Age returns differently one day, organized of course, but perhaps not managed.

Notes

1 This chapter is based on (2009) 'Space Age Management', *Management and Organizational History* 4/3: 317–332.
2 Not as common a term at that time, when 'management' was still trying to distinguish itself from 'administration'.
3 Though a few pages later, he appears to contradict himself again, suggesting that 'the large complex endeavour cannot allow the executive such freedom of personal choice' (Webb 1969, 145). In context, he seems referring to middle managers, not 'leaders'.
4 For an account of politics, bureaucracy and culture in NASA forty years on, see Klerkx 2004, 142 *passim*.
5 For a revealing and relatively uncensored view of space shuttle era NASA from the point of view of an astronaut, see Mullane 2006.
6 For more on the political conjuring trick that allowed Keynesianism and market liberalism to coexist in the post-war US, see Barbrook 2007, 110 *passim*.
7 From W.H. Auden's poem 'Moon Landing'.

14

THE CIRCUS

I was driving from Stoke-on-Trent to Leicester in the English Midlands, on the long flat ribbon that slumps south of Derby, when I started to pass a fair in transit.[1] First a big truck, with a trailer carrying some kind of collapsible ride. A car and oversized caravan, a brightly painted truck, then another, and another. I passed about thirty vehicles, spread along ten or fifteen miles, most emblazoned with the name of the owner of the fair. An organization then, on the move, following the money.

Many organizations aren't very mobile. Universities, for example, tend to be solid things that grow themselves into the ground with imagined ivy and, leaving the ontological problems aside, appear to be located in one or two places. Other organizations might be multiple, but still sedentary, such as banks, shops, factories and so on. And then there are some organizations that can move. They fold themselves away, and roll away, later to unfold somewhere else. Some of the simpler ones don't unfold much, like mobile libraries and ice cream vans, others decant themselves and their bags into new spaces, like hairdressers or plumbers who visit you in your home. More complex nomadic organizations often require some sort of infrastructure that they can hook up to, such as a travelling production arriving at a theatre, or a sports team at a stadium. These latter examples remind us that organizations are often necessarily entangled with other organizations. So when the Formula 1 Grand Prix arrives in town, the organization that runs the racetrack becomes merged with the organizations that run the cars, and the one that own the franchise (as well as a host of other organizations that pitch up and sell hot dogs, run the security, organize the social media and so on).

Circuses are complex organizations but from the outside, they appear to require only permission, space and an audience.[2] Everything else they bring

DOI: 10.4324/9781032714288-19

The Circus **251**

with them – the ticket booth, the generator, the tent, the candy floss, the performers. There are over a thousand circuses worldwide, with Italy and Germany having particular concentrations, and India having some of the largest (Stoddart 2000, 43; Cottle 2006, 119). According to the Association of Circus Proprietors, in 2008 there were about thirty circuses touring the UK. Not everything will necessarily be carried by the circus – the mobile toilets might be sourced locally, for example – but everything has to be moved. Afterwards, all they leave is yellowed grass and tyre tracks, and bag mountains of litter to be taken to the local dump. As the US saying goes 'nothing left but wagon tracks and popcorn sacks' (Ogden 1993, 338).

This spatial mobility is unusual, but what makes it even more interesting is that it seems to be aimed at making all sorts of categories become mobile too. Circuses are places where bodies do extraordinary things, and extraordinary things are done to bodies. The voice, whether talking or singing, takes second place to more visceral forms of sensation and expression – the scream, the roar, provoked by the sight of something awe-ful or amazing. Humans do things that only animals can do – balance, fly, carry heavy weights – human bodies are subjected to inhuman treatment, and animals show human intelligence. Food is excessively large or sweet, noises are loud and painful, smells are intense, colours are bright, and insincerity and violence are masked by a red nose.

In this chapter, I am interested in the circus as both an excessive organization, and a mobile one, and I want to understand something about the relation between these two features. I will explore the circus as a powerful cultural representation of otherness, of an irreducible strangeness, but also a business that makes money by moving people and things around. I want to show how magic and miracles are produced through economic and institutional mechanisms and, as with so many of the chapters in this book, that disorganization requires organization and vice versa (Cooper 1986). I will begin with the magic, and then pull the curtain aside to see the machine that systematically produces disorder. Though I am mostly concerned with the circus, I will also necessarily mention fairs, carnivals and freak shows. At different times, and in different places, the four forms have been related, and it is difficult to make a clear distinction between them. Finally, most of my examples are from the US and UK, which reflects my pitch and my ignorance. There are plenty of circuses in other parts of the world, and I do mention them occasionally, but they are not under the spotlight here.

Representing the Circus

Whatever we say about the circus as an organization, about its economics or its anthropology, it is difficult not to notice its strangeness. A social-scientific description of the circus might somehow miss the myth, would fail to catch the very weirdness that it welcomes. Consider, for example, Rudy Horn, who would balance six cups of tea on his head whilst riding an unicycle, flick the sugar cubes in with his foot, and then finally flick the spoon into the top cup (Cottle 2006, 8). In a Mexican circus, Hickman reports seeing four boxing chimps looking like old men, but with babies' nappies underneath their boxing shorts (2001, 36). In 1792, there are mentions of an act involving someone riding around in a wig made from bees (Stoddart 2000, 90), whilst in 1972, Freddy Knie Jr presented a tiger riding on a rhinoceros. Or Schmarlowski the animal trainer, who dresses a woman in a fur coat that suddenly dissolves into dozens of live polecats with a fox playing the part of a collar (Stevens 2004, 9, 22). This is the stuff of dreams and nightmares, of surreal juxtapositions and motivations hidden by greasepaint.

What makes it even stranger is that this is also a work organization which became a standard setting for wholesome ideas about childhood too. Rather like cowboys and pirates for boys, and horse-riding schools and ballet companies for girls, the circus was a place for stories (and toys, comics and lunchboxes), which were exciting and moral. In children's fiction and television, such as Enid Blyton's English circus books, or the US TV show *Circus Boy*, baby elephants go missing, tents are threatened by storms, and children ensure that the show goes on. Here, the circus was a community, in which clowns can be kindly uncles and lion tamers have mysterious pasts. More widely, the circus provided a comprehensible backdrop for characters, plots and songs that were simultaneously exotic and homely. TV shows such as *Circus of the Stars*, films and plays such as *Annie Get Your Gun*, *Barnum* and *Dumbo* could be realized in an immediately recognizable way and provide plenty of opportunities for someone brave and pure of heart to save the day.

This rather sanitized version of the circus was certainly encouraged by circus owners from the late nineteenth century onwards. Partly to counter the various moral and gender panics that accompanied the organization in its wanderings, the marketing often stressed the intensity of the physical discipline required, as well as the family nature of the circus as an entertainment (Davis 2002, 35). Yet despite the successful construction of the sawdust and sequins, its more troubling side never went away. As we have seen, many work organizations have been represented in a 'gothic' style at various times and, for at least the last 150 years, the circus has often been depicted as a dangerous, excessive and secretive place. In Dickens' *Hard Times* of 1854, it is counterposed to the grim industrial city but suffused with an otherness that is often a little frightening, partly because it is a space of freedom, but also of mystery and difference. By the late nineteenth century, sensationalist English novels such as Amy Reade's 1892 *Slaves of the Sawdust* were presenting it as a place of coercion and fear for women and children. The book contributed to the passing of legislation which announced that only men could engage in dangerous performances, preventing cruelty to children and unbecoming behaviour in women (Stoddart 2000, 74).

By the twentieth century, the circus has two very different lives – one as a happy place for children, and another as a place of monstrosity. As an early example of the latter, in the cult film *Freaks* (1932), Tod Browning produced a movie about a group of sideshow circus performers who turn violent; the film was banned in the UK for thirty years on the grounds that it was simply too disturbing. Later in the century, the circus films of Frederico Fellini use the brightly lit ring and its outer darkness to manifest psychological interiors, in the same way that the haunted house came to be used in many horror films. In literature, Ray Bradbury's 1963 novel *Something Wicked This Way Comes* provides us with a demonic railway circus which sweeps into an innocent mid-Western town. Its sideshows whisper of temptation and fear – 'Mademoiselle Tarot', 'The Dangling Man', 'The Demon Guillotine', 'The Skeleton', 'The Illustrated Man'. The hall of mirrors, the merry-go-round and the discordant scream of the calliope, together with the psychotic leer of the clown, have been used in many thriller and horror films since. Twenty years later, Angela Carter's *Nights at the Circus* (2006) plays with the same cast of characters, but turns them into a feminist baroque, in which strong men discover their emotions, tigers dance with tears in their eyes, the monkeys negotiate contracts, and a clown gradually goes insane, provoking the audience to laugh even harder.

Yet the circus is a secular organization. There are no ancient gods or scented candles being invoked and the performer escapes injury and death through their own skill: not through divine or demonic intervention, or tradition, but through the machineries of reason and training. Chaos is prevented through discipline (Stoddart 2000, 13) or, as Carter puts it, this is a celebration of 'the triumphs of man's will over gravity and over rationality' (2006, 121). Of course, the knowledge of the fall, the knife hitting the assistant, or the lion's jaws closing must always haunt every successful performance. Order and disorder, organization and disorganization, the light and the dark, are in close relation, with one seeming to invite the other as a precondition of being there in the ring. Other separations are blurred too. Whether it involves flying people or hats made from bees, the act performs an event or thing that could belong in at least two different categories. So something normal is performed upside down, or on a high wire, or boxing monkeys blur culture and nature, animal and human (Carmeli 2003). Being shot from a cannon, putting your head in the mouth of a lion – these are all things that no rational person would attempt, but are performed as demonstrations of the extension of reason, not the love of god or the devil.

The circus is a place of anomalies. Unlike the neighbours and workmates you saw yesterday and will see tomorrow, this is a gathering of transients who cannot be entirely understood or trusted. Both their mobility and their ostentation present problems to the settled locals. The word 'mountebank' (like *banquiste* and *saltimbanco*) comes to us as a way of describing someone who stood on a bench or table to entertain, and would often be regarded as a disreputable character. This is someone who draws attention to themselves, but may not be the person that they pretend to be. The deception might be cold-eyed and driven by cash, but could also be tragic, as when we refer to the tears of a clown, and the sadness behind the painted smile. In Katie Hickman's account of a Mexican circus, Mundo Bell performs as a clown just after hearing that his father has died in a caravan behind the tent. 'But, ah!' Mundo says, 'If you are not *del circo* it is almost impossible to explain it. Perhaps I should not even try [...] Even though the tears were running down my face, the next moment I was out there, out in the ring as usual' (Hickman 2001, 242; see also Davis 2002, 99, for a similar story). Pretence is at the heart of such performances. The clown, coming from the old English for clod, clot, or lump – so a clumsy or stupid bumpkin – must pretend stupidity in order to earn a living; just as the *aerialiste* must make her strength seem effortless; and the lion tamer ensure that the half-blind and toothless big cat growls convincingly. These are people who are 'dressing in spangles yet living in tents and trailers' (Hoagland 2004, 3). Circuses trade on things not being what they seem, and make inauthenticity and transience into a way of life.

No surprise then that the circus has been thought as an example of both prohibition and transgression (Adams 2001, Davis 2002). Like the carnival – the idea of the world turned upside down (Bakhtin 1984) – the debate seems to be the question of whether the circus, freak show and fair are forms of entertainment which simply propagate ideology, or whether they simultaneously question it. Transgression is not a particularly helpful word here, however fashionable it has become, because any 'transgression' could be taken to both mark the boundary that cannot be crossed, at the same time that it shows that it *can* be crossed. Witnessing an act which transgresses a cultural or material boundary does not necessarily make the audience into subversives. 'Reading' the circus is more complex than this. We can admire the discipline that allows someone to have a hat made from bees, without ourselves wanting a hat made from bees. The phrase 'don't do this at home' can be understood as both stern prohibition and seductive invitation, or another version of the necessary relation between order and disorder. The circus, it seems to me, neatly shows us that disorder must be organized, and that any boundary crossing is also a boundary marking.[3]

Take, for example, the ways in which the circus presented what Rachel Adams calls the 'ethnographic freak': 'Framed in pseudoethnographic language by showmen who called themselves "doctors" and "professors", anthropological exhibits at the freak show often provided American audiences with their primary source of information about the non-Western world' (Adams 2001, 28).

By using the legitimacy of the academy, as well as the endless restatement of words like 'true', 'genuine' and 'authentic', entrepreneurs like Barnum hoped to bring new middle-class customers to their entertainments. A century ago, circuses, museums, zoos and sideshows were all potentially places to find knowledge, and all were capable of deploying ideas about nature and evolution in order to justify exhibiting animals and human-animal hybrids, as well as scientifically curious human beings.[4] The Bronx Zoo exhibited the man Ota Benga, a member of the African Batwa tribe, in a cage with a trained orangutan; Barnum posing a 'What is it?' supposing Benga to be half-man and half-monkey. The Yahi Indian Ishi lived for a while in the University of California Hearst Museum of Anthropology, and was studied by Alfred Kroeber (Adams 2001, 31–56; see also Davis 2002, 131). Exhibits like this travelled with circuses, displayed as part of the 'midway' that led to the circus' Big Top. For Adams, all were trading on the idea that the 'wild man' allows us to identify civilized man, and to position the audience as part of the geographical and historical superiority of the white northern peoples. In other words, the circus was selling the myths of racism and imperialism, and perhaps could therefore be safely filed as part of the ideological apparatus.

This seems to be a critique of many of the exotic aspects of the circus – of the juggling Italians and balancing Indians who are closer to nature than the civilized audience. Adams, here relying on the work of Judith Butler, also suggests that the freak show tells us about the ways in which the figure of the Other is constructed. There is nothing 'natural' about the unnaturalness of the freak, and our definitions of difference depend on our socially located senses of who we are, and who we are not (Adams 2001, 6; see also Goffman 1963, Bogdan 1988). Davis argues that women growing beards or sewing with their feet, midgets dressed as royalty and people swallowing swords, all invite the viewer to question normality, not simply reinforce it (2002, 27). Audience is also important here, as when the North American customers might have been recently freed black slaves, paying to stare at people rattling spears or wearing head-dresses. Some of the exhibits may have been born elsewhere, but most were just as likely to be poor US blacks themselves, paid to snarl and tear at raw meat (Adams 2001, 166).[5] This nudges at the idea that we are all freaks. Whilst it is certainly true that circuses can trade on an idea of learned skill rather than pre-existing difference, freakishness is common and mutable. Elephants used to be freakish, tattooed men and ethnographic others have been freaks, and the freakishness of physical prowess heavily depends on changing assumptions about social identities.

Growing out of the ruins of the railroad circuses, the 'new circus' of the 1970s onwards often seemed to articulate a counter-cultural sensibility. They tended to be smaller, more community oriented, collective in decision making, communal in living practices, and cooperative in structure. Club-juggling routines might satirize assembly-line speed-up techniques, and a bohemian sensibility would shape aspects of the show (Albrecht 1995, 22, 26; Hartzman 2005, 236 *passim*). The new circus was much more explicit about its transgressions, with bearded lady stand-up comedians making jokes about patriarchy; freaks who are using surgery and tattoos to turn themselves into lizards or cats, whilst the sideshow sells books by Deleuze, Ballard and Foucault (Adams 2001, 219). By the early 1990s, groups like 'Archaos' and 'The Circus of Horrors' were self-consciously aiming to shock, as well as aiming at a younger audience (Cottle 2006, 249). Using what might be described as a 'metal gothic' aesthetic, they featured exploding cars, roaring motorbikes, scrapyard pyromania, and a female clown who bit the heads off raw mackerel and spat them into the audience (Albrecht 1995, 90). This seemed to be a circus which was challenging conventions, perhaps even self-consciously engaged in ideology critique, and not simply reproducing the dull racist or sexist routines.

The circus can not be staked once and for all for or against a particular politics, but perhaps it can always be understood as an institutionalized questioning of stability and classification. It necessarily relies on the prior existence of assumptions about gender, gravity, animals and cannons in order to do its work, and it must simultaneously confirm and deny what we assume in order to produce amazement. If we didn't make assumptions about human bodies, then we could not be amazed by a small black person with a spear, or someone with no legs who walks on their hands. If we thought that humans could fly and animals could reason, the *aerialiste* would leave us uninterested and the educated pig seem stupid. Stunts will only work if our understanding is stunted, if our imagination is constrained and our prejudices in place. At the same time, the existence of the anomaly produces a space into which doubt is invited. In Angela Carter's *Nights at the Circus*, the central conceit is that the *aerialiste* (like an angel) has wings and can really fly. So if women can perform athletic feats like this, what else could they do? If chimps can box, might they be like us? The circus demands that we see disorder from the viewpoint of order. At the beginning of *Thus Spake Zarathustra*, Nietzsche describes man as a rope stretched between 'beast and Superman'. The rope is the human, a crossing which he, in typical fashion, describes as perilous and trembling. Presumably, for Nietzsche, we begin as dull beast, and might end as Superman, if our nerves are strong enough. Leaving such humanist heroism aside, the materialist point is that the tightrope joins things that are separate and allows the wire-walker to demonstrate both gravity and its overcoming. It joins the earthbound animal and the sequinned angel.

Community

The circus is a place of danger, dissimulation and confusion:

> The circus is a jealous wench. Indeed, that is an understatement. She is a ravening hag who sucks your vitality as a vampire drinks blood – who kills the brightest stars in her crown and who will allow no private life to those who serve her; wrecking their homes, ruining their bodies, and destroying the happiness of their loved ones by her insatiable demands. She is all of these things, and yet, I love her as I love nothing else on earth.
>
> *(Henry Ringling North, in Feiler 1995, 9)*

This is because there are many accounts of the circus that treat it as a community, with all the virtues which that implies. Ron Beadle, for example, has used the circus as a way of suggesting that this is a life which is substantially an end in itself. In Alasdair MacIntyre's terms, it is a community aimed at the excellence of the practice which sustains the community (Beadle 2003). Beadle's account provides a philosophical gloss for the idea that the circus is not only a machine for questioning categories, but also a way of life. Like other isolated or intense occupations, the story then told is one that stresses cultural distinctiveness. This produces a kind of anthropology of practices, superstitions and argot (Cottle 2006, 91). For example, Harry Crews gives an account of 'Carney' – a language made by deliberately inserting extra syllables into English words so that beer becomes bee-a-zeer and so on (2004, 54). It seems that the point of using Carney, as well as the many specific and exclusionary terms commonly used in the circus, is to demonstrate something about 'us' and 'them'. In most cases, those excluded are the slack-jawed crowds – 'the "lot lice", the Elmers, rubes, towners, hayseeds, hicks, yokels' (Hoagland 2004, 2). It is their dumb stupidity that justifies their exclusion, and that they deserve to have their credulity exploited and their pockets picked. Most of all though, it is their immobility that condemns them to boredom, and allows the circus performer to laugh at them behind his hand: 'Eat your heart out, rube, was part of his message. We'll be gone tomorrow. We'll see Chicago. We'll be in Florida. You stay here and milk your cows!' (ibid., 10).

Yet mobility is not the only difference that can be deployed, because it is also common to distinguish circus people from the fair, or the carnival. As Gerry Cottle, a circus owner himself, puts it, fairs have a less settled workforce who tend to be 'younger jack the lads who have joined for the girls' (Cottle 2006, 79). According to Cottle, in the UK, there is no love lost between the 'Association of Circus Proprietors' and 'The Showman's Guild', which represents fun fairs, in terms of the control of pitches and routes (Cottle 2006, 237). Compared to carneys, circus people are professionals. Internal to many circuses is another 'us' and 'them': that of the family. The idea, both as a metaphor and a description of actual kin relations, is very common indeed (Davis 2002, 72; Feiler 1995, 100). Being outside the family, being a 'josser' (Beadle 2003), however long your relation with the circus, was a category that could be deployed to explain or exclude. Even for circus owners (Cottle 2006, 33), ethnographers (Carmeli 2001), and participant observers (Hickman 2001), the warmth of being accepted is always haunted by this ineradicable difference.

Bruce Feiler describes the circus he stayed with for a year as unified against others, but also internally divided because of its 'fundamentally liberal' ethos. He depicts a workplace that was remarkably diverse and tolerant, but where everyone gossips about everything in quite vicious terms, and in which people ultimately survive by minding their own business (Feiler 1995, 237–239). There is some evidence for this view of the circus as a libertarian community. Gay and lesbian relationships, often-long term ones, appear quite often in accounts (Feiler 1995, 122; Cottle 2006, 69, 84), as do stories about male transvestites performing as women (Davis 2002, 115). Circuses were also routinely ethnically diverse workplaces, with 'exotic' ethnicities being marketed as positive features – even if they sometimes had to be manufactured with stage names. Compared to other labour markets, there was even a relative parity of reward between male and female stars, and even non-white and disabled performers being able to command income and prestige which would have been denied to them in the immobile world (Stoddart 2000, 50):

> An alligator girl can't be a waitress, or a receptionist, or a nurse, or a babysitter. How many job opportunities are open to Siamese twins? How many personnel managers are looking for monkey-faced boys? Would you climb into a taxi driven by a dwarf with a pointed head, or a guy nine feet tall?
>
> *(Dick Best, a freak-show booking agent, in Hartzman 2005, 5)*

Of course the idea of the community of outsiders is only partly true, because we can also find accounts of cruelty, racism and discrimination (Feiler 1995, 186; Crews 2004, 58). In Ogden's dictionary of the circus, there is a story about a prostitute who was running a 'line up joint' in which workers queued for sex when the circus was raided by the police. Instead of admitting to prostitution, she claimed that she had been raped by four Black workers, and they were all immediately lynched, and hung from the light poles on the showground (Ogden 1993, 234). But even if the circus is never isolated from the brutalities of the outside world, it is still seen as a place where people can go and be different. For an US author such as Feiler, this means that the circus exemplifies the American liberal melting pot and 'a dream to do what they wanted in a place that was free, a desire to carve out a little corner of the world where they could be themselves' (Feiler 1995, 270). Stripping the westering ethnocentrism from this account, we are left with a version of the circus as a place where the romantic outsider can find fellow travellers. The grey stabilities of normal life can be escaped, and a life lived with danger and authenticity. Even Karl Marx was seduced by the image:

> When we see the back of an individual contorted in fear and bent in humiliation, we cannot but look around and doubt our very existence, fearing lest we lose ourselves. But on seeing a fearless acrobat in bright costume, we forget about ourselves, feeling that we have somehow risen above ourselves and reached the level of universal strength. Then we can breathe easier.
>
> *(in Albrecht 1995, 8)*

Mobility

The idea of the circus as a community of outsiders is related to the phenomena that I began with, its mobility. When the 15-year-old Gerry Cottle ran away to join the Roberts Brothers Circus in 1961, he left this little note: 'Please do not under any circumstances try to find me. I have gone forever. I have joined the circus. You do not understand me. You are not listening to me. I do not need O levels where I am going. I am going to join the circus. I have gone' (Cottle 2006, 1). All accounts of circuses are predicated on this sense of flight. Of endless movement across and between, and necessarily leaving somewhere called 'home'. Perhaps this involves escaping from prejudice and history, and into some sort of tolerant community – a place where there will be no credit checks, qualifications, or drug tests. So the travelling circus brings to mind refugees, a straggling line of the dispossessed, at the same time as it is a romantic gypsy caravan:

> In one way or another the circus is full of the enchanted: many come here for love, both girls and men; others are orphans, runaways, or simply nomads, such as myself. Our presence occasions neither comment nor surprise: it is expected, because it has always been so.
>
> *(Hickman 2001, 16)*

Perhaps for performers and audience, there is a 'shared illusion of escape' (Feiler 1995, 176). In Charles Dickens' *Hard Times*, the vitality and spontaneity of the circus is contrasted to the repetitive narrowness of industrial experience, whether at school or at work. In some sense, the golden age of circus makes sense only in distinction to stable times and places, and its appearance coincides with urbanization. The circus moves between towns, and settles in marginal places, appearing and disappearing overnight. In England, the first tents were made by sail-makers with masts for poles (Stevens 2004, 15), all held under tension in order to mimic the action of the billowing wind. Even the work of circus people seems to be like play, happening during high days and holidays, perhaps looking like the sorts of things that children might do, provoking the gasps and laughter not found in the boredom of the factory or office.

Though circuses are mobile, they are not quite temporary. The idea of a temporary organization is usually one that is brought together for a specific project, and takes the form of a coalition made, for example, to build a skyscraper or make a film (Bryman et al. 1987, Kenis et al. 2009). Though in the long term, all organizations are temporary, project organizations usually announce that they will wind themselves up into their constituent parts once a particular goal has been achieved, and are best characterized as 'multi-firm temporary networks' (Kavanagh 1998), in which the component parts have a degree of permanence that the whole doesn't have. This isn't quite true of the circus, since it usually assembles its singular organization once a year, for the touring season, employing various people from a network of performers and labourers and adding them to a core of people who are the same from year to year. There are echoes here of the dissolution of permanence augured by terms such as post-Fordism, clusters and networks, but are probably best characterized as a seasonal numerical flexibility. The 'rolling show' (Davis 2002, 16) has a cyclical connection to space and time, repeating its dissolution and assembly between a series of places, and also annually as it re-paints and re-stitches for next year.

However, the idea of the circus as a caravan of Bohemians doesn't really fit with the history of the institution. Though fairs and menageries were mobile, and the former certainly involved various forms of entertainment, like their ancient antecedents, the first modern circuses were one element of the static entertainments of the industrial city. What is normally defined as the first circus in the UK dates to 1768, and in the US to 1793, but both were based in amphitheatres and circular parade grounds; it wasn't until 1825 that the first mobile tented circus started to perform in the US (Davis 2002, 16; Feiler 1995, 38), and in the 1840s in England. The early circus was essentially a display of the disciplined mobility of the horse, and the skills of the rider, sometimes combined with military or historical pageant. An 1827 poster for Astley's Circus in London notes that the 'unpractised eye' might not appreciate the 'scientific management of the Rein' that was being deployed in the show (Stoddart 2000, 68). That the move from hippodrome to big tent happens first in the US might reflect the cultural influence of the medicine shows with attached performers, as well as the menageries and rodeos which were already moving across the expanding territories by this period. The golden age of mobility again really begins in the US with the train circuses that haltingly began in 1856 and, by the close of the century, had become in size and complexity 'the city that moves by night'.

For these giant circuses, the contrast with the modern sense of the word 'circus' as chaos and disorganization is remarkable. A commentator in *The Times* writes about Phineas T. Barnum's *12,000*-seat 1889 show in London in the following way:

> Things being ordered on such a scale, one reads without surprise in the programme that the establishment comprises no fewer than 1,200 "people" and 380 horses. In all its branches the great enterprise [...] works with a smoothness implying a high degree of departmental organization and efficiency. It consists of almost as many departments as the United States Government itself ... .
>
> *(in Cook 2005, 229)*

The scale itself seemed to become part of the spectacle. According to the Ringling Brothers Golden Jubilee programme in 1933, the show travelled over 20,000 miles in over a hundred double-length railroad cars, with 1,500 employees, 735 horses, six herds of elephants and a thousand other wild animals. The circus had its own lawyer, doctor, dentists and detectives, and its kitchen served 4,800 meals a day, cooking 10,000 pancakes for breakfast (Wood 2002, 215; see also Davis 2002, 38). It is said that the US Army and Kaizer Wilhelm were observing the logistics of circuses from the 1890s onwards (Davis 2002, 78; Feiler 1995, 55). The production of a mobile fantasy required a considerable degree of planning.

Economics

The modern circus was produced by a combination of entrepreneurial capitalism, mass marketing, urbanization and mass transport. When Barnum visited an English fair at Greenwich in 1844, he expressed disgust at the disorganization, the noise, the crowded public transport – 'an English "fair" in these degenerate days is the most *foul* place a man could easily get into' (in Cook 2005, 64). In the same year, he visited Franconi's summer circus in Paris, and was impressed with the neo-classical design and size, and the pricing of the 6,000 seats (ibid., 72–73). By the 1870s, he is touring his own 'Greatest Show on Earth', a gigantic consolidation which he confidently expects will force smaller 'one-horse concerns' to 'hide their diminished heads in the cross-roads and back woods' (ibid., 148). 'P.T. Barnum's Grand Travelling Museum, Menagerie, Caravan, and Circus' travelled by rail to large towns and trumpeted its arrival as noisily as possible in order to ensure that ticket sales covered its huge expenses. These shows became part of a global supply chain which (like the zoo) needed to source animals, as well as people for acts, was doing frequent foreign tours, had franchises, agents and acts around the world and, by the time Barnum died in 1891, employed a staff of thousands.

The contemporaneous coining of the words 'Barnumize', or 'Barnumism' reflected the general sense that a new kind of hyperbolic puff was emerging (Stevens 2004, 12). To a certain extent, the need for the puff was driven by risk. The more Barnum spent on his shows, logistics and supply chain, the more he had to spend on marketing in order to bring the punters crowding in. For all the big circuses, the majority of the marketing was print based and involved covering towns with posters. As the circus developed, there were also increasingly sophisticated efforts to gain local media coverage through PR exercises and strategic sponsorship. This required that every large circus ran a timed series of advance railroad cars with a staff who engineered publicity, as well as sourcing supplies and local labour, arranging accommodation and licences, disbursing bribes, as well as putting up the posters (Davis 2002, 43). Competition with other shows was fierce. The advance parties would also try find out about the movements of other circuses, attempting to arrive in town a week before their competitors and, if needed, 'night riders' might deface or post over existing publicity[6]. If another circus had already posted, 'Wait' paper might be posted on top, usually simple white sheets instructing the reader to 'Wait for the Big One' and not to waste their money on the earlier competitor (Ogden 1993, 362).

For all the circuses, there was also a general need to counter bad publicity, given the widespread perceptions of small-scale criminality and immorality that were associated with its arrival. Janet Davis writes about the social panics associated with circuses, and the moral decline that they were seen to inaugurate, particularly in terms of gender and the partly clad female performer (2002, 30, 85). There was a clear need to market the respectability of the circus and to assert its role in nation building, tradition and some sort of childlike innocence. The expense of scale meant that it was necessary to market a wholesome product to families, but so too was the need for efficient disassembly, transport and reassembly. Because of the size of the daily audience required, movement was necessary since the local market was quickly exhausted, however intense and effective the publicity. The more rapidly the big show could move, the more efficiently it could extract profits from many different towns. Connecting this necessary mobility and size back to marketing was the marketing of mobility and size itself. Circuses would parade through town on arrival, often for hours, and encourage locals to come and see the Big Top being erected, as well as circulating puff which stressed the sheer scale and variety of the attractions on offer. Size, mobility and advertising were all entangled in a necessary relation in order to ensure that the circus could continue to roll.

Less visible was the complex division of labour within the circus which allowed for a tent to be erected, candy floss to be sold and a show to be performed. Like many organizations, circuses were sites of complex formal and informal hierarchies. For example, the larger circuses used numbered identity badges, and different colours of uniform, in order to identify different categories of worker (Davis 2002, 41). The wages of workers, and performers, depended on their position in the hierarchy. Even freaks were paid differently, depending on their relative freakishness and rarity (Adams 2001, 256). Spatially, there were codes that determined the position that a performer had in the dressing tents (Davis 2002, 65), very commonly with clowns segregated into a 'clown alley', aerialists deemed higher status than equestrians and so on. The same sort of arrangements determined where people sat in the cookhouse, or whether you ate in the cookhouse at all (Odgen 1993, 114), as well as the luxury of your sleeping compartment. Feiler, reporting on his year in a contemporary US circus, even writes about the invisible hierarchy that took your caravan away from the noise of the generator, or divided heavy lifting labour from the more glamorous ringside props labour (Feiler 1995, 55, 250).

Perhaps mindful of these divisions, in the large US circuses, there were attempts at constructing early organizational culture programmes, pretty much at the same time that Ford and others were worrying about the morals of their workforce (Beder 2000). There were specified rules for behaviour, alcohol consumption and dress, and even organized sports, picnics and recreation seemingly aimed at instilling loyalty (Davis 2002, 76–77).[7] At the bottom, and perhaps the real subject of these behavioural controls, were the roustabout labourers who hauled ropes in the middle of the night, and slept three to a bunk on lice-infested mattresses in the noisiest part of the train. This was hard labour for hobos. Sometimes, the circus could even get locals to work for nothing, or next to nothing, with promises of tickets to see the show. This was commonly called 'Chinese labour', with the derogatory terms 'punk pusher' or 'kid worker' being applied to the people who hired them (Ogden 1993, 73, 224). For a century, the pay and conditions of cheap muscle was what allowed the circuses to be mobile and profitable. There was little stardust involved at this end of the hierarchy;

> People are juggling themselves, hand-to-mouth, in brassy penury, in the circus, not just tossing torches or chancing an awful clawing. Then they'll live in back-street rented rooms during the winter until they can take to the road again.
>
> *(Hoagland 2004., 3)*

In the US, there were attempts at unionization from the American Federation of Labour from the late 1930s onwards, but they were all unsuccessful until the stand-off between the Teamsters, the American Guild of Variety Artists, and the Ringling Brothers and Barnum and Bailey Circus in 1956 (Davis 2002, 229; Odgen 1993, 295). The union victory and the consequent announcement that Ringling would no longer travel was widely reported as an example of the destructive power of unions attacking a traditional American institution, though it could just as easily be taken to demonstrate that one element of circus economics was the exploitation of manual labour.

There was also much money to be made selling candyfloss and popcorn,[8] as well as rigged games of chance and tickets to sideshows. The people who ran concessions paid a 'privilege' to management in order to be able to set up next to the circus. Though usually they would be selling food or toys, or exhibiting freaks or curios, often enough the concessions would be for grift – shell and card games in which the punter had no chance of winning. Grift could also mean that people were effectively given cover for shortchanging or pickpocketing. The 'lucky boys' who 'got the X' for a particular concession paid management, and in turn sometimes part of this cash might be used to bribe local officials and police officers in order to turn a blind eye to the complaints of aggrieved punters (Ogden 1993, 183, 377). As well as these sorts of scams for making money off locals, Feiler describes a complex series of economic relationships between people working in the circus. Collectively referred to as 'cherry pie', he details how workers augmented their salaries by buying and selling services, work and commodities from each other, as well as doing little extras around the site (Feiler 1995, 58–59). The thriving internal economy of the circus was again one of the ways in which low pay could be justified by circus management.

What might be called the 'business model' of the circus relies on a series of complex relations between mobility, size and marketing, as well as a clear division of labour with a star system at the top and exploitation at the bottom. The outlaw swagger, as well as the mysteries and anomalies, are made possible precisely because the circus is such a highly organized place. The greasepaint and sequins might distract us from questions of management, organization and economics, but they are visible enough if you look (Beadle and Konyot 2006). Like NASA, this is a place where miracles are engineered for money.

Finale

Nowadays, I think the circus is constituted by a certain nostalgia. Like eggs and community, it was better in the old days:

> Houses were good, it being the tail end of what they call the Golden Age of the Circus, before roads and cars offered people in small towns choices.

When we came to town, banks closed, as did all schools and businesses. Attendance was routinely more than 80 percent of the people in any given town.

(Hough 2004, 288)

Much post-golden age writing now stresses the various crises which are facing the institution (Truzzi 1968, Albrecht 1995, Stoddart 2000, 75; Beadle 2003). The rise of concern about animal welfare, together with increasingly interventionist regulatory regimes, means that it is more and more difficult for the circus to use animals, particularly the iconic exotic ones. Criticisms of the use of animals in the circus go back to at least the 1930s (Albrecht 1995, 201), but now mass urbanization, and a general distance from all but a few species (apart from those in the freezer cabinet), has resulted in a romanticized welfarism which effectively ended the classic circus in much of the Western world (Albrecht 1995, 222). Regulatory regimes applied to labour have put up costs, and increasingly dense urbanization has made it more difficult to get a cheap pitch near a large population. Health and safety rules, transportation costs and trade unions make the circus more and more expensive, and the stability of the zoo and theme park a capital intensive alternative. Finally, there is the question of audience, and the idea that people don't really recognize a good circus anymore. The short film 'cinema of attractions' originally screened in sideshows has grown to become the glittering array of stars that is Hollywood (Stoddart 2000, 27; Adams 2001, 64). Charlie Chaplin and Buster Keaton made the switch from circus to cinema early, and the growth of the film industry in the twentieth century turned film stunts into special effects. Now, the attractions of digital gaming, computer-generated animation and take-away meals delivered thanks to an immigrant on a bicycle mean that the audience is no longer minded to appreciate the secular skills displayed in the ring. Why pay to watch someone jumping around on a horse when you could stay in and watch battles involving mythological creatures, or superheroes flying into buildings?[9]

But perhaps the best circus was always in the past, and the contemporary crisis is nothing that new. In 1919, Lenin declared the Russian circus a national treasure, and his first people's Minister of Education A.V. Lunacharsky said, 'Our primary task must be to wrest the circus away the opportunists who play to the baser tastes of the public. Once it is free of this influence, it will certainly become what it must be: an academy of physical beauty and merriment' (in Albrecht 1995, 8).

Elements of the new circus movement have a similar distaste for the cheapening effects of commercialism on the circus, and stress its community building and family values elements – 'the inherent honesty, purity and dignity of Circus are perverted by exhibitionism, the easy or dishonest trick, or commercial exploitation' (Alan Slifka, in Albrecht 1995, 50). Beset by alternative and morally cheapening entertainments, the circus must be defended. This myth, whether in the USSR then or the US now, avoids any account of the economy and organization of the circus, of the labour practices, hyperbolic marketing and routine grift that have accompanied the travelling mountebanks. Barnum's puff for his 'Parliament of Peculiar and Puzzling Physical Phenomena and Prodigies' (in Hartzman 2005, 23) sits uneasily with the idea of the circus as a form of inspirational athletics, a callisthenics for the education of the citizen, or even a celebration of queer bodies.

The problem with a nostalgic account is that the sanitized and morally wholesome circus only ever existed in the books where children save baby elephants. The actual circus was always much more complicated, dirtier and much more interesting. Like fairs and carnivals, it is necessarily a highly organized place; otherwise, it wouldn't be able to move, or perform after it had moved, or pack itself up and move again. Normally, the organization is supposed to be invisible to the audience, who are expected not to want to see the machinery in operation. Sometimes, of course, it is seen. One English review of the Barnum and Bailey Circus in 1889 complained that 'the spectator feels himself oppressed by the variety of efforts made for his entertainment ... He will perhaps be constrained to imagine himself in some vast factory, with its endless spindles and revolving shafts and pulleys. (in Cook 2005, 231).

Nowadays, Cirque du Soleil, with air-conditioned tents, performers' green rooms, computerized ticketing and haute cuisine cookhouse, presents the same sort of highly ordered experience of disorder. The fact that it might be sold to management away-days or corporate events just adds to a sense that the magic has gone. We can't believe our eyes, but we know that an experience has been produced for us using a complex division of labour and advanced forms of technology.

Yet even though these sorts of descriptions are important, the circus is not reducible to a set of economic or organizational relations.[10] The circus, like so many of the cultural forms in this book, exceeds its machinery, even if we need to understand mobility, marketing and divisions of labour in order to know how the circus is produced. The mysteries that I began with, as well as the romantic notion of a mobile community,[11] are produced as a result of economics and organization. Yet, in an oddly non-reversible way, the economics and organization cannot explain them away. Indeed, the paradox is now built into the very word. 'Circus' is now often used as a term for something chaotic, multiple and incapable of meeting its ends. That is the trick, because if you can see behind the curtain to the economics and the organization, the effect is harder to produce. What Carmeli describes as 'a precarious and precious modern dream' (2001, 163; 2003) is produced as durable through the meticulous planning of time and space. The very possibility of disorder, disorganization – of the opening-up of categories of human, normal, gravity, reason – happens at the same time that the temporary institution has been built (Cooper 1986):

> That's what we try to do, isn't it? Keep rolling, keep juggling and strutting our stuff, honouring our gods; then take a bow and exit smiling? But magic seldom happens unless a structure has been erected – whether a church or a tent – that is hospitable to it.
>
> *(Hoagland 2004, 8)*

The questioning of natural and social 'law', of tradition, of common sense, that makes the circus work, doesn't come from nowhere. It is the production of a complex mobile assembly which questions stability in order to make money:

> Once every hour, ladies and gentlemen, Hubert's museum proudly presents none other than Professor Heckler's trained flea circus. In this enclosure you're going to see dozens of real, live trained performing fleas. Fleas that juggle, jump through hoops, play football, tiny little fleas hitched to a chariot, they actually run a race. But the predominating feature of the entire show is little fleas dressed in costume dancing to the strains of music. It is without doubt the most fascinating sight you will ever see. Now, the Professor is on the inside, ready and waiting to give the performance. There will be no show out on these stages until it is all over. If you would like to go, there is a small admission. We do not apologize, it is only nine cents. Fleas that juggle, jump through hoops … .

That was Bobby Reynolds, whilst pitching at Hubert's Museum in New York City in the 1940s (in Hartzman 2005, 207). The flea circus that Bobby Reynolds was pitching worked because a lot of time and effort had gone in to constructing the illusion. Even if there were real fleas in Professor Heckler's circus (because sometimes magnets and mechanisms were used), the illusion was often produced by gluing fleas to the ring, and then fastening things to the fleas. The application of heat to the underside made the fleas struggle to escape. Any circus, perhaps any form of culture, requires that the machinery is partly hidden, because if we can see the economics and the organization too clearly, the miracle begins to look like mere trickery, even cruelty.

Notes

1 This chapter is based on (2011) 'Organizing the Circus: The Engineering of Miracles', *Organization Studies* 32/4: 555–569.
2 The same is also true of music festivals. The links between festival and circus are suggestive, particularly in terms of the rock-and-roll celebration of nomadism and

excess, but they are not my focus here. Trains, planes and cars are as often the subject of songs as drink, drugs and sex.

3 Which reminds me of Emile Durkheim's arguments about the 'functions' of crime and deviance (1895/1982).

4 Just as medical photography, and the hospital and the asylum, began to produce a form of knowledge about mutants and the normal human body.

5 Forms of stereotyping which Helen Stoddart identifies in a 1989 Ringling Brothers Circus programme too, with acts brought from the 'Dark Continent of Africa' and so on (Stoddart 2000, 104)

6 In the UK, there are even accounts of teams sabotaging the route markers left to direct competitor circuses to their pitch (Cottle 2006, 14, 79).

7 For a similar account of rules at Disneyland, see Van Maanen (1991).

8 Cottle (2006, 60) appears to suggest that selling product before, during and after the show was all that was keeping his circus afloat at times.

9 If you were minded, you could add to this a diagnosis of mass production, reproduction and the culture industries. The unpredictable and embodied entertainer gives way to the production of mechanical commodities which are aimed at generating profits for the entertainment industry (Adorno 1991).

10 For work on the circus from the Business School, see Chan Kim et al. (2005) and Cummings and St. Leon (2009).

11 Again, the comparison with touring rock-and-roll bands is interesting here.

PART VI
Reorganization

15

THE ORDER OF THINGS

A second-hand bookshop in Tenby, Pembrokeshire. The scene of family holidays for decades, always prefigured by the quick recognition of a silhouette known by heart, pastel houses grandly surveying a beach, whiffs of chips and the jingle of an amusement machine. Down some stone steps from the main square, past the shop that sells honey and scent made by monks from Caldey Island, and you will find a one-room bookshop. The window is cluttered with postcards of old Tenby, and over the years the bookshop has collected so much stock it is barely possible to get inside. Ten years ago, perhaps, you could enter and follow a narrow path through shelves and piles into the heart of the place. The smell of old paper, and a vague sense of an attempt to keep order. Detectives, history, science fiction, transport, romance. Then, the old man who ran it seemed to know roughly what he had, and if asked, for a book on angels, or the circus, or cranes, could furrow his brows and then shamble off into the shadows, coming back with something vaguely relevant which I would feel I had to buy.

Five years ago, the corridors into the shop were becoming difficult to pass down. I was in there, and a woman was on the other side of a bookshelf from me. Every five minutes, one of us would reach for something and set off a little bookalanche, a slide of book scree that further disorganized the shelves, boxes and teetering piles that everywhere threatened to bury you in words. I didn't stay long, because the disorder had become so great that it was no longer possible to find something I wanted. The detectives and the romances were interleaved, war and science were stacked on top of each other, and I could see philosophy and religion, but couldn't get anywhere near it because Westerns were in the way.

DOI: 10.4324/9781032714288-21

Last year, I couldn't even get in, and neither could the proprietor. Instead, he sat on a folding chair on the pavement, smiling solemnly at those who passed, and nodding at those who tried to go in. If you did enter, a revolving stand with novels was pretty much all that you could get to. The paths in and out had become blocked by new stacks and falls. You could see where they used to be, but navigation was simply too hazardous. I stood in the doorway, idly turning the stand of Penguins and Corgi and Mills and Boon. Beyond was chaos, a moonscape of paper. Any order that there had been was drowned, with towers and shelves teetering in the gloom, and the smell of browning mouldering books, covers torn, twisted by the sedimentary weight of the layers above. Inaccessible, except to thought and imagination. Useless as a bookshop.

One of the themes in this book has been that organization and disorganization are co-produced, made in the same moment. We can understand this assertion as both conceptual and practical, a feature of both thought and action which means that the sublime is engineered and ordering is haunted by mystery. My fascination with the things here very often began with a feeling that there is something strange and excessive about whatever has caught me, and so I gnaw at it for years, enjoying the sparks of excitement. The soar of the skyscraper or thunder of a rocket, conundrums of angels and containers, the confusion caused by art or the circus. Eventually though, when I have tired of the images, and think I have solved the riddle and understood the machinery, the magic disappears. This is the tragedy at the end of my method, that it always ends in disappointment, boredom, even revulsion, and then I have to repeat the same cycle with something new. And again, and again. Once I feel I have understood something about the organization of the things, then the seduction of disorganization recedes. I have seen the little bald man behind the curtain and he is not the Great and Powerful Oz, just a conman, a common huckster trying to sell me something that he claims to be sublime. 'Fleas that juggle, jump through hoops … .' The promise of the disorder is what drives me to want to understand its ordering but when I think I do (understand) I desire some other disorder again.

As this book shows, one of the consequences of this compulsion, this repetition, is that it seems to disorganize conventional versions of academic discipline too. My catalogue of things doesn't fit together well as a recognizable example of a particular form of knowing which could be mapped onto one of the buildings that make up the university. The plan of the university, a view from a balloon, shows us its epistemology made into brick and concrete, gives us subjects like biology, theology, politics, engineering and (of course) business. Like the map of a zoo, the humans and non-humans are all boxed into separate structures, and usually into spatially defined areas too. This allows students and staff to organize their worlds, to know where things belong, and also where they belong. But this book, which begins with objects and images rather than disciplinary questions, seems to produce a cabinet of curiosities, a *Wunderkammer* which reflects the idiosyncratic interests of the collector and which I display for my delight, and perhaps yours as well. It is a symptom of inadequate discipline and this book is an example of what has gone wrong with the business school if people like me are employed within it.

I was asked once, at a conference after I had done a talk on cowboys, Westerns and the outlaw, what my argument was. It's all very nice, and interesting, they said, but what are you trying to tell us? Why does it matter, for us thinkers of organization? I didn't know what to say, but I had recently been on a holiday to Tenby and had been collecting things on the beach that attracted me – a few shells, a crab claw, some pretty pebbles. I used this as my reply, suggesting that I had been beachcombing and was bringing some of the things that I had found together for people to see. Look what I have found? Do you like these things? Would you like to keep them? I'm not sure that the questioner thought much of what I said, perhaps thinking that what I had brought them was actually some pieces of shit with no value or meaning whatsoever.

I don't really know who this book is for. Who wants to know this stuff? Who is the reader? When you walk into a bookshop or a library, you experience classification. Shelves for children, for readers interested in war or romance, travel, gardening or social science. Books kept apart and kept together, like animals in the zoo. The entire publishing process is shaped by the same impulse to categorize, from the submission of a proposal through the selection of readers, reviewers and covers, all the way to the shelves in the shop, books are channelled into their containers. Romance, mystery, young adult, science fiction. In academic publishing, it is no different. Specialist editors look after different lists which themselves map onto the map of the buildings of the university. And when they receive a proposal, despite decades of talk of intertranspostdisciplinarity, it is easiest to commission a book when there are courses that already teach this 'subject', 'topic', 'theme', 'area', 'speciality', all words that point to something taxonomically specific, something bounded and defined. A market which is understood, because it is much easier to write books than to sell them. If there are other texts that compete with this one, even better, because this one can be like those ones, and sit next to them on websites and be tagged with the same metadata on search engines. It is simplest when it can be claimed that this book belongs in this shelf in this building and is likely to be read by this sort of person.

This book is written from the English business school, and though it bears the imprints of a struggle with that particular genealogy, ungrateful child that I am, I think it does not fit well within it. Rather it is a version of Borges list – Art, The Zoo, Tower Cranes, Angels, Skyscrapers, Superflat, Gothic, Secret Societies, James Bond, Shipping Containers, Rockets, The Circus, and things that, from a distance, resemble flies. Things that caught my eye when beachcombing. Remember Foucault again, when he refers to the 'laughter that shattered' as:

> I read the passage, all the familiar landmarks of thought—our thought, the thought that bears the stamp of our age and our geography—breaking up all the ordered surfaces and all the planes with which we are accustomed to tame the wild profusion of existing things and continuing long afterwards to disturb and threaten with collapse our age-old definitions between the Same and the Other.
>
> *(Foucault 1989a, xvi)*

Foucault would never claim that we can do without discipline, as if knowledge could be an open field in which fulgarites nestled next to ballet dancers, corporate strategy and necromancy were taught in the same class, and we could study a small picture made of the root of an olive tree upon which nature had wrought a human figure which sat in a vitrine next to a mummified monkey's claw. What Borges' list and the cabinet of curiosities do is, not to invite us to do away with classification, but to shake the dice on the forms of order that seem evident to us, in order that different connections can be made apparent. In disorder, different connections.

The novelist Aldous Huxley, in his collection of essays *Brave New World Revisited* (1958/2004) rails against 'over-organization', against the compulsive will to order everything. He reluctantly recognizes that we need organization, in both thought and everyday life, but insists that too much of it crushes individuality and the human spirit:

> ... the theoretical reduction of unmanageable multiplicity to comprehensible unity becomes the practical reduction of human diversity to subhuman uniformity, of freedom to servitude. In politics the equivalent of a fully developed scientific theory or philosophical system is a totalitarian dictatorship. In economics, the equivalent of a beautifully composed work of art is the smoothly running factory in which the workers are perfectly adjusted to the machines. The Will to Order can make tyrants out of those who merely aspire to clear up a mess. The beauty of tidiness is used as a justification for despotism.
>
> *(Huxley 1958/2004, 30)*

Huxley's suspicion about the 'will to order', written in the shadow of the Second World War and the rise of mass consumerism, echoes many romantic condemnations of modernity. It also echoes the rather more nuanced arguments of thinkers like Zygmunt Bauman (1989, 1993) and James Scott (1985, 1998), in which the politics of organizing construct separations and forms of visibility that allow for the hygienic cleansing of the Other and the production of brave new worlds. In a book which begins by begins by nodding at Foucault's *Order of Things* (1989a), Gibson Burrell more generously terms this the 'will to form', developing an argument in which patterns, stabilizations and formalization are simultaneously necessary and limiting (2013). As he says, just as we need the home, the dwelling, for warmth and protection, so does the structure of a building constrain who we can be with, how we eat and live. Without stability and predictability, human lives would be short and confused. Nevertheless, Burrell's desire (like Foucault's) is to flirt with danger, to play with the chaos that always lurks, to disorganize that which is organized.

Organization, ordering, classification, is a way of seeing and of not seeing. It produces visibilities and intelligibilities, and correspondingly also produces invisibility and incomprehension. This is not just an epistemological point, a broadly constructionist, poststructuralist, or relational sense that our conceptual and material tools make our world, but also a political one, because in seeing certain possibilities we do not see others. Academic disciplines are ways of making such a cut, deciding in advance what the problem looks like, and what tools might be used to address it. They tend to produce what Thomas Kuhn famously called 'normal science' – the routine gap spotting and problem solving which occurs within the core of a discipline, and which is mostly unremarkable apart from its function in administering the glass-bead game of academic hierarchy. Normal science that, as Kuhn (1996, 52) asserted, 'does not aim at novelties of fact or theory and, when successful, finds none'.

Kuhn's point suggests that disciplines tend to reproduce the same, they rehearse and reinforce common understandings of the materials and mechanisms that are relevant to a particular domain of inquiry. But the order of things, as Foucault intimated in all his work, can always be different because what is understood as disorder is itself a question of standpoint, of perspective, of classification. This is the sting in the tail for the Business School. Dominant forms of organization are taught within the (at least) 13,000 business schools on the planet and as a result, they tend to replicate rather than innovate. (Despite claiming the opposite, loudly and relentlessly, as if they had something to hide.) They teach certain assumptions about what it means to be human, about the times and spaces of organizing that make entities and their relations, about the associations between humans and non-humans and more-than-humans, about the categories and classifications that we use to imagine phenomena like 'markets', 'technology', 'exchange', 'production' and so on.

And why does this matter? Because if we humans, holobionts that we already are, wish to participate in a longer-term future on the lively and encrusted surface of this planet, we need to think and do organizing in different ways. We need to grow the cabinet of curiosities.

REFERENCES

Abbot, E. (1884/1992) *Flatland: A Romance of Many Dimensions*. New York: Dover Publications.

Ackroyd, S. and Thompson, P. (1999) *Organisational Misbehaviour*. London: Sage.

Acuto, M. (2010) 'High-Rise Dubai: Urban Entrepreneurialism and the Technology of Symbolic Power', *Cities* 27/4: 272–284.

Adams, R. (2001) *Sideshow USA: Freaks and the American Cultural Imagination*. Chicago, IL: University of Chicago Press.

Adorno, T. (1991) *The Culture Industry*. London: Routledge.

Albrecht, E. (1995) *The New American Circus*. Gainesville, FL: University Press of Florida.

Allen, J. (2005) *Opus Dei: Secrets and Power Inside the Catholic Church*. London: Allen Lane.

Alvarez, R. (2009) *The Wire: Truth Be Told*. Edinburgh: Canongate.

Amin, A. and Thrift, N. (eds) (2004) *Cultural Economy Reader*. Oxford: Blackwell.

Amis, K. (1965) *The James Bond Dossier*. London: Jonathan Cape.

Appleyard, B. (2006) *Aliens*. London: Scribner.

Arendt, H. (1958/1998) *The Human Condition*. Chicago, IL: University of Chicago Press.

Artforum (2007) 'The Art of Production', *Artforum* special issue, October.

Astel, C. (2005) *Discovering Angels*. London: Duncan Baird.

Azuma, H. (2000) 'Super Flat Speculation', in T. Murakami (ed.), *Super Flat* (pp. 138–151). Tokyo: Madra Publishing Company.

Bachman, O., Cohrs, H.-H., Whiteman, T. and Wislicki, A (1997) *The History of Cranes*. Wadhurst, East Sussex: KHL International.

Bain, A. (2005) 'Constructing an Artistic Identity', *Work, Employment and Society* 19/1: 25–46.

Bakhtin, M. (1984) *Rabelais and His World*. Bloomington: Indiana University Press.

Baldick, C. (1987) *In Frankenstein's Shadow*. Oxford: Clarendon Press.

Bankowsky, J., Gingeras, A. and Wood, C. (2009) *Pop Life: Art in a Material World*. London: Tate Publishing.

Banks, I. (2009) *Transition*. London: Little, Brown.

Barad, K. (2007) *Meeting the Universe Halfway*. Durham, NC: Duke University Press.

Baratay, E. and Hardouin-Fugier, E. (2004) *Zoo. A History of Zoological Gardens in the West*. London: Reaktion Books.

Barbrook, R. (2007) *Imaginary Futures*. London: Pluto.

Barthes, R. (1957/2000) *Mythologies*. London: Vintage.

Bauman, Z. (1993) *Modernity and Ambivalence*. Cambridge: Polity Press.

Bauman, Z. (1989) *Modernity and the Holocaust*. Oxford: Blackwell.

Beadle, R. (2003) 'The Discovery of a Peculiar Good', *Journal of Critical Postmodern Organization Science* 2/3: 60–68.

Beadle, R. and Konyot, D. (2006) 'The Man in the Red Coat', *Culture and Organization* 12/2: 127–137.

Beardsworth, A. and Bryman, A. (2001) 'The Wild Animal in Late Modernity', *Tourist Studies* 1/1: 83–104.

Becker, H. (1963/1982) *Art Worlds*. Berkeley: University of California Press.

Beder, S. (2000) *Selling the Work Ethic: From Puritan Pulpit to Corporate PR*. London: Zed Books.

Beliefnet (ed.) (2003) *The Big Book of Angels*. Dingley, VIC: Hinkler Books.

Bell, E. (2008) *Reading Management and Organization in Film*. Basingstoke: Palgrave Macmillan.

Benjamin, M. (2004) *Rocket Dreams*. London: Vintage.

Benjamin, W. (1999) *Illuminations*. London: Pimlico.

Bennett, T. (1995) *The Birth of the Museum*. Abingdon: Routledge.

Bennett, T. and Woollacott, J. (1987) *Bond and Beyond: The Political Career of a Popular Hero*. London: Routledge.

Berger, P. (1966) *Invitation to Sociology: A Humanistic Perspective*. Harmondsworth: Pelican.

Berger, J. (1972) *Ways of Seeing*. London: BBC/Penguin.

Berger, P. (2009) 'Why Look at Animals?', in J. Berger (ed.), *Why Look at Animals?* (pp. 12–37). London: Penguin.

Bergin, P. (1967) 'Andy Warhol: The Artist as Machine', *Art Journal* 26/4: 359–363.

Bergson, H. (1911) *Matter and Memory* (trans. by Nancy Margaret Paul and W. Scott Palmer). London: George Allen and Unwin.

Berinato, S. (2011) 'Inside the Global Hacker Service Economy', in N. Gilman, J. Goldhammerand S. Weber (eds), *Deviant Globalization: Black Market Economy in the 21st Century* (pp. 215–231). London: Continuum.

Beyes, T. (2024) *Organizing Colour: Towards a Chromatics of the Social*. Stanford, CA: Stanford University Press.

Bhaskar, R. (1978) *A Realist Theory of Science*. Brighton: Harvester Press.

Bingham, N., Carolin, C., Cook, P. and Wilson, R. (2004) *Fantasy Architecture*. London: Heyward Gallery/Royal Institute of British Architects.

Birchall, C. (2011) 'Introduction to "Secrecy and Transparency": The Politics of Opacity and Openness' Theory, *Culture and Society* 28/7–8: 7–25.

Bissell, D. (2007) 'Animating Suspension: Waiting for Mobilities', *Mobilities* 2/2: 277–298.

Bissell, D. and Fuller, G. (eds) (2010) *Stillness in a Mobile World*. London: Routledge.

Bizony, P. (2006) *The Man Who Ran the Moon*. Cambridge: Icon Books.

Blaug, R. (1999) 'The Tyranny of the Visible', *Organisation* 6/1: 33–56.

Blom, P. (2004) *To Have and to Hold. An Intimate History of Collectors and Collecting*. Woodstock, NY: Overlook Press.

Bobbit, P. (2002) *The Shield of Achilles*. London: Allen Lane.

Boccioni, U. (1912/2009) 'Technical Manifesto of Futurist Sculpture', in L. Rainey, C. Poggi and L. Wittman (eds), *Futurism: An Anthology* (pp. 113–119). New Haven, CT: Yale University Press.

Bogdan, R. (1988) *Freak Show*. Chicago, IL: University of Chicago Press.

Boin, A. (2006) 'On the Rise and Fall of NASA', *British Journal of Management* 17/3: 257–260.

Bold, C. (2009) ' "Under the Very Skirts of Britannia": Re-Reading Women in the James Bond novels', in C. Lindner (ed.), *The James Bond Phenomenon: A Critical Reader* (pp. 205–219). Manchester: Manchester University Press.

Bolt, R. (1960) *A Man for All Seasons*. London: Heinemann.

Boltanski, L. and Chiapello, E. (2005) *The New Spirit of Capitalism*. London: Verso.

Bookchin, M. (1982) *The Ecology of Freedom*. Palo Alto, CA: Cheshire Books.

Booth, M. (1991) *The Triads*. London: Grafton Books.

Borges, J. L. (1942/1964) 'The Analytical Language of John Wilkins', in idem, *Other Inquisitions (1937–1952)*. Austin, TX: University of Texas Press.

Botting, F. (1996) *Gothic*. London: Routledge.

Bourdieu, P. (1984) *Distinction: A Social Critique of the Judgement of Taste*. London: RKP.

Bowring, J. (ed.) (1843) *The Works of Jeremy Bentham: Vol X*. Edinburgh: William Tait. http://oll.libertyfund.org/titles/2085, accessed March 2018.

Bowry, S. (2014) 'Before Museums: The Curiosity Cabinet as Metamorphe', *Museological Review* 18: 30–42.

Brabazon, T. (2009) 'Britain's Last Line of Defence: Miss Moneypenny and the Desperations of Filmic Feminism', in C. Lindner (ed.), *The James Bond Phenomenon: A Critical Reader* (pp. 238–250). Manchester: Manchester University Press.

Bradbury, R. (2015) *Something Wicked This Way Comes*. London: Orion.

Bradley, M. (2005) *The Secret Societies Handbook*. London: Cassell Illustrated.

Bratton, W. (1989) 'The New Economic Theory of the Firm', *Stanford Law Review* 41: 1471–1527.

Braverman, I. (2012) *Zooland: The Institution of Captivity*. Stanford, CA: Stanford University Press.

Broeze, F. (2002) *The Globalisation of the Oceans: Containerisation from the 1950s to the Present*. St John's, Newfoundland: International Maritime Economic History Assocation.

Brown, C. (1997) 'Figuring the Vampire: Death, Desire and the Image', in S. Golding (ed.), *The Eight Technologies of Otherness* (pp. 117–133). London: Routledge.

Brown, R. K. (1992) *Understanding Industrial Organizations*. London: Routledge.

Bruccoli, M. and Baughman, J. (eds) (2004) *Conversations with John le Carré*. Jackson: University Press of Mississippi.

Brunsson, N. and Jacobsson, B. (2002) *A World of Standards*. Oxford: Oxford University Press.

Bryman, A. (1999) 'The Disneyization of Society', *The Sociological Review* 47/1: 25–47.

Bryman, A., Bresnen, M., Beardsworth, A., Ford, J. and Keil, E. (1987) 'The Concept of the Temporary System', *Research in the Sociology of Organizations* 5: 253–283.

Burke, E. (1990) *A Philosophical Enquiry.* Oxford: Oxford University Press.

Burrell, G. (1993) 'The Organization of Pleasure', in M. Alvesson and H. Willmott (eds), *Critical Management Studies* (pp. 66–89). London: Sage.

Burrell, G. (1997) *Pandemonium: Towards a Retro-Organization Theory.* London: Sage.

Burrell, G. (2013) *Styles of Organizing: The Will to Form.* Oxford: Oxford University Press.

Burrell, G. and Parker, M. (eds) (2016) *For Robert Cooper: Collected Work.* London: Routledge.

Burroughs, W. (1999) *Word Virus. The Williams Burroughs Reader.* London: Flamingo.

Byatt, A. (1993) *Angels and Insects.* London: Vintage.

Cacciari, M. (1994) *The Necessary Angel.* Albany: State University of New York Press.

Calder, A. (1932) 'Comment réaliser l'art?', *Abstraction-Création, Art Non Figuratif* 1/6. http://calder.org/life/system/downloads/texts/1932-How-Can-Art-P0337.pdf.

Calvino, I. (1974) *Invisible Cities.* London: Secker and Warburg.

Cameron, A. (2014) 'Modelling Headless: Finance, Performance Art and Paradoxy', *Journal of Critical Globalization Studies* 7: 102–121.

Campion-Vincent, V. (2003) 'The Enemy Within: From Evil Others to Evil Elites' *Ethnologia Europaea* 33/2: 23–31. Campion-Vincent, V. (2004) 'From Evil Others to Evil Elites', in G. A. Fine, V. Campion-Vincent and C. Heath (eds), *Rumor Mills: The Social Impact of Rumor and Legend* (pp. 103–122). New York: Aldine De Gruyter.

Cantor, N. (1970) *The Age of Protest: Dissent and Rebellion in the Twentieth Century.* London: Allen and Unwin.

Carmeli, Y. (2001) 'Circus Play, Circus Talk, and the Nostalgia for a Total Order', *Journal of Popular Culture* 35/3: 157–164.

Carmeli, Y. (2003) 'Lion on Display', *Poetics Today* 24/1: 65–90.

Carter, A. (2006) *Nights at the Circus.* London: Vintage.

Castells, M. (2000) *The Information Age: The Rise of the Network Society.* London: Blackwell.

Cawelti, J. and Rosenberg, B. (1987) *The Spy Story.* Chicago, IL: University of Chicago Press.

Chan Kim, W. and Mauborgne, R. (2005) *Blue Ocean Strategy.* Cambridge, MA: Harvard Business School Press.

Chancellor, H. (2005) *James Bond: The Man and His World.* London: John Murray.

Chapman, J. (2007) *License to Thrill: A Cultural History of the James Bond Films.* London: I.B. Tauris.

Chapple, J. (1970) *Documentary and Imaginative Literature 1880–1920.* London: Blandford Press.

Chomsky, N. (1989) *Necessary Illusions: Thought Control in Democratic Societies.* Boston, MA: South End Press.

Cohen, P. (1972/1997) 'Subcultural Conflict and Working Class Community', in K. Gelder and S. Thornton (eds), *The Subcultures Reader* (pp. 90–99). London: Routledge.

Cohen, S. (2005) *Boom Boxes: Shipping Containers and Terrorists, Berkeley Roundtable on the International Economy Working Paper 169*. Berkeley: University of California Press.

Cohen, S. and Taylor L. (1976/1992) *Escape Attempts*. London: Routledge.

Cohn, N. (1970) *The Pursuit of the Millennium*. Oxford: Oxford University Press.

Colby, A., Ehrlich, T., Sullivan, W. and Dolle, J. (2011) *Rethinking Undergraduate Business Education*. San Francisco, CA: Jossey-Bass.

Cook, J. (ed.) (2005) *The Colossal P.T. Barnum Reader*. Urbana, IL: University of Illinois Press.

Cook, R. and Oleniuk, M. (2007) *Around the World in Forty Feet*. Hong Kong: WordAsia/NYK Group.

Cooke, B. (2003) 'The Denial of Slavery in Management Studies', *Journal of Management Studies* 40/8: 1895–1918.

Cooper, R. (1986) 'Organization/Disorganization', *Social Science Information* 25/2: 299–335. Reprinted in Burrell, G. and Parker, M. (eds) (2016) *For Robert Cooper: Collected Work*. London: Routledge.

Cooper, R. (1989) 'The Visibility of Social Systems', in M. Jackson, P. Keys and S. Cropper (eds), *Operational Research in the Social Sciences*. New York: Plenum.

Cooper, R. (2006) 'Making Present: Autopoeisis as Human Production' *Organization* 13/1: 59–81.

Cooper. R. (2010) 'Georg Simmel and the Transmission of Distance' *Journal of Classical Sociology* 10/1: 69–86.

Cooper, R. and Burrell, G. (1988) 'Modernism, Postmodernism and Organizational Analysis' *Organization Studies* 9/1: 91–112.

Cooper, R. and Law, J. (1995) 'Organisation: Proximal and Distal Views', *Research in the Sociology of Organizations* 13: 237–74.

Costas, J. and Grey, C. (2014) '*Bringing Secrecy into the Open*', *Organization Studies* https://doi.org/10.1177/0170840613515470

Cottle, G. (2006) *Confessions of a Showman*. London: Vision Paperbacks.

Cowie, H. (2014) *Exhibiting Animals in Nineteenth-Century Britain*. Basingstoke: Palgrave Macmillan.

Cox, S. (2004) *Cracking the Da Vinci Code*. London: Michael O'Mara Books.

CPA (2008) *Tower Crane Operator's Handbook*. London: Construction Plant-Hire Association/Tower Crane Interest Group.

Cram, R. (1909) *Gothic Architecture, The Catholic Encyclopedia, Volume VI. Online edition 1999*. www.newadvent.org/cathen/06665b.htm, accessed 31 October 2003.

Crews, H. (2004) 'Carney', in: N. Knaebel (ed.), *Step Right Up: Stories of Carnivals, Sideshows and the Circus* (pp. 47–71). New York: Carrol and Graf Publishers.

Cudahy, B. (2006) *Box Boats: How Container Ships Changed the World*. New York: Fordham University Press.

Cummings, L. and St Leon, M. (2009) 'Juggling the Books: The Use of Accounting Information in Circus in Australia', *Accounting History* 14/1–2: 11–33.

Czarniawska, B (1992) *Exploring Complex Organizations: A Cultural Perspective*. London: Sage.

Czarniawksa, B. (2011) 'Business Fiction. Global Economy by William Gibson', in F.-R. Puyou, P. Quattrone, C. McLean and N. Thrift (eds), *Imagining Organizations: Performative Imagery in Business and Beyond* (pp. 31–52). London: Routledge.

Czarniawska, B. and Hernes, T. (eds) (2005) *Actor-Network Theory and Organizing.* Copenhagen: Copenhagen Business School Press.

Dahm, A. (2015) 'Ideal Elevation', *International Cranes and Specialised Transport* April: 17–18.

Dale, K. (2009) 'Ideal Homes? Managing the Domestic Dream', in P. Hancock and M. Tyler (eds), *The Management of Everyday Life*. Basingstoke: Palgave Macmillan.

Dale, K. and Burrell, G. (2008) *Spaces of Organization and the Organization of Space.* Basingstoke: Palgrave Macmillan.

Danto, A. (1964) 'The Artworld', *Journal of Philosophy* 61/19: 571–584.

Daraul, A. (1965) *Secret Societies*. London: Tandem.

Darley, G. (2003) *Factory*. London: Reaktion.

Darton, E. (2011) Divided We Stand: A Biography of the World Trade Center. New York: Basic Books.

Davenport-Hines, R. (1998) *Gothic. Four Hundred Years of Excess,* Horror, Evil *and Ruin* . New York: North Point Press.

Davidson, G. (1971) *A Dictionary of Angels, Including the Fallen Angels.* New York: Free Press.

Davis, J. (2002) *The Circus Age.* Chapel Hill, NC: University of North Carolina Press.

de Certeau, M. (1984) *'Walking in the City'. In The Practice of Everyday Life.* Berkeley: University of California Press.

De Cock, C. and O'Doherty, D. (2017) 'Ruin and Organization Studies', *Organization Studies* 38/1: 129–150.

DeGroot, G. (2007) *Dark Side of the Moon. The Magnificent Madness of the American Lunar Quest.* London: Jonathan Cape.

Deleuze, G. and Guattari, F. (1984) *Anti-Oedipus: Capitalism and Schizophrenia.* London: Athlone Press.

Deleuze, G. and Guattari, F. (1988) *A Thousand Plateaus*. London: Continuum.

Deleuze, G. and Guattari, F. (1994) *What is Philosophy?* London: Verso.

DeLillo, D. (2007) *Falling Man*. London: Picador.

Deloitte Real Estate (2015) *The London Office Crane Survey: Appetite for Construction.* London: Deloitte. www2.deloitte.com/content/dam/Deloitte/uk/ Documents/real-estate/london-office-crane-survey-summer-2015.pdf.

Denning, M. (1987) *Cover Stories. Narrative and Ideology in the British Spy Thriller.* London: Routledge and Kegan Paul.

Dewey, J. (1980) *Art as Experience*. New York: Perigree Books.

Dickens, C. (1853/1993) *Bleak House*. Ware: Wordsworth Editions.

Dickens, C. (1854/1994) *Hard Times*. London: Penguin.

Dickens, C. (1857/1994) *Little Dorrit*. London: Penguin.

Dickens, P. and Ormrod, J. (2007) *Cosmic Society: Towards a Sociology of the Universe.* London: Routledge.

Dickie, G. (1997) *Art Circle: A Theory of Art*. Chicago, IL: Spectrum Press.

Dickie, J. (2004) *Cosa Nostra: A History of the Sicilian Mafia*. London: Hodder and Stoughton.

Dillon, B. (ed.) (2013) *Curiosity. Art and the Pleasures of Knowing*. London: Hayward Publishing.

Domosh, M. (1992) 'Corporate Cultures and the Modern Landscape of New York City', in K. Anderson and F. Gale (eds), *Inventing Places* (pp. 72–86). Melbourne: Longman Cheshire.

Donovan, A. and Bonney, J. (2006) *The Box That Changed the World*. East Windsor, NJ: Commonwealth Business Media.

Dorrian, M. (2006) 'Cityscape with Ferris Wheel', in C. Lindner (ed.), *Urban Space and Cityscapes* (pp. 18–37). London: Routledge.

Douglas, M. (1966/2002) *Purity and Danger*. New York: Routledge.

Draper, E. (2009) *Tate and Lyle: Sugar Love*. www.bbc.co.uk/legacies/work/england/liverpool/article_1.shtml

du Gay, P. and Pryke, M. (eds) (2002) *Cultural Economy*. London: Sage.

Duncan, G. (2002) *I, Lucifer*. London: Scribner.

Duncombe, S. (1997) *Notes from Underground*. Bloomington, IN: Microcosm Publishing.

Dupré, J. (1996) *Skyscrapers*. New York: Black Dog and Leventhal.

Durkheim, E. (1895/1982) *The Rules of Sociological Method*. London: Macmillan.

Dyer, R. (1977/1993) 'Entertainment and Utopia', in S. During (ed.), *The Cultural Studies Reader* (pp. 271–283). London: Routledge.

Eco, U. (1979/2009) 'Narrative Structures in Fleming', reprinted in C. Lindner (ed.) (2009) *The James Bond Phenomenon: A Critical Reader* (pp. 34–55). Manchester: Manchester University Press.

Ehrenzweig, A. (1967) *The Hidden Order of Art*. Berkeley: University of California Press.

Ellis, N. (2008) '"What the Hell is That?"', *Organization* 15/5: 705–723.

Erickson, B. (1981) 'Secret Societies and Social Structure', *Social Forces* 60/1: 188–210.

Erickson, P. (1979) 'The Role of Secrecy in Complex Organizations: From Norms of Rationality to Norms of Distrust', *Cornell Journal of Social Relations* 14/2: 121–138.

Etchells, T. (2009) 'Time Served', in A. Heathfield and T. Hsieh (eds) *Out of Now* (pp. 355–361). London and Cambridge, MA: Live Art Development Agency and MIT Press.

Fainstein, S. (2001) *The City Builders: Property Development in New York and London*. Lawrence: University Press of Kansas.

Farley, P. and Symmons Roberts, M. (2011) *Edgelands. Journeys into England's True Wilderness*. London: Jonathan Cape.

Fenske, G. (2005) 'The Beaux-Arts Architect and the Skyscraper', in R. Moudry (ed.) *The American Skyscraper: Cultural Histories* (pp. 19–37). New York: Cambridge University Press.

Fenster, M. (2008) *Conspiracy Theories: Secrecy and Power in American Culture*. Minneapolis: University of Minnesota Press.

Ferguson, E. (2008) 'I'm Looking Down on You', *The Guardian*, 27 July.

Ferree, M. and Martin, P. (eds) (1995) *Feminist Organizations*. Philadelphia, PA: Temple University Press.

Feiler, B. (1995) *Under the Big Top*. New York: Scribner.

Fine, L. (2005) 'The Female "Souls of the Skyscraper"', in R. Moudry (ed.), *The American Skyscraper: Cultural Histories* (pp. 63–82). New York: Cambridge University Press.

Flack, A. (2018) *The Wild Within: Histories of a Landmark British Zoo*. Charlottesville: University of Virginia Press.

Forster, G. (2006) ' "Just a stupid policeman": Bond and the Rule of Law', in J. South and J. Held (eds), *Questions Are Forever: James Bond and Philosophy* (pp. 121–137). Chicago, IL: Open Court.

Foucault, M. (1986) 'Of Other Spaces', *Diacritics* 16/1: 22–27.

Foucault, M. (1989a) *The Order of Things*. London: Routledge.

Foucault, M. (1989b) *Madness and Civilisation*. London: Routledge.

Foucault, M. (1991) *Discipline and Punish*. London: Penguin.

Fournier, V. and Grey, C. (2000) 'At the Critical Moment: Conditions and Prospects for Critical Management Studies', *Human Relations* 53/1: 7–32.

Frank, W., Mumford, L., Norman, D., Rosenfield, P. and Rugg, H. (1934) *America and Alfred Steiglitz: A Collective Portrait*. New York: Doubleday, Doran and Company.

Franklin, H. (1990) 'Visions of the Future in Science Fiction Films from 1970 to 1982', in A. Kuhn (ed.), *Alien Zone: Cultural Theory and Contemporary Science Fiction Cinema* (pp. 19–31). London: Verso.

Friedman, T. (2005) *The World Is Flat*. New York: Farrar, Straus and Giroux.

Frongia, A. (2005) 'The Shadow of the Skyscraper', in R. Moudry (ed.), *The American Skyscraper: Cultural Histories* (pp. 217–233). New York: Cambridge University Press.

Frost, P., Moore, L., Louis, M., Lundberg, C. and Martin J. (eds) (1991) *Reframing Organizational Culture*. Newbury Park, CA: Sage.

Fuller, G. (2009) '>store>forward: Architecture of a Future Tense', in S. Cwerner, S. Kesselring and J. Urry (eds), *Aeromobilities* (pp. 63–75). London: Routledge.

Gan, A. (1922/1974) 'Constructivism', in S. Bann (ed.), *The Tradition of Constructivism* (pp. 32–42). New York: Viking.

Garrett, B. (2014) *Explore Everything: Place Hacking the City*. London: Verso.

Garrett, E. (2014) *Why Do We Go to the Zoo?* Lanham, MD: Rowman and Littlefield/ Fairleigh Dickinson University Press.

Garrick, J. and Clegg, S. (2000) 'Organizational Gothic: Transfusing Vitality and Transforming the Corporate Body through Work-Based Learning', in C. Symes and J. McIntyre (eds), *Working Knowledge*. Buckingham: SRHE/ Open University Press.

Gaskell, E. (1855/1995) *North and South*. London: Penguin.

Gelder, K. (1994) *Reading the Vampire*. London: Routledge.

Gergen, K. (1992) 'Organisation Theory in the Postmodern Era', in M. Reed and M. Hughes (eds), *Rethinking Organisation* (pp. 207–226). London: Sage.

Gerth, H. and Mills, C. (eds) (1948) *For Max Weber*. London: Routledge and Kegan Paul.

Gibson, W. (2007) *Spook Country*. London: Penguin.

Gibson-Graham, J. K. and Dombroski, K. (eds) (2000) *The Handbook of Diverse Economies*. Cheltenham: Edward Elgar.

Gillbank, L. (1996) 'A Paradox of Purposes. Acclimatization Origins of the Melbourne Zoo', in R. J. Hoage and W. A. Deiss (eds), *New Worlds, New Animals: From Menagerie to Zoological Park in the Nineteenth Century* (pp. 73–85). Baltimore, MD: Johns Hopkins University Press.

Gilman, N., Goldhammer, J. and Weber, S. (eds) (2011) *Deviant Globalization: Black Market Economy in the 21st Century*. London: Continuum.

Gingeras, A. (2009) 'Lost in Translation: The Politics of Identity in the Work of Takashi Murakami', in J. Bankowsky, A. Gingeras and C. Wood (eds), *Pop Life: Art in a Material World* (pp. 77–87). London: Tate Publishing.

Glynn, J (1849) *Rudimentary Treatise on the Construction of Cranes and Machinery.* London: John Weale.

Godfrey, R., Jack, G. and Jones, C. (2004) 'Sucking, Bleeding, Breaking: On the Dialectics of Vampirism, Capital And Time', *Culture and Organisation* 10/1: 25–36.

Goffman, E. (1963) *Stigma.* Englewood Cliffs, NJ: Prentice-Hall.

Goodman, M. (2011) 'What Business Can Learn from Organized Crime', *Harvard Business Review* November: 27–30.

Goss, J. (1988) 'The Built Environment and Social Theory', *Professional Geographer* 40/4: 392–403.

Goss, J. (1992) 'Modernity and Post-modernity in the Retail Landscape', in K. Anderson and F. Gale (eds), *Inventing Places* (pp. 159–177). Melbourne: Longman Cheshire.

Graham, B. (1976) *Angels: God's Secret Agents.* London: Hodder and Stoughton.

Grayson, R., Carolin, C., and Cardinal, R. (2006) *A Secret Service: Art, Compulsion, Concealment.* London: Hayward Gallery Publishing.

Gray, C. (2012) *The Russian Experiment in Art: 1863–1922,* (revised and enlarged by M Burleigh-Motley). London: Thames and Hudson.

Grey, C (2012) *Decoding Organization.* Cambridge: Cambridge University Press.

Grey, C. and Garsten, C. (2002) 'Organized and Disorganized Utopias', in M. Parker (ed.), *Utopia and Organization.* Oxford: Blackwell.

Griffiths, J. (1980) *Three Tomorrows: American, British and Soviet Science Fiction.* London: Macmillan.

Grigson, C. (2016) *Menagerie. A History of Exotic Animals in England* (pp. 1100–1837). Oxford: Oxford University Press.

Groening, M. (1986) *Work is Hell.* New York: Pantheon Books.

Grunenberg, C. (ed.) (1997) *Gothic. Transmutations of Horror in Late Twentieth Century Art.* Cambridge, MA: MIT Press.

Guillen, M. (2008) *The Taylorised Beauty of the Mechanical.* Princeton, NJ: Princeton University Press.

Halberstam, J. (2011) *The Queer Art of Failure.* Durham, NC: Duke University Press.

Hall, S., and Jefferson, T. (eds) (1976) *Resistance through Rituals.* London: Hutchinson.

Hall, S., Hobson, D., Lowe, A. and Willis, P. (eds) (1980) *Culture, Media, Language: Working Papers in Cultural Studies, 1972–1979.* London: Routledge.

Hamilton, V. and Parker, M. (2016) *Daniel Defoe and the Bank of England: The Dark Arts of Projectors.* Ripley, Hants: Zer0 Books.

Hancock, P. (2008) 'Fear and (Self) Loathing in Coleridge Close', *Organization* 15/5: 685–703.

Hancock, P. (2023) *Organizing Christmas.* New York: Routledge.

Hannam, K., Sheller, M. and Urry, J. (2006) 'Editorial: Mobilities, Immobilities and Moorings', *Mobilities* 1/1: 1–22.

Hansen, J. (2005) *First Man: The Life of Neil Armstrong.* London: Simon & Schuster.

Hanson, E. (2004) *Animal Attractions. Nature on Display in American Zoos.* Princeton, NJ: Princeton University Press.

Harding, N. (2005) *Secret Societies.* Harpenden: Pocket Essentials.

Hartzman, M. (2005) *American Sideshow.* New York: Tarcher/Penguin.

Harvey, D. (1985) *The Urbanization of Capital.* Baltimore, MD: Johns Hopkins University Press.

Hassard, J. and Holliday, R. (eds) (1998) *Organization – Representation*. London: Sage.

Hatherley, O. (2011) *A Guide to the New Ruins of Great Britain*. London: Verso.

Hazelrigg, L. (1969) 'A Reexamination of Simmel's "The Secret and the Secret Society"', *Social Forces* 47/3: 323–330.

Heath, J. and Potter, A (2004) *Rebel Sell*. Chichester: Capstone Publishing.

Heathfield, A. and Hsieh, T. (2009) *Out of Now*. London and Cambridge, MA: Live Art Development Agency and MIT Press.

Hebdige, D. (1979) *Subculture. The Meaning of Style*. London: Methuen.

Hebdige, D. (1998) 'The Bottom Line on Planet One: Squaring Up to the Face', in D. Hebdige (ed.), *Hiding in the Light*. London: Comedia.

Helin, J., Hernes, T., Hjorth, D. and Holt, R. (eds) (2014) *The Oxford Handbook of Process Philosophy and Organization Studies*. Oxford: Oxford University Press.

Hennessy, P. (2003) *The Secret State: Whitehall and the Cold War*. London: Penguin.

Hernes, T. and Matlis, S. (eds) (2010) *Process, Sensemaking and Organization*. Oxford: Oxford University Press.

Hersch, M. (2009) 'Checklist: The Secret Life of Apollo's "Fourth Crewmember"', in D. Bell and M. Parker (eds), *Space Travel and Culture: From Apollo to Space Tourism*. Oxford: Blackwell.

Hesmondhalgh, D. (2018) *The Cultural Industries*. London: Sage.

Hetherington, K. (1997) *The Badlands of Modernity*. London: Routledge.

Hibbert, C. (1979) *The Rise and Fall of the House of Medici*. Harmondsworth: Penguin.

Hickman, K. (2001) *Travels with a Circus*. London: Flamingo.

Hill, H. (with G. Russo) (2004) *Gangsters and Goodfellas*. Edinburgh: Mainstream Publishing.

Hill, S. (1976) *The Dockers: Class and Tradition in London*. London: Heinemann.

Hitchcock, H. and Johnson, P. (1966) *The International Style*. New York: The Norton Library.

Hoagland, E. (2004) 'Circus Music', in N. Knaebel (ed.), *Step Right Up: Stories of Carnivals, Sideshows and the Circus* (pp. 1–12). New York: Carrol and Graf Publishers.

Hobsbawm, E. (1965) Primitive Rebels. New York: W.W. Norton & Co.

Hofstadter, R. (1966) *The Paranoid Style of American Politics and Other Essays*. New York: Knopf.

Hofstede, G. (1991) *Culture and Organisations: The Software of the Mind*. New York: McGraw Hill.

Hohn, D. (2011) *Moby Duck*. New York: Viking.

Hollington, M. (1984) *Dickens and the Grotesque*. London: Croom Helm.

Holmes, B. (2011) 'Do Containers Dream of Electric People?' *Continental Drift*. https://brianholmes.wordpress.com/2011/08/19/do-containers-dream-of-electric-people/, accessed 31 July 2024.

Hopkins, N. (2011) 'Welcome to Camp Bastion', *The Guardian*, G2 section, 16 August, 7–9.

Horkheimer, M. and Adorno, T. (1944/2002) 'The Culture Industry', in *Dialectic of Enlightenment* (pp. 94–136). Stanford, CA: Stanford University Press.

Horn, E. (2011) ' "Logics of Political Secrecy' Theory', *Culture and Society* 28/7–8: 103–122.

Hosey, G., Melfi, V. and Pankhurst, S. (2013) *Zoo Animals. Behaviour, Management and Welfare*. Oxford: Oxford University Press.

Hough, R. (2004) 'The Final Confession of Mabel Stark', In N. Knaebel (ed.), *Step Right Up: Stories of Carnivals, Sideshows and the Circus* (pp. 275–289). New York: Carrol and Graf Publishers.

HRH Charles, Prince of Wales (1989) *A Vision of Britain*. London: Doubleday.

Hsieh, T. (2009) 'An Exchange with Tehching Hsieh', in A. Heathfield and T. Hsieh (eds), *Out of Now* (pp. 319–338). London and Cambridge, MA: Live Art Development Agency and MIT Press.

Huxley, A. (1958/2004) *Brave New World Revisited*. London: Vintage Classics.

ICC International Maritime Bureau (2011) *Piracy and Armed Robbery against Ships*. Annual Report. London: International Chamber of Commerce.

Isherwood, R (2010) *Tower Crane Incidents Worldwide (Research Report RR820)*. Norwich: HSE Books/HMSO.

Ito, T. (2014) *London Zoo and the Victorians*. Woodbridge: Royal Historical Society/ Boydell Press.

Jacobs, J. (2006) 'A Geography of Big Things', *Cultural Geographies* 13/1: 1–27.

Jacobs, J., Cairns, C. and Strebel, I. (2007) 'A Tall Storey ... but, a Fact Just the Same', *Urban Studies* 44/3: 609–629.

Jacques, R. (1996) *Manufacturing the Employee: Management Knowledge from the 19th to 21st Centuries*. London: Sage.

Jameson, F. (2005) *Archaeologies of the Future*. London: Verso.

Jameson, F. (2008) 'The Square Peg in the Round Hole or the History of Spaceflight', *Critical Enquiry* 34/supplement: 172–183.

Jancovich, M. (1992) *Horror*. London: Batsford.

Johnson, S. (2002) *The Secret of Apollo*. Baltimore, MD: Johns Hopkins University Press.

Jones, M. (2006) *The Good Life in the Scientific Revolution: Descartes, Pascal, Leibniz and the Cultivation of Virtue*. Chicago, IL: University of Chicago Press.

Jungk, R. (1954) *Tomorrow is Already Here*. London: Rupert Hart-Davis.

Kafka, F. (1925/1953) *The Trial*. Harmondsworth: Penguin.

Kafka, F. (1926/1957) *The Castle*. London: Penguin.

Kane, P. (2004) *The Play Ethic*. London: Macmillan.

Kaulingfreks, R., Spoelstra, S. and ten Bos, R. (2011) 'Wonders Without Wounds: On Singularity, Museum and Organization', *Management and Organizational History* 6/3: 311–327.

Kavanagh, D. (1998) *Multi-firm, Temporary Networks: A Study of Process*. Unpublished PhD, Department of Marketing, Lancaster University.

Keck, D. (1998) *Angels and Angelology in the Middle Ages*. New York: Oxford University Press.

Kenis, P., Janowicz, M. and Cambré, B. (eds) (2009) *Temporary Organizations*. Cheltenham: Edward Elgar.

King, A. (2004) *Spaces of Global Cultures*. London: Routledge.

Klein, N. (2008) *The Shock Doctrine*. London: Penguin.

Klerkx, G. (2004) *Lost in Space*. London: Secker and Warburg.

Knight, P. (2000) *Conspiracy Culture: From Kennedy to the X Files*. London: Routledge.

Knowles, S. (2004) *five days out of seven*. Falmouth: R. Booth Ltd.

Knox, H., O'Doherty, D. P., Vurdubakis, T., and Westrup, C. (2015) 'Something Happened: Spectres of Organization/Disorganization at the Airport', *Human Relations* 68(6):1001–1020.

Korczynski, M. (2014) *Songs of the Factory: Pop Music, Culture and Resistance.* Ithaca, NY: Cornell University Press.

Kornberger, M., Rhodes, C. and ten Bos, R. (2006) 'The Others of Hierarchy', in M. Fugelsang and B. Meier Sorensen (eds), *Deleuze and the Social* (pp. 58–74). Edinburgh: Edinburgh University Press.

Krantz, G. (2000) *Failure Is Not an Option.* New York: Berkley Books.

Kuhn, T. (1996) *The Structure of Scientific Revolutions* (3rd edn). Chicago, IL: Chicago University Press.

Lamborn Wilson, P. (1980) *Angels.* London: Thames and Hudson.

Lambright, W. H. (1995) *Powering Apollo: James E. Webb of NASA.* Baltimore, MD: Johns Hopkins University Press.

Land, C., Loren, S. and Metelmann, J. (2014) 'Rogue Logics: Organization in the Grey Zone', *Organization Studies* 35/2: 233–253.

Landa, I. (2006) 'James Bond: A Nietzchean for the Cold War', in J. South and J. Held (eds), *Questions Are Forever: James Bond and Philosophy.* Chicago, IL: Open Court, 79–93.

Landau, S. and Condit, C. (1996) *The Rise of the New York Skyscraper.* New Haven, CT: Yale University Press.

Lange, A. (1998) 'Hellfire: Getting the Most from a Lethal Missile System', *Armor* Jan./Feb.: 25–30.

Langley, A. and Tsoukas, H. (eds) (2016) *The SAGE Handbook of Process Organization Studies.* Thousand Oaks, CA: SAGE Publications.

Latham, R. (2002) *Consuming Youth: Vampires, Cyborgs and the Culture of Consumption.* Chicago, IL: University of Chicago Press.

Latour, B. (2005) *Reassembling the Social.* Oxford: Oxford University Press.

Leach, N. (ed.) (1997) *Rethinking Architecture.* London: Routledge.

Leavitt, D. (1986) *The Lost Language of Cranes.* New York: Knopf.

Lee, P. (2007) ' "Economies of Scale" in The Art of Production', *Artforum* October (Special Issue): 337–343.

Levine, A. (1982) *Managing NASA in the Apollo Era.* Washington, DC: NASA. http://history.nasa.gov/SP-4102/sp4102.htm, accessed 24 November 2008.

Levinson, M. (2006) *The Box: How the Shipping Container Made the World Smaller and the World Economy Bigger.* Princeton, NJ: Princeton University Press.

Lévi-Strauss, C. (1963) *Structural Anthropology.* London: Penguin.

Lévi-Strauss, C. (1966) *The Savage Mind.* London: Weidenfeld and Nicholson.

Levitt, S. and Dubner, S. (2006) *Freakonomics.* London: Penguin.

Lewis, J. (2008) *Cultural Studies.* London: Sage.

Lindner, C. (2006) 'New York Vertical', *American Studies* 47/1: 5–29.

Lindner, C. (ed.) (2009) *The James Bond Phenomenon: A Critical Reader.* Manchester: Manchester University Press.

Longrigg, C. and McMahon, B. (2006) 'Fresh Cheese and Sweet Nothings', *The Guardian*, April 15.

Lovink, G. and Scholz, T. (2007) *The Art of Free Cooperation.* Brooklyn, NY: Autonomedia.

Luibheid, C. (trans.) (1987) *Pseudo-Dionysius: The Complete Works.* New York: Paulist.

MacDonald, F. (2007) 'Anti-Astropolitik: Outer Space and the Orbit of Geography', *Progress in Human Geography* 31/5: 592–615.

Maeseneer, Y. (2003a) 'Horror angelorum', *Modern Theology* 19/4: 511–527.

Maeseneer, Y. (2003b) 'Un ange passe ...', *Literature and Theology* 17/4: 374–387.

Mailer, N. (1971) *A Fire on the Moon.* London: Pan Books.

Marqusee, M. (ed.) (1988) *New York: An Illustrated Anthology.* London: Conran Octopus.

Marshall, P. (1993) *Demanding the Impossible: A History of Anarchism.* London: Fontana Books.

Marshall, P. and Walsham, A. (2006) 'Migrations of Angels in the Early Modern World', in P. Marshall and A. Walsham (eds), *Angels in the* Early Modern World. Cambridge: Cambridge University Press.

Martin, C. (2011) 'Desparate Passage: Violent Mobilities and the Politics of Discomfort', *Journal of Transport Geography* 19: 1046–1052.

Marx, G and Muschert, G (2009) 'Simmel on Secrecy'. In C. Rol and C. Papilloud (eds), *Soziologie als Möglichkeit.* Wiesbaden, Germany: Verlag für Sozialwissenschaften, 217–33.

Marx, K. (1876/1976) *Capital , Volume 1.* Harmondsworth: Penguin.

Massey, D. (2005) *For Space.* London: Sage.

Matanle, P., McCann, L., and Ashmore, D. (2008) 'Men Under Pressure', *Organization* 15/5: 639–664.

Mauriès, P. (2002) *Cabinets of Curiosities.* London: Thames and Hudson.

May, J. and Thrift, N. (eds) (2001) *Timespace: Geographies of Temporality.* London: Routledge.

McGrath, P. (1997) 'Transgression and Decay', in: C. Grunenberg (ed.), *Gothic. Transmutations of Horror in Late Twentieth Century Art* (pp. 158–153). Cambridge, MA: MIT Press.

McKenna, V., Travers, W. and Wray, J. (eds) (1987) *Beyond the Bars. The Zoo Dilemma.* Wellingborough, Northants: Thorsons.

McNeill, D. (2005) 'Skyscraper Geography', *Progress in Human Geography* 29/1: 41–55.

Melville, F. (2001) *The Book of Angels.* London: Quarto.

Millegan, K. (ed.) (2004) *Fleshing Out Skull and Bones: Investigations into America's Most Powerful Secret Society.* Walterville, OR: TrineDay.

Milne, A. (ed.) (2017) *Correspondence of Jeremy Bentham: Volume 4.* London: UCL Press.

Mol, A. (2003) *The Body Multiple.* Durham, NC: Duke University Press.

Molesworth, H. (2003) *Work Ethic.* University Park, PA: Pennsylvania State University Press.

Moniot, D. (1976) 'James Bond and America in the Sixties', *Journal of the University Film Association* XXVIII/3: 25–33.

More, T. (1516/1965) *Utopia.* London: Penguin.

Moretti, F. (1983) 'Dialectic of Fear', in F. Moretti et al. (eds), *Signs Taken for Wonders* (pp. 83–108). London: Verso.

Moudry, R. (ed.) (2005) *The American Skyscraper: Cultural Histories.* New York: Cambridge University Press.

References **289**

Mullane, M. (2006) *Riding Rockets*. New York: Scribner.

Murakami, T. (2000) *Super Flat*. Tokyo: Madra Publishing Company.

Murakami, T. (2011) *A Message*. http://english.kaikaikiki.co.jp/whatskaikaikiki/mess age, accessed 14 February 2011.

Naess, A. (1989) *Ecology, Community and Lifestyle*. Cambridge: Cambridge University Press.

Neilson, B. and Rossiter, N. (2010) 'Still Waiting, Still Moving: On Labour, Logistics and Maritime Industries', in D. Bissell and G. Fuller (eds), *Stillness in a Mobile World* (pp. 51–68). London: Routledge.

Néret, G (2003) *Devils*. Köln: Taschen.

Néret, G. (2004) *Angels*. Köln: Taschen.

Neuse, S. (1982) 'Bureaucratic Malaise in the Modern Spy Novel: Deighton, Greene and Le Carré', *Public Administration* 60: 293–306.

Nietzsche, F. (2007) 'The Antichrist', in *Twilight of the Idols*. Ware, Hertfordshire: Wordsworth.

Nye, D. (1994) *American Technological Sublime*. Cambridge, MA: MIT Press.

Nye, D. (2005) 'The Sublime and the Skyline', in R. Moudry (ed.), *The American Skyscraper: Cultural Histories* (pp. 255–269). New York: Cambridge University Press.

Ogden, Y. (1993) *Two Hundred Years of the American Circus*. New York: Facts on File Inc.

Oliveri, F. (2014) 'Acts of Citizenship against Neo-liberalism: The New Cycle of Migrant Struggles in Italy', in N.-K. Kim (ed.), *Multicultural Challenges and Sustainable Democracy in Europe and East Asia*. London: Palgrave.

Origen, E. and Golen, G. (2010) *The Adventures of Unemployed Man*. New York: Little, Brown and Company.

Page, M. (2005) 'The Heights and Depths of Urbanism', in R. Moudry (ed.), *The American Skyscraper: Cultural Histories* (pp. 165–184). New York: Cambridge University Press.

Palmer, J. (1979) *Thrillers: Genesis and Structure of a Popular Genre*. New York: St. Martin's Press.

Papadopoulos, D., Stephenson, N. and Tsianos, V. (2008) *Escape Routes: Control and Subversion in the 21st Century*. London: Pluto.

Parish, J. (2000) 'From the Body to the Wallet: Conceptualising Akan Witchcraft at Home and Abroad', *Journal of the Royal Anthropological Institute* 6/3: 487–500.

Parish, J. and Parker, M. (eds) (2001) *The Age of Anxiety: Conspiracy Theory and the Human Sciences*. Oxford: Blackwell.

Parker, M. (2000) *Organizational Culture and Identity*. London: Sage.

Parker, M. (2001) 'Human Science as Conspiracy Theory', in J. Parish and M. Parker (eds), *The Age of Anxiety: Conspiracy Theory and the Human Sciences* (pp. 191–207). Oxford: Blackwell.

Parker, M. (2002a) 'Queering Management and Organisation', *Gender, Work and Organisation* 9/2: 146–166.

Parker, M. (2002b) *Against Management*. Oxford: Polity.

Parker, M. (2007) 'After the Space Age: Science, Fiction and Possibility', in M. Grebowicz (ed.), *SciFi in the Mind's Eye: Reading Science through Science Fiction* (pp. 275–288). Chicago, IL: Open Court.

Parker, M. (2008) 'Memories of the Space Age: From Apollo to Cyberspace', *Information, Communication and Society* 11/6: 846–860.

Parker, M. (2009) 'Capitalists in Space', in D. Bell and M. Parker (eds), *Space Travel and Culture: From Apollo to Space Tourism*. Oxford: Blackwell.

Parker, M. (2012) *Alternative Business: Outlaws, Crime and Culture*. London: Routledge.

Parker, M. (2014) 'Writing: What Can Be Said, by Who, and Where?', in E. Jeanes and T. Huzzard (eds), *Critical Management Research: Reflections from the Field* (pp. 211–226). London: Sage.

Parker, M (2018) *Shut Down the Business School*. London: Pluto.

Parker, M., Cheney, G., Fournier, V. and Land, C. (eds) (2014) *The Companion to Alternative Organization* (p. 384). London: Routledge.

Parker, M., Fournier, V. and Reedy, P. (2007) *The Dictionary of Alternatives: Utopianism and Organization*. London: Zed.

Parkinson, C. Northcote (1958) *Parkinson's Law*. London: John Murray.

Peake, M. (1972) *Mr Pye*. London: Penguin.

Peake, M. (1946/1983) *Titus Groan*. Harmondsworth: Penguin.

Pelikan, J. (1987) 'The Odyssey of Dionysian Spirituality', in *Pseudo-Dionysius: The Complete Works* (trans. by C. Luibheid) (pp. 11–24). New York: Paulist.

Pelzer, P. and Pelzer, M. (1996) 'The Gothic Experience', paper presented at 14th SCOS Conference, UCLA, Los Angeles, July.

Penny, L. (2015) 'Pity the Boys Raised to Admire James Bond', *New Statesman*, 5 November, p. 31.

Penzler, O. (2008) 'Foreword', in O. Penzler (ed.), *Pulp Fiction: The Villains*. London: Quercus.

Philips-Birt, D. (1970) *The Future of Ships*. Saint Ives, Huntingdon: Imray Laurie Norie and Wilson.

Pilger, J. (2002) *The New Rulers of the World*. London: Verso.

Plester, B. (2016) *The Complexity of Workplace Humour: Laughter, Jokers and the Dark Side of Humour*. Cham, Switzerland: Springer.

Popper, K. (1945/2002) *The Open Society and Its Enemies*. London: Routledge.

Pred, A. (ed.) (1981) *Space and Time in Geography: Essays in Honour of Torsten Hägerstrand*. Lund: Gleerup.

Purdon, J. (2013) 'Electric Cinema, Pylon Poetry', *Amodern* 2. http://amodern.net/

Purdon, J. (2013) 'Pylons', in *Jesus College Annual Report* (pp. 24–25). Cambridge: Jesus College.

Pye, M. (1993) *Maximum City*. London: Picador.

Quattrone, P. (2004) 'Accounting for God: Accounting and Accountability Practices in the Society of Jesus', *Accounting, Organizations and Society* 29: 647–683.

Rainey, L., Poggi, C. and Wittman, L. (eds) (2009) *Futurism: An Anthology*. New Haven, CT: Yale University Press.

Rand, A. (1993) *The Fountainhead*. New York: Signet.

Reed, M. (1997) 'In Praise of Duality and Dualism', *Organization Studies*, 18/1: 21–42.

Rees, D. (2004) *My New Filing Technique Is Unstoppable*. London: Penguin.

Reichenbach, H. (1996) 'A Tale of Two Zoos. The Hamburg Zoological Garden and Carl Hagenbeck's Tierpark', in R. Hoage and W. Deiss (eds), *New Words, New*

Animals. From Menagerie to Zoological Park in the Nineteenth Century (pp. 51–62). Baltimore, MD: Johns Hopkins University Press.

Reis, E. (2001) 'The Trouble with Angels', *Common-Place* 1/3. www.common-place.org

Rhodes, C. (2001) 'D'Oh: The Simpsons, Popular Culture and the Organizational Carnival', *Journal of Management Inquiry* 10/4: 374–383.

Rhodes, C. (2007) 'Outside the Gates of Eden: Utopia and Work in Rock Music', *Group and Organization Management* 32/1: 22–49.

Rhodes, C. and Parker, M. (2008) 'Images of Organizing in Popular Culture', *Organization* 15/5: 627–637.

Rhodes, C. and Lilley, S. (eds) (2012) *Organization and Popular Culture*. London: Routledge.

Rhodes, C. and Westwood, R. (2008) *Critical Representations of Work and Organization in Popular Culture*. London: Routledge.

Richardson, L. and St. Pierre, E. A. (2005) 'Writing: A Method of Inquiry', in N. K. Denzin and Y. S. Lincoln (eds), *The Sage Handbook of Qualitative Research* (pp. 959–978). Thousand Oaks, CA: Sage.

Ridley, G. (2004) *Clara's Grand Tour. Travels with a Rhinoceros in Eighteenth Century Europe*. London: Atlantic Books.

Ritvo, H. (1997) *The Platypus and the Mermaid and Other Figments of the Classifying Imagination*. Cambridge, MA: Harvard University Press.

Robbins, L. (2002) *Elephant Slaves and Pampered Parrots: Exotic Animals in Eighteenth-Century Paris*. Baltimore, MD: Johns Hopkins University Press.

Roland, A. (2007) 'Essay Review: Containers and Causality', *Technology and Culture* 48/2. DOI: 10.1353/tech.2007.0087.

Ronson, J. (2001) *Them: Adventures with Extremists*. London: Picador.

Rorty, R. (1990) *Objectivity, Relativism and Truth*. Cambridge: Cambridge University Press.

Rossbach, S. (1996) 'Gnosis, Science and Mysticism', *Social Science Information* 35/2: 233–255.

Rothfels, N. (2002) *Savages and Beasts. The Birth of the Modern Zoo*. Baltimore, MD: Johns Hopkins University Press.

Roy, D. (1959) '"Banana Time": Job Satisfaction and Informal Interaction', *Human Organization* 18: 158–168.

Rubin, B. (1979) 'Aesthetic Ideology and Urban Design', *Annals of the Association of American Geographers* 69/3: 339–361.

Ruskin, J. (1985) 'The Nature of Gothic', in C. Wilmer (ed.), *Unto This Last and Other Writings* (pp. 77–109). London: Penguin.

Sabbagh, K. (1989) *Skyscraper: The Making of a Building*. London: Papermac/Macmillan.

Sagan, C. (1996) *The Demon Haunted World*. London: Headline.

Saviano, R. (2008) *Gormorrah: Italy's Other Mafia*. London: Pan.

Schleier, M. (2005) 'The Skyscraper, Gender and Mental Life', in R. Moudry (ed.), *The American Skyscraper: Cultural Histories* (pp. 234–254). New York: Cambridge University Press.

Schoeneborn, D. and Scherer, A. (2012) 'Clandestine Organizations, al Qaeda and the Paradox of (In)Visibility', *Organization Studies* 33/7: 963–971.

Scott, D. and Leonov, A. (with Toomey, C.) (2004) *Two Sides of the Moon*. London: Simon & Schuster.

Scott, J. (1985) *Weapons of the Weak: Everyday Forms of Peasant Resistance*. New Haven, CT: Yale University Press.

Scott, J. (1990) *Domination and the Arts of Resistance*. New Haven, CT: Yale University Press.

Scott, J. (1998) *Seeing Like a State*. New Haven, CT: Yale University Press.

Sekula, A. (1991) 'War Without Bodies', *Artforum* November: 107–110.

Serres, M. (1995) *Angels: A Modern Myth*. Paris: Flammarion.

Shaw, P. (2006) *The Sublime*. London: Routledge.

Shaxon, N. (2011) *Treasure Islands*. London: Bodley Head.

Shelton, A. (1994) 'Cabinets of Transgression: Renaissance Collections and the Incorporation of the New World', in J. Elsner and R. Cardinal (eds), *The Cultures of Collecting* (pp. 177–203). Cambridge, MA: Harvard University Press.

Shukaitis, S. (2009) 'Space Is the (Non)Place', in D. Bell and M. Parker (eds), *Space Travel and Culture: From Apollo to Space Tourism*. Oxford: Blackwell.

Siegal, K. and Mattick, P. (2004) *Money*. London: Thames and Hudson.

Simmel, G. (1906) 'The Sociology of Secrecy and of Secret Societies', *American Journal of Sociology* 11: 441–498.

Slawik, H., Bergmann, J., Buchmeier, M. and Tinney, S. (2010) *Container Atlas: A Practical Guide to Container Architecture*. Berlin: Gestalten Verlag.

Sleight, C. (2015) 'Olympic Lifters', *International Cranes and Specialised Transport* April: 45–46.

Smircich, L. (1983) 'Concepts of Culture and Organisational Analysis', *Administrative Science Quarterly* 28: 339–359.

Smith, A. (2005) *Moondust. In Search of the Men Who Fell to Earth*. London: Bloomsbury.

Smith, A. (2001) 'Reading Wealth in Nigeria: Occult Capitalism and Marx's Vampires', *Historical Materialism*, 9 : 39–59.

Smith, W., Higgins, M., Parker, M. and Lightfoot, G. (eds) (2001) *Science Fiction and Organisation*. London: Routledge.

Sorkin, M. and Zukin, S. (eds) (2012) *After the World Trade Center: Rethinking New York City*. New York: Routledge.

South, J. and Held, J. (eds) (2006) *Questions are Forever: James Bond and Philosophy*. Chicago, IL: Open Court.

Southwell, D. (2005) *Secrets and Lies: Exposing the World of Cover-Ups and Deception*. London: SevenOaks.

Sparks, R. (1996) 'Masculinity and Heroism in the Hollywood Blockbuster', *British Journal of Criminology* 36/3: 348–360.

Spotte, S. (2006) *Zoos in Postmodernism*: Signs and Simulation. Cranbury, NJ: Fairleigh Dickinson University Press.

Stallybrass, P. and White, A. (1986) *The Politics and Poetics of Transgression*. Ithaca, NY: Cornell University Press.

Starr, A. (2000) *Naming the Enemy: Anti-Corporate Movements Confront Globalisation*. London: Zed Books.

Sterling, C. (1991) *The Mafia*. London: Grafton.

Stevens, G. (2004) *Circus Dictionary*. Buntingford, Herts: Aardvark Publishing.

Steyaert, C. and Michels, C. (2018) 'Atmosphere', in T. Beyes and J. Metelmann (eds), *The Creativity Complex: A Companion to Contemporary Culture* (pp. 43–47). Bielefeld: Transcript Verlag.

Steyaert, C., Beyes, T. and Parker, M. (eds) (2016) *The Companion to Reinventing Management Education*. London: Routledge.

Stock, P. (2009) 'Dial 'M' for Metonym: Universal Exports, M's Office Space and Empire', in C. Lindner (ed.), *The James Bond Phenomenon: A Critical Reader* (pp. 251–267). Manchester: Manchester University Press.

Stoddart, H. (2000) *Rings of Desire*. Manchester: Manchester University Press.

Stohl, C. and Stohl, M. (2011) 'Secret Agencies: The Communicative Constitution of a Clandestine Organization', *Organization Studies* 32/9: 1197–1215.

Storey, J. (1993) *An Introductory Guide to Cultural Theory and Popular Culture*. Hemel Hempstead: Harvester Wheatsheaf.

Streeter, M. (2008) *Behind Closed Doors: The Power and Influence of Secret Societies*. London: New Holland.

Sturgeon, T. (1978) 'It Opens the Sky', in *A Touch of Strange*. Feltham: Hamlyn.

Sudjic, D. (2006) *The Edifice Complex: How the Rich and Powerful Shape the World*. London: Penguin.

Thrift, N. (2005) *Knowing Capitalism*. London: Sage.

Tiryakian, E. (1992) 'Dialectics of Modernity: Reenchantment and Dedifferentiation as Counter Processes', in H. Haferkamp and N. Smelser (eds), *Social Change and Modernity* (pp. 78–93). Berkeley, CA: University of California Press.

Tisdall, C. and Bozzolla, A. (1996) *Futurism*. London: Thames and Hudson.

Tolliver, J. and Coleman, D. (2001) 'Metropolis, Maslow and the Axis Mundi', in W. Smith, M. Parker and G. Lightfoot (eds), *Science Fiction and Organisation*. London: Routledge.

Truzzi, M. (1968) 'The Decline of the American Circus', in M. Truzzi (ed.), *Sociology and Everyday Life* (pp. 314–321). Englewood Cliffs, NJ: Prentice-Hall.

Tupitsyn, M. (1999) 'Back to Moscow', in M. Tupitsyn (ed.), *El Lissitzky: Beyond the Abstract Cabinet*. New Haven, CT: Yale University Press.

Turnbull, P. and Wass, V. (1994) 'The Greatest Game No More – Redundant Dockers and the Demise of "Dock Work"', *Work, Employment and Society* 8/4: 487–506.

Uddin, L. (2015) *Zoo Renewal. White Flight and the Animal Ghetto*. Minneapolis, MN: University of Minnesota Press.

Urry, J. (2007) *Mobilities*. Cambridge: Polity.

Van Maanen, J. (1991) 'The Smile Factory', in P. Frost, L. Moore, M. Louis, C. Lundberg and J. Martin (eds), *Reframing Organizational Culture* (pp. 58–76). Newbury Park: Sage.

Vattimo, G. (1992) *The Transparent Society*. Oxford: Polity.

Vevers, G. (1976) *London's Zoo*. London: The Bodley Head.

Virilio, P. (1999) *Politics of the Very Worst: An Interview with Philippe Petit*. New York: Semiotext(e).

Ward, L., and Steeds, W. (2005) *Angels: A Glorious Celebration of Angels in Art*. London: Sevenoaks.

Warhol, A. (2007/1975) *The Philosophy of Andy Warhol*. London: Penguin.

Watts, S. (2005) 'Built Languages of Class', in R. Moudry (ed.), *The American Skyscraper: Cultural Histories* (pp. 185–200). New York: Cambridge University Press.

Webb, J. (1969) *Space Age Management: The Large Scale Approach*. New York: McGraw Hill.

Weber, M. (1930) *The Protestant Ethic and the Spirit of Capitalism*. London: Allen and Unwin.

Wells, H. G. (2005/1903) *A Modern Utopia*. London: Penguin.

Wells, M. (2005) *Skyscrapers: Structure and Design*. London: Lawrence King.

Westwood, B. and Rhodes, C. (eds) (2007) *Humour, Organization and Work*. London: Routledge.

Whyte, W. H. (1961) *The Organisation Man*. Harmondsworth: Penguin.

Williams, R. (1976) *Keywords*. London: Flamingo.

Willis, C. (1995) *Form Follows Finance: Skyscrapers and Skylines in New York and Chicago*. New York: Princeton Architectural Press.

Willis, H. and Ortiz, D. (2004) *Evaluating the Security of the Containerized Supply Chain*. Santa Monica, CA: RAND Corporation.

Willis, P. (1977) *Learning to Labour*. Farnborough: Saxon House.

Wilson, J. (1988) *Carriage of Goods by Sea*. London: Longman.

Wilson, M. (2014) *Rules without Rulers*. Winchester: Zed Books.

Winder, S. (2006) *The Man Who Saved Britain. A Personal Journey into the Disturbing World of James Bond*. London: Picador.

Wolf, R. (1980) *New York*. Köln: Taschen.

Wood, G. (2002) *Living Dolls*. London: Faber & Faber.

Woods, A. (2018) 'Doctors in the Zoo', in A. Woods, M. Bresalier, A. Cassidy, R. Mason Dentinger (eds), *Animals and the Shaping of Modern Medicine* (pp. 27–62). Cham, Switzerland: Springer Nature/Palgrave Macmillan.

Woollacott, J. (2009) 'The James Bond Films: Conditions of Production', in C. Lindner (ed.), *The James Bond Phenomenon: A Critical Reader* (pp. 117–135). Manchester: Manchester University Press.

Ziolkowski, T. (2013) *Lure of the Arcane: The Literature of Cult and Conspiracy*. Baltimore, MD: Johns Hopkins University Press.

Zola, E. (1885/1954) *Germinal*. Harmondsworth: Penguin.

Zytaruk, M. (2011) 'Cabinets of Curiosities and the Organization of Knowledge', *University of Toronto Quarterly* 80/1: 1–23.

INDEX

Printed in the United States
by Baker & Taylor Publisher Services